AMERICAN BAR ASSOCIATION
Defending Liberty
Pursuing Justice

STREET LEGAL

A GUIDE TO PRE-TRIAL CRIMINAL PROCEDURE *for* POLICE, PROSECUTORS, AND DEFENDERS

Ken Wallentine

Criminal Justice Section

Cover design by ABA Publishing

11 10 09 08 07 5 4 3 2 1

Cataloging-in-Publication data is on file with the Library of Congress

Street legal: a guide to pre-trial criminal procedure for police, prosecutors, and defenders / Wallentine, Ken
ISBN: 978-1-59031-8225/978-1-59031-822-6

Discounts are available for books ordered in bulk. Special consideration is given to state bars, CLE programs, and other bar-related organizations. Inquire at Book Publishing, ABA Publishing, American Bar Association, 321 North Clark Street, Chicago, Illinois 60610.

www.ababooks.org

CONTENTS

ACKNOWLEDGMENTS

I am foremost grateful to my wife and her understanding of long hours at the keyboard, highlighted case reports spread across the desk and floor, and meals eaten while balanced over pages of notes. Thanks to my children, at home and afar, for keeping me grounded in the important stuff.

I am deeply indebted to a collection of fine prosecutors, civil rights attorneys, and criminal defense attorneys who helped shape this book into a usable reference work. Thanks to Kirk Torgensen, Loni DeLand, Peter "Rocky" Rognlie, and Paul Amann for their enlightening comments and able critiques along the way. Lt. Ed Spann and Sgt. Dave Hatch (Las Vegas Metro Police Department, retired) provided invaluable help with investigative checklists. The Spanish-language appendix was written by Davis Wallentine, a soldier who exemplifies loyalty, duty, respect, selfless service, honor, integrity, and personal courage, and who is an outstanding son.

I am constantly humbled and sustained by the examples of criminal defense attorneys, prosecutors, judges, and public safety officers who live and work in faithful obedience to the United States Constitution. As the final pages of this book were written, my former student, employee, and friend, Corporal Kevin Orr, joined those who gave their lives in defense of what is right. All give some and some give all. This book is dedicated to them.

Any errors are entirely my own.

NOTE CONCERNING CITATIONS

Although this book is intended for officers working the streets and as quick reference for criminal defenders and prosecutors, some readers may want to actually read court decisions supporting the author's conclusions. Short-form citation is used, not intended to comply with formal rules. Ellipses are eliminated in quotes. The citations are included so that readers may find and read the entire case.

ABOUT THE AUTHOR

Ken Wallentine is the Chief of Law Enforcement for the Utah Attorney General. He formerly served as administrative counsel at the Utah Department of Public Safety. Mr. Wallentine is the former Chief Deputy Uintah County Attorney. He regularly teaches use of force liability, search and seizure, laws of arrest, and other legal subjects at the Utah State Police Academy. He is on the faculty of Excelsior College of Albany, New York.

Mr. Wallentine is affiliated with the American Inns of Court, where he serves as a Master of the Inns and is president-elect of America's first Inn of Court. He is the author of numerous peer-reviewed articles and books, including *Preparing and Executing Search Warrants* (UPOA 1998), and is a co-author of *Lobbying, PACs, and Campaign Finance* (West Publishing 1992), as well as *Life in the Law: Answering God's Interrogatories* (Deseret Book 2001). His most recent book is *Criminal Procedure: A Street Cop's Guide* (Aspen Press 2005).

CHAPTER 1

INVESTIGATIVE DETENTION

Introduction

Not all police/citizen contacts require specific legal justification for the contact. However, most police/citizen contacts are not purely voluntary and do involve some degree of detention. To determine whether the encounter was lawful, courts examine whether the officer has effected a seizure, the motive for the contact, and the quantum of information (such as reasonable suspicion or probable cause) known to the officer at the time of the encounter. Courts generally describe police/citizen contacts by reference to one of three levels: level one, a purely voluntary encounter; level two, an investigative detention; and level three, a custodial arrest. Traffic detentions will be covered in a separate chapter.

Voluntary Encounters

Street contacts

An officer may approach a citizen and have a conversation and ask questions without any level of suspicion—as long as no detention is involved. An officer/citizen contact remains "voluntary" as long as the officer does not restrict the freedom of the citizen, either by physical conduct or verbal direction. Another question courts consider in assessing the voluntariness of an officer/citizen contact is whether a reasonable person would feel free to turn and walk away from the encounter. As long as a reasonable person believes that he or she can "disregard the police and go about his or her business," the encounter remains voluntary. *Florida v. Bostick,* 501 U.S. 429 (1991). If a reasonable person in similar circumstances would not feel free to leave, then the encounter has turned into a "seizure." *United States v. Ringold,* 335 F.3d 1168 (10th Cir. 2003), *cert. denied,* 540 U.S. 1026 (2003). Simply asking a citizen for identification, without any command or show of force, remains a voluntary encounter. *Hiibel v. Sixth Judicial Dist. Court of Nev., Humboldt County,* 542 U.S. 177 (2004) ("In the ordinary course a police officer is free to ask a person for identification without implicating the Fourth Amendment."); *United States v. Drayton,* 536 U.S. 194 (2002). "A police officer does not have to inform the citizen they are free to disregard any further questioning for the encounter to be consensual." *United States v. Manjarrez,* 348 F.3d 881 (10th Cir. 2003), *cert. denied,* 541 U.S. 911 (2004).

The United States Supreme Court has ruled that mere questioning by police does not create a detention. *Muehler v. Mena,* 544 U.S. 93 (2005). The Supreme Court upheld the officers' questioning of Mena, whom they were detaining while officers executed a search warrant in her residence. Officers asked Mena questions about her immigration status during a search for weapons and suspects connected to a shooting. The lower court ruled that the officers were required to have independent reasonable suspicion in order to question her about her immigration status because her status was not related to the purpose of the search warrant. The Supreme Court reversed, holding that "mere police questioning does not constitute a seizure" under the Fourth Amendment. "Even when officers have no basis for suspecting a particular individual, they may generally ask questions of that individual; ask to examine the individual's identification; and request consent to search his or her luggage." Though Mena was detained and handcuffed for approximately three hours, the questioning about her immigration status did not prolong her detention and did not create an additional seizure. Therefore, no independent reasonable suspicion was required to support the questioning. The Court relied on its decision in *Illinois v. Caballes,* wherein the Court ruled that conducting a drug detector dog sniff during a traffic stop does not violate the Fourth Amendment if it does not extend the stop beyond the time normally required to complete the purpose of the original detention. *Illinois v. Caballes,* 543 U.S. 405 (2005).

For example, an officer walks up to a group of high school students at a football game, suspicious that some of the students may have been throwing water balloons into the crowd. The officer greets the students and asks their names. As long as the officer does not do anything such as block the exit path, give nonverbal signals of detention, or use command language, the encounter remains voluntary. The officer may ask the students if they were involved in the balloon tossing or if they have any information, and still no detention will be created.

If the officer approaches the students and tells them not them not to move, or waves them to stop or come toward him, the officer has exercised enough control that the encounter may well be ruled a seizure. Thus, reasonable suspicion of criminal activity will be required to make the detention lawful. The difference between seizure and voluntary encounter, as well as the difference between encouraging cooperation or generating hostility, often depends on the officer's tone and language. Remember: you can be perfectly tactically aware with a smile on your face!

Community Caretaking

An officer may approach a person to check on the person's welfare, without any criminal investigative purpose, and the encounter is not an investigatory detention. For example, if an officer sees a person slumped over the steering wheel of a car with the engine running, the officer may check on the person's welfare without creating a detention. *In re Matter of Clayton,* 748 P.2d 401 (Idaho 1988). Knocking on the window, waking the person, and asking the person to step out and show identification will not create a detention when the purpose is to check on welfare. *People v. Murray,* 560 N.E.2d 309 (Ill. 1990); *State v. Kersh,* 313 N.W.2d 566 (Iowa 1981).

Officers found a crash victim seated, staring straight ahead, and completely unresponsive to questions about how he was doing. In an effort to find something that might explain the driver's odd condition and to find some identification, one of the officers opened the glove box and found an illegally possessed handgun. The court upheld the search under the community caretaker doctrine. Because there was no Fourth Amendment violation, the gun could be admitted into evidence against the driver. *United States v. Johnson,* 410 F.3d 137 (4th Cir. 2005).

Investigative Detention

Reasonable suspicion

An investigative detention must be based on reasonable suspicion of criminal activity. *United States v. Cortez,* 449 U.S. 411 (1981). The first question is whether there was even a seizure by the officer. If so, the second question is whether the seizure was supported by adequate reasonable suspicion.

What constitutes a "seizure"?

A seizure of a person occurs when a reasonable person, considering the totality of the circumstances, would not believe that he or she is free to leave. *Florida v. Royer,* 460 U.S. 493 (1991). A seizure does not automatically happen when a person flees from an officer. No seizure occurs until the officer touches the person in an attempt to seize him or her ("Tag, you're it!"), or until the person submits to the officer. *California v. Hodari D.,* 499 U.S. 621 (1991). A seizure is not accomplished until "there is a governmental termination of freedom of movement through means *intentionally applied." County of Sacramento v. Lewis,* 523 U.S. 833 (1998). A person who flees upon seeing officers, without any commands or actions by officers, is not seized even when officers follow. *Michigan v. Chesternut,* 486 U.S. 567 (1988). However, even a brief submission to a command to stop—followed by immediate flight—can constitute a seizure, even though the officer may not have been able to grab the suspect. *United States v. Coggins,* 986 F.2d 651 (3d Cir. 1993). Other factors that would likely lead to a ruling that a seizure occurred, even when the subject did not try to flee, include the threatening presence of several officers, the display of a weapon by an officer, or the use of language or tone of voice indicating that compliance with the officer's request might be compelled. *United States v. Mendenhall,* 446 U.S. 544 (1980).

Concerned about gang members frequenting his business, the owner of a roller rink installed a metal detector at the entrance. The owner hired off-duty, uniformed police officers to staff the entrance and monitor the metal detector. No dump site for illegal weapons was provided. If a person approached the metal detector and decided to leave rather than pass through the detector, no officer would follow or stop the person. When a man holding cash and cocaine activated the metal detector, he was not "seized." When the man attempted to leave, was stopped by the off-duty officer and told to raise his hands, the man was "seized." *United States v. Ford,* 333 F.3d 839 (7th Cir. 2003).

A man was loading cardboard boxes into a car trunk. There had been several burglaries in the area. An officer drove by and saw the man at the same time that the man began to back out of the single-lane driveway. The officer pulled into the driveway, blocking the exit. The officer approached the car, and the man got out and walked up to the officer and produced identification without being asked to do so. Shortly thereafter, the officer discovered a methamphetamine lab in the barn at the end of the driveway. The man was "seized" when the officer pulled into the driveway, blocking his exit. Thus, all information and evidence gathered after the seizure was suppressed because the court found that there was no reasonable suspicion for the seizure. *United States v. Kerr,* 817 F.2d 1384 (9th Cir. 1987).

What made the difference between the *Kerr* case's outcome and that of the following case? An officer stopped a car for speeding. While the officer wrote a warning and waited for computer warrant checks, the driver told the officer that he needed to use the bathroom. The officer told the driver that he was "free to go," and then followed him to a gas station. The officer told him that he would stop him again if the computer showed that he was a wanted person. The officer drove into the gas station parking lot and parked, though not directly behind the suspect's car. The officer approached the driver and told him that he had been informed of a criminal conviction for drug distribution. The officer asked for consent to search the car, and the driver refused. The driver then went into a restaurant. The officer called for a narcotics detector dog. A canine sniff indicated the odor of controlled substances. A warrant search subsequently revealed 20 pounds of marijuana in the car. The court refused to suppress the drugs, ruling that the driver was not seized at the time of the dog sniff or at the time of the search. *State v. Gronau,* 31 P.3d 601 (Utah App. 2001); *United States v. Ringold,* 335 F.3d 1168 (10th Cir. 2003) (driver not seized when officer parked at an angle to and not blocking the driver's car parked at gas station), *cert. denied,* 540 U.S. 1026 (2003).

A seizure of property, covered in depth in a later section, occurs when "there is some meaningful interference with an individual's possessory interests in that property." *United States v. Karo,* 468 U.S. 705 (1984); *United States v. Jacobsen,* 466 U.S. 109 (1984).

What does "reasonable suspicion" mean?

An officer may stop a person when the officer has reasonable suspicion to believe that the person has committed or is committing or is attempting to commit a crime. *United States v. Jones,* 432 F.3d 34 (1st Cir. 2005). Courts have attempted to define reasonable suspicion on many occasions; however, no court has been able to provide a black-letter, one-size-fits-all definition of reasonable suspicion. "Articulating precisely what 'reasonable suspicion' means is not possible. It is a commonsense, nontechnical conception that deals with the factual and practical considerations of everyday life on which reasonable and prudent men, not legal technicians, act." *Illinois v. Gates,* 462 U.S. 213 (1983).

Reasonable suspicion is substantially less than probable cause and considerably less than proof of wrongdoing by preponderance of evidence. *Immigration & Naturalization Service v. Delgado,* 466 U.S. 210 (1984). Reasonable suspicion is always more than a simple "hunch" or "mere suspicion." *United States v. Williams,* 876 F.2d 1521 (11th Cir. 1989). Reasonable suspicion must be particular; that is, it must be directed at a specific person in order to detain that person. *Ybarra v. Illinois,* 444 U.S. 85 (1979).

Reasonable suspicion requires "specific and articulable facts which, taken together with rational inferences from those facts, reasonably warrant" a detention. *Terry v. Ohio,* 392 U.S. 1 (1968). Reasonable suspicion is measured by the "totality of the circumstances" and from the collective knowledge of the officers involved in the stop. *United States v. Sokolow,* 490 U.S. 1 (1989). Both the quantity and quality of the information are important to assessing reasonable suspicion. *United States v. Forte,* 412 F. Supp. 2d 258 (W.D.N.Y. 2006). Courts recognize that what may not be suspicious to a citizen could be suspicious to an officer. An officer is entitled to use experience and training in formulating reasonable suspicion to detain. *United States v. Tinoco,* 304 F.3d 1088 (11th Cir. 2002), *cert. denied sub nom. Hernandez v. United States,* 538 U.S. 909 (2003); *United States v. Williams,* 271 F.3d 1262 (10th Cir. 2001).

Can an officer demand that a person identify himself?

There is no expectation of privacy in one's identity. *Commonwealth v. Campbell,* 862 A.2d 659 (Pa. Super. 2004), *appeal denied,* 882 A.2d 1004 (Pa. 2005) ("A person's name, like his voice or handwriting, is revealed in a variety of daily interactions and there is no legitimate expectation of privacy associated with one's identity."). The United States Supreme Court has held that a person detained upon reasonable suspicion of criminal activity may be compelled to give his or her name. *United States v. Hiibel,* 543 U.S. 177 (2004). Nevada rancher Larry Hiibel was detained after a report that a man in a pickup truck was assaulting a woman. The officer asked for Hiibel's name, and Hiibel refused. As the officer tried to persuade Hiibel to identify himself, Hiibel put his hands behind his back and told the officer to arrest him and book him in jail. Hiibel claimed that he had done nothing illegal. He was convicted of willfully obstructing an officer. No charges of assault against the woman (who turned out to be his daughter) were filed. The Court stated: "Knowledge of identity may inform an officer that a suspect is wanted and help clear a suspect and allow the police to concentrate their efforts elsewhere."

Not all states have statutes requiring that a person identify himself or herself to law enforcement officers. Though *Hiibel* holds that there is no Fourth Amendment right to refuse to identify oneself, that does not mean that an officer may arrest for failure to identify. Such an arrest must be authorized by statute. *Marrs v. Tuckey*, 362 F. Supp. 2d 927 (E.D. Mich. 2005). The *Hiibel* decision does not go so far as to uphold a requirement that a suspect give an explanation of his or her actions, and the Fifth Amendment privilege against self-incrimination still applies. Thus, an officer may detain a person for failure to provide a name, assuming that there is reasonable suspicion of a criminal activity, but should not arrest a person for failure to provide a name, address, or explanation of actions without specific statutory authority. The detention can last as long as the officer is making reasonable efforts, through whatever means, to identify the suspect.

When an officer requests identification documents from a person, the documents should be returned as soon as possible. Consider writing down the name, date of birth, and driver license number and immediately returning it to the person. Holding onto the license may itself create a seizure where no seizure is intended. *Florida v. Royer*, 460 U.S. 491 (1983); *United States v. Mendez*, 118 F.3d 1426 (10th Cir. 1997) ("officer must return a driver's documentation before the detention can end"); *United States v. Turner*, 928 F.2d 956 (10th Cir. 1991) ("If the officer retains the driver's license, he or she must have reasonable and articulable suspicion to question the driver about drugs or weapons."), *cert. denied*, 502 U.S. 881 (1991). Not all courts share this view. The Fourth Circuit Court of Appeals noted that "while it is without question that a driver's license is one of the most valuable pieces of personal identification possessed by any citizen, it does not logically follow that any time an officer retains someone's driver's license that such retention blossoms into an unconstitutional seizure. Under the totality of the circumstances, however, something more is required." *United States v. Weaver*, 282 F.3d 302 (4th Cir.), *cert. denied*, 537 U.S. 847 (2002).

How long may a reasonable suspicion detention last?

A detention may last as long as it takes to investigate the circumstances that led to the initial stop. However, even a momentary detention requires reasonable suspicion. *Florida v. Royer*, 460 U.S. 491 (1983). The detention may be extended if the officer develops additional reasonable suspicion of criminal activity. While investigating the original reason for the detention, the wise approach is to limit the intrusiveness and the length of the detention as much as possible while keeping the officer and public safe.

Many courts have found 20 minutes to be a reasonable amount of time for an investigative detention. However, the Supreme Court has refused to set any hard-and-fast time limit on the length of an investigative stop, ruling that whether the stop is too long depends on the circumstances of each case. *United States v. Sharpe*, 470 U.S. 675 (1985); *United States v. Soto-Cervantes*, 138 F.3d 1319 (10th Cir. 1998). Even longer detentions may be appropriate when calling for a drug-detector dog (*see Canine Search chapter*). A key issue is whether officers are "diligently pursuing their investigation." Extending the detention beyond the time required to investigate may diminish the reasonableness of the detention. *Byndloss v. State*, 893 A.2d 1119 (Md. 2006).

Sources of reasonable suspicion

Reasonable suspicion usually arises from a number of related factors. Even if each fact appears to have an innocent and legitimate explanation, courts look at the totality of the circumstances, including the officer's training and experience. *United States v. Sokolow*, 490 U.S. 1 (1989); *Oliver v. Woods*, 209 F.3d 1179 (10th Cir. 2000). The fact that an event may have an innocent explanation does not necessarily defeat a conclusion of reasonable suspicion. *Cibula v. Driver and Motor Vehicle Services Branch*, 123 P.3d 382 (Or. App. 2005), *cert. denied*, 132 P.3d 28 (Or. 2006). Factors that commonly lead to reasonable suspicion include:

- **Time of day.** Obviously, a person loitering outside a business late at night when the business is closed is more suspicious than a person hanging around the front door when the business is open or is about to open. *Bennett v. City of Eastpointe*, 410 F.3d 810 (6th Cir. 2005). Courts are generally more likely to find reasonable suspicion in late-night and early-morning stops. Being in a high-crime area late at night, without other indicators of criminal activity, may not be enough for a detention. *Brown v. Texas,* 443 U.S. 47 (1979).

- **Dress.** A person in a black ninja suit will surely generate suspicion at any time of day (except, perhaps, while near a martial arts studio). *People v. Jackson,* 742 P.2d 929 (Colo. App. 1987). Almost as suspicious is a person wearing unusually heavy or bulky clothing in warm weather. *United States v. Williams,* 714 F.2d 777 (8th Cir. 1983).
- **Suspicious conduct.** The *Terry* decision was based on a case where a veteran detective saw suspicious behavior, believed that a crime was about to occur, and detained and frisked a suspect. An officer may, indeed must, apply experience and training to determine whether conduct is "suspicious." *United States v. Lujan,* 188 F.3d 520 (10th Cir. 1999).
- **Crimes in the area.** The crime history of an area, particularly recently reported criminal activity, is an important factor in assessing reasonable suspicion. *State v. Griffin,* 61 P.3d 112 (Kan. App. 2003). There may also be correlation between the type of crime (auto burglaries), the suspect (a person walking alone with tools in his back pocket), and the conduct (walking through the aisles of a parking lot) to further add to the reasonable suspicion. Mere presence in a high-crime area is not sufficient suspicion for a detention. *Illinois v. Wardlow,* 528 U.S. 119 (2000).
- **Location.** A person walking in a Wal-Mart parking lot will be less suspicious than a person walking through a manufacturing business parking lot, particularly if it is not a meal or break time at the manufacturing plant. If the area is fenced and the property owner has posted trespass warnings, the presence of a person in the area may be a more significant factor. *Griffin v. Runyon,* ___F. Supp. 2d___, 2006 WL 1344818 (M.D. Ga. 2006) (climbing residential yard fence a factor in reasonable suspicion calculation); *State v. Little,* 806 P.2d 749 (Wash. 1991) (breaching posted trespass warnings contributes to reasonable suspicion).
- **Known criminal history.** *State v. Thirty Thousand Six Hundred Sixty Dollars,* 136 S.W.3d 392 (Tex. App. 2004). Any reasonable officer will be very interested in the activity of a person previously convicted of burglary when the officer spots the convicted burglar in a neighborhood other than the burglar's. Similarly, a registered sex of-

fender might arouse particular suspicions at a park or school function. Knowledge of a criminal history by itself usually will not justify a detention. *United States v. Johnson*, 427 F.3d 1053 (7th Cir. 2005).

- **Tips.** Information that a suspect is about to commit a crime, when sufficiently detailed and reliable, can offer sufficient reasonable suspicion to detain. The more detailed, the more recent, and the more reliable the source, the stronger the reasonable suspicion. *Commonwealth v. Kelly*, 180 S.W.3d 474 (Ky. 2005).
- **Nervousness.** Considered by itself, nervous behavior at the sight of law enforcement officers is *never* enough to create reasonable suspicion to detain. Many people who are violating no law become nervous around law enforcement officers. Even so, an officer should not discount an averted gaze, changed direction, lack of eye contact, or other nervous behavior. Nervousness is of "limited significance" in the reasonable suspicion calculation. *United States v. Wood*, 106 F.3d 942 (10th Cir. 1997). Refusal to voluntarily cooperate with officers also cannot establish reasonable suspicion.
- **Unprovoked flight upon seeing police.** *Illinois v. Wardlow*, 528 U.S. 119 (2000); *Whitfield v. Commonwealth*, 576 S.E.2d 463 (Va. 2003) (flight when illuminated by police car spotlight); *Wilson v. United States*, 802 A.2d 367 (D.C. 2002) (suspect twice walking rapidly away from different sets of officers within moments held to justify stop). As repeatedly cited by the United States Supreme Court, "The wicked flee when no man pursueth." *Illinois v. Wardlow*, 528 U.S. 119 (2000) (quoting *Proverbs* 28:1). Although running from the police cannot, by itself, constitute reasonable suspicion to detain, it is a significant factor.
- **Walking away from officers.** A suspect's attempt to walk away has been held to be a valid factor supporting a finding of reasonable suspicion. *United States v. Holloway*, 962 F.2d 451 (5th Cir. 1992); *Lee v. Immigration and Naturalization Service*, 590 F.2d 497 (3d Cir. 1979).
- **Wanted flyers.** As long as the issuing officer or agency has reasonable suspicion to issue a wanted flyer or radio broadcast, a person meeting the description may be stopped and detained in order to determine identity and involvement in the crime under investigation. *Ornelas v. United States*, 517 U.S. 690 (1996).

- **Collective knowledge of multiple officers.** "Officers are entitled to rely upon information relayed to them by other officers in determining whether reasonable suspicion exists to justify an investigative detention." *United States v. Mullane*, 123 Fed. Appx. 877 (10th Cir. 2005); *United States v. Cervine*, 347 F.3d 865 (10th Cir. 2003) (In determining reasonable suspicion, the court looks to the knowledge of all the police involved in the criminal investigation.).

Homeland security detentions

An officer cannot stop persons solely on the basis that they are, or appear to be, aliens. *United States v. Brignoni-Ponce*, 422 U.S. 873 (1975) ("Except at the border and its functional equivalents, officers on roving patrol may stop vehicles only if they are aware of specific articulable facts that reasonably warrant suspicion that the vehicles contain aliens who may be illegally in the country."). That is not to say that officers must ignore suspects' ethnicity, particularly if the description of the wanted person includes a specific ethnicity, or if the crime itself suggests an ethnicity. *United States v. Vite-Espinoza*, 342 F.3d 462 (6th Cir. 2003) (ethnicity could be considered when Mexicans were found at home under investigation for counterfeit immigration and identification documents); *United States v. Montero-Camargo*, 208 F.3d 1122 (9th Cir. 2000), *cert. denied sub nom. Sanchez-Guillen v. United States*, 531 U.S. 889 (2000). If the persons appear to be aliens, and there is some additional articulable suspicious factor, then an investigative detention is proper. *United States v. Cortez*, 449 U.S. 631 (1981).

Although there are many political issues surrounding local officers' enforcement of immigration laws, a state or local officer may lawfully detain undocumented aliens. *United States v. Vasquez-Alvarez*, 176 F.3d 1294 (10th Cir.), *cert. denied*, 528 U.S. 913 (1990) ("The plain language and legislative history of § 1252c reflect that Congress intended the provision to displace perceived Federal limitations on the authority of state and local officers to arrest criminal illegal aliens."). The United States Code provides that a state or local officer may detain and arrest a person if: (1) the person is illegally present in the United States; (2) the person has previously been convicted of a felony in the United States and since left the country or was deported (known as "aggravated re-entry"); (3) the officer obtains "appropriate confirmation" from federal officials of the immigration status of the person; and (4) the officer only detains the person for as long as is reasonably required for federal officials to take custody of the person for deportation or removal from the United States. 8 U.S. Code § 1252c(a).

With appropriate confirmation, tips from citizens or informants can lead to a detention of a suspected undocumented alien. One New York City police officer detained a man dressed as a postal carrier after citizens had observed the man placing items in mailboxes. When the citizens followed him, the "postal carrier" tried to avoid them. *United States v. Mohammad Shadid Ullah,* No. 02 CR. 899(JFK), 2003 WL 1396300 (S.D.N.Y. March 20, 2003). Though the citizens thought the suspect was an alien terrorist planting anthrax in mailboxes, he was actually involved in a mail fraud scheme. The court upheld the detention as reasonable, based on the suspect's impersonating a mail carrier and attempting to avoid contact.

Reliable information that a person is purchasing materials commonly used to make explosive devices can certainly also support a detention. *United States v. Keith,* 375 F.3d 346 (5th Cir.) (retailer informed police that suspect was purchasing material for a bomb, and suspect was on probation for related offenses), *cert. denied,* 543 U.S. 950 (2004). In a case involving an anonymous tip of a juvenile carrying a gun, the Supreme Court commented that "a report of a person carrying a bomb need not bear the indicia of reliability we demand for a report of a person carrying a firearm before the police can constitutionally conduct a frisk. Nor do we hold that public safety officials in quarters where the reasonable expectation of Fourth Amendment privacy is diminished, such as airports, *see Florida v. Rodriguez,* 469 U.S. 1 (1984), and schools, *see New Jersey v. T.L.O.,* 469 U.S. 325 (1985), cannot conduct protective searches on the basis of information insufficient to justify searches elsewhere." *Florida v. J.L.,* 529 U.S. 266 (2000).

Following the Supreme Court's lead in *Florida v. J.L.,* several courts have ruled that a report of a bomb will afford officers greater freedom to detain and frisk than a report of a concealed gun, particularly in schools, airports, and other vulnerable areas. *Cuesta v. School Board of Miami-Dade County,* 285 F.3d 962 (11th Cir. 2002) (violent drawings accompanied by threatening words were sufficient to create reasonable suspicion to detain student); *Williams v. Cambridge Board of Educ.,* 186 F. Supp. 2d 808 (S.D. Ohio 2002), *aff'd,* 370 F.3d 560 (6th Cir. 2004) (finding probable cause for detention of students who told other students that they were considering bringing guns and bombs to school); *Stockton v. City of Freeport,* 147 F. Supp. 2d 642 (S.D. Tex. 2001) (discovery of threatening letter on school property justified detention of suspected students), *aff'd,* 37 Fed. Appx. 712 (5th Cir.), *cert. denied,* 537 U.S. 1030 (2002). One hapless drug smuggler carried an electronic scale next to his drugs in his carry-on luggage. When a screening agent became concerned that the electronic device might be connected to a bomb, the bag was searched and methamphetamine was found. The court found the detention and search to be reasonable. In this time of rampant terrorism, "an individual who enters an airport security area may be searched even on a mere suspicion of possible illegal activity." *State v. Crisanti,* 470 S.E.2d 314 (Ga. App. 1996). Another court has noted that merely fitting the profile of a terrorist is sufficient grounds for detention at an airport. *United States v. Lopez-Pages,* 767 F.2d 776 (11th Cir. 1985).

Threats of chemical or biological exposure may also lead to reasonable suspicion. A pharmacist with access to chemicals and drugs who was a member of an animal rights activist group sent a suspicious-looking letter to a university. When a university employee opened the letter, she and others present immediately felt a burning sensation in their throats. This event happened during the wave of national anthrax-related incidents and shortly after other animal-rights-activist terrorist attacks at the same university. The court found that these circumstances created reasonable suspicion to forcibly detain those present when the envelope was opened. *Allison v. Michigan State University,* 2005 WL 2123852 (W.D. Mich. 2005).

Informant issues

In order to use an informant to build reasonable suspicion, the officer must consider the reliability of the information. Informants can be generally categorized as anonymous (including known, but unwilling to provide a name), paid or coerced, and good-citizen informants. When the information comes from an informant, reliability may be assessed by viewing "the credibility or veracity of the informant, the basis of the informant's knowledge, and the extent to which the police are able independently to verify the reliability of the tip." *United States v. Leos-Quijada,* 107 F.3d 786 (10th Cir. 1997). The lower the reliability of the informant, the more information that is required to create reasonable suspicion. *United States v. Cortez,* 449 U.S. 411 (1981). *See Traffic Detention chapter for discussion of traffic stops based on informants' tips.*

The anonymous informant creates the greatest concern for the officer, because the officer usually cannot verify the basis for the information or the reliability of the informant. For example, officers received an anonymous phone tip that a young black man wearing a plaid shirt was standing at a particular bus stop and that he had a concealed gun. Officers went to the bus stop and saw three black males, one of whom wore a plaid shirt. Officers had no information about criminal activity other than the anonymous call. The officers frisked all three men and found a gun on the man with the plaid shirt. The evidence of the gun was suppressed. "Unlike a tip from a known informant whose reputation can be assessed and who can be held responsible if her allegations turn out to be fabricated, an anonymous tip alone seldom demonstrates the informant's basis of knowledge or veracity." *Florida v. J.L.,* 529 U.S. 266 (2000).

The paid informant, or "twist" (one who is promised leniency on criminal charges in exchange for information), will generally be known to the officer. The officer can interrogate the paid informant about the basis for the tip. The reliability of the informant will depend largely on the informant's track record in providing truthful information.

In another case, an informant told an officer about drugs in a car. The officer knew the informant by name and had received reliable information from the informant on approximately 10 other occasions. The informant stated that the drugs would be in an older green Buick Riviera driven by a male, with a female passenger. The informant gave the license plate number, though the informant was not certain about one of its six characters. The informant also provided the last known location of the car. The court ruled that there was ample reasonable suspicion to stop the car. *State v. Grovier,* 808 P.2d 133 (Utah App. 1991).

A citizen informant enjoys a presumption of reliability. *United States v. Harris,* 403 U.S. 573 (1971). The citizen informant usually gains knowledge by being either a witness or a victim of a crime. Because there is generally a strong basis of knowledge and the information is volunteered for motives of civic concern, courts give great deference to reasonable suspicion established from a citizen informant's statements. *Carattini v. State,* 774 So. 2d 927 (Fla. App. 2001).

An unnamed citizen informant who provides information face-to-face to officers is not considered the same as an anonymous tipster. *United States v. Romain,* 393 F.3d 63 (1st Cir. 2004), *cert. denied,* 545 U.S. 1122 (2005). Thus, officers do not have the same duty to confirm the citizen informant's information before acting on it. A citizen waved over an officer, reported drug dealing in a parking lot, and described the suspect, truck, and location. The officer immediately went to the parking lot and saw the truck leaving. The officer stopped the truck and located methamphetamine. The court noted that a "face-to-face encounter provides police officers with the opportunity to perceive and evaluate personally an informant's mannerisms, expressions, and tone of voice and thus, to assess the informant's veracity more readily than can be done from a purely anonymous phone tip." *Commonwealth v. Priddy,* 184 S.W.3d 501 (Ky. 2005).

Detentions for Identification

Officers investigating a fresh crime (committed within the past few minutes or hours) may detain a potential suspect on the basis that the suspect matches a description provided by a victim or witness. A common investigative tool is to bring the victim or witness to the suspect for a contemporaneous eyewitness identification. This is known as a "show-up" identification. Unlike a line-up conducted after a defendant is charged with a crime, the suspect has no right to an attorney before submitting to a show-up identification. *United States v. Abshire,* 471 F.2d 116 (5th Cir. 1972); *Faulkner v. Makel,* 839 F. Supp. 1242 (E.D. Mich. 1993).

If a suspect is identified in the show-up process, the court will generally hold a hearing to determine whether the show-up was conducted in an impermissibly suggestive manner. This is often called a *Wade* hearing, after the case of *United States v. Wade,* 388 U.S. 218 (1967). If the process is "so unnecessarily suggestive and conducive to irreparable mistaken identification that the defendant was denied due process of law," the eyewitness testimony will be excluded. *Stovall v. Denno,* 388 U.S. 293 (1967). The court first considers whether the show-up was too suggestive and then considers whether the show-up is inherently reliable. The first factor focuses on law enforcement conduct, while the second factor focuses on the circumstances of the crime and the identifying witness.

Whenever possible, the witness should be taken to the suspect. Transporting the suspect may lend weight to a later argument that the suspect had been arrested rather than merely detained. Not forcing the suspect to return to the scene of the crime may lessen the inherent suggestiveness of the show-up. However, the location of the show-up is not a critical issue for a reviewing court. *United States v. Butler*, 970 F.2d 1017 (2d Cir.), *cert. denied*, 506 U.S. 980 (1992). If circumstances suggest that there will be a significant delay, consider photographing the suspect for later identification. *State v. Flores*, 706 A.2d 628 (Md. App.1998) (police may photograph a person during an investigatory detention). A photograph will have the added advantage of making a photo line-up possible.

When conducting a show-up, officers should tell the witness that a "potential suspect" has been located rather than "we got the guy that did this to you." The fact that the suspect is handcuffed or standing next to a uniformed officer will not invalidate the show-up. *United States v. Nelson*, 931 F. Supp. 194 (W.D.N.Y. 1996), *aff'd*, 131 F.3d 132 (2d Cir. 1997). Show-ups should be conducted as soon as possible after the crime, but even a show-up several hours after the crime, where the suspect was taken to the witness's business for identification, has been upheld. *People v. Drayton*, 288 N.E.2d 922 (Ill. App. 1972); *Hoover v. Slayton*, 341 F. Supp. 317 (W.D. Va. 1972).

Distinguishing detention basis from frisk basis

An officer may stop and detain a person whenever the officer has reasonable suspicion to believe that the person has committed a crime, is committing a crime, or is about to commit a crime. *Illinois v. Wardlow*, 528 U.S. 119 (2000). The detention may last only as long as it takes to determine whether a crime has been committed, is being committed, or is about to be committed, but no longer. In other words, the scope of the detention must be reasonably related to the original reason for the stop. *Florida v. Royer*, 460 U.S. 491 (1983).

A level two, or reasonable suspicion, detention does not automatically mean that the officer may frisk the person. The reasonableness of the detention and the lawfulness of the frisk are two separate legal issues. *State v. Kester*, 51 P.3d 457 (Idaho App. 2002). An officer may see a person acting suspiciously, have reasonable suspicion to detain the person, and still not be able to lawfully frisk the person.

An adult man walking back and forth in front of an elementary school appears to be watching young girls on the playground. Perhaps he is looking for his daughter or granddaughter; or perhaps not. He's been there for 15 minutes. None of the teachers recognize him, and he seems not to be concentrating on any particular child. When the officer drives up in response to a call from a teacher, the man turns away from the officer and drops his head. He begins to run. Most officers would conclude that there is a basis for an investigatory detention. The man makes no movements toward his pockets. He's not wearing bulky clothing and makes no threatening movements or statements. In other words, there is no reason to believe that he is armed. Therefore, the detention may be lawful but a frisk would be unlawful.

Terry v. Ohio

In *Terry v. Ohio,* 392 U.S. 1 (1968), the United States Supreme Court approved the stop-and-frisk practice. Generally known as the "*Terry* frisk" doctrine, it is a very limited and narrow exception to the Fourth Amendment warrant requirement. An officer may conduct a pat-down frisk of a person only when the officer reasonably believes the person to be *armed and presently dangerous to the officer or others.* Even before the frisk, the officer must have a legitimate reason to stop the person. There is only one lawful purpose to a *Terry* frisk: to remove weapons that threaten the officer or others. *Michigan v. Long,* 463 U.S. 1032 (1983). A *Terry* frisk is not intended to explore for drugs or other contraband.

Courts have considered a variety of factors that officers use to justify a *Terry* frisk. Following are some examples:

- Bulges in the clothing that might hide a weapon. *United States v. Hill,* 545 F.2d 1191 (9th Cir. 1976); *State v. Lafond,* 68 P.3d 1043 (Utah App. 2003). As one court noted, pockets were made to carry things, and an undefinable bulge alone generally will not create a reason to frisk. *People v. Howard,* 542 N.Y.S.2d 536 (1989). A heavy bulge that causes pockets to swing, though indefinable as a weapon by appearance alone, may offer sufficient reasonable suspicion to frisk. *People v. Miles,* 242 Cal. Rptr. 107 (Cal. App. 1987).
- Bulky clothing worn on a warm day. A frisk was upheld when an officer testified that drug couriers often wore heavy, bulky coats in warm weather to better conceal

illegal drugs. *United States v. Varela,* 2006 WL 120263 (D. Utah, Jan. 17, 2006). One officer literally shook down a suspect when the suspect's excessively baggy clothes could not be effectively frisked. A vial of cocaine rolled out. The court allowed the shaking, finding it reasonable and perhaps less intrusive than a traditional frisk. *State v. Triplett,* 707 N.W.2d 881 (Wis. App. 2005).

- Flight upon seeing the officer, coupled with some other factor suggesting that the suspect is armed. *United States v. Lane,* 909 F.2d 895 (6th Cir. 1990) (flight and suspect reaching into pocket); *United States ex rel. Richardson v. Rundle,* 461 F.2d 860 (3d Cir. 1972) (flight from drugstore at closing time combined with furtive movement); *Commonwealth v. E.M.,* 735 A.2d 654 (Pa. 1999) (flight coupled with a single officer confronting suspect in dark alley).
- Furtive gestures clearly made in response to police action. *United States v. Edmonds,* 240 F.3d 55 (D.C. Cir. 2001). Suspicious movements alone do not generally constitute a basis to frisk. *United States v. Edmonds,* 240 F.3d 55 (D.C. Cir. 2001).
- Tip from a reliable informant that the suspect is armed. *Adams v. Williams,* 407 U.S. 143 (1972).
- Crime reported involved use of a weapon, such as armed robbery or burglary where weapons were likely stolen. *State v. Belieu,* 773 P.2d 46 (Wash. 1989).
- Matching the description of persons using weapons in a crime. *United States v. Campbell,* 178 F.3d 345 (5th Cir. 1999).
- Where one weapon is found, there may be others. *United States v. Christian,* 187 F.3d 663 (D.C. Cir. 1999) ("The presence of one weapon may justifiably arouse concern that there may be more in the vicinity, as turned out to be the case here."), *cert. denied,* 529 U.S. 1030 (2000); *State v. Olsson,* 895 P.2d 867 (Wash. 1995).
- Suspicion of commission of serious crimes. Certain crimes have been viewed as virtually automatically justifying a *Terry* frisk. *United States v. Cortez,* 449 U.S. 411 (1981) (when deciding whether to frisk, officers can make "common-sense conclusions about the modes or patterns of operation of certain kinds of lawbreakers"); *Terry v. Ohio,* 392 U.S. 1 (1968) ("The right to frisk must be immediate and automatic if the reason for the stop is an articulable suspicion of a crime of violence."); *People v. Shackelford,* 546 P.2d 964 (Colo. 1976) (rape); *State v. Kea,* 606 P.2d

1329 (Haw. 1980) (assault with a deadly weapon); *State v. Gilchrist,* 299 N.W.2d 913 (Minn. 1981) (homicide); *Mays v. State,* 726 S.W.2d 937 (Tex. App. 1986), *cert. denied,* 484 U.S. 1079 (1988) (burglary); *Russell v. State,* 415 So. 2d 797 (Fla. App. 1982), *review denied,* 427 So. 2d 737 (Fla. 1983). Though the *Terry* Court did not go so far as to authorize frisks for all drug crime detentions, many courts agree that drug trafficking has become so dangerous that officers may frisk all persons detained for suspicion of drug dealing (though not necessarily possession). *United States v. Trullo,* 809 F.2d 108 (1st Cir.) (frisk for weapons may accompany seizure of drug-dealing suspect), *cert. denied,* 482 U.S. 916 (1987); *United States v. Vasquez,* 634 F.2d 41 (2d Cir. 1980) (officers justified in making a protective frisk, "particularly in view of the violent nature of narcotics crime"); *United States v. Oates,* 560 F.2d 45 (2d Cir. 1977) (guns are "tools of the trade" of drug dealers). Suspicion of drug *possession* alone will not justify a frisk. *People v. Rivera,* 650 N.E.2d 1084 (Ill. App.), *appeal denied,* 660 N.E.2d 1277 (Ill. 1995); *State v. White,* 856 P.2d 656 (Utah App. 1993).

- Single officer dealing with an aggressive suspect. *State v. McGill,* 609 N.W.2d 795 (Wis. 2000). Single officer dealing with suspect with a felony record. *State v. Wilkinson,* 785 P.2d 1139 (Wash. App.), *review denied,* 791 P.2d 534 (Wash. 1990).
- Officer's knowledge that suspect has a history of being armed. *State v. Valentine,* 636 A.2d 505 (N.J. 1994).
- Stop made in a remote location by a single officer. *State v. Collins,* 847 P.2d 919 (Wash. 1993).
- Stop is made in an area known for violent crime. *United States v. McCoy,* 428 F.3d 38 (1st Cir. 2005).
- Suspect associated with a violent gang. *United States v. Strahan,* 984 F.2d 155 (6th Cir. 1993).
- Suspect's placement of hand into pocket as if reaching for (or holding) a weapon. *United States v. Michelletti,* 991 F.2d 183 (5th Cir. 1993), *cert. denied,* 513 U.S. 829 (1994); *United States v. Quarles,* 955 F.2d 498 (8th Cir.), *cert. denied,* 504 U.S. 944 (1992).
- Refusal to make hands visible. *United States v. Harris,* 313 F.3d 1228 (10th Cir. 2002) (suspect's refusal to remove hands from pockets justified weapons frisk); *United States v. Taylor,* 716 F.2d 701 (9th Cir. 1983) (frisk of passenger upheld, in part because passenger twice disobeyed an order to raise his hands).

- Officer's subjective belief that the suspect is armed. This is generally not a significant factor in the court's analysis of the frisk. *State v. Warren,* 78 P.3d 590 (Utah 2003). One court ruled that a suspect's admission that he had a pocket knife, considered alone, was not a sufficient reason for a frisk. *State v. Henage,* ___ P.3d ___, 2007 WL 194665 (Idaho 2007).
- Department policy requires a frisk before transporting in a patrol car. *State v. Wheeler,* 737 P.2d 1005 (Wash. 1987). One court noted that when an officer places a traffic violator in the officer's car for some valid reason, a frisk may be appropriate without any further reason. *United States v. McCargo,* 464 F.3d 192 (2d Cir. 2006). However, officers should not place violators in patrol cars merely in an effort to establish a basis to frisk. *State v. Varnado,* 582 N.W.2d 886 (Minn. 1998).
- Person entering the area where a search warrant for drugs or evidence of dangerous crimes is being executed. *United States v. Proctor,* 148 F.3d 39 (1st Cir. 1998); *Rivera v. United States,* 928 F.2d 592 (2d Cir. 1991); *Dashiell v. State,* 821 A.2d 372 (Md. 2003). *See Search Warrant chapter.*

Once the dangerous circumstance that might justify a frisk is no longer present, neither is the justification for the frisk. For example, in the course of searching a room, an officer discovered a suspect who was hiding. The suspect, who was taken outside of the house, left his jacket behind. After the suspect left, an officer frisked the jacket for weapons, finding illegal drugs. Because the suspect (being outside) could not have reached into the jacket to obtain a weapon, the frisk was improper and the drugs were not admissible. *State v. Peterson,* 77 P.3d 646 (Utah App. 2003), *aff'd,* 110 P.3d 699 (Utah 2005).

Plain touch in the course of a Terry *frisk*

While frisking for weapons, an officer may feel an item that is obviously a bag of marijuana. The officer may reach in and seize the marijuana under the plain touch doctrine. As long as the officer is conducting a lawful frisk, the incriminating nature of the item is immediately apparent to the touch, and the officer can lawfully access the item and seize it. *Minnesota v. Dickerson,* 508 U.S. 366 (1993). Because the incriminating nature must be *immediately apparent,* an officer cannot squeeze or manipulate the item to determine whether or not it is a bag of marijuana or a twist of cocaine. However, if the officer cannot immediately determine that the item is *not* a weapon, the officer may manipulate the item—but only to decide if it is a weapon. Some courts have allowed reaching into pockets when the clothing is too bulky to be effectively frisked and items in pockets cannot be identified. *State v. Kyles,* 675 N.W.2d 449 (Wis. 2004).

Use of force to detain and to frisk

When a suspect does not comply with verbal commands to assume a tactically sound position for frisking, force may be used to gain compliance. *Brandon v. Village of Maywood,* 157 F. Supp. 2d 917 (N.D. Ill. 2001). The officer should be very careful to limit the force to only what is necessary to effect the detention and frisk. The greater the force, the more likely that the temporary seizure of the frisk will be construed as an arrest, thus requiring a higher standard of probable cause and not merely reasonable suspicion. Courts have ruled that displaying a weapon will not always turn an investigatory detention into an arrest. *United States v. Melendez-Garcia,* 28 F.3d 1046 (10th Cir. 1994) ("The use of firearms, handcuffs, and other forceful techniques does not necessarily transform a *Terry* detention into a full custodial arrest—for which probable cause is required—when the circumstances reasonably warrant such measures."). When there is a high probability that the suspect has a gun or knife, police display of guns is lawful and makes good sense from a safety perspective. When an officer knows that the suspect is wanted for a violent crime or has a history of being armed, a weapon may be drawn without great fear that the detention will become an arrest based solely on the officer's display of the gun. *United States v. Campbell,* 178 F.3d 345 (5th Cir. 1999) (drawn guns and handcuffing reasonable steps in detention of suspected armed burglar); *United States v. Shareef,* 100 F.3d 1491 (10th Cir. 1996) (handcuffing of suspects wanted for federal weapons violations); *United States v. Bautista,* 684 F.2d 1286 (9th Cir. 1982) (handcuffing during *Terry* stop when suspect posed flight risk). Nor will the application of handcuffs, where justified, transform a detention into an arrest. *United States v. Blackman,* 66 F.3d 1572 (11th Cir. 1995).

When a suspect is detained at gunpoint and frisked after handcuffing, the scope of the detention in both time and intensity (how long the suspect is confined in handcuffs or in a police car) will be strictly scrutinized. *United States v.*

Navarrete-Baron, 192 F.3d 786 (8th Cir. 1999). Other factors that may support the display of weapons or handcuffing include multiple suspects, suspects at large after fleeing, suspect posing a flight risk, prior conviction for violent assault, suspects outnumbering officers, and detention of suspects in a vehicle believed to be involved in a violent crime. The landmark case of *Graham v. Connor* (discussed in the Use of Force chapter) established factors for measuring the proper use of force, such as the severity of the crime under investigation, whether the suspect poses a threat to the public or officers, and whether the suspect is actively resisting or attempting to escape.

CHAPTER 2

TRAFFIC DETENTIONS

Introduction

Initial Detention

- Reasonable suspicion of a violation
- Length and scope of detention

Pretextual Detentions

- *United States v. Whren*
- Tension between pretext stops and profiling stops
- Stops based on drug courier profiles
- Stops based on terrorist profiles
- Stops based on anonymous tips of impaired driving or other violations

After the Initial Detention

- Questioning about non-traffic matters
- Asking about drugs and alcohol
- Drug interdiction indicators
- Seeking consent to search
- Ordering driver and occupants out of the car or to remain in the car
- Stopping passengers from walking away from a traffic detention
- Identification and warrant checks for passengers
- Vehicle "frisks"
- Canine sniffs

Roadblocks

- *Michigan v. Sitz*
- Investigative roadblocks
- Administrative traffic checkpoints
- Avoiding a checkpoint as a basis for detention
- Public housing checkpoints
- Roadblock ruse operations
- "Hand-off" or "wall stops"

Introduction

Officers may stop and detain a vehicle upon reasonable suspicion of a traffic offense or crime. Probable cause to believe that a crime or traffic violation has been committed is *not* required. The scope of the traffic detention will depend on the reason for the initial stop, as well as facts developed during the stop. A court will always look first at the reason for the stop; if the reason was not lawful, all of the evidence obtained during the stop will likely be suppressed.

Initial Detention

Reasonable suspicion of a violation

Any traffic violation, no matter how insignificant, and whether a moving violation or non-moving violation, justifies a traffic stop. *United States v. Botero-Ospina,* 71 F.3d 783 (10th Cir. 1995). Even a minor parking violation may lead to a lawful traffic detention. *United States v. Burton,* 334 F.3d 514 (6th Cir. 2003), *cert. denied,* 540 U.S. 1135 (2004). The stop may also be based on a reasonable suspicion that the driver has a suspended driver's license or is the subject of an arrest warrant. Equipment violations may justify a stop. The following are examples of equipment violation stops that have been allowed by courts:

- License tag light out, where state law requires a light. *State v. Weinheimer,* 2004 WL 323186 (Ohio App. 2004); *State v. Patefield,* 927 P.2d 655 (Utah App.1996). License plate obscured or not visible from a reasonably safe distance. *United States v. Edgerton,* 438 F.3d 1043 (10th Cir. 2006).
- Turn signal on for an extended distance. *State v. Marshall,* 791 P.2d 880 (Utah App. 1990). Some courts have disallowed a stop on this basis where no specific state statute controls. *United States v. Miller,* 146 F.3d 274 (5th Cir. 1998).
- Wobbly wheel, which may have posed safety concern. *State v. O'Brien,* 959 P.2d 647 (Utah App. 1998).
- Bouncing (skipping on pavement) tire. *State v. Harrison,* 533 P.2d 1143 (Az. 1975).
- Bulging or balding tires. *State v. Myers,* 580 N.E.2d 61 (Ohio App. 1990).

- Missing mirror. *State v. Thompson,* 816 A.2d 550 (Vt. 2002).
- Brake light out. *State v. Chevre,* 994 P.2d 1278 (Utah App. 2000).
- Blinking headlight. *State v. Pinkham,* 565 A.2d 318 (Me. 1989).
- Improper bumper height. *State v. Shiley,* 598 N.E.2d 775 (Ohio App. 1991).
- Lack of mud flaps and tires extending beyond body. *United States v. Cotton,* 223 F. Supp. 2d 1039 (D. Neb. 2002).
- Cracked windshield. Some courts have sustained traffic stops for cracked windshields only where the officer could see that the crack was unsafe or violated the equipment statute. *United States v. Callarman,* 273 F.3d 1284 (10th Cir. 2001) (traffic stop was allowed where officer had reasonable suspicion that crack obstructed the driver's vision), *cert. denied,* 535 U.S. 1072 (2002). Most courts, however, allow a stop upon observation of any crack. *United States v. Cashman,* 216 F.3d 582 (7th Cir. 2000) (cracked windshield provided basis for stop even if the crack was not large enough to violate equipment statute); *State v. Vera,* 996 P.2d 1246 (Ariz. App. 1999) (stop proper even though no Arizona statute specifically prohibits cracks).
- Parking violation. An officer may detain a vehicle and driver to investigate a parking violation even if a state treats parking violations as civil, rather than criminal. The pretext stop doctrine established in *Whren v. United States,* 517 U.S. 806 (1996), does not distinguish between criminal and civil traffic violations. *United States v. Choudhry,* 461 F.3d 1097 (9th Cir. 2006). Other courts have reached similar conclusions, including a case where officers did not stop a vehicle until following it several blocks from the scene of the illegal parking. *United States v. Copeland,* 321 F.3d 582 (6th Cir. 2003).

In addition to an observed parking or moving violation, registration violation, or equipment violation, the driver's identity may provide the basis for the stop. Stops may also be justified by:

- Knowledge, or reasonable suspicion, that the driver or passenger is the subject of an arrest warrant. *State v. Lopes,* 552 P.2d 120 (Utah 1976).

- Recognizing the driver as having a suspended driver's license. *United States v. Hope*, 906 F.2d 254 (7th Cir. 1990) (officer knew that license suspended as of one week prior to the stop); *United States v. Sandridge*, 385 F.3d 1032 (6th Cir. 2004) (officer knew that license was suspended 22 days before the stop); *State v. Decoteau*, 681 N.W.2d 803 (N.D. 2004) (officer stopped same subject one week prior and learned of suspended license); *State v. Wilkinson*, 785 P.2d 1139 (Wash. App.), *review denied*, 791 P.2d 534 (Wash. 1990). The court had no trouble invalidating a stop where the officer's most recent contact with the driver had been at least four months prior and there was no testimony of whether the driver's license was suspended at that time or how long prior to that stop the officer knew that the license was suspended. *United States v. Laughrin*, 438 F.3d 1245 (10th Cir. 2006).
- Running a registration check and learning that the registered owner has a suspended license. *State v. Reno*, 840 A.2d 786 (N.H. 2003); *State v. Halvorson*, 997 P.2d 751 (Mt. 2000).
- Running a registration check and learning that an arrest warrant has been issued for the registered owner, when the driver reasonably could be the registered owner. *State v. Penfield*, 22 P.3d 293 (Wash. 2001) (stop must terminate when driver is found not to be registered owner); *State v. Oshkeshequoam*, 503 N.W.2d 23 (Wis. App. 1993).
- No reasonable suspicion is required to run a registration check. There is no expectation of privacy in a license plate number visible to the public. *United States v. Ellison*, 462 F.3d 557 (6th Cir. 2006); *Hallstein v. City of Hermosa Beach*, 87 Fed. Appx. 17 (9th Cir. 2003); *United States v. Sparks*, 37 Fed. Appx. 826 (8th Cir. 2002); *Olabisiomotosho v. City of Houston*, 185 F.3d 521 (5th Cir. 1999).

An officer can always stop a vehicle for speeding, a red light violation, following too closely, a stop sign violation, or some other obvious violation. This is particularly true of serious traffic violations that normally result in citations or written warnings. Many traffic stops that result in an arrest for driving under the influence of alcohol or drugs begin with a far more subtle violation or even no violation at all. Often, weaving, improper lane change, or slow driving are cited as the basis for the stop of an impaired driver. An officer may also rely on tips from citizens about violations or suspected impaired drivers. *See Informant Issues in the Investigative Detention chapter.* Following are examples of some of these stops that courts have considered.

- Weaving outside of lane divider, breakdown lane, or fog lines. *Rowe v. State,* 769 A.2d 879 (Md. 2001); *State v. Smith,* 21 S.W.3d 251 (Tenn. App. 1999).
- Weaving within the lane of travel. Note that most courts require some other violation or impairment clue, even the most minor, such as slow driving. *State v. Dorendorf,* 359 N.W.2d 115 (N.D. 1984). Repeated weaving within the lane may support a stop. *Neal v. Commonwealth,* 498 S.E.2d 422 (Va. 1998). Where the weaving is not significant, and there is no other violation, there is generally not sufficient reasonable suspicion for a stop. *United States v. Colin,* 314 F.3d 439 (9th Cir. 2002); *State v. Bello,* 871 P.2d 584 (Utah App. 1994) (seizure of large load of drugs suppressed when the only basis for the stop was a single incident of weaving); *Warrick v. Commissioner of Public Safety,* 374 N.W.2d 585 (Minn. App. 1985) ("subtle" weaving of the vehicle within its own lane did not create reasonable suspicion for stop). One federal court noted: "If failure to follow a perfect vector down the highway were sufficient reason to suspect a person of driving while impaired, a substantial portion of the public would be subject each day to an invasion of their privacy." *United States v. Lyons,* 7 F.3d 973 (10th Cir. 1993).
- Prolonged stop with no apparent reason and no other violation observed. *State v. Guthmiller,* 499 N.W.2d 590 (N.D. 1993). This may be particularly significant at night.
- Stopping at a green light or stopping for no apparent reason. *State v. Schriml,* 1997 WL 531219 (Ohio App. 1997) (remained stopped for 10 seconds after light turned green); *Parent v. Commissioner of Motor Vehicles,* 1994 WL 723048 (Conn. Super. 1994); *State v. Goeman,* 431 N.W.2d 290 (N.D. 1988). A brief delay in starting after a light turns green may not be sufficient reasonable suspicion for a traffic detention. *State v. Roberson,* 592 S.E.2d 733 (N.C. App. 2004) (8- to 10-second delay in starting after light change not sufficient for stop); *State v. Emory,* 809 P.2d 522 (Idaho App. 1991) (five- to six-second delay not sufficient for a stop).
- Driving significantly below the speed limit when not warranted by conditions. *State v. Haataja,* 611 N.W.2d

353 (Minn. App. 2000) (reasonable suspicion found when car drove slowly for a quarter of a mile and impeded traffic); *State v. Ratliff,* 728 P.2d 896 (Or. App. 1986) (driving at least 10 miles per hour below speed limit may be impairment clue and gives basis to stop), *aff'd,* 744 P.2d 247 (Ore. 1987); *Sell v. State,* 496 N.E.2d 799 (Ind. App. 1986) (reasonable suspicion found when driver drove 15 to 20 miles per hour below the speed limit for two to three minutes).

A stop may also be based on a request from another law enforcement officer. *State v. Bruce,* 779 P.2d 646 (Utah 1989). As long as the requesting officer observed reasonable suspicion for the detention, a second officer who has not seen factors to support a stop may detain the vehicle. *United States v. Celio,* 945 F.2d 180 (7th Cir. 1991) (officers could lawfully stop suspected drug traffickers based solely on request from Drug Enforcement Agency to stop vehicle).

Length and scope of detention

The traffic detention must last no longer than necessary to resolve the suspected traffic violation, either by warning, citation, or hearing an explanation from the driver. *Florida v. Royer,* 460 U.S. 491 (1983). The detention and investigation must be reasonably related to the initial reason for the stop, unless other factors support additional reasonable suspicion. *United States v. Gil,* 204 F.3d 1347 (11th Cir.), *cert. denied,* 531 U.S. 951 (2000). Any further detention must be supported by reasonable suspicion of more serious criminal activity. *United States v. Davis,* 430 F.3d 345 (6th Cir. 2005). The following steps are permitted for every traffic stop made for a valid reason:

- Require the driver to produce a driver's license and vehicle registration. *United States v. Clayborn,* 339 F.3d 700 (8th Cir. 2003), *cert. denied,* 541 U.S. 1019 (2004). If the registered owner is not in the car, the driver may be required to show a right to possess and drive the car. *United States v. Zabalza,* 346 F.3d 1255 (10th Cir. 2003).
- Require proof of insurance for the vehicle. *United States v. Brigham,* 343 F.3d 490 (5th Cir. 2003) ("Officer is authorized to require the driver of the vehicle to produce a valid driver's license and documentation establishing the ownership of the vehicle and that required public liability insurance coverages are in effect on such vehicle."),

rev'd on other grounds, 382 F.3d 500 (5th Cir. 2004); *State v. Romero,* 48 P.3d 102 (N.M. App. 2002); *State v. Hansen,* 63 P.3d 650 (Utah 2002).

- Check the *driver* for a valid license and for warrants. *United States v. Barragan,* 379 F.3d 524 (8th Cir. 2004); *United States v. Holt,* 264 F.3d 1215 (10th Cir. 2001). Warrant checks of passengers are discussed below.
- Request a computer check of the *driver's* criminal history. The check should be requested at the initial stage of the stop, at the same time that driver's license and registration checks are requested, and may not unreasonably delay the stop. *United States v. Estrada,* 459 F.3d 627 (5th Cir. 2006); *United States v. Salazar,* 454 F.3d 843 (8th Cir. 2006); *United States v. Purcell,* 236 F.3d 1274 (11th Cir. 2001); *United States v. McRae,* 81 F.3d 1528 (10th Cir. 1996).
- Inspect the VIN (vehicle identification number) in the least intrusive manner and compare it to the VIN shown on registration documents or computer records. *New York v. Class,* 475 U.S. 106 (1986). An officer may require the driver to move an item blocking the view of the VIN. *United States v. Caro,* 248 F.3d 1240 (10th Cir. 2001). If the VIN on the dashboard is obscured or unreadable, the officer may open the door to check the VIN. *Morgan v. State,* 906 S.W.2d 620 (Tex. App. 1995), *cert. denied,* 519 U.S. 865 (1996). Most courts hold that opening the door and inspecting the door VIN plate or looking under the car at the frame VIN does not violate a reasonable expectation of privacy. *People v. Piper,* 427 N.E.2d 1361 (Ill. App. 1981). However, a few courts require at least some basis to suspect that the VIN has been altered or the car is stolen. *State v. Romero,* 48 P.3d 102 (N.M. App.), *cert. denied,* 49 P.3d 76 (N.M. 2002); *State v. Castner,* 825 P.2d 699 (Utah App. 1992).
- Visually inspect the "plain view" interior of the car. *Colorado v. Bannister,* 449 U.S. 1 (1980).
- Ask about travel plans, particularly if the stop is for the suspicion of impairment and the driver's drowsiness may be an explanation for the driving pattern. *United States v. Kopp,* 45 F.3d 1450 (10th Cir.), *cert. denied,* 514 U.S. 1076 (1995). Most courts allow routine questions about travel plans. *United States v. Martin,* 422 F.3d 597 (7th Cir. 2005) (officer may ask questions unrelated to the initial purpose for the stop, provided that the questions do not unreasonably extend the amount of time that the

subject is detained); *United States v. Hernandez,* 93 F.3d 1493 (10th Cir. 1996) (officer may ask questions regarding travel plans "as a matter of course without exceeding the proper scope of a traffic stop"); *United States v. Gonzalez-Lerma,* 14 F.3d 1479 (10th Cir.), *cert. denied,* 511 U.S. 1095 (1994). The officer may inquire of both the driver and passengers. *United States v. Rivera,* 867 F.2d 1261 (10th Cir. 1989) (officer could ask about the identity and travel plans of the driver and passenger, and inconsistent answers provided by each supported the finding of reasonable suspicion to detain further).

- Ask about the relationship of the driver to any passengers. *United States v. Rivera,* 867 F.2d 1261 (10th Cir. 1989); *United States v. Galindo-Gonzales,* 4 F. Supp. 2d 1016 (D.N.M. 1996), *aff'd* 142 F.3d 1217 (10th Cir. 1998).
- Ask the driver to sit in the patrol car for questioning and for issuance of a citation. *United States v. Ramos,* 42 F.3d 1160 (8th Cir. 1994), *cert. denied,* 514 U.S. 1134 (1995). Though lawful, bringing the driver back to the car may or may not be tactically sound.
- A traffic stop resulting in only a citation and not a custodial arrest will not allow a search of the vehicle. *Knowles v. Iowa,* 525 U.S. 113 (1998). *See Search and Seizure chapter.*

If the officer finds a reasonable explanation for the initial stop, or finds that he or she is mistaken about the reason for the stop, the driver cannot be detained. One court recently ruled that an officer who stopped a car because the temporary license tag was not visible, but then clearly saw the tag as he approached the driver, should have done nothing more than explain the reason for the stop. The officer conversed with the driver, obtained consent to search the car, and found 20 kilograms of cocaine. The court of appeals ruled that the traffic detention was unlawful. *United States v. Edgerton,* 438 F.3d 1043 (10th Cir. 2006). A Colorado state trooper stopped a car because no license plate was visible. As the trooper walked up to the car, he saw a valid paper temporary tag in the window. Nonetheless, the trooper asked the driver for license and registration. As the driver was getting his license, he dropped a small bindle of methamphetamine. The Colorado Supreme Court ruled that the drugs had to be suppressed because the stop became invalid once the officer realized that he was mistaken about the lack of vehicle registration. *People v. Redinger,* 906 P.2d 81 (Colo. 1995).

Courts are divided over the result of mistakes about the applicability of commercial vehicle regulations to particular vehicles. A New Hampshire state trooper stopped a truck believing that the truck was a commercial vehicle and subject to random inspection under 49 C.F.R. §§ 390 (2005). The truck had dual axles and Massachusetts commercial vehicle plates. As the trooper approached the truck, he smelled residual marijuana odor. The trooper saw a marijuana cigarette in the driver side door pocket, arrested the driver, and found additional illegal drugs. He later discovered that the truck did not weigh enough to be considered a commercial vehicle. The Department of Transportation Motor Carrier Safety rules authorize officers to conduct routine safety inspections of commercial motor vehicles. The court ruled that an officer may stop a vehicle upon a reasonable belief that the vehicle is subject to commercial vehicle regulations. In this case, the truck appeared to be sufficiently heavy, and the truck had commercial vehicle plates from another state. Thus, the stop was reasonable, and the seizure of evidence and the arrest were proper. *State v. Livingston*, 897 A.2d 977 (N.H. 2006).

The Court of Appeals for the Tenth Circuit came to the opposite conclusion when a Kansas trooper stopped a truck believing that it was subject to commercial vehicle regulations. The court refused to allow the officer's reasonable mistake as justification for the stop. The court reasoned that stops for inspections of commercial vehicles are premised on the theory that a trucker consents to the stop by engaging in a regulated business. One who does not intend to engage in a regulated business and who does not operate a vehicle subject to commercial vehicle regulation cannot be said to have given implied consent for a stop. *United States v. Herrera*, 444 F.3d 1238 (10th Cir. 2006).

Officers are required to know certain laws of other states, particularly license plate regulations. For example, if a neighboring state does not require the display of a front license plate, a vehicle properly registered in the neighboring state cannot be stopped for the lack of a front license plate. *United States v. Twilley*, 222 F.3d 1022 (9th Cir. 2000). A good-faith error of law may not invalidate a stop. A highway patrol trooper stopped a car because of a large air freshener hanging from the mirror. The trooper was aware that the law prohibits items on the windshield that might obstruct the driver's vision. However, according to the applicable statute, the item must be "affixed" to the windshield.

Thus, there was no actual traffic law violation upon which a stop might be based. As the trooper spoke with the driver, he smelled the strong odor of marijuana. A subsequent search revealed over five pounds of marijuana and a sizable amount of cash. The court held that it was a reasonable mistake and refused to suppress the evidence. *People v. White et al.*, 132 Cal. Rptr. 371 (Cal. App. 2003).

Pretextual Detentions

United States v. Whren

In *Whren v. United States,* the United States Supreme Court ruled that no Fourth Amendment violation occurs for a traffic stop based on a minor violation when the violation is a pretext rather than the actual motivation for the stop. *Whren v. United States,* 517 U.S. 806 (1996). In *Whren,* officers saw a man leaving a high drug crime area in a vehicle, but lacked enough information to make a reasonable suspicion detention. A short time later, the officers saw the vehicle make an illegal turn, and the officers stopped the vehicle. Eventually, officers found drugs and made an arrest. The defendant claimed that the traffic stop for the illegal turn was a pretext to look for a drug crime; the officers essentially agreed that was their motivation. The pretext rule of the *Whren* case allows an officer to stop a vehicle any time that the officer has reasonable suspicion of a violation, even if the officer has hopes or intentions of finding evidence of a more serious crime. The Supreme Court reaffirmed its rejection of subjective pretext as an unreasonable basis for a stop in *Arkansas v. Sullivan,* 532 U.S. 769 (2001) (reversing the Arkansas Supreme Court's decision that a legitimate traffic stop became invalid when motivated by intent to search for drugs).

Many state courts have followed the *Whren* decision and applied the pretext doctrine under state law. *State v. Ryon,* 108 P.3d 1032 (N.M. 2005); *People v. Robinson,* 741 N.Y.S.2d 147 (N.Y. 2001); In fact, the Utah Supreme Court adopted the pretext doctrine years before the *Whren* decision in *State v. Lopez,* 873 P.2d 1127 (Utah 1994). Other states have been more restrained. For example, the Washington Supreme Court, relying on their state constitution, has ruled that officers cannot use the pretext stop doctrine. *State v. Ladson,* 979 P.2d 833 (Wash. 1999) (state constitution "forbids use of pretext as a justification for a warrantless search or seizure. In the case of pretext, the actual reason for the stop is inherently unreasonable, otherwise the use of pretext would be unnecessary."). After the United States Supreme Court reversed the Arkansas Supreme Court in *Arkansas v. Sullivan,* the Arkansas Court again found pretextual traffic stops to be unlawful under the independent grounds of the Arkansas State Constitution. *State v. Sullivan,* 74 S.W.3d 215 (Ark. 2002).

Tension between pretext stops and profiling stops

The *Whren* decision did not create an unlimited pretext rule. An officer should never base a traffic stop or any other detention solely on the race or ethnicity of a person. *United States v. Brignoni-Ponce,* 422 U.S. 873 (1975) (involving border checkpoints); *United States v. Avery,* 137 F.3d 343 (6th Cir. 1997) (airport detentions based on race not proper). Under *Whren,* a stop motivated by an improper racial bias would not necessarily violate the Fourth Amendment ban on unreasonable seizures. However, a stop primarily based on the subject's race, national origin, or ethnicity would violate the Fourteenth Amendment Equal Protection Clause. *Whren v. United States,* 517 U.S. 806 (1996); *United States v. Botero-Ospina,* 71 F.3d 783 (10th Cir. 1995), *cert. denied,* 518 U.S. 1007 (1996). An officer or department would face a potential lawsuit from the subject and possibly even federal criminal charges for a racially motivated seizure. *Wilson v. Dep't of Public Safety,* 66 Fed. Appx. 791 (10th Cir. 2003). A racially motivated pretext stop may also result in suppression of the criminal evidence gathered at the stop. *People v. Hester,* 14 Cal. Rptr. 3d 377 (Cal. App. 2004); *People v. Dickson,* 690 N.Y.S.2d 390 (N.Y. Sup. 1998) (in suppressing evidence, court quoted officer: "shouldn't have left the one white guy behind").

In a case addressing reasonable suspicion for a traffic detention, the Tenth Circuit Court of Appeals sent a not-too-subtle message about its perception of racial profiling and selective enforcement. In the past, the court has been prompt to suppress evidence when the defendant shows that there was selective enforcement. The court noted that 34 percent of the particular officer's stops in a two-year period were of Hispanic drivers. The court stated that "this evidence has substantial appeal." "Although direct evidence establishes that the officer was not motivated by race in his decision to stop Mr. Alcaraz-Arellano, the stop statistics that Mr. Alcaraz-Arellano has presented are disturbing. We assume that in future investigations federal prosecutors will take the utmost care to assure themselves that racial profiling is not lurking behind such statistics." *United States v. Alcaraz-Arellano,* 441 F.3d 1252 (10th Cir. 2006). Officers must take particular care that the flexibility of the pretext doctrine does not fall victim to court decisions combating bias-based policing.

Stops based on drug courier profiles

A "drug courier profile" is nothing more than a collection of characteristics frequently seen in persons or vehicles carrying illegal drugs. The principal problem with stopping a vehicle based on a drug courier profile is that the characteristics can easily change from one locale to another or from one drug to another and with the passage of time. Merely meeting a drug courier profile is not a sufficient basis for a stop. *Reid v. Georgia,* 448 U.S. 438 (1980).

When an officer finds a vehicle matching drug courier profile characteristics, the officer should find some independent reason for making a traffic stop. Though the drug courier profile should not be the basis for the stop, it may direct the investigation and support detention beyond the scope of the traffic-related reason for the stop. *Florida v. Royer,* 460 U.S. 1 (1983) (traveling under false name and matching a drug courier profile supplied reasonable suspicion for an investigative stop); *United States v. Cervine,* 347 F.3d 865 (10th Cir. 2003) (typical drug courier countersurveillance behavior justified detention for drug dog sniff); *State v. Stovall,* 788 A.2d 746 (N.J. 2002) (profile characteristics may support detention beyond original scope to allow investigation of possible drug crime). *See Drug Interdiction Factors, below.*

Drug courier profile stops are closely scrutinized when race or ethnicity is made part of the claimed profile. *United States v. Restrepo,* 890 F. Supp. 180 (E.D.N.Y. 1995) (stop violated the Fourth Amendment because the basis for stop was that car had out-of-state license plates and driver appeared to be Hispanic); *Whitfield v. Board of County Comm'rs,* 837 F. Supp. 338 (D. Colo. 1993) (highway drug interception program illegal where vehicles were stopped because of out-of-state license plates and the race of the occupants). Not only is there a risk of a Fourteenth Amendment constitutional violation, but assuming that drugs are carried by only a particular race or ethnicity is simply poor law enforcement practice.

Stops based on terrorist profiles

Though the world of security and law enforcement changed dramatically after the events of September 11, 2001, few changes have been made to the laws that affect local officers. Some federal statutes give officers additional power to control the borders, but these laws are generally not applicable to traffic stops. Homeland Security Act of 2002, 6 U.S. Code §§ 101, *et seq.*; USA PATRIOT Act, 18 U.S. Code §§ 2331, *et seq.* The same principles that apply to drug courier profile stops, particularly that the stop must be based on some independent reason, also apply to stops of suspected terrorists. *See Investigative Detention chapter* for a more thorough discussion of reasonable suspicion factors for terrorist interdiction.

Stops based on anonymous tips of impaired driving or other violations

Though the Supreme Court limited investigatory detentions based on uncorroborated anonymous tips in *J.L. v. Florida,* 529 U.S. 266 (2000), most courts generally uphold stops based on anonymous reports of an impaired driver when the tipster provides a sufficient quantity and quality of information about the vehicle and the reason for suspicion. When the tip is anonymous, some courts require that the officer personally observe impaired driving or a traffic violation to justify a stop. *Kaysville City v. Mulcahy,* 943 P.2d 231 (Utah App. 1997). One court justified upholding an arrest stemming from an anonymous tip with details of highly erratic driving by comparing an impaired driver to a "time bomb" on a public highway. *United States v. Wheat,* 278 F.3d 722 (8th Cir. 2001), *cert. denied,* 537 U.S. 850 (2002). Another cited the "awesome carnage" wrought by impaired drivers. *State v. Gollotta,* 837 A.2d 359 (N.J. 2003). Generally, a description of the vehicle color and style, accompanied by details of the erratic driving, will justify a stop if the officer is able to confirm the details provided and the stop occurs within a reasonable time of the anonymous report.

After a citizen reported the vehicle type, color, direction of travel, road number on which the vehicle was traveling, and reported that the vehicle was swerving across lanes, an officer stopped the vehicle before observing any erratic driving to confirm the suspicion of an impaired driver. The court upheld the stop, noting that the "report of a possibly intoxicated highway driver, 'weaving all over the roadway,' poses a far more grave and immediate risk to the public than a report of mere passive gun possession" as reported in *J.L. v. Florida. People v. Wells,* 136 P.3d 801 (Cal. 2006). Moreover, a traffic stop imposes less embarrassment and intrusion than a stop and physical frisk on the sidewalk. Many other courts have reached similar conclusions, even when officers saw no erratic driving pattern. *Kellems v. State,* 842 N.E.2d 352 (Ind. 2006) (officer confirmed vehicle type, color, and license plate); *State v. Scholl,* 684 N.W.2d 83 (S.D. 2004) (officer verified vehicle type and color and license plate number before stop); *Bloomingdale v. State,* 842 A.2d 1212 (Del. Super. 2004) (officer confirmed vehicle make, model, and color, and race of driver before stop); *State v. Gollotta,* 837 A.2d 359 (N.J. 2003) (officer confirmed partial plate, vehicle style and color).

After the Initial Detention

Questioning about non-traffic matters

As part of a routine traffic stop, an officer may request a driver's license and vehicle registration, conduct a computer check for warrants, and issue a citation. *United States v. Zabalza,* 346 F.3d 1255 (10th Cir. 2003); *Diltz v. State,* 172 S.W.3d 681 (Tex. App. 2005). Once these steps are concluded, however, the person must be allowed to depart. *Ferris v. State,* 735 A.2d 491 (Md. 1999). Further temporary detention for investigative questioning after fulfilling the purpose for the initial traffic stop constitutes an illegal seizure, unless an officer has reasonable suspicion or probable cause of a further illegality. *Florida v. Royer,* 460 U.S. 491 (1983). Additional detention without additional reasonable suspicion is the evil to avoid. As long as the additional questions do not extend the length of the detention, there is no Fourth Amendment issue about the subject matter of the questions. *United States v. Alcaraz-Arellano,* 441 F.3d 1252 (10th Cir. 2006).

Some suspicionless incidental questioning is also permissible as long as it does not unreasonably extend the traffic detention. *Ohio v. Robinette,* 519 U.S. 33 (1996). In *Muehler v. Mena,* 544 U.S. 93 (2005), the Supreme Court held that questioning unrelated to the purpose of an initial detention did not create an independent seizure as long as the supplemental questioning did not unreasonably extend the initial seizure. As part of the traffic stop, an officer may ask the vehicle occupants a "moderate number of questions" and request their identification. *Berkemer v. McCarty*, 468 U.S. 420 (1984). Officers may also ask about the ownership of the car and the right to use it. *United States v. Alcaraz-Arellano*, 441 F.3d 1252 (10th Cir. 2006). It may well be that the officer's questions "efficiently determine whether a traffic violation has taken place, and if so, whether a citation or warning should be issued or an arrest made." *United States v. Brigham*, 382 F.3d 500 (5th Cir. 2004).

Following the Supreme Court's decision in *Muehler v. Mena*, several courts have questioned whether there are any limitations on questions not directly related to the original purpose of the traffic stop. *United States v. Alcaraz-Arellano*, 441 F.3d 1252 (10th Cir. 2006); *United States v. Hernandez*, 418 F.3d 1206 (11th Cir. 2005) ("Although the seizure in *Muehler* was conducted pursuant to a search warrant, we believe that the focus on duration and not scope of questioning is just as applicable to a lawful traffic stop."); *United States v. Torres-Monje*, 433 F. Supp. 2d 1028 (D.N.D. 2006) (applying reasoning of *Muehler*, officer could ask about immigration status following a stop for speeding); *Commonwealth v. Briggs*, 2006 WL 850667 (Va. App. 2006) ("officer may question the person on subjects not directly related to the reasons that provided the basis for the stop, even if he lacks reasonable suspicion as to the unrelated subjects"). The Georgia Supreme Court recently ruled that asking for consent to search a vehicle does not impermissibly extend the traffic detention, and thus consent to search may be routinely sought at traffic stops. *Salmeron v. State*, 632 S.E.2d 645 (Ga. 2006). As defendants raise additional challenges to officers' questioning at traffic stops, the direction from the Supreme Court in *Muehler v. Mena* suggests that the subject matter of the questions is no longer relevant to analyzing the lawfulness of the detention.

Most courts find that questions about travel plans fit within the scope of a traffic detention. *United States v. Gonzalez*, 328 F.3d 755 (5th Cir. 2003); *United States v. Givan*, 320 F.3d 452 (3d Cir. 2003) ("questions relating to a driver's travel plans ordinarily fall within the scope of a traffic stop"); *United States v. Linkous*, 285 F.3d 716 (8th Cir. 2002) ("officer does not violate the Fourth Amendment by asking the driver his destination and purpose, checking the license and registration, or requesting that the driver step over to the patrol car"); *United States v. Holt*, 264 F.3d 1215 (10th Cir. 2001) (questions relating to a motorist's travel plans are ordinarily related to the reason for the stop); *United States v. Hill*, 195 F.3d 258 (6th Cir. 1999) (officer's questioning driver about "moving plans at the outset of the stop was reasonable in that the questions related to driver's purpose for traveling"). If the answers about travel plans are suspicious, the officer may inquire further. *People v. Williams*, 696 N.W.2d 636 (Mich. 2005). The officer may also ask the passengers about their intended travel plans. *United States v. Johnson*, 58 F.3d 356 (8th Cir. 1995).

Asking about drugs and alcohol

Questions about drugs and alcohol that delay the traffic detention must be premised on reasonable suspicion. If there are specific elements that point to the presence of alcohol or illegal drugs, such as an odor, or physical clues from the driver or passengers, an officer may ask about possession and consumption of drugs or alcohol. *Nickelson v. Kansas Dept. of Revenue*, 102 P.3d 490 (Kan. App. 2004); *State v. Lafond*, 68 P.3d 1043 (Utah App. 2003). Obviously, smelling alcohol presents reasonable suspicion to ask questions about impairment or open containers. *In re Z.C.B.*, 669 N.W.2d 478 (N.D. 2003); *State v. Ottesen*, 920 P.2d 183 (Utah App. 1996). Many courts go so far as to rule that the odor of alcohol gives probable cause to search the vehicle for open containers of alcohol (assuming a state statute that prohibits open containers in a vehicle). *State v. Wigginton*, 125 P.3d 536 (Idaho App. 2005); *State v. Haibeck*, 685 N.W.2d 512 (N.D. 2004); *State v. Peterson*, 407 N.W.2d 221 (S.D. 1987).

The additional detention and not the questioning alone is the triggering factor in requiring reasonable suspicion. *State v. Meeks*, 118 P.3d 177 (Kan. App. 2005) (relying on *Muehler v. Mena* and holding that questions about drugs and alcohol were permissible during traffic stop). However, a state is always free to impose a more restrictive rule under its state constitution. For example, even in light of the Supreme Court decision in *Muehler v. Mena* and acknowledging the departure from a majority of jurisdictions, the Minnesota Supreme Court recently ruled that reasonable suspicion is required before asking questions about drugs and alcohol during a traffic stop. Moreover, the odor of alcohol alone did not support reasonable suspicion for the officer to ask for voluntary consent to search the vehicle for alcohol. *State v. Burbach*, 706 N.W.2d 484 (Minn. 2005). New Jersey has also imposed similar requirements. *State v. Elders*, 899 A.2d 1037 (N.J. Super. 2006). Still other courts have rejected a rule requiring reasonable suspicion before merely asking about alcohol or drugs when asked to consider the question under their state constitutions. *State v. Cox*, 171 S.W.3d 174 (Tenn. 2005).

Questions about transporting illegal drugs or precursors that extend the scope of the stop beyond its original purpose must also be based on reasonable suspicion. *United States v. Jones*, 44 F.3d 860 (10th Cir. 1995). Information suggesting that vehicle occupants purchased drug precursors will support reasonable suspicion to detain. *People v. Leighty*, 837 N.E.2d 1022 (Ill. App. 2005), *cert. denied*, 844 N.E.2d 969 (Ill. 2006). A citizen's report that a suspect bought two gallons of iodine (a methamphetamine precursor) is reasonable suspicion to stop and question. *United States v. Araque*, 255 F. Supp. 2d 1010 (D. Neb. 2003); *People v. Reatherford*, 802 N.E.2d 340 (Ill. App. 2003) (purchase of 46 boxes of pseudoephedrine sufficient reasonable suspicion); *State v. Vereb*, 643 N.W.2d 342 (Minn. App. 2002) (reasonable suspicion when two men bought 30 boxes of pseudoephedrine from store). *But see State v. Bulington*, 802 N.E.2d 435 (Ind. 2004) (insufficient reasonable suspicion for stop when two men each purchased three boxes of pseudoephedrine in two separate grocery lines); *Williamson v. State*, 876 So. 2d 353 (Miss. 2004) (purchase of "several boxes" of pseudoephedrine insufficient reasonable suspicion). Recent federal legislation restricting pseudoephedrine purchasers to no more than 3.6 grams per day or 9 grams per 30 days provides additional grounds for reasonable suspicion of criminal activity when purchases exceed the limits. Many states have similar restrictions.

Drug interdiction indicators

During the course of a traffic stop, an officer may detect clues of illegal drug activity. Assembled together, these clues may provide the additional reasonable suspicion required to detain for further investigation. There is usually no single factor justifying further detention. Each individual factor, considered separately, may well have an innocent explanation, but still suggest illegal activity when considered in the aggregate. *United States v. Arvizu*, 534 U.S. 266 (2002) (multiple innocent facts considered together may amount to reasonable suspicion of criminal act). Following is a sampling of factors that courts have accepted as supporting reasonable suspicion of illegal drug trafficking:

- Nervousness, considered alone, is *never* sufficient to establish reasonable suspicion, and courts accept that most motorists are nervous when stopped by police. However, **extreme nervousness** should not be discounted. *United States v. Williams,* 403 F.3d 1203 (10th Cir. 2005) (suspect's "hands were shaking, his voice was cracking, he could not sit still, and his heart was beating so fast that Trooper Hyde was able to see his chest jerk"); *United States v. Carel,* 133 Fed. Appx. 497 (10th Cir. 2005) (hands and knees were trembling more than the average driver); *United States v. Lebrun,* 261 F.3d 731 (8th Cir. 2001) (sweating profusely on a cold day); *United States v. Bloomfield,* 40 F.3d 910 (8th Cir. 1994) (suspect perspiring, swallowing and breathing heavily, constantly moving his feet and fingers), *cert. denied,* 514 U.S. 1113 (1995); *State v. Huth,* 836 N.E.2d 623 (Ohio App. 2005) (panicky behavior and unusual fidgeting behind the wheel).
- **Implausible travel plans.** *United States v. Santos,* 403 F.3d 1120 (10th Cir. 2005); *United States v. Carel,* 133 Fed. Appx. 497 (10th Cir. 2005) (suspect driving his employer's vehicle from California to Indiana to search for another job); *United States v. Corona-Ramirez,* 125 Fed. Appx. 78 (8th Cir. 2005) (cost-effectiveness of a New Mexico wrecker transporting a utility vehicle to Georgia to fix a transmission); *United States v. Guerrero,* 379 F. Supp. 2d 1138 (D. Kan. 2005) (man dressed in business clothing driving from Los Angeles to Kansas City to work as building framer; man had no tools).
- **Conflicting explanations** or statements of purpose or destination. *United States v. Sowers,* 136 F.3d 24 (1st Cir. 1998) (detention of 30 minutes justified because driver and passenger told conflicting stories and were nervous); *United States v. Guerrero,* 379 F. Supp. 2d 1138 (D. Kan. 2005).
- **Criminal history** for driver or passengers of drug violations. *United States v. Santos,* 403 F.3d 1120 (10th Cir. 2005) (lying about prior criminal history of drug trafficking was "powerful" factor in establishing reasonable suspicion); *United States v. Lindsey,* 160 Fed. Appx. 708 (10th Cir. 2005) (lying about criminal history and denying knowledge of current arrest warrant); *United States v. Finke,* 85 F.3d 1275 (7th Cir. 1996).
- **Lack of familiarity** with the registered owner of the vehicle. *United States v. Carrate,* 122 F.3d 666 (8th Cir.

1997); *United States v. Guerrero,* 379 F. Supp. 2d 1138 (D. Kan. 2005).

- **Probability of hidden compartment**—based on external observation by the officer. *United States v. Wallace,* 429 F.3d 960 (10th Cir. 2005) (distance from trailer floor to underside suggested hidden compartment); *United States v. Corona-Ramirez,* 125 Fed. Appx. 78 (8th Cir. 2005) (compartment visible under wheel bed); *United States v. Leal,* 385 F. Supp. 2d 540 (W.D. Pa. 2005) (window would not roll down, suggesting that drugs could be hidden in the door panel).
- **Driving a rental vehicle**, particularly with a short-term rental. *State v. DeMarco,* 952 P.2d 1276 (Kan. 1998).
- **Religious statues and stickers.** *United States v. Guerrero,* 379 F. Supp. 2d 1138 (D. Kan. 2005) (religious symbols often used by drug dealers to convince police that the vehicle occupants are good people); *State v. Alverez,* 111 P.3d 808 (Utah App.), *cert. granted,* 124 P.3d 624 (Utah 2005) (statues and pictures of Jesus Malverde, pseudo-saint of drug dealers, suggest drug trafficking).
- **Driving from a known drug source city** to a drug destination city. *United States v. Carel,* 133 Fed. Appx. 497 (10th Cir. 2005) (driving from "California, a known drug source, and traveling to Indiana, a delivery point along route I-70, a common drug route"); *United States v. Foreman,* 369 F.3d 776 (4th Cir. 2004) (considering officer's prior drug interdiction experiences on Route 13 as a factor in reasonable suspicion of drug activity); *United States v. Morgan,* 270 F.3d 625 (8th Cir. 2001) (driving from Arizona, a marijuana source state, to Michigan with large, new duffle bags); *United States v. Carrate,* 122 F.3d 666 (8th Cir. 1997) (driving from California to Chicago); *United States v. Leal,* 385 F. Supp. 2d 540 (W.D. Pa. 2005) (driving from Texas border town to Philadelphia); *United States v. Guerrero,* 379 F. Supp. 2d 1138 (D. Kan. 2005) (driving from Los Angeles to Kansas City); *State v. DeMarco,* 952 P.2d 1276 (Kan. 1998) (driving from California to Kansas on I-70, a "known drug corridor").
- **Time of travel.** *United States v. Brown,* 334 F.3d 1161 (D.C. Cir. 2003) (interdiction stop in a high-crime area "is further compounded by the lateness of the hour"); *United States v. Lender,* 985 F.2d 151 (4th Cir. 1993) (lateness of hour on the road may be a factor in reasonable suspicion of drug trafficking); *United States v. Samaguey,* 180 F.3d 195 (5th Cir. 1999) (though "traveling at an usual

time of day alone may not give rise to a reasonable suspicion, it is a permissible consideration" in assessing reasonable suspicion).

- **Excessive air fresheners** or other odor-masking substances. *United States v. Grier,* 127 Fed. Appx. 712 (5th Cir. 2005) (strong odor of fabric softener); *United States v. Bloomfield,* 40 F.3d 910 (8th Cir. 1994) (deodorant later identified as "Stick-Ups" and "Renuzit" and dog repellant, pet deodorizer and ammonia), *cert. denied,* 514 U.S. 1113 (1995); *United States v. Morgan,* 270 F.3d 625 (8th Cir. 2001) (intense smell of cigar smoke and deodorizer and/or perfume); *United States v. Pollington,* 98 F.3d 341 (8th Cir. 1996) (laundry detergent); *United States v. Torres,* 2005 WL 3546677 (S.D. Ohio 2005) (Febreze).
- **Rental car company stickers** or contracts suggesting that the car was rented as a local rental only, yet driven long distances or across state lines. *Castaneda v. Commonwealth,* 376 S.E.2d 82 (Va. App. 1989) (bumper sticker from a local car rental company known for restricting rentals to local area supported investigatory detention of drug courier stopped outside of normal rental area).
- **Presence of multiple cell phones** in the vehicle, presence of a cell phone not belonging to the vehicle occupants, or two-way radio in the car. *United States v. Windrix,* 405 F.3d 1146 (10th Cir. 2005) (court relied on officer's statement that drug traffickers often use multiple cell phones to find probable cause for warrant); *United States v. Foreman,* 369 F.3d 776 (4th Cir. 2004); *United States v. Slater,* 351 F. Supp. 2d 1214 (D. Utah 2005) (drug couriers often provided with cell phones by dealer so that dealer may monitor the trip, and couriers may not know the phone number); *United States v. Chavira,* 2005 WL 1213670 (D. Kan. 2005) (discovery of second cell phone supported reasonable suspicion to detain); *United States v. White,* 42 F.3d 457 (8th Cir. 1994) (radar detector and ham radio in car).
- **Vehicles traveling in tandem.** *United States v. Owens,* 101 F.3d 559 (8th Cir. 1996) (driving in tandem "is one factor to be considered in determining whether reasonable suspicion exists"); *United States v. Ocampo,* 937 F.2d 485 (9th Cir. 1991) ("tandem driving, though oftentimes explicable on entirely innocent grounds, may likewise indicate criminal activity").
- **Lack of luggage for a long trip.** *United States v. Corona-Ramirez,* 125 Fed. Appx. 78 (8th Cir. 2005); *United States*

v. Hernandez, 418 F.3d 1206 (11th Cir. 2005); *United States v. Corona-Ramirez,* 125 Fed. Appx. 78 (8th Cir. 2005). In one case, the court cited excessive luggage as supporting reasonable suspicion to detain, where the suspect had taken a brief trip to a nearby destination. *People v. Lewis,* 649 N.W.2d 792 (Mich. App. 2002).

- **Luggage carried on the back seat,** suggesting a load of illegal drugs may be in the trunk. *United States v. Orsolini,* 300 F.3d 724 (6th Cir. 2002); *United States v. Ivey,* 313 F. Supp. 2d 1242 (D. Utah 2004).
- **Fast-food wrappers or food containers** suggesting a trip with few or no stops. *United States v. Lebrun,* 261 F.3d 731 (8th Cir. 2001); *LeBlanc v. State,* 138 S.W.3d 603 (Tex. App. 2004); *State v. Day,* 87 S.W.3d 51 (Mo. App. 2002). Due to the plethora of drive-through fast-food restaurants, several courts have declared fast-food wrappers on the car floors to be non-factors for a reasonable suspicion detention. *United States v. Smith,* 263 F.3d 571 (6th Cir. 2001).
- **Weapons questions.** There is a trend in courts to allow officers to ask the driver and passengers about weapons without any reasonable suspicion that there are weapons in the vehicle. In a recent and often-cited case from the Tenth Circuit Court of Appeals, the court ruled that the officer conducting a traffic stop is always allowed to ask about the presence of weapons in a vehicle. *United States v. Holt,* 264 F.3d 1215 (10th Cir. 2001) ("We therefore conclude that allowing officers to ask about the presence of loaded weapons in a lawfully stopped vehicle will promote the government's 'legitimate and weighty' interest in officer safety."). The court cited the number of assaults and deaths of officers stemming from traffic stops as part of the basis for its decision. Another court allowed questions about weapons when the car was a rental car, the driver admitted to drug-trafficking convictions, and the stop was in a high-crime area. *United States v. Purcell,* 236 F.3d 1274 (11th Cir. 2001).

  Note: the basis to ask weapons-related questions is slightly different from the basis to "frisk" the vehicle (see Vehicle Frisk section, below).

Seeking consent to search

Just as mere questioning does not create a detention, asking for consent to search a vehicle does not independently create a detention. Thus, most courts rule that no reasonable suspicion is required prior to asking for voluntary consent to search a vehicle at a traffic detention. *United States v. Burton*, 334 F.3d 514 (6th Cir. 2003) (holding police could, during the course of a traffic stop, ask driver whether he would consent to a search of the automobile); *United States v. Purcell*, 236 F.3d 1274 (11th Cir. 2001) (officer may ask for consent to search during "routine traffic stop"); *State v. Akuba*, 686 N.W.2d 406 (S.D. 2004) (officers properly seek consent to search at traffic stops "thousands of times daily across the nation" and "that is not an unreasonable law enforcement strategy" because persons can decline to answer); *People v. Moore*, 792 N.E.2d 836 (2003) (request for consent to search vehicle was legal, and reasonable suspicion was unnecessary); *James v. State*, 102 S.W.3d 162 (Tex. App. 2003) (after giving a warning ticket for minor traffic offenses, officer could ask for consent to search); *State v. Harris*, 590 N.W.2d 90 (Minn.1999) (absent a seizure, reasonable suspicion prior to request for consent to search is unnecessary); *State v. Middleton*, 43 S.W.3d 881 (Mo. App. 2001) (during traffic stop, officer may ask for consent to search for drugs in the absence of reasonable suspicion or probable cause). However, the prosecution carries a heavy burden to show that the consent was truly voluntary. *United States v. Flores*, 48 F.3d 467 (10th Cir.), *cert. denied*, 516 U.S. 839 (1995). A few courts hold that an officer may not ask for consent to search a vehicle during a routine traffic stop because the request exceeds the permissible scope of the stop. *State v. Elders*, 899 A.2d 1037 (N.J. Super. 2006) (relying on New Jersey Constitution); *State v. Mogen*, 52 P.3d 462 (Utah App. 2002).

Consent to search may also be requested if the encounter between the officer and the driver detention is ended and the encounter becomes purely voluntary. Returning the driver's documents (i.e., license, registration, insurance card) to the driver, issuing a citation or warning, and using a casual, conversational tone will generally convert the traffic stop into a consensual encounter. *United States v. West*, 219 F.3d 1171 (10th Cir. 2000) ("A traffic stop may become a consensual encounter, requiring no reasonable suspicion, if the officer returns the license and registration and asks questions without further constraining the driver by an overbearing show of authority.").

To convert a traffic detention into a consensual encounter, the first step is to return all documents to the driver. *United States v. Gregory*, 79 F.3d 973 (10th Cir. 1996); *United*

States v. Gonzalez-Lerma, 14 F.3d 1479 (10th Cir.), *cert. denied,* 511 U.S. 1095 (1994). Many courts view the act of returning the driver's license and other documents as a threshold question; if the documents are not returned, the encounter has not become consensual. *United States v. Urrea-Leal,* 322 F. Supp. 2d 1213 (D. Kan. 2004); *Daniel v. State,* 597 S.E.2d 116 (Ga. 2004). Moreover, if the officer has written a citation or a warning, that document should be delivered to the driver prior to attempting a voluntary encounter. *Faulkner v. State,* 567 S.E.2d 754 (Ga. App. 2002) (encounter not consensual where questioning began before driver was given copy of traffic ticket). Returning the driver's documents does not guarantee a finding of a voluntary encounter. When an officer returned the driver's license but continued to ask accusatory questions of the driver, and another officer had allowed the passenger to leave, the court found that there was a continued detention. *State v. Huffstutler,* ___ P.3d ___, 2006 WL 1096281 (Idaho App. 2006).

Though it is not required, telling a person that he or she is free to go effectively ends the detention. *Ohio v. Robinette,* 519 U.S. 33 (1996). Some states have required that the officer inform the suspect of the right to refuse consent. *State v. Todd,* 809 A.2d 818 (N.J. App. 2002). Other factors that courts consider: whether the officer displayed a weapon (not just wearing, but holding it or hand placed on the grip), presence of more than one officer, firm or commanding tone of voice, physical touching by the officer, and issuing a citation or warning—or failure to do so. *United States v. Elliott,* 107 F.3d 810 (10th Cir. 1997); *United States v. Turner,* 928 F.2d 956 (10th Cir.), *cert. denied,* 502 U.S. 881 (1991). In contrast, using a friendly and casual tone supports a conclusion of a voluntary encounter. *United States v. Drayton,* 536 U.S. 194 (2002); *People v. Heilman,* 52 P.3d 224 (Colo. 2002).

One court found that a traffic stop *did not* convert to a consensual detention where a second officer showed up at a traffic stop before the primary officer asked for consent to search and parked behind the primary officer with flashing lights. The primary officer initially told the defendant that the stop was for an improper lane change, yet when the officer returned the documents to the defendant, the officer did not mention either a citation or warning on the improper lane change. The court also noted that the primary officer did not inform the defendant that he was free to leave and did not have to answer the officer's questions. *State v.*

Hansen, 63 P.3d 650 (Utah 2002). This case shows how hard it is to legally convert a detention into a consensual encounter. Though it may seem a small point, the case might have come out differently if the officer had issued a warning or citation on the initial violation. It is not enough just to hand back the documents and immediately ask for consent to search. Further, any back-up officer should take care to have only the rear flashing lights illuminated.

Ordering driver and occupants out of the car or to remain in the car

In 1977, the United States Supreme Court laid down a bright-line rule that an officer may always require a driver to get out of a lawfully stopped vehicle. *Pennsylvania v. Mimms*, 434 U.S. 106 (1977). The Court balanced the privacy interests of the driver and the safety interests of the officer in reaching this conclusion. The officer need not state any particular suspicion or fear to require the driver to get out of the vehicle. Twenty years later, the Court extended its ruling to all passengers in a lawfully stopped car in *Maryland v. Wilson*, 519 U.S. 408 (1997). However, a handful of states have rejected the *Mimms/Wilson* rule on state constitutional grounds. *Commonwealth v. Gonsalves*, 711 N.E.2d 108 (Mass. 1999) (rejecting *Mimms/Wilson*); *State v. Mendez*, 970 P.2d 722 (Wash. 1999) (affirming acceptance of *Mimms* under Washington Constitution, though explicitly refusing to extend to passengers); *State v. Caron*, 586 A.2d 1127 (Vt. 1990) (court upholds exit order on the basis that police had reasonable suspicion that person stopped was armed and dangerous); *State v. Kim*, 711 P.2d 1291 (Haw. 1985) (rejecting *Mimms*).

Conversely, courts have relied on *Maryland v. Wilson* to rule that officers may require the driver and passengers to *remain inside* the car. "It follows from *Maryland v. Wilson* that a police officer has the power to reasonably control the situation by requiring a passenger to remain in a vehicle during a traffic stop, particularly where, as here, the officer is alone and feels threatened." *Rogala v. District of Columbia*, 1616 F.3d 44 (D.C. Cir. 1998). Officers may also require the driver and passengers to keep hands in plain sight during the traffic stop. *United States v. Moorefield*, 111 F.3d 10 (3d Cir. 1997); *King v. State*, 696 So. 2d 860 (Fla. App. 1997).

Stopping passengers from walking away from a traffic detention

Maryland v. Wilson did not answer the question of whether an officer could stop a passenger who wished to walk away from the scene of a traffic detention. For obvious and overwhelming safety reasons, officers should be able to keep driver and passengers in view and control their movements during the detention. *State v. Shearin,* 612 S.E.2d 371 (N.C. App. 2005) (citing studies of dangers presented to officers at traffic stops). Though courts have been divided on the issue, the majority view allows the officer to control the passengers' movements until the end of the traffic stop. *United States v. Williams,* 419 F.3d 1029 (9th Cir. 2005) ("It is reasonable for an officer to order a passenger back into an automobile that he voluntarily exited because of concerns for officer safety originally announced in *Wilson* and, specifically, the need for officers to exercise control over individuals encountered during a traffic stop outweighs the marginal intrusion on the passenger's liberty interest."); *Coffey v. Morris,* 401 F. Supp. 2d 542 (W.D. Va. 2005); *People v. Forbes,* 728 N.Y.S.2d 64 (N.Y. A.D. 2001); *State v. Hodges,* 631 N.W.2d 206 (S.D. 2001); *People v. Dixon,* 21 P.3d 440 (Colo. App. 2000); *People v. Gonzalez,* 704 N.E.2d 375 (Ill. 1998), *cert. denied,* 528 U.S. 825 (1999); *Carter v. State,* 494 S.E.2d 108 (Ga. App. 1997); *State v. Webster,* 824 P.2d 768 (Ariz. App. 1991) (An order to passenger to return to the car imposes no greater intrusion on the passenger's freedom than an order directing a passenger inside a stopped car to get out; the threat to the officer does not dissipate when a passenger gets out of a stopped car.).

Washington has turned to its state constitution to reject this view. *State v. Mendez,* 970 P.2d 722 (Wash. 1999) (police might be able to stop passenger if the passenger behaved in threatening or potentially dangerous fashion). A few other courts have relied on the open language of *Maryland v. Wilson* to limit police authority to stop passengers who wish to walk away from a traffic detention. *F.J.R. v. State,* 922 So. 2d 308 (Fla. App. 2006); *Castle v. State,* 999 P.2d 169 (Alaska App. 2000) (officer could not order passenger to return to the car, either as a potential witness to the traffic violation or for officer safety); *Dennis v. State,* 693 A.2d 1150 (Md.) (acknowledging open question left by *Maryland v. Wilson* and ruling that a passenger in a lawfully stopped vehicle could only be detained if there was a showing that it was safer for the officer to detain the passenger than allow him to walk away), *cert. denied*, 522 U.S. 928 (1997).

Identification and warrant checks for passengers

Whether an officer could ask a passenger for identification, or at least ask the passenger's name, has been the subject of a minor debate. Acknowledging the confusion, one court recently relied on the Supreme Court decision in *Muehler v. Mena*, 544 U.S. 93 (2005), to establish the bright-line rule that an officer may ask a passenger for identifying information. *United States v. Hernandez*, 418 F.3d 1206 (11th Cir. 2005) ("Arguments that the trooper asked questions unrelated to either officer safety, the speeding offense, or processing the citation are not determinative of our evaluation of the constitutionality of the seizure here. We are to look only at the duration of the seizure given all the circumstances: was it for an unreasonable time?"). A passenger who is committing no crime and does not fall into one of the categories listed below is generally free to decline to provide identifying information. *State v. Griffith*, 613 N.W.2d 72 (Wis. 2000). Even so, the officer is still free to ask without fear that the inquiry itself is improper. *United States v. Slater*, 411 F.3d 1003 (8th Cir. 2005); *United States v. Torres-Monje*, 433 F. Supp. 2d 1028 (D. N.D. 2006). A minority of state courts require reasonable suspicion to ask a passenger's name for investigatory purposes. *State v. Rankin*, 92 P.3d 202 (Wash. 2004) (applying state constitution); *State v. Affsprung*, 87 P.3d 1088 (N.M. 2004).

The driver of a car stopped by police is clearly seized for purposes of the Fourth Amendment. *Whren v. United States*, 517 U.S. 806 (1996). Many courts hold that passengers are also seized incident to seizure of the driver. *United States v. Perez*, 440 F.3d 363 (6th Cir. 2003); *United States v. Grant*, 349 F.3d 192 (5th Cir. 2003). A minority of courts rule that the passengers are not automatically seized during a traffic stop and instead analyze individual relevant factors to determine whether the passengers have been seized. *People v. Brendlin*, 136 P.3d 845 (Cal. 2006); *People v. Jackson*, 39 P.3d 1174 (Colo. 2002). The balance of authority on this issue may well shift as courts heed the principles of *Muehler v. Mena*. However, under current law, if the officer commands passengers to remain in the car or at the scene of the traffic stop and the passengers submit to the command, the officer has effectively seized the passengers. When an officer commands passengers to remain, the officer should take particular care to ensure that compliance with requests for passenger identification is voluntary, or that one of the circumstances below applies.

Courts have allowed record and warrant checks on passengers in a variety of circumstances. Following are examples of proper requests:

- Legitimate need to find a properly licensed driver in the car. *State v. Griffith*, 613 N.W.2d 72 (Wis. 2000); *State v. Higgins*, 884 P.2d 1242 (Utah 1994).
- Compliance with request for passenger identification is voluntary. *State v. Smith*, 683 N.W.2d 542 (Iowa 2004) (voluntariness of request shown by the officer's casual and conversational tone of voice, lack of demanding language, non-threatening manner, lack of weapons, and officer's court testimony that passenger could have refused to show identification); *State v. Williams*, 590 S.E.2d 151 (Ga. App. 2003); *People v. Jackson*, 39 P.3d 1174 (Colo. 2002); *People v. O'Neal*, 32 P.3d 533 (Colo. App. 2000).
- Passengers trying to hide from the officer's view inside the vehicle. *United States v. Lopez-Martinez*, 25 F.3d 1481 (10th Cir. 1994) (passenger peered through back window, stared at officer, and then sank back out of sight); *United States v. Garcia*, 732 F.2d 1221 (5th Cir. 1984) (passengers tried to hide by ducking and scrambling in vehicle); *United States v. Ramirez-Cubillas*, 223 F. Supp. 2d 1049 (D. Neb. 2002).
- Driver's statement that passengers are not United States citizens. *United States v. Rodriguez-Arreola*, 270 F.3d 611 (8th Cir. 2001); *United States v. Santana-Garcia*, 264 F.3d 1188 (10th Cir. 2001) (driver had no license, was not registered vehicle owner, stated passengers had come from Mexico and admitted they were not legal residents).
- Passenger has committed some violation, such as not wearing a seatbelt or having an open container of alcohol. *State v. Chelly*, 970 P.2d 376 (Wash. App.), *review denied*, 989 P.2d 1138 (Wash. 1999).
- Officer's request for passenger's information is for the purpose of making an accurate report of what happened on the traffic stop and identifying witnesses. *State v. Jones*, 5 P.3d 1012 (Kan. App. 2000), *aff'd*, 17 P.3d 359 (Kan. 2001); *State v. Chagaris*, 669 N.E.2d 92 (Ohio App. 1995) (voluntary request "so we know who we're talking to" without demand or show of force was permissible, be-

cause "detention, not questioning" is the "evil" to avoid); *People v. Grant,* 266 Cal. Rptr. 587 (Cal. App. 1990) (officer needed to identify passenger as witness to traffic citation of driver).
- Alcohol is in the vehicle, or the driver has been drinking, and there is reasonable suspicion that underage passenger has also been drinking. *State v. Ottesen,* 920 P.2d 183 (Utah App. 1996).

Once the officer obtains the passenger's identifying information, through whatever legitimate means, the officer may perform a warrant check as long as the detention is not unreasonably extended. *State v. Chagaris,* 669 N.E.2d 92 (Ohio App. 1995); *State v. Higgins,* 884 P.2d 1242 (Utah 1994). Then, if the warrant check reveals an active warrant, a valid arrest can result. If the officer has some reasonable suspicion that the passenger has given false information, further detention and investigation is appropriate. *People v. O'Neal,* 32 P.3d 533 (Colo. App. 2000) (passenger complied with officer's request for passenger's name, and once the officer had reasonable suspicion that the passenger had given a false name, the officer could investigate, which led to the discovery of the outstanding warrants).

Vehicle "frisks"

A vehicle may be given a quick, cursory inspection for weapons, also known as a "vehicle frisk," when there is reasonable suspicion that there are weapons in the vehicle. *Michigan v. Long,* 463 U.S. 1032 (1983). The frisk can include closed containers accessible to passengers. *United States v. Cervantes,* 19 F.3d 1151 (7th Cir. 1994), *cert. denied,* 513 U.S. 1086 (1995). Ordering the driver and passengers to exit the car may diminish the justification for frisking the vehicle. *State v. Warren,* 78 P.3d 590 (Utah 2003).

Several factors work in favor of a permissible vehicle frisk. These include:

- **Observing furtive movement,** particularly a movement fairly characterized as hiding something under the seat or taking something out from under the seat. *State v. Wilkins,* 692 A.2d 1233 (Conn. 1997); *Commonwealth v. Morris,* 644 A.2d 721 (Pa.) (quick movement toward feet at time of the stop), *cert. denied,* 513 U.S. 1031 (1994).
- **Ammunition in plain view.** *United States v. Baker,* 47 F.3d 691 (5th Cir.) (box of ammunition on the floorboard

made permissible a quick visual inspection of the car), *cert. denied,* 515 U.S. 1168 (1995).

- **Suspicion of a particularly dangerous crime** or crime involving a weapon. *See discussion of pedestrian frisk factors in the Investigative Detentions chapter. United States v. Rowland,* 341 F.3d 774 (8th Cir. 2003) (occupants driving stolen car reasonably presumed to be car thieves and reasonably presumed to be armed); *United States v. Rodriquez,* 750 F. Supp. 2d 1272 (W.D.N.C. 1990), *aff'd sub nom. United States v. Rodriquez-Morales,* 972 F.2d 343 (4th Cir. 1992) (officer had reasonable belief that the car's occupants were armed, where officer knew that drug dealers are frequently armed); *State v. Strickling,* 844 P.2d 979 (Utah App. 1992) (reasonable to frisk vehicle carrying burglary suspects). Some courts have authorized vehicle frisks upon reasonable suspicion that the occupants are dealing in drugs from the vehicle. *United States v. Sakyi,* 160 F.3d 164 (4th Cir. 1998) (reasonable suspicion that car contained illegal drugs supported frisk of occupants); *United States v. Brown,* 913 F.2d 570 (8th Cir. 1990).
- **Information that there are weapons in the car.** *State v. Sheldon,* 88 P.3d 1220 (Idaho App. 2003); *Maddox v. United States,* 745 A.2d 284 (D.C. 2000).
- **Vehicle occupant known to carry a weapon.** *United States v. Dennison,* 410 F.3d 1203 (10th Cir. 2005) (occupant known to be subject of arrest warrant for gun charges and to have been involved in recent domestic violence); *United States v. Holmes,* 376 F.3d 270 (4th Cir. 2004) (occupant belonged to gang whose members were known to carry guns); *State v. Chapman,* 921 P.2d 446 (Utah 1996) (but finding weapon not sufficient cause alone to justify computer check of weapon serial number).
- **Occupants are aggressive toward officers** (not merely rude or uncooperative). *State v. Clyburn,* 462 S.E.2d 538 (N.C. App. 1995).
- **Car windows are heavily tinted** and officer cannot see through windows. *United States v. Stanfield,* 109 F.3d 976 (4th Cir.) (officers conducting traffic stop of vehicle having windows so heavily tinted as to render officers unable to view interior of stopped vehicle may open door of vehicle and visually inspect its interior), *cert. denied,* 522 U.S. 857 (1997).
- **Pursuit and high-speed response driving cautions:** When the traffic violator doesn't stop, or when an officer be-

gins a pursuit for any reason, the suspect is not really "seized." Though it may be an attempt to seize, the suspect is not yet restrained or submitting to police authority, and no Fourth Amendment seizure occurs. *County of Sacramento v. Lewis,* 523 U.S. 833 (1998). That said, officers are urged to use the greatest discretion and caution in initiating and continuing a vehicular pursuit. Though no seizure may occur, there is still tremendous risk of enormous civil liabilities. Officers who kill and injure people in crashes may also face criminal liability. The risk of going to jail for an improper pursuit is very real.

Approximately 40 percent of law enforcement pursuits end in a crash, killing over 200 suspects in a year and an average of over 100 bystanders. Every year, more officers are killed in vehicle crashes than by gunfire. So even though there is no constitutional ban on beginning a pursuit for a speeding violation or some minor misdemeanor, consider the odds of death and injury to the officer, to uninvolved and innocent bystanders, and to suspects.

Canine sniffs

A canine sniff of the exterior of a vehicle found in a public location is not a "search" within the meaning of the Fourth Amendment. *United States v. Place,* 462 U.S. 696 (1983). "The exterior of a car is thrust into the public eye, and thus to examine it does not constitute a 'search.'" *New York v. Class,* 475 U.S. 106 (1986). *See Canine Search and Seizure chapter* for a thorough discussion of when and where a drug detector canine can be deployed. A canine sniff of the exterior of a vehicle may generally be conducted any time a vehicle is lawfully stopped and if the scope and duration of the detention is not extended by the sniff. *Illinois v. Caballes,* 543 U.S. 405 (2005). Some courts have allowed a very brief delay in a traffic detention without reasonable suspicion of drug possession to accomplish a dog sniff when a dog was at the scene of the traffic stop. *United States v. Alexander,* 448 F.3d 1014 (8th Cir. 2006); *United States v. $404,905.00 U.S. Currency,* 182 F.3d 643 (8th Cir. 1999), *cert. denied,* 528 U.S. 1161 (2000).

If there is reasonable suspicion to believe that the vehicle contains drugs, then the vehicle may be detained for a brief time to await the arrival of a drug-detection dog.

United States v. McFarley, 991 F.2d 1188 (4th Cir.), *cert. denied,* 510 U.S. 949 (1993). Courts routinely allow detentions of 30 minutes or more. *United States v. Villa-Chaparro,* 115 F.3d 797 (10th Cir.) (finding that a 48-minute detention was not unreasonable while awaiting canine unit), *cert. denied,* 522 U.S. 926 (1997); *Commonwealth v. Feyenord,* 833 N.E.2d 590 (Mass. 2005) (30-minute detention was reasonable, citing numerous cases of longer detention), *cert. denied,* ___ U.S. ___, 126 S. Ct. 1369 (2006). The key issue is that the canine is promptly called and promptly responds when there is reasonable suspicion of a drug crime.

If the canine sniff is being conducted with no reasonable suspicion of a drug crime, it is critical that the detention not be extended even briefly to get the dog to the scene to conduct the sniff. Several courts have allowed canine sniffs that create a slight (two- to three-minute) increase in the detention time when the canine is already at the scene of the traffic stop. *United States v. $404,905.00 in U.S. Currency,* 182 F.3d 643 (8th Cir. 1999), *cert. denied,* 528 U.S. 1161 (2000); *State v. DeLaRosa,* 657 N.W.2d 683 (S.D. 2003). Thus, a drug detector dog handler may enjoy slightly more latitude to detain at a routine traffic stop. As with any accommodation extended by courts, abuse leads to loss, and care in performing a sniff promptly is strongly advised.

Roadblocks

Michigan v. Sitz

The United States Supreme Court has specifically approved the use of limited sobriety checkpoints, also called DUI roadblocks, to combat impaired drivers. *Michigan v. Sitz,* 496 U.S. 444 (1990). The Court held that sobriety checkpoints must: (1) present only a slight intrusion; (2) operate according to a plan that limits participating officers' discretion; and (3) be aimed at curbing the problem of impaired drivers. Some states have adopted statutes that control sobriety checkpoints.

The Court had previously approved roadblocks as a part of border enforcement in *United States v. Martinez-Fuerte,* 428 U.S. 543 (1976) (allowing fixed Border Patrol checkpoints to intercept undocumented aliens). Courts have also approved checkpoints for driver's licenses. *State v. Mitchell,*

592 S.E.2d 543 (N.C. 2004); *State v. Orr,* 745 N.E.2d 1036 (Ohio 2001). Roadblocks to enforce fish and game regulations are also permissible. *State v. Tourtillott,* 618 P.2d 423 (1980), *cert. denied,* 451 U.S. 972 (1981); *State v. Thurman,* 996 P.2d 309 (Idaho App. 1999); *State v. Albaugh,* 571 N.W.2d 345 (N.D. 1997). Administrative planning and approval, coupled with neutral criteria for stopping vehicles, is required. *State v. Knowles,* 917 So. 2d 1262 (La. App. 2005); *State v. Legg,* 536 S.E.2d 110 (W. Va. 2000). Port of entry or weigh station checkpoints are also permissible. *State v. Jutte,* 968 P.2d 334 (N.M. App. 1998).

Investigative roadblocks

General crime control roadblocks—i.e., fishing expeditions—are not lawful. *City of Indianapolis v. Edmond,* 531 U.S. 32 (2000). In *Edmond,* the Court ruled that the police department roadblocks to catch drug offenders violated the Fourth Amendment because the roadblock's primary purpose was essentially the same as a general interest in crime control. A dragnet roadblock to round up all the usual suspects cannot withstand constitutional scrutiny. "We have never approved a checkpoint program whose primary purpose was to detect evidence of ordinary criminal wrongdoing. Rather, our checkpoint cases have recognized only limited exceptions to the general rule that a seizure must be accompanied by some measure of individualized suspicion. Each of the checkpoint programs that we have approved was designed primarily to serve purposes closely related to the problems of policing the border or the necessity of ensuring roadway safety." The *Edmond* case teaches that a roadblock's primary purpose cannot be to identify or deter "ordinary criminal activity."

A temporary roadblock can be operated to cordon off an area and search for suspects. *United States v. O'Mara,* 963 F.2d 1288 (9th Cir. 1992) (roadblock after shots fired in campground); *United States v. Davis,* 43 F. Supp. 2d 1302 (M.D. Ala. 2001) (roadblock to apprehend six known suspects believed to be traveling particular road), *aff'd,* 288 F.3d 1262 (11th Cir.), *cert. denied,* 537 U.S. 1094 (2002); *Commonwealth v. Grant,* 783 N.E.2d 455 (Mass. App) (roadblock set up after shooting in neighborhood), *review denied,* 786 N.E.2d 394 (Mass. 2003).

In a slight variation on that theory, police in Lombard, Illinois, placed a roadblock at the scene a week after a 70-year-old bicyclist was killed in a hit-and-run crash in hopes of finding a witness. Officers stopped all cars traveling in the direction of the crash, detaining the motorists for about 15 seconds, handing out a flyer about the crash and asking if they had seen anything that might help the investigation. As the minivan driven by Robert Lidster approached the roadblock, Lidster almost struck one of the officers. Subsequent investigation resulted in Lidster's arrest and conviction for driving under the influence of alcohol. The Supreme Court ruled that these so-called "special needs" roadblocks are constitutional if the law enforcement need outweighs severity of the intrusion. *Illinois v. Lidster,* 540 U.S. 419 (2004). The *Lidster* roadblock was valid because the investigation was for a serious crime (vehicular homicide), the investigation had no other leads to follow, the roadblock was a last-chance effort to find a witness, and the roadblock had a reasonable chance of success. The Court found that the intrusion was minimal and that the roadblock was designed to minimize anxiety and alarm.

A checkpoint with the primary purpose of disseminating information to citizens constitutes a Fourth Amendment seizure but is constitutional. An officer staffing a checkpoint at the main entry to a public recreation area stopped all motorists to explain regulations governing fires, litter, and alcohol. A driver challenged his conviction for possession of an open container of alcohol (as well as marijuana and drug paraphernalia), claiming that the checkpoint was an unlawful general crime-control roadblock similar to the one struck down in *City of Indianapolis v. Edmond.* The court ruled that the checkpoint was more similar to the information-gathering checkpoint upheld in *Illinois v. Lidster* than to the unconstitutional general crime-control roadblock in *Edmond.* The court found that the primary purpose of the checkpoint was to disseminate information about the area, not to promote general crime control. *United States v. Faulkner,* 450 F.3d 466 (9th Cir. 2006).

Administrative traffic checkpoints

In response to a number of court decisions addressing sobriety checkpoints, many states adopted administrative traffic checkpoint laws to define the operation of sobriety (and other purpose) checkpoints. *See, e.g.,* Haw. Rev. Stat. 286-162.5, 286-162.6; Mont. Code Ann. 46-5502; Nev. Rev. Stat. Ann. 484.359; N.H. Rev. Stat. Ann. 265:1-a; Utah Code Ann. §§ 77-23-101 *et seq.* Over three-quarters of the states allow sobriety checkpoints by statute or under judicial decisions.

Sobriety Checkpoint State Case Law Summary (Nat'l Highway Traffic Safety Admin. 2000).

The critical measure of any sobriety checkpoint, whether established by statute or allowed by judicial decision, is the limitation on the discretion of officers in the field. *Commonwealth v. Worthy*, 903 A.2d 576 (Pa. Super. 2006) ("central concern in balancing the opposing interests is protecting the individual from arbitrary invasions at the unfettered discretion of officers in the field"); *State v. Levitt,* 73 S.W.3d 159 (Tenn. App. 2001) ("most important attribute of a reasonable roadblock is the presence of genuine limitations upon the discretion of the officers in the field"). Limitations on field officers' discretion are created when administrative officers determine where to situate the checkpoint and when administrative officers prescribe procedures to be used in operating the checkpoint. *State v. Levitt,* 73 S.W.3d 159 (Tenn. App. 2001).

The usual purpose for an administrative checkpoint is to deter and apprehend impaired drivers, thereby enhancing the safety of the motoring public. A roadblock with the primary purpose of detecting evidence of ordinary criminal wrongdoing, such as illegal drug trafficking, violates the Fourth Amendment. *City of Indianapolis v. Edmonds,* 531 U.S. 32 (2000). Most courts are very skeptical of mixed-motive roadblocks. *United States v. Morales-Zamora,* 974 F.2d 149 (10th Cir. 1992) (roadblock premised on driver's license checks but actually focusing on drug interdiction was unreasonable). However, one federal circuit court has adopted a totally objective standard for roadblock purposes. As long as one of the purposes of the roadblock is authorized by law, it does not matter that officers are actually pursuing narcotics enforcement. *Merrett v. Moore,* 58 F.3d 1547 (11th Cir. 1995), *cert. denied,* 519 U.S. 812 (1996) (driver's license checkpoint's significant purpose to detect drug activity held permissible).

Problems arise when officers relying on administrative traffic checkpoint statutes stray from the intent and language of the authorizing statute. The Utah Supreme Court struck down a checkpoint with seven stated purposes and 11 checks to effect those seven purposes. *State v. Abell,* 70 P.3d 98 (Utah 2003). The court stated: "We permit checkpoints in order to advance the singular purpose of 'promoting the safe use of the highways.' Each element of the checkpoint plan must be 'narrowly tailored' to serve this limited interest alone." This does not mean that an officer must ignore obvious violations unrelated to the purpose of the checkpoint, as long as the primary purpose is that the focus and the judicially approved plan is followed. *State v. Aguinaldo,* 782 P.2d 1225 (Haw. 1989) (request to see driver's license and insurance card at a sobriety checkpoint was reasonable). When a person stopped at a game enforcement checkpoint, an officer asked to see her driver's license. After learning that it was suspended, the officer cited her. She argued that a driver's license check was beyond the scope of a game checkpoint. The court disagreed, noting that a request to see a license was reasonable even though not part of the checkpoint plan. *State v. Tourtillott,* 618 P.2d 423 (Ore. 1980).

Avoiding a checkpoint as a basis for detention

The roadblock should be planned to allow lawful avoidance of the checkpoint stop. *State v. Gerschoffer,* 763 N.E.2d 960 (Ind. 2002) ("In evaluating the degree of intrusion, we also consider whether the roadblock was avoidable. The more avoidable a roadblock is, the less it interferes with the liberty of individual drivers."). It is not an essential constitutional requirement that the roadblock be unavoidable. *State v. Hester,* 584 A.2d 256 (N.J. Super. 1990). However, the best practice is to allow motorists to avoid the checkpoint while still observing such motorists and stopping them as necessary on the grounds of traffic violations other than avoiding the checkpoint.

A traffic checkpoint statute may prohibit intentional failure to stop at a checkpoint, but what about motorists who see the checkpoint and try to avoid it? Merely making a U-turn to avoid the checkpoint, assuming that the U-turn is lawfully executed, is not sufficient grounds for a stop. However, officers do not need to completely ignore the U-turn. They may choose to follow the car and watch for other violations. "We do not mean to suggest that flight from a checkpoint must be entirely ignored. Flight may heighten an officer's general suspicion and provide added justification for a stop. We merely hold that 'flight,' *alone,* is not sufficient to create an articulable suspicion for a stop." *State v. Talbot,* 792 P.2d 489 (Utah App. 1990). At least one court has ruled that exiting a highway where no services are present and there is no other reasonable purpose to exit creates adequate reasonable suspicion for a stop. *State v. Mack,* 66 S.W.3d 706 (Mo. 2002).

The Indiana Court of Appeals noted that to require that officers not consider avoidance of a roadblock in evaluating reasonable suspicion would be to "ignore reality." *Snyder v. State,* 538 N.E.2d 961 (Ind. App. 1989). Remember, "the wicked flee where no man pursueth." *California v. Hodari D.,* 499 U.S. 621 (1991) (quoting *Proverbs* 28:1). Several courts have found reasonable suspicion to stop when a driver avoids an actual roadblock and commits a minor traffic violation in the process. *Stanley v. State,* 382 S.E.2d 686 (Ga. App. 1989); *Jones v. State,* 723 P.2d 984 (Okla. App. 1986).

Public housing checkpoints

Following the explicit prohibition on general crime-control roadblocks of *City of Indianapolis v. Edmonds,* it is evident that roadblocks at public housing project access points are unlawful. Chattanooga Housing Authority police officers conducted random, regular checkpoints to identify whether persons entering a public housing zone were residents and were bringing drugs or other contraband into the housing project. Hayes was stopped at a checkpoint and found to unlawfully possess alcohol. Prosecutors tried to distinguish the housing checkpoints from *Edmonds* by arguing that the checkpoints were intended to exclude non-resident trespassers and deter crime, not to identify crimes already committed. The court found the housing access checkpoints to be unconstitutional under *Edmonds. State v. Hayes,* 188 S.W.3d 505 (Tenn. 2006).

But an otherwise lawful checkpoint is not unconstitutional just because it is conducted on public housing access roads. A county sheriff held a contract with a local housing authority to provide security at the housing project. The sheriff set up a checkpoint at a major intersection in the public housing project, stopping all vehicles to check driver's license s, automobile insurance documentation, and vehicle safety devices such as seatbelts. The court found that this was reasonable under the Fourth Amendment because the primary purpose was lawful. *Ex parte Jackson,* 886 So. 2d 155 (Ala. 2004).

Roadblock ruse operations

Creative officers have placed highway signs indicating that a drug enforcement roadblock would be waiting down the road when no roadblock is actually being operated. "Spotters" watch the road from a hidden position near the signs to observe persons tossing out drugs and alcohol. *United States v. Klinginsmith,* 25 F.3d 1507 (10th Cir.), *cert. denied,* 513 U.S. 1059 (1994); *United States v. McGee,* 816 F. Supp. 1511 (D. Kan. 1993). The roadblock ruse technique can be very productive. However, there are several limitations that must be carefully observed.

Ruse operations that entice motorists to exit the freeway to avoid the checkpoint and then stop motorists who exit are not proper. *United States v. Huguenin,* 154 F.3d 547 (6th Cir. 1998). However, a motorist is not "seized" when a roadblock ruse sign prompts the motorist to exit the freeway. When a motorist saw such a sign, left the freeway, and tossed out a package of methamphetamine, officers recovered the package and subsequently stopped and arrested the driver. The driver claimed that he did not voluntarily abandon the package of methamphetamine because he was compelled to do so by the roadblock ruse. The court disagreed and allowed admission of the illegal drugs at trial. *United States v. Flynn,* 309 F.3d 736 (10th Cir. 2002).

Ruse operations must be limited to stops where there is a clearly articulable violation observed by an officer. Under the pretext doctrine of *United States v. Whren,* the officer's subjective motivation for the stop is not an issue as long as there is an underlying violation of traffic or criminal laws to support the stop. Officers must also limit ruse operations where state statutes prohibit them. In such cases, officers may consider placing ruse signs at some distance before an actual checkpoint and having spotters watch for violations of the law, such as littering or unlawful U-turns.

"Hand-off" or "wall stops"

One form of a pretext stop is known as a hand-off or wall stop. This stop is based on a legitimate traffic violation motivated by a belief that illegal drugs or other contraband will be found in the vehicle, and designed to preserve the confidentiality of a continuing investigation that provided the initial information. The term "wall stop" is based on the theory that there is a wall between the stopping officers and the investigators who give the tip to the stopping officers. Essentially, the investigators have "handed off" the information to the stopping officers. These are not stops intended just to gather intelligence about who may be driving a load of drugs or other information; rather, they are intended to lead to an independently prosecutable case. Often, the information leading to the suggestion for a stop comes from a confidential and continuing wiretap operation.

In a wall stop, the stopping officers must find their own reasonable suspicion to stop the vehicle and their own probable cause to arrest and/or search. Though investigators should never withhold information affecting officer safety issues, they should give only the bare minimum information to the stopping officers. This encourages, indeed requires, the stopping officer to develop independent cause for the stop. Moreover, if the stopping officers are not told what to look for—beyond evidence of criminal activity—then the prosecutor's ability to keep the ongoing investigation confidential will be greatly enhanced. Naturally, the investigators may point out that the vehicle's registration is expired, or the tires are balding, or some other violation. There may also be plans to have a drug detector dog nearby, thus eliminating the waiting period and potential issue of expanding the detention. Even though many wall stops are impromptu and reactive to surveillance, as much prior planning as possible enhances safety and success probabilities.

Note: An officer or agency using wall stops should be trained on how to develop the stop from the observed violation all the way through the writing of the report. This section is merely an introduction to the technique as part of the discussion of permissible pretext stops under *United States v. Whren.*

CHAPTER 3

ARREST

Introduction

Making an Arrest

Defining an arrest and when an arrest is considered to have been effected
Defining probable cause
Sources of probable cause to arrest
Constructive possession and probable cause to arrest
Misdemeanor arrests
Felony arrests
Use and preparation of arrest warrants
Place of arrest
Exceptions to the rule of *Payton* and *Steagald:* Consent, exigency, and hot pursuit
Fresh pursuit and peace officer authority
Vienna Convention arrest and detention issues
Diplomatic immunity
Fingerprinting and photographing

Introduction

Restricting a person's liberty in a significant way is a seizure. Classifying a seizure as either an investigatory detention or an arrest is important to determine: a) whether *Miranda* applies, and b) whether a person may be lawfully searched incident to arrest. **All arrests are seizures, but not all seizures are arrests.**

It is possible for an officer to unintentionally arrest a person. If an officer arrests a person without sufficient probable cause, this is often called a "false arrest." The consequences of an improper arrest can include suppression of any testimonial statements by the suspect, suppression of physical evidence, and personal civil liability for the officer.

Making an Arrest

Defining an arrest and when an arrest is considered to have been effected

The traditional definition of arrest by an officer includes four elements:

- Intent to arrest communicated by words or actions of the officer,
- Show of the officer's authority,
- Submission to custody or sufficient force to effect custody by the officer, and
- The person's understanding that he or she is under arrest.

Most states statutorily define an arrest simply as "the taking of a person into custody when and in the manner authorized by law, including restraint of the person or the person's submission to custody." Iowa Code § 804.5 (2005); Cal. Penal Code § 834 ("taking a person into custody, in a case and in the manner authorized by law"); Texas Code Crim. Proc. Ann. Art. 15.22 (2003) (arrest occurs when person is actually restrained or taken into custody); Arizona Rev. Stat. § 13-3881 (2001) ("arrest is made by an actual restraint of the person to be arrested, or by his submission to the custody of the person making the arrest").

An arrest occurs when an officer deprives a person of liberty in a significant way, and to the degree traditionally associated with a formal arrest. To decide if an arrest was made, a court considers whether "in view of all the circumstances surrounding the incident, a reasonable person would have believed that he was not free to leave." *United States v. Mendenhall,* 446 U.S. 544 (1980). An arrest must be based upon probable cause to believe that a crime was committed and that the arrestee committed it. *Beck v. Ohio,* 379 U.S. 89 (1964).

An arrest may occur even where the officer does not subjectively intend to arrest. Several factors are considered in weighing whether a de facto arrest has occurred. One court noted that "no scientific formula exists" to distinguish between investigative stops and arrests. *United States v. McGuire,* 359 F.3d 71 (1st Cir. 2004). The principal question is whether a reasonable person would feel free to leave under the circumstances. In making this assessment, courts consider a variety of factors, including:

- **Display of weapons by officers.** *United States v. Merkley,* 988 F.2d 1062 (10th Cir. 1993) (guns and handcuffs reasonable; "a law enforcement agent, faced with the possibility of danger, has a right to take reasonable steps to protect himself and an obligation to ensure the safety of innocent bystanders, regardless of whether probable cause to arrest exists"); *United States v. Merritt,* 695 F.2d 1263 (10th Cir. 1982) (displaying shotguns when making an investigatory stop of a suspect they reasonably believed was heavily armed and dangerous did not create arrest), *cert. denied,* 461 U.S. 916 (1983); *United States v. Taylor,* 716 F.2d 701 (9th Cir. 1983) (no arrest occurred when police approached suspects with drawn guns after having been warned that suspects were dangerous).
- **Presence of numerous officers.** *United States v. Quinn,* 815 F.2d 153 (1st Cir. 1987) (presence of five officers arriving at various times showed that investigation was serious, but did not create arrest); *United States v. Fernandez Santana,* 975 F. Supp. 135 (D. P.R. 1997).
- **Physical restraint or touching of the person.** *United States v. Maguire,* 359 F.3d 71 (1st Cir. 2004) (physically grabbing a robbery suspect did not create arrest); *United States v. Zapata,* 18 F.3d 971 (1st Cir. 1994) ("modest laying-on of hands" does not create arrest); *United States v. Alvarado-Rodriguez,* 59 F. Supp. 2d 329 (D. P.R. 1999) (brief touching of suspect during detention did not create an arrest); *Curry v. State,* 699 S.W.2d 331 (Tex. App. 1985) (suspect was arrested when the officer "grabbed" suspect's arm).

- **Blocking a suspect's exit route.** *United States v. Young,* 105 F.3d 1 (1st Cir. 1997) (blocking a suspect's path a factor in deciding whether a reasonable person would feel free to leave); *People v. McHugh,* 14 Cal. Rptr. 3d 142 (Cal. App. 2004) (pointing a gun at suspect and blocking suspect's car did not reach level of arrest when suspect appeared inclined to flee and the officer's gun was displayed only long enough to seize car keys). However, a person may be contained (though not restrained) and still not be under arrest. For example, in *People v. Treier,* 630 N.Y.S.2d 224 (N.Y. Co. Ct. 1995), a suspect who had taken hostages and was surrounded by a SWAT team claimed that his statements to the hostage negotiator should be suppressed. He asserted that he was under arrest and had not received a *Miranda* warning. The court ruled that, though contained and blocked, he could not be under arrest because he was not yet actually restrained by officers. A reasonable person would not have considered holding a gun on a hostage, though surrounded by police, as being under arrest.
- **Use of handcuffs or other restraints.** *United States v. Miller,* 974 F.2d 953 (8th Cir. 1992) (handcuffs on dangerous suspect approved); *United States v. Del Vizo,* 918 F.2d 821 (9th Cir. 1990) (where drug-trafficking suspect did not resist arrest, officers exceeded the bounds of an investigative stop by ordering him from his car at gunpoint and handcuffing him); *United States v. Hastamorir,* 881 F.2d 1551 (11th Cir. 1989); *United States v. Bautista,* 684 F.2d 1286 (9th Cir. 1982) (handcuffing justified by possibility that another suspect lurked in the vicinity), *cert. denied,* 459 U.S. 1211 (1983); *Adams v. State,* 830 So. 2d 911 (Fla. App. 2002) (jumping on suspect without warning and handcuffing suspect strong factors in finding that arrest had occurred).
- **Tone of voice and authoritative commands**. *State v. Ketchum,* 34 P.3d 1006 (Haw. 2001) (ordering suspects to raise hands contributes to finding of arrest); *United States v. Brown,* 313 F. Supp. 2d 1108 (D. Kan. 2004) (tone suggesting compliance is a required factor in determining detention or voluntary encounter).
- **Accusatory nature of questioning.** *United States v. Fernandez Santana,* 975 F. Supp. 135 (D. P.R. 1997) (generic nature of questioning in a public area suggests an investigatory stop and not an arrest).

- **Confining the suspect in a patrol car.** *United States v. Dickson,* 58 F.3d 1258 (8th Cir. 1995) (confinement in car for 15 minutes does not automatically create an arrest), *cert. denied,* 516 U.S. 1064 (1996); *United States v. Bloomfield,* 40 F.3d 910 (8th Cir. 1994) (confinement of one hour a factor, but no arrest occurred), *cert. denied,* 514 U.S. 1113 (1995); *United States v. Maltais,* 295 F. Supp. 2d 1077 (D. N.D. 2003) (placing in car for one and one-half hours while waiting for a drug dog a factor to consider, but no arrest created).
- **Moving the suspect from the scene of detention.** *Florida v. Royer,* 460 U.S. 491 (1983) (not all movements of suspect create arrest; "there are undoubtedly reasons of safety and security that would justify moving a suspect from one location to another during an investigatory detention"); *United States v. Hernandez,* 825 F.2d 846 (5th Cir. 1987) (removal of suspect from scene of the stop to police headquarters usually marks the point at which the investigative stop becomes a de facto arrest), *cert. denied,* 484 U.S. 1068 (1988); *United States v. Gonzalez,* 763 F.2d 1127 (10th Cir. 1985) (*forcing* suspect to go to the police station crosses the line into de facto arrest); *United States v. Jones,* 759 F.2d 633 (8th Cir. 1985) (moving suspect for the purposes of protecting officers does not elevate the detention to the level of arrest); *Swift v. State,* 899 A.2d 867 (Md. 2006) (moving suspect and segregating from others a factor to consider in assessing a seizure).
- **Length of detention.** *United States v. Walker,* 47 Fed. Appx. 851 (9th Cir. 2002) (37-minute detention strong factor in creating an arrest, not an investigatory detention). There is no magic time limit that transforms a detention into an arrest. *United States v. Sharpe,* 470 U.S. 675 (1985).
- **Reciting of *Miranda* warning.** *Baggett v. State,* 849 So. 2d 1154 (Fla. App. 2003) (reading *Miranda* warnings and handcuffing suspect created de facto arrest); *Saturnino-Boudet v. State,* 682 So. 2d 188 (Fla. App. 1996) (giving *Miranda* warnings during detention, when not required, did not elevate detention into an arrest).

Defining probable cause

Probable cause to arrest exists when the facts known to the officer and the inferences that can fairly be drawn there-

from would cause a reasonable and prudent person to believe that the suspect had committed a crime. *Beck v. Ohio,* 379 U.S. 89 (1964). The United States Supreme Court defines probable cause justifying an arrest as "facts and circumstances within the officer's knowledge that are sufficient to warrant a reasonable person in believing, in the circumstances shown, that the suspect has committed, is committing, or is about to commit an offense." *Michigan v. DeFillippo,* 443 U.S. 31 (1979). In essence, probable cause is a reasonable belief that a suspect is about to commit, is committing, or imminently will commit a crime. Probable cause is a far lower standard than evidence sufficient to convict. An acquittal on a criminal charge does not mean that probable cause was lacking. *Williams ex rel. Allen v. Cambridge Bd. of Education,* 370 F.3d 630 (6th Cir. 2004). The probable cause standard is lower, even, than a preponderance of the evidence standard used in civil cases. *Biddle v. Martin,* 992 F.2d 673 (7th Cir. 1993); *United States v. 221 Dana Avenue,* 261 F.3d 65 (1st Cir. 2001).

Sources of probable cause to arrest

- **Crime in the officer's presence.** An officer can always arrest a person for a crime committed in the officer's presence, no matter how minor the crime. *Atwater v. City of Lago Vista,* 532 U.S. 318 (2001).
- **Arrest warrant.** An arrest warrant is a judicial command, issued by a court of competent jurisdiction, to arrest a particular person on a particular charge. The judge has already determined that there is probable cause for an arrest. Either a written or verbal arrest warrant is generally sufficient. *Trapp v. U.S. Marshals Service,* 2005 WL 3179471 (D. Kan. 2005). Some states require a written warrant to validate the arrest. *Commonwealth. v. Muller,* 18 Mass. L. Rptr. 483 (Mass. Super. 2004); *State v. McKee,* 958 P.2d 700 (Mont. 1998). The officer generally does not need to have the written warrant in hand before making an arrest. *United States v. Buckner,* 717 F.2d 297 (6th Cir. 1983) (officer's lack of the warrant in hand was of "no consequence" where officer had reliable knowledge that a warrant had been issued); Fed. R. Crim. P. 4(c)(3)(A).
- **Informants.** When an informant is relied upon for probable cause for an arrest warrant or a warrantless arrest, the officer must have a basis for the truthfulness of the informant's statement. *Illinois v. Gates,* 462 U.S. 213 (1983). The court will consider the totality of the circum-

stances to determine whether the informant's tip, together with the officer's corroborating observations, provided probable cause to arrest. This is similar to the rule requiring verification of an informant's information to support a search warrant. *See Search Warrant chapter.*

- **Crime observed by another officer.** An officer may rely on information received from a fellow officer in determining probable cause to arrest. *United States v. Ventresca,* 380 U.S. 102 (1965).
- **An officer may rely on specialized training** or experience to help establish probable cause to arrest. For example, smelling freshly burned marijuana during a traffic stop, smelling the odors of a clandestine lab, or seeing a substance that appears to be methamphetamine all can provide probable cause to arrest. *United States v. Eaton,* 99 Fed. Appx. 85 (9th Cir. 2004) (officer's detection of odor of methamphetamine production from outside of known drug user's apartment created probable cause to arrest); *United States v. Scroger,* 98 F.3d 1256 (10th Cir. 1996) (officer's detection of odor consistent with methamphetamine manufacturing when defendant opened door constituted probable cause); *Blake v. State,* 772 So. 2d 1200 (Ala. App. 2000); *State v. Overby,* 590 N.W.2d 703 (N.D. 1999) (officer had probable cause to arrest defendant where officer smelled odor of burning marijuana emanating from vehicle during traffic stop); *Brunson v. State,* 940 S.W.2d 440 (Ark. 1997) (odor of marijuana from a legally stopped vehicle gave probable cause to arrest all four occupants of the vehicle), *cert. denied,* 522 U.S. 898 (1997); *State v. Mitchell,* 482 N.W.2d 364 (Wis. 1992) (odor of burned or burning marijuana and presence of smoke inside an automobile provided probable cause to arrest both driver and passenger); *State v. Hammond,* 603 P.2d 377 (Wash. App. 1979) (officers detected odor of burning marijuana coming from an automobile, giving probable cause to arrest the vehicle occupants).

Constructive possession and probable cause to arrest

One common probable cause issue in drug arrests arises when drugs are found in a room or vehicle occupied by multiple persons. Rarely does the question "Who owns the dope?" result in a complete and honest answer. To show that a suspect constructively possesses contraband and therefore may be arrested, an officer must have facts demonstrating a sufficient connection between the suspect and the drugs or other contraband to infer that the suspect had both the power and the intent to exercise dominion and control over the contraband. *Commonwealth v. Clarke,* 692 N.E.2d 85 (Mass. App. 1998). The Supreme Court recently ruled that when cocaine was found in the glove box of a car occupied by three persons late at night and all three denied ownership, there was a probable cause basis to arrest all three. *Maryland v. Pringle,* 540 U.S. 366 (2004). Remember, probable cause to arrest does not necessarily ensure a conviction.

A number of factors will help show constructive possession of contraband, including:

- **Proximity to the contraband,** though not necessarily in plain view. *State v. Salas,* 820 P.2d 1386 (Utah App. 1991). Testimony of witnesses who see the suspect near the contraband is also helpful. *State v. Hopkins,* 989 P.2d 1065 (Utah 1999). Proximity to large quantities of drugs strongly supports constructive possession. *United States v. Romero,* 452 F.3d 610 (6th Cir. 2006).
- **Contraband in plain view near suspect.** *Gee v. State,* 810 N.E.2d 338 (Ind. 2004); *Miller v. State,* 6 S.W.3d 812 (Ark. App. 1999).
- **Drug packaging materials** similar to those found in a suspect's possession may indicate constructive possession of other drugs. *State v. Taylor,* 818 P.2d 561 (Utah App. 1991).
- **Suspect's fingerprints on packaging material.** *State v. Cashen,* 666 N.W.2d 566 (Iowa 2003).
- **Suspect's flight from the area near contraband.** *Gee v. State,* 810 N.E.2d 338 (Ind. 2004); *Jenkins v. State,* 76 S.W.3d 709 (Tex. App. 2002).
- **Suspect's suspicious behavior at time that the contraband is found.** *Miller v. State,* 6 S.W.3d 812 (Ark. App. 1999).
- **Suspect's knowledge of hidden compartment** where contraband is located. *Vargas v. State,* 883 S.W.2d 256 (Tex. App. 1994).
- **Suspect's residence at location where contraband is found.** *Commonwealth v. Clarke,* 692 N.E.2d 85 (Mass. App. 1998) (constructive possession found where suspect had apartment keys and ran toward bedroom when police arrived, suspect's identification in the bedroom, sus-

pect retrieved shirt from the bedroom); *Commonwealth v. Handy*, 573 N.E.2d 1006 (Mass. App. 1991).

- **Suspect's ownership of the vehicle in which contraband is found.** *Mings v. State*, 884 S.W.2d 596 (Ark. 1994).
- **Suspect's personal belongings found mixed with contraband.** *Gee v. State*, 810 N.E.2d 338 (Ind. 2004); *State v. Cashen*, 666 N.W.2d 566 (Iowa 2003).
- **Suspect found in possession of drug paraphernalia,** large amounts of cash, or other characteristics of drug user or seller. *State v. Cashen*, 666 N.W.2d 566 (Iowa 2003); *Jenkins v. State*, 76 S.W.3d 709 (Tex. App. 2002).
- **Voluntary presence where drugs are in open use** can support a finding of constructive possession. *State v. Anderton*, 668 P.2d 1258 (Utah 1983).

Though a variety of creative factors may be argued, the ultimate test is always whether the suspect intends, and is able, to exercise dominion and control over the contraband.

Misdemeanor arrests

Both statute and the common law give authority to arrest for a misdemeanor committed in the officer's presence. *United States v. Watson*, 423 U.S. 411 (1976) (recognizing "the ancient common-law rule that a peace offiscer was permitted to arrest without a warrant for a misdemeanor or felony committed in his presence"). The common-law power of a peace officer to make a warrantless arrest for an offense committed in the officer's presence dates to the *Magna Carta*, or perhaps as early as the Norman Conquest of England. *Commonwealth v. Leet*, 641 A.2d 299 (Pa. 1994). Most states have statutory provisions codifying this common-law rule. *E.g.*, Cal. Penal Code § 836 (officer may arrest when he or she has probable cause to believe that the person has committed a public offense in the officer's presence); N.Y. Crim. Proc. Law § 140.10 (officer may arrest a person for any offense when he has reasonable cause to believe that such person has committed such an offense in his presence); R.I. Stat. § 12-7-3 (officer may effect warrantless arrest if the criminal act has been or is being committed in the officer's presence); Utah Code Ann. § 77-7-2(1) (peace officer may arrest a person for any public offense committed or attempted in the presence of the officer); Wyo. Stat. § 31-5-233 (peace officer may arrest for a misdemeanor, without a warrant, when any criminal offense is being committed in the officer's presence by person to be arrested).

Grounds for misdemeanor arrests include the following:

- **Crime committed in officer's presence.** *United States v. Lugo,* 170 F.3d 996 (10th Cir. 1999) (officer's observation of suspect committing misdemeanor offense gave probable cause and legitimate basis to arrest suspect). "Presence" means crimes perceived through direct sight as well as smell, *Seldon v. State,* 824 A.2d 999 (Md. App.) ("knowledge gained from the sense of smell of cocaine alone may be of such character as to give rise to probable cause for a belief that a crime is being committed in the presence of an officer"), *cert. denied,* 832 A.2d 206 (Md. 2003); hearing, *Goodwin v. Allen,* 78 S.E.2d 804 (Ga. App. 1953) (hearing screams and cries for help provides probable cause of crime committed in officer's presence), and touch, *Minnesota v. Dickerson,* 508 U.S. 366 (1993) (officer may seize contraband detected through sense of touch). An arrest made for a crime committed out of the officer's presence, assuming no saving statutory provision, may invalidate the arrest. However, it will not create federal civil rights liability. *Vargas-Badillo v. Diaz-Torres,* 114 F.3d 3 (1st Cir. 1997) ("neither the Supreme Court nor this circuit ever has held that the Fourth Amendment prohibits warrantless arrests for misdemeanors not committed in the presence of arresting officers"); *United States v. Smith,* 73 F.3d 1414 (6th Cir. 1996); *Fields v. City of South Houston,* 922 F.2d 1183 (5th Cir. 1991).
- **Crime committed within the officer's jurisdiction.** The common law allowed an officer to arrest for a misdemeanor committed within the officer's jurisdiction and further required that the arrest be effected within the jurisdiction. *Commonwealth v. O'Hara,* 571 N.E.2d 51 (Mass App. 1991). Many states preserve the common-law rule and do not allow an officer to make a misdemeanor arrest outside of the officer's geographic jurisdiction. *Perry v. State,* 794 S.W.2d 141 (Ark. 1990). A number of states have abandoned the common-law rule and provide statutory authority for extraterritorial arrests. *County of Los Alamos v. Johnson,* 776 P.2d 1252 (N.M. 1989); *State v. Englehardt,* 465 So. 2d 1366 (Fla. App. 1985); *State v. Cochran,* 372 A.2d 193 (Del. 1977). Most states recognize that an officer may make an arrest outside of his or her geographic boundaries on the same grounds as a citizen arrest. *State v. Miller,* 896 P.2d 1069 (Kan. 1995); *People v. Niedzwiedz,* 644 N.E.2d 53 (Ill.

App. 1994); *People v. Meyer*, 379 N.W.2d 59 (Mich. 1985).

- **Fresh pursuit of a misdemeanor suspect.** Most courts recognize the common-law rule of fresh pursuit of a misdemeanor suspect crossing jurisdictional lines, even in the absence of a specific state statute. *Seip v. State*, 835 A.2d 187 (Md. App. 2003). The arrest must follow the crime within a reasonable amount of time.
- **Factors allowing arrest for crime not in officer's presence.** Common law generally prohibited misdemeanor arrests when the crime was committed outside the officer's presence. Exceptions were often made when the arrestee posed a danger of harm to others or a likelihood of flight from the jurisdiction. This rule continues in many states today. *State v. Hughes*, 607 N.W.2d 621 (Wis.) (officer may arrest for misdemeanor committed outside of the officer's presence for "(1) an arrest made in 'hot pursuit,' (2) a threat to safety of a suspect or others, (3) a risk that evidence will be destroyed, and (4) a likelihood that the suspect will flee"), *cert. denied*, 531 U.S. 856 (2000); *State v. Harmon*, 910 P.2d 1196 (Utah 1995) (arrest proper for misdemeanor outside of officer's presence when suspect may (a) flee or conceal himself to avoid arrest; (b) destroy or conceal evidence of the commission of the offense; or (c) injure another person or damage property belonging to another person); Md. Code Crim. Proc. § 2-203 (officer may arrest for misdemeanor not committed in the officer's presence when, unless the person is arrested immediately, the person may not be apprehended; the person may cause physical injury or property damage to another; or the person may tamper with, dispose of, or destroy evidence).
- **Co-habitant abuse.** In 1994, Congress passed a comprehensive act aimed at curbing domestic violence and improving local government response to domestic violence complaints. Violence Against Women Act, Pub. L. 103-322, 108 Stat. 1796 (1994). Many states responded with statutes requiring that an arrest be made in certain domestic violence circumstances even when the crime did not happen in the presence of the officer. N.Y. Crim. Proc. Law § 140.10(4); 18 Pa. Const. Stat. Ann. § 2711; S.C. Code Ann. § 16-25-70(A); Wash. Rev. Code § 10.31.100.
- **Shoplifting.** Many states have retail theft statutes permitting an officer to arrest for shoplifting not committed in the officer's presence. If the officer has probable cause

to arrest, usually based on statements by the merchant who has detained the suspect, the officer may arrest. *State v. Walker*, 138 P.3d 113 (Wash. 2006); *Penn v. Commonwealth*, 412 S.E.2d 189 (Va. App. 1991), *aff'd*, 420 S.E.2d 713 (Va. 1992); *SuperX Drugs of Kentucky, Inc. v. Rice*, 554 S.W.2d 903 (Ky. App. 1977).

Felony arrests

An officer can generally arrest without a warrant for a felony *not* committed in the officer's presence, as long as there is probable cause to believe that a felony was committed and the suspect committed it, and the arrest is in a public place. *Maryland v. Pringle*, 540 U.S. 366 (2003) ("A warrantless arrest of an individual in a public place for a felony is consistent with the Fourth Amendment if the arrest is supported by probable cause."). Most states have incorporated this principle in statutes. Ala. Code § 15-10-3(a); Fla. Stat. Ann. § 901.15(2); Md. Code Crim. Proc. § 2-202; Minn. Stat. Ann. § 629.34. Some states impose a slight additional requirement of knowledge that a felony has been committed. Alaska Stat. § 12.25.030(a).

Use and preparation of arrest warrants

- **Drafting probable cause affidavits.** A proper affidavit supporting an arrest warrant must state facts sufficient to establish that a crime has been committed and a reasonable belief that the suspect committed it. *Whiteley v. Warden, Wyo. State Penitentiary*, 401 U.S. 560 (1971). The affidavit does not have to establish a prima facie case against the suspect. The core of the affidavit must state the officer's experience and training that relate to the inferences stated in the affidavit, statements from witnesses or other officers, and the reasonable inferences that can be drawn from the known facts.
- Some court decisions, particularly from federal courts, use the term **"fair probability"** in place of "probable cause." *See, e.g., Illinois v. Gates*, 462 U.S. 213 (1983). Others use the wording of a "substantial probability that a crime has been committed and that a specific individual committed the crime." *Taylor v. Meacham*, 82 F.3d 1556 (10th Cir.), *cert. denied*, 519 U.S. 871 (1996). Courts recognize that these terms essentially mean the same as "probable cause." *Stacey v. Emery*, 97 U.S. 642 (1878); *State v. Clark*, 20 P.3d 300 (Utah 2001); *People v. Chaney*,

686 N.Y.S.2d 871 (N.Y. App. Div. 1998) ("reasonable cause means probable cause").

- **Benefits of arrest warrants.** The U.S. Supreme Court has ruled that whenever possible, arrests by warrant are preferred over warrantless arrests. *Aguilar v. Texas*, 378 U.S. 108 (1964). An officer enjoys substantial protection against civil liability when he or she arrests under the authority of a warrant. If the arrest is later found to be without probable cause, the officer will be protected from liability. That is not necessarily the case with a warrantless arrest. An arrest warrant also make its easier to send out a general notice that the suspect is wanted, so that any officer encountering the suspect may make the arrest.
- **Constitutional and statutory provisions.** A warrantless arrest for a misdemeanor should be made as promptly as possible. A warrantless arrest for a felony may be made at any point the officer has sufficient probable cause. *United States v. Watson*, 423 U.S. 411 (1976). When tactical considerations permit, the officer should consider avoiding a warrantless arrest to take advantage of the liability protection offered by an arrest warrant.
- **Time limitations.** The Colonists' experience with the British created a strong sentiment against nighttime arrests. *O'Rourke v. City of Norman*, 875 F.2d 1465 (10th Cir. 1989). Most states restrict arrests under misdemeanor warrants to the daytime, unless a judge specifically authorizes nighttime service or the suspect is found in a public place. Cal. Penal Code § 840; Minn. Stat. § 629.31.

Place of arrest

A suspect may be arrested for a felony in any public place in which the suspect is found, whether the arrest is with a warrant or upon probable cause and without a warrant. However, different rules apply to arrests made in residences. **Unless there is an actual exigency, an officer cannot enter a residence for the purpose of making a warrantless felony (or misdemeanor) arrest**. *Payton v. New York*, 445 U.S. 573 (1980). The prosecution has a particularly heavy burden of showing in court that an entry into a home to effect a warrantless arrest is based on sufficient probable cause ***and*** exigent circumstances. *Welsh v. Wisconsin*, 466 U.S. 740 (1984). A suspect standing in the doorway, or in the public or common areas of apartment buildings, is not considered to be "in the home." *United States v. Santana*, 427 U.S. 38 (1976).

An officer may walk up to the door or approach on the driveway or other areas where a reasonable citizen might approach the residence. *State v. Reyna,* 130 P.3d 1162 (Idaho App. 2005); *State v. Prewitt,* 38 P.3d 126 (Idaho App. 2001) ("there is an implied invitation for the general public to use and enter access routes to a house such as pathways, driveways, parking lots"). *See Use of Force chapter.*

A valid felony arrest warrant carries the inherent authority to enter the named suspect's home. To allow a proper entry into the home, two questions must be considered. First, is there a reasonable belief that the home to be searched is the suspect's dwelling, and second, is there a reasonable belief that the suspect is within the home at the time of entry? *Valdez v. McPheters,* 172 F.3d 1220 (10th Cir. 1999). The Supreme Court has not defined the necessary level of certainty that the home is the suspect's residence and that the suspect is at home. Most courts have ruled that the standard is a "reasonable belief" and is less than probable cause. *See United States v. Route,* 104 F.3d 59 (5th Cir.), *cert. denied,* 521 U.S. 1109 (1997); *United States v. Risse,* 83 F.3d 212 (8th Cir. 1996) ("officers executing an arrest warrant must have a 'reasonable belief that the suspect resides at the place to be entered and reason to believe that the suspect is present' at the time the warrant is executed"). No matter what the justification may be for entering a home to make an arrest, the officer should announce his or her authority and presence unless doing so would pose a safety risk. *Richards v. Wisconsin,* 520 U.S. 385 (1997).

Misdemeanor arrest warrants usually present less urgency and public interest in prompt apprehension of the suspect. The *Payton* rule that an arrest warrant is generally required to enter the suspect's home applies to both felonies and misdemeanors. Thus, a misdemeanor arrest warrant carries the authority to enter the *suspect's* home to effect an arrest. *Shreve v. Jessamine County Fiscal Court,* 453 F.3d 681 (6th Cir. 2006) (misdemeanor arrest warrant allowed forced entry into suspect's home at 12:50 a.m. when suspect refused to answer); *Kain v. Nesbitt,* 156 F.3d 669 (6th Cir. 1998) (misdemeanor arrest warrant for traffic offenses authorized officers to forcibly enter the residence and arrest the person named in the warrant); *Smith v. Tolley,* 960 F. Supp. 977 (E.D. Va. 1997) ("Once that judicial approval was given, it makes no federal, constitutional difference that the warrant was issued in the form of a bench warrant for failure to appear on a misdemeanor offense, as opposed to a felony offense.").

An officer must have a search warrant to enter a third party's home to make an arrest, even if the officer possesses an arrest warrant. *Steagald v. United States,* 451 U.S. 204 (1981). Some exceptions apply and are discussed below. In order to lawfully enter a third party's home to arrest a suspect, an officer must have either a search warrant (in addition to the arrest warrant for the suspect), consent by the third-party homeowner or other person with authority to grant consent to enter, or exigent circumstances. The amount of force that may be used to enter the home is discussed elsewhere. *See Use of Force chapter.*

The *Steagald* rule is based on the homeowner's fundamental right to protect his or her home from government intrusion, the core value of the Fourth Amendment. If an arrest warrant were a sufficient reason to enter and search for a suspect, law enforcement could conceivably use the arrest warrant to search the homes of all of the suspect's family members and friends. Once law enforcement informs the homeowner that the person sought inside the home is a wanted suspect, then the homeowner might be guilty of harboring a fugitive or obstructing justice. However, the homeowner's related crime, *if any,* still would not allow warrantless entry into the home. The far safer and smarter course is to set a perimeter watch and take the time to obtain a telephonic search warrant or to just wait for the suspect to come out.

Not only third-party homes are covered by the *Steagald* rule. *Pembaur v. City of Cincinnati,* 475 U.S. 469 (1986) ("Plaintiff's theory was that, absent exigent circumstances, the Fourth Amendment prohibits police from searching an individual's home *or business* without a search warrant even to execute an arrest warrant for a third person. We agreed with that proposition in *Steagald.*"). Officers should carefully consider a search warrant to enter any premises, business or home where a third party holds a legitimate expectation of privacy. *O'Rourke v. Hayes,* 378 F.3d 1201 (11th Cir. 2004).

Exceptions to the rule of Payton *and* Steagald: *Consent, exigency, and hot pursuit*

The homeowner or other person in authority over the home can always **consent** to entry by law enforcement. *Steagald v. United States,* 451 U.S. 204 (1981). Even if the wanted suspect protests, the homeowner's consent is a valid basis for entry to arrest the suspect. By consenting, the homeowner takes the risk that officers may see something in plain view that may be incriminating, such as drugs or paraphernalia.

Another exception is **exigent circumstances**. A non-criminal traffic offense, where the officer is not in immediate pursuit of the suspect, is not sufficiently exigent to allow warrantless entry to arrest. *Welsh v. Wisconsin,* 466 U.S. 740 (1984). Exigency to enter to arrest may include probable cause to believe that destruction of evidence may be imminent; the need to prevent a suspect's escape; or the need to protect persons inside the home into which the suspect has fled—all considered in light of the "risk of danger, the gravity of the crime and the likelihood that the suspect is armed." *Minnesota v. Olson,* 495 U.S. 91 (1990). In the *Olson* case, the Court ruled that there was *not sufficient exigency* to enter a home to arrest when, in the course of investigating a murder, the suspect sought was not believed to be the killer, the murder weapon was in police possession, the home was surrounded by numerous officers, there was no avenue of escape, the time of day was 3:00 p.m., and there was no suggestion that the home's occupants were endangered by the suspect. This case illustrates how strictly courts limit the application of the exigent circumstances basis to enter a third party's home to make an arrest.

Closely related to exigent circumstances is the doctrine of **hot pursuit**. The hot pursuit exception to the warrant requirement states that a suspect may not defeat a proper arrest simply by getting home one or two steps ahead of pursuing police. *United States v. Santana,* 427 U.S. 38 (1976). "Hot pursuit" implies an immediate pursuit of a suspect fleeing from officers. Hot pursuit may justify warrantless entry to arrest for both felonies and misdemeanors. *United States v. Williams,* 354 F.3d 497 (6th Cir. 2003) ("hot pursuit of a fleeing felon" as an exigency exception to the warrant requirement); *Middletown v. Flinchum,* 765 N.E.2d 330 (Ohio 2002) (officers in hot pursuit of a suspect who flees to a house in order to avoid arrest "may enter without a warrant, regardless of whether the offense for which the suspect is being arrested is a misdemeanor").

A suspect standing in a public place who sees officers and runs into a private premises may be pursued into the private place, even when officers have no reason to believe that the location is the suspect's residence. *State v. Thomas,* 124 P.3d 48 (Kan. 2005); *United States v. Williams,* 2004 WL 1637021 (S.D.N.Y. 2004). In *Thomas,* officers were chasing Prouse, the subject of an arrest warrant. When Prouse ran into Thomas's house, officers saw a clandestine methamphetamine lab. Because the entry was permissible under the hot pursuit doctrine, any evidence seen in plain view while pursuing Prouse was admissible in a trial against Prouse, the third-party occupant.

Hot pursuit to arrest and entry into a home under the doctrine of exigent circumstances to preserve or obtain evidence, such as in the case of a suspected impaired driver, are closely related but distinct legal concepts. "Only when the 'totality of the circumstances' supports a finding that the officer 'was confronted with an emergency, in which the delay necessary to obtain a warrant, under the circumstances, threatened 'the destruction of evidence'" will hot pursuit into a home to *obtain evidence* be allowed. *City of Orem v. Henrie,* 868 P.2d 1384 (Utah App. 1994). *See Search and Seizure chapter.*

The question of the lawfulness of a warrantless entry into a home to effect an arrest frequently arises in the context of investigating complaints of impaired drivers. One recent California case is typical. A citizen found Thompson parked in her reserved stall; he was passed out behind the wheel. She woke him and asked him to leave. Seeing that he was highly intoxicated, she followed him and called police. She reported his numerous dangerous traffic violations, but lost sight of him. Shortly thereafter, an officer found Thompson's car parked in his driveway. Though officers could see him in the house and his companion confirmed that he was home, Thompson would not come out of the house. Officers entered and arrested him for DUI. *People v. Thompson,* 135 P.3d 3 (Cal. 2006). The California Supreme Court upheld the entry and arrest.

In *Welsh v. Wisconsin,* 466 U.S. 740 (1984), the Supreme Court disallowed a warrantless entry into a home to make a DUI arrest, based on the fact that the Wisconsin law provided for only a civil penalty for a first DUI offense. The Court said that "an important factor to be considered when determining whether any exigency exists is the gravity of the underlying offense for which the arrest is being made." In *Thompson,* the California Supreme Court ruled that the public interest in preserving the blood alcohol evidence created sufficient exigent circumstances to enter Thompson's home without a warrant. Most courts allow warrantless entry to effect an arrest for a criminal violation as long as it is a "jailable" offense. *Rideout v. State,* 122 P.3d 201 (Wyo.

2005); *Cherry v. Commonwealth*, 605 S.E.2d 297 (Va. App. 2004); *State v. Nikola*, 821 A.2d 110 (N.J. App. 2003); *Beaver v. State*, 106 S.W.3d 243 (Tex. App. 2003); *State v. Legg*, 633 N.W.2d 763 (Iowa 2001); *State v. Hughes*, 607 N.W.2d 621 (Wis. 2000); *Mendez v. People*, 986 P.2d 275 (Colo. 1999); *Dolan v. Salinas*, 1999 WL 566943 (Conn. Super. 1999); *Threatt v. State*, 524 S.E.2d 276 (Ga. App. 1999); *State v. Paul*, 548 N.W.2d 260 (Minn. 1996); *Beachwood v. Sims*, 647 N.E.2d 821 (Ohio App. 1994); *City of Orem v. Henrie*, 868 P.2d 1384 (Utah App. 1994); *Goines v. James*, 433 S.E.2d 572 (W. Va. 1993); *State v. Griffith*, 808 P.2d 1171 (Wash. App. 1991); *People v. Lagle*, 558 N.E.2d 514 (Ill. App. 1990); *People v. Odenweller*, 527 N.Y.S.2d 127 (1988); *City of Kirksville v. Guffey*, 740 S.W.2d 227 (Mo. App. 1987); *State v. Ellinger*, 725 P.2d 1201 (Mont. 1986); *State v. Roberts*, 706 P.2d 564 (Or. App. 1985). The reasonableness of the warrantless entry will only be enhanced when the officer pauses to attempt to gain consent to enter.

Fresh pursuit and peace officer authority

The common-law doctrine of fresh pursuit allows an officer to pursue a suspect and effect a warrantless arrest outside of the officer's jurisdictional boundaries for crimes committed in the officer's presence within a reasonable time after the commission of the crime. *Gattus v. State*, 105 A.2d 661 (Md. 1954). Beginning in 1937, the majority of the states adopted the Uniform Act on Fresh Pursuit. The Act gives officers from other states limited powers of arrest in the state into which an officer pursues a *felony* suspect.

A representative section of the Act provides:

> Any member of a duly organized state, county, or municipal peace unit of another state of the United States who enters this state in fresh pursuit, and continues within this state in such fresh pursuit, of a person in order to arrest him on the ground that he is believed to have committed a felony in such other state, shall have the same authority to arrest and hold such person in custody, as has any member of any duly organized state, county or municipal peace unit of this state, to arrest and hold in custody a person on the ground that he is believed to have committed a felony in this state. Idaho Code § 19-701.

As long as the out-of-state officer is pursuing a felony suspect and acting without unreasonable delay and the officer would have the power to arrest the suspect in the officer's home state, then the arrest is valid. Normal extradition procedures apply; the out-of-state officer cannot immediately transport the suspect back over the border.

Fresh pursuit is not the same as hot pursuit. The Act provides that pursuit should be "continuous and without unreasonable delay," but does not require instant pursuit. As long as officers are diligently seeking the suspect, they need not be right on the suspect's heels in an active pursuit. *United States v. Getz,* 381 F. Supp. 43 (E.D. Pa. 1974), *aff'd,* 510 F.2d 971 (3d Cir.), *cert. denied,* 421 U.S. 950 (1975) ("officer need not engage in a bumper to bumper, 'fender-smashing Hollywood-style chase'").

Vienna Convention arrest and detention issues

The history of diplomatic immunity and the notion of special privileges for consular operations dates to the relations between ancient Rome and Greece. Today, consular relations are principally governed by the Vienna Convention on Consular Relations, generally referred to as the "Vienna Convention" or "VCCR." One hundred and seventy nations are party to the VCCR. The United States became subject to the VCCR in 1969, and it is binding on all state, local, and federal law enforcement officers. The VCCR addresses the operations of consulates and embassies, but also governs the way foreign citizens arrested in the United States are treated by law enforcement.

Officers should get into the habit of asking a simple question when arresting or detaining for a period traditionally associated with a formal arrest: "Are you a citizen of the United States?" If the answer is "yes," the VCCR simply does not apply. If the answer is "no," the officer must follow the provisions of the VCCR and associated treaties. Because the VCCR does not apply to temporary investigative detentions, it is generally not necessary to inquire about citizenship or resident alien ("green card") status.

For law enforcement officers, the key provision of the VCCR, coupled with related treaties, requires certain notifications to be made when an officer arrests a foreign national or is investigating a death or aircraft crash or shipwreck involving a foreign national. The arresting officer is the person primarily responsible for making the appropriate notification under the VCCR. The fundamental VCCR provisions are:

- A detained person must be promptly advised that the person's home nation's consulate *may* be notified of the person's detention, at the detainee's request, *unless* the detainee is from a mandatory notification nation (*see Appendix*).
- The detained person must be given the opportunity to decide whether or not the consulate should be notified. If the detainee requests it, the officer must ensure that prompt notification is given to the nearest consulate or embassy of the detainee's country.
- Consular officials must be given access to detainees.
- Any communication from detainees to consular officials must be promptly forwarded.
- Consular officials may visit and communicate with detained nationals freely and *may* arrange legal counsel for them, but consular officials cannot act as attorneys for detainees.

For mandatory notification nations, the officer *must* notify consular officials, even if the detainees do not wish that notification be made. In fact, a belief that notification is not in the best interest of the detainee or may place the detainee in danger does not excuse the officer's obligation to make notification. However, officers *should not* notify consular officials if the detainee is seeking asylum in the United States. *See Appendix VCCR and Diplomatic Immunity.*

Recent judicial decisions have addressed the remedies available for an arresting officer's noncompliance with the VCCR. The U.S. Supreme Court recently ruled that suppression of evidence is not an appropriate remedy for VCCR violations. *Sanchez-Llamas v. Oregon*, ___ U.S. ___, 126 S. Ct. 2669 (2006). In 2000, Germany sued the United States following the execution of two German citizens denied consular assistance. Though the World Court ruled against the United States, the executions were not delayed.

Officers may be sued for VCCR violations. Jogi served six years in prison and was then deported to India. No one advised him of his VCCR right to consular assistance. He learned of the VCCR in prison and filed suit against the arresting officers. While diplomatic treaties do not generally create individual rights, the court allowed Jogi to sue the officers and the prosecutor for VCCR noncompliance. The court noted that Jogi did not have to show that the violation was "shockingly egregious" in order to enforce his rights and collect money damages. The rules of consular notification following detention of a foreign national are fairly straightforward. When officers violate the rules, they risk personal liability as well as damage to the prosecution process. *Jogi v. Voges*, 425 F.3d 367 (7th Cir. 2005).

Diplomatic immunity

The theory of diplomatic immunity is based on the belief that foreign government representatives can more effectively represent their governments' interests when unhindered by local restrictions. The United States extends diplomatic immunity with the expectation that its own diplomats will enjoy full diplomatic immunity when sent abroad to foreign nations. Reciprocity of respect and obedience to diplomatic immunity principles are critical to the protection of U.S. interests throughout the world.

Diplomatic immunity is often misunderstood to mean that foreign nationals representing their governments may not be detained, arrested, or charged for criminal acts. In truth, some senior officials enjoy nearly that much protection, but most do not, and in all cases, law enforcement may act to prevent violence and protect lives and property. Moreover, foreign government officials are still obligated to obey U.S. laws, and methods exist to hold them responsible for their actions.

The highest level of diplomatic immunity is granted to diplomatic agents. These are the top officials at diplomatic missions (embassies). In most cases, law enforcement officers can quickly determine the level of diplomatic immunity that a subject enjoys through examination of an identification card issued by the State Department. Diplomatic passports and visas are *not* proof of diplomatic status and immunity. *See Appendix VCCR and Diplomatic Immunity.* Diplomatic agents enjoy the following privileges:

- May not be detained, arrested, or handcuffed (handcuffing can be done only in *extraordinary circumstances*), but may be cited for violations.
- Vehicles, personal property, and homes are "inviolable" and cannot be entered or searched.
- Cannot be compelled to testify as witnesses, even as crime victims.
- Cannot be prosecuted for any crime, no matter how serious, unless immunity is waived.
- Protections also apply to their family members.

Consular officers enjoy a very different type of immunity. Consular officers enjoy immunity only for their official acts. Their property is not inviolable, meaning that it can be searched if an otherwise lawful basis exists. They can be arrested, but only with a judicial warrant, and only for a felony. They can be cited for felonies and misdemeanors. Their families enjoy no immunity.

Even if a person who is entitled to diplomatic immunity cannot be detained or arrested, they can in many cases be charged with a crime. An officer can, and should, act to protect the public in any case of diplomatic immunity. For example, if an officer stops a diplomatic agent suspected of driving under the influence of alcohol or drugs, the officer should attempt to investigate the act as with any other case. The diplomatic agent can be cited, but not arrested. The officer can ask the diplomatic agent to perform field sobriety tests but cannot require performance of the tests. Rather than allow an impaired driver to drive, the officer can arrange for a ride or take the person to his or her destination.

Fingerprinting and photographing

Arrestees have no right to refuse to cooperate with fingerprinting and photographs. Taking an arrestee's fingerprints is usually mandated by state law. Though the common remedy is to leave an arrestee in custody until he or she cooperates with the normal booking process, at least one court has approved a charge of obstructing justice when the arrestee would not be photographed or fingerprinted. *Fillmore v. Ordonez,* 829 F. Supp. 1544 (D. Kan. 1993), *aff'd,* 17 F.3d 1436 (10th Cir. 1994).

CHAPTER 4

USE OF FORCE

Force to make a felony arrest
Excessive force
Force to make a misdemeanor arrest
Force to maintain order or gain compliance
Force in an officer's self-defense
Resisting arrest
Deadly force against a stun gun or pepper spray
Measuring the appropriate application of force
Force to enter a suspect's home
Force to enter a third party's home
Specialized applications of force
Alternative force tools
Use of force to obtain evidence
Use of force in correctional facilities
Reporting use of force
Consequences of improper use of force

Force to make a felony arrest

An officer may use no more force than is reasonably necessary to make an arrest. Deadly force may be used only when lesser force is not reasonable and when the suspect presents an imminent threat of death or serious bodily injury to the officer or the public. Deadly force may be used to prevent an escape by a fleeing felon when:

- **the officer has probable cause to believe that the suspect committed a crime involving the threat of death or serious bodily injury, AND;**
- **deadly force is reasonably necessary to prevent the escape, AND;**
- **the officer gives a warning prior to the use of force, whenever feasible.**

The traditional common law rule of force allowed an officer to use whatever force necessary, including deadly force, to make a felony arrest. The common law rule was modified in many states during the 1960s and 1970s, and in 1985, the United States Supreme Court banned the use of deadly force against a fleeing felon who does not pose an immediate threat to officers or the public. *Tennesee v. Garner,* 471 U.S. 1 (1985). Deadly force may still be used on some fleeing felons in very limited circumstances (*see* blackletter rule above).

All use of force lawsuits are measured by standards established by the Supreme Court in *Graham v. Connor,* 490 U.S. 386 (1989). In the *Graham* case, the Court instructed lower courts to always ask three questions to measure the constitutionality of a particular use of force. First, what was the severity of the crime that the officer believed the suspect to have committed or to be committing? Second, did the suspect present an immediate threat to the safety of officers or the public? Third, was the suspect actively resisting arrest or attempting to escape? The Supreme Court also stated that the use of force should be measured by what the officer knew at the scene.

If officers create the situation requiring deadly force, they may be liable for resulting injuries. Responding to a suicide call, deputies approached a woman loading a gun. They retreated, and one deputy then approached to within a few feet, thinking that he was hidden from her. She saw him and turned her weapon in his direction. He fired three times, killing the woman. The court held that the deputy was liable because he "voluntarily and negligently placed himself in a position of peril where he had no other choice than to use deadly force." *Quezada v. County of Bernalillo,* 944 F.2d 710 (10th Cir. 1991).

Excessive force

An officer may use only that force which is both *reasonable* and *necessary* to effect an arrest or detention. Any more force is *excessive force.* In addition to the three questions asked by the *Graham v. Connor* case, courts consider the *need* for the application of force, the *relationship* between the need and amount of force used, and the *extent of the injury* inflicted by the officer's force. The *Graham v. Connor* factors govern both the amount of force used, as well as the force method, tool, or weapon used. *United States v. Dykes,* 406 F.3d 717 (D.C. Cir. 2005).

Force to make a misdemeanor arrest

An officer may use whatever nondeadly force is reasonably necessary to make a misdemeanor arrest. *Dauffenbach v. City of Wichita,* 667 P.2d 380 (Kan. 1983). Deadly force may *never* be used to make a misdemeanor arrest. *Day v. State ex rel. Utah Dept. of Public Safety,* 980 P.2d 1171 (Utah 1999); *Schumann v. McGinn,* 240 N.W.2d 525 (Minn. 1976). Even so, a situation that begins as a misdemeanor, such as a minor shoplifting complaint, may rapidly evolve into a felony arrest, depending on the degree of resistance offered by the suspect or whether the suspect uses a dangerous weapon. The crime involved could develop to include an aggravated assault, or perhaps even attempted murder. The situation would then be analyzed under rules applying to felony arrests where the suspect poses a threat of death or serious bodily injury.

Force to maintain order or gain compliance

The use of force is one factor that courts consider when faced with the question of whether an encounter is a detention or an arrest. Using force to maintain order or gain compliance does not automatically create an arrest. *See Arrest chapter.* An officer may draw a weapon or use force to enforce lawful orders. For example, during a traffic stop, a driver gets out of the car, approaches the officer in a threatening manner, and repeatedly ignores the officer's orders to return to the car. The officer could reasonably draw a weapon to order compliance. *Courson v. McMillian*, 939 F.2d 1479 (11th Cir. 1991) (officer acted reasonably in pointing shotgun when suspect approached the officer's car, made threats, waved arms, and was told to get down); *Gainor v. Douglas County*, 59 F. Supp. 2d 1259 (N.D. Ga. 1998) (pointing a gun at suspect and later drawing a baton was reasonable when suspect would not stay back from officer and would not obey order to get on the ground).

Law enforcement officers often cannot allow a stalemate to continue. A dilemma arises when a suspect passively and persistently resists arrest or detention efforts. Officers may use force to gain compliance. A suspect who refuses to assume a position for searching and handcuffing may be physically forced to comply with either direct force, pepper spray, or an electronic tool. *Archer v. City of Portland*, 2006 WL 1643507 (D. Or. 2006) (shooting bean bag rounds at suspect was reasonable when assault suspect refused to show hands); *Willkomm v. Mayer*, 2006 WL 582044 (W.D. Wis. 2006) (application of Taser proper when DUI suspect refused to be handcuffed); *Reese v. Herbert*, 2006 WL 1892026 (N.D. Ga. 2006) (pepper spray not unreasonable force when suspect refused to present arms for handcuffing); *Mitchell v. Yeadon Borough*, 2002 WL 265021 (E.D. Pa. 2002) (pepper spray was reasonable when suspect snatched his arm away from the arresting officer on first attempt to arrest and control); *Passino v. State*, 260 A.D.2d 915 (N.Y. 1999) (pepper spray reasonable when suspect stood rigid and would not be handcuffed). A suspect who refuses to get out of a car may similarly be forced. *Lawyer v. City of Council Bluffs*, 361 F.3d 1099 (8th Cir. 2004) (pepper spray in driver's face when driver refused to unlock car door was reasonable). An arrestee who refuses to get into a patrol car may be sprayed to gain compliance. *Vinyard v. Wilson*, 311 F.3d 1340 (11th Cir. 2002) ("Using pepper spray is reasonable where the suspect was either resisting arrest or refusing police requests, such as requests to enter a patrol car."); *Gainor v. Douglas County*, 59 F. Supp. 2d 1259 (N.D. Ga. 1998).

Force in an officer's self-defense

When an officer is attempting a lawful arrest, the officer has no obligation to retreat if the suspect resists. *Commonwealth v. Boden*, 507 A.2d 813 (Pa. 1986). The officer must first ensure that the arrest is lawful, and that the officer is not provoking the use of force by the suspect. When the suspect places the officer in the dilemma of using force or backing off from a lawful arrest, the officer may use whatever force is reasonably necessary to protect the officer in making the arrest.

Resisting arrest

Common law allowed a citizen to resist an unlawful arrest. This rule made some sense when an unlawful arrest might result in a lengthy incarceration under poor conditions and before the constitutionally guaranteed rights of bail and speedy process became integral to the judicial system. The overwhelming majority of states have rejected this rule and now hold that a citizen has no right to resist an arrest, as long as the officer is acting within the scope of his or her authority. The fact that the initial arrest may later be ruled to have been made without probable cause will not defeat a charge of resisting the initial arrest. *Jurco v. State,* 825 P.2d 909 (Alaska App. 1992); *Robinson v. State,* 814 N.E.2d 704 (Ind. App. 2004); *City of Wichita v. Cook,* 89 P.3d 934 (Kan. App. 2004); *Commonwealth v. Moreira,* 447 N.E.2d 1224 (Mass. 1983); *People v. Ventura,* 686 N.W.2d 748 (Mich. App. 2004); *State v. Merritt,* 805 S.W.2d 337 (Mo. App. 1991); *Columbus v. Fraley,* 324 N.E.2d 735 (Ohio 1975); *State v. Trane,* 57 P.3d 1052 (Utah 2002); *Commonwealth v. Hill,* 570 S.E.2d 805 (Va. 2002); *State v. Hobson,* 577 N.W.2d 825 (Wis. 1998); Cal. Penal Code § 834a; 720 Ill. Comp. Stat. 5/7-7; Ky. Rev. Stat. § 520.090.

A few states hold to the common law rule and allow citizens to forcibly resist unlawful arrests and detentions. *Akron v. Callaway,* 835 N.E.2d 736 (Ohio App. 2005). Washington has judicially limited the statutory right to resist an arrest to allow an arrestee to defend against injury, but not against the actual arrest. *State v. Valentine,* 935 P.2d 1294 (Wash. 1997).

To help ensure the suspect's ultimate conviction for resisting arrest, the officer must be certain that the suspect knows that the officer is a law enforcement officer and that the officer is placing the suspect under arrest. If the officer is in uniform, the suspect cannot likely claim that the officer's identity as a law enforcement officer was unclear. Officers not in uniform should plainly identify themselves as law enforcement officers, verbally and by displaying identification prior to the arrest whenever practical. Even though the circumstances may make it obvious, it is always helpful to clearly inform the suspect that he or she is under arrest.

Deadly force against a stun gun or pepper spray

Difficult questions arise when an officer is confronted by a suspect armed with nonlethal weapons, such as a stun weapon or pepper spray. In any struggle with a suspect, there is always at least one gun present: the officer's handgun. Is it reasonable for an officer to use deadly force against a threat of being sprayed with OC spray? Or stunned by an electronic weapon? Nearly one-fifth of officers shot are shot with their own weapons after having the weapon taken away. What if the officer's weapon is taken away?

Officers can rarely, if ever, be certain of an armed suspect's intent; therefore, officers must assume an intent to assault and escape. An officer simply cannot assume that a suspect who incapacitates the officer with pepper spray will calmly turn and walk away without committing further assault and violence. Moreover, the suspect may well pose a threat to third persons, a threat significantly increased if the suspect takes the officer's weapon. There is no certain rule for using deadly force against a suspect with an incapacitating, nonlethal weapon. Following are some factors to be considered when faced with such weapons:

- What is the underlying crime that led to the confrontation?
- What threats, verbal or physical, has the suspect made against officers?
- Consider the relative physical size and condition and defensive tactics skills of the officer and suspect, as well as relative numbers of backup officers present or readily available.
- What other weapons are available to the suspect? Even if the officer can retain his or her weapon, are there tools or other items available to the suspect, such as impact or edged weapons?
- Can the officer work through the effects of the non-lethal weapon? Has the officer experienced a dose of pepper spray or application of an electronic weapon so that he or she knows the effects firsthand?

Measuring the appropriate application of force

Many law enforcement agencies use some form of a use of force continuum. This approach presents force in a ladder, or step fashion, escalating from one extreme to the other. A commonly used continuum looks like this:

Officer Presence → Verbal Command → Hand Control → Impact Tool → Deadly Force

One of the obvious criticisms of the continuum approach is the possible implication that an officer must progress through the steps on the continuum before using deadly force. That approach may be appropriate if the suspect's actions progress from one level to another.

As an alternative to the use of force continuum, the force options chart is gaining popularity. This approach places the focus of measuring force directly on the suspect. Ultimately, it is the suspect's action that determines the level of reasonably necessary force. The force options approach is expressed in Exhibit 4-1.

Exhibit 4-1
Force Options

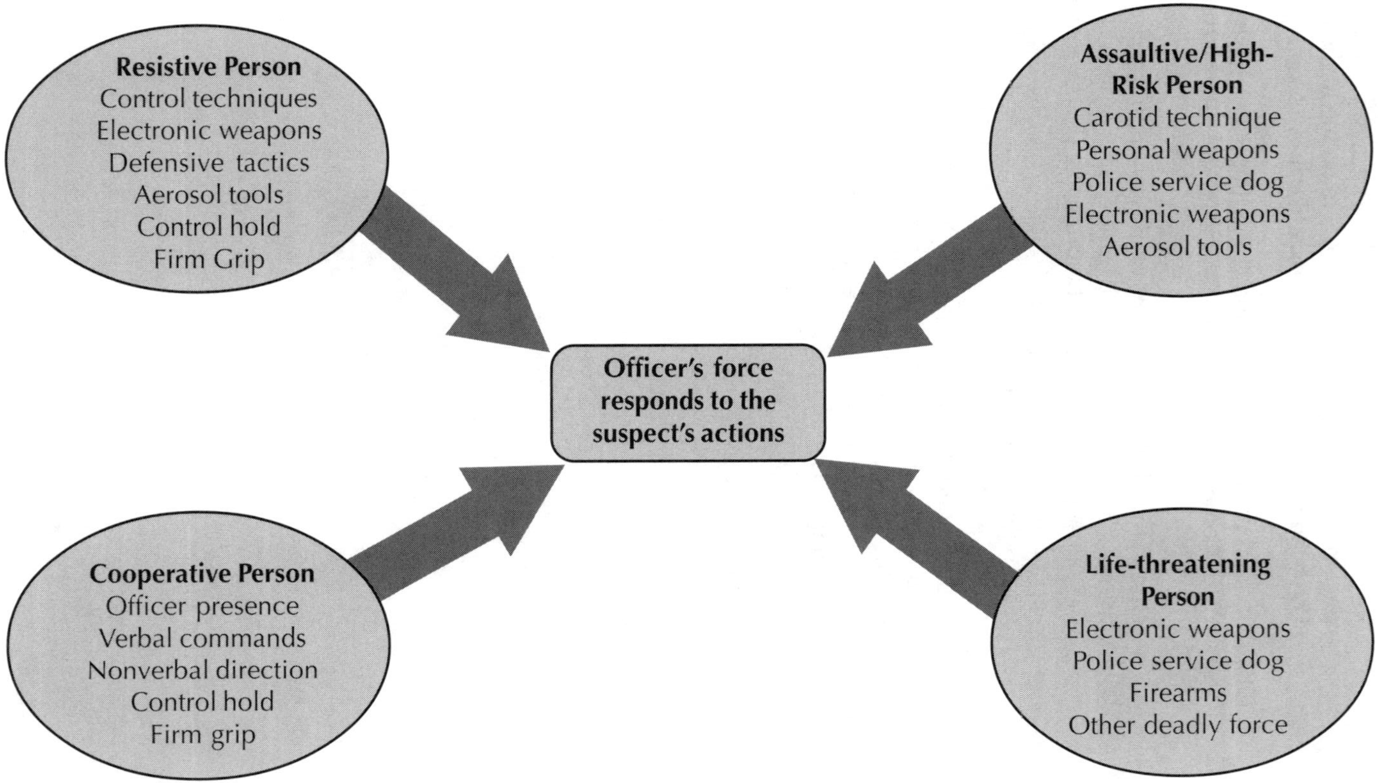

The numerous approaches to diagramming use of force in response to a suspect's action all help the officer express the necessity and the reasonableness of the force. No matter what force options model is used, an officer should be confident in the following four areas before using any force:

- Is the officer's intervention fully legal? Is the intervention based on a lawful objective, such as a valid arrest, detention, search, frisk, community caretaker custodian of mentally ill, defense of an officer or a citizen, or to prevent escape?
- Is the use of force proportional to the person's resistance? Even though there is no duty to retreat, could the officer use lesser force and still safely accomplish the lawful objective?
- Is the officer well-trained and confident and competent with all force tools authorized by the public safety agency?
- Does the officer's conduct appear to be objectively reasonable? Did the officer's conduct precipitate the use of force? Is the officer's language or behavior inappropriate or unprofessional?

Force to enter a suspect's home

When an officer has a reasonable belief that a felony suspect is inside *and* has a valid felony arrest warrant for the suspect, the officer may forcibly enter a suspect's home to arrest him or her. An officer may use whatever force is reasonably necessary to force entry when the officer has a lawful right to do so. Even if the officer believes that there is an independent legal right to enter, the officer should, whenever possible, obtain consent to enter from the resident. Consent to enter may well defeat later claims of unlawful entry for both criminal prosecution and civil liability purposes.

The U.S. Supreme Court has ruled that a valid felony arrest warrant carries the authority to forcibly enter a suspect's home when an officer has a reasonable belief that the dwelling is actually the suspect's residence and the suspect is in the home. *Payton v. New York,* 445 U.S. 573 (1980). This rule does not apply to common areas in an apartment or condominium complex.

The plain language of the *Payton* decision addresses the officer's right to enter the suspect's home by force with a valid *felony* arrest warrant. A few courts have invalidated forced entry into a suspect's home to arrest the suspect on a *misdemeanor* arrest warrant. However, the prevailing interpretation of the *Payton* case is that there is no distinction between felony and misdemeanor arrest warrants for purposes of authorizing entry into a suspect's home. *Howard v. Dickerson,* 34 F.3d 978 (10th Cir. 1994); *United States v. Meindl,* 83 F. Supp. 2d 1207 (D. Kan. 1999). *See Arrest chapter.* A note of caution, however: most courts view misdemeanor offenses with greater scrutiny when they balance constitutional interests of law enforcement and the Fourth Amendment protection given to a person in a home.

An officer must generally knock and announce the officer's presence and authority before using force to enter a residence. Although an officer may have a lawful right to enter and even force entry, the officer must generally first allow the suspect the opportunity to grant peaceable entry. *Wilson v. Arkansas,* 514 U. S. 927 (1995). Failure to give notice may lead to civil liability, but it should not generally require suppression of evidence. *Hudson v. Michigan,* ___ U.S. ___, 126 S. Ct. 2159 (2006). An officer need only wait a "reasonable time" for the suspect to open the door. The United States Supreme Court ruled that a 15- to 20-second wait at two o'clock in the afternoon was a reasonable wait. Officers knocked and announced with no answer, and then broke in. The suspect was in the shower. The Court ruled that the reasonableness of the wait would be measured by what the officers knew and not some later claim that the resident was in the shower, or listening to loud music, or otherwise unable to hear a reasonably loud knock and announcement. The Court also acknowledged that drug dealers might well store their drugs near a toilet or drain, and one factor to consider was the time that it would take for a suspect to get to a drain and dispose of evidence. Another factor to weigh is whether there is a necessity to actually break in and cause damage to property. *United States v. Banks,* 540 U.S. 31 (2003).

The reasonableness of the wait time will vary with the type and size of dwelling, and even the crime under investigation. When seeking to arrest or enter the residence of a drug dealer, an officer may "reasonably infer refusal [to enter] more readily than under other circumstances." *United States v. Bonner,* 874 F.2d 822 (D.C. Cir. 1989). If officers hear or see signs that the suspect is trying to escape or destroy evidence, the wait requirement is waived. *United States v. Gillaum,* 372 F.3d 848 (7th Cir.) (officers heard footsteps running away from the front door), *cert. denied,* 543 U.S. 969 (2004). Even without a no-knock warrant, the wait time may also be shorter if officers are placed at risk. *United States v. Crippen,* 371 F.3d 842 (D.C. Cir.) (information that suspect had rocket launcher created exigency and entry four seconds after knocking and announcing was justified), *cert. denied,* 543 U.S. 970 (2004).

Forced entry without knocking and announcing has been approved by courts in a variety of situations, such as when the officer is reasonably sure that the suspect knows of the officer's presence, when knocking and announcing may endanger the officer, or in the course of a suspect escaping custody and fleeing into his or her home. *United States v. Bynum,* 362 F.3d 574 (9th Cir. 2004) (finding no-knock entry valid when officers knew suspect had a gun readily accessible and suspect's answering the door in the nude and pointing a pistol only a few hours prior to the raid created reasonable suspicion that he might become violent). Forced entry may also be appropriate when there is a likelihood that the suspect will destroy evidence. It is not enough that a drug crime is being investigated and that drugs may easily be flushed down toilets and drains. The Supreme Court refused to create a blanket forced-entry rule for drug crimes, ruling that each case must be considered in light of what the officer knows about the home and suspects. *Richards v. Wisconsin,* 520 U.S. 385 (1997). Evasive action by the suspect, sounds of flushing, or apparent fortification of the home are factors that may support forced entry without knocking and announcing.

Force to enter a third party's home

When an officer has a reasonable belief that a felony suspect is inside a *third party's* home *and* the officer has a valid felony arrest warrant for the suspect, the officer must also secure a *search warrant* to forcibly enter the third party's home to arrest the suspect. Although most of the time it will be easier and more practical to wait a suspect out, an officer has the obligation to obtain both an arrest warrant and a search warrant to enter the home of anyone other than the suspect, absent exigent circumstances. This is true even if the officer knocks on the door, tells the homeowner that the officer has an arrest warrant for the suspect, and the homeowner refuses consent to enter. Most officers then think to arrest the homeowner on a charge of some type of obstruction of justice. Generally, that is not a wise course. The defense will claim, probably successfully, that the homeowner was simply exercising a Fourth Amendment right to a search warrant. Additionally, arrest of the homeowner still does not grant the officer the right to enter and search the entire home. One court allowed an exception when a third party knowingly allowed a fleeing felon to enter the third party's home, the officer arrested the third party for a state law violation of harboring a fugitive, and the suspect was found within the scope of a valid search incident to arrest. *United States v. Donaldson,* 793 F.2d 498 (2d Cir. 1986), *cert. denied,* 479 U.S. 1056 (1987). However, most courts have rigorously applied the *Steagald* rule and have dismissed charges against third parties arrested after refusing entry to police. *State v. Howard,* 600 N.E.2d 809 (Ohio App. 1991). *See Arrest chapter.*

Under search and seizure doctrine, if the suspect shares a home with one or more roommates, any one of the lawful tenants may consent, or not, to a search of the common areas of the residence. In such cases, none of the lawful tenants can refuse entry, or demand a search warrant. Even though the co-tenants are "third parties," the key issue is that there is an arrest warrant and the suspect lives at that residence. *See Warrantless Search and Seizure chapter.*

Specialized applications of force

SWAT teams have force options often not available to patrol officers. This leads to additional legal considerations of the appropriate level of force and additional policy needs. The same general rules discussed above govern specialized weapons and diversionary devices. Some lawsuits have unsuccessfully sought to ban devices such as battering rams and armored vehicles. The Supreme Court has ruled that the method of executing a warrant, including the type of force, is generally a question left to the discretion of the police. *Dalia v. United States,* 441 U.S. 238 (1979). However, extreme measures such as armored vehicles and tank-mounted battering rams should be specifically authorized in a warrant, absent exigent circumstances. *Langford v. Gates,* 729 P.2d 822 (Cal.), *cert. denied,* 484 U.S. 824 (1987).

Some criminal defendants have argued that seizures of evidence following entry with diversionary devices make the subsequent search unreasonable. Colorado officers executed a search warrant on a crack house where the dealer was believed to be armed. Officers ignited a diversionary device immediately prior to entry. A large quantity of cocaine and several weapons were seized. The defendant claimed that the force to execute the search was unreasonable because officers did not have specific information that the defendant could rapidly dispose of the cocaine, and because he had not actually threatened to use firearms against police. The court quickly dismissed his claim, noting that no one was injured in the entry and that police could reasonably fear for their safety by the mere presence of a weapon in the drug house. *United States v. Green,* 25 F.3d 1058 (10th Cir.), *cert. denied,* 513 U.S. 893 (1994).

Diversionary devices do not constitute excessive force when used by trained personnel under circumstances not likely to produce any significant injury and when they may be useful to prevent armed resistance. *Bing v. City of Whitehall,* 456 F.3d 555 (6th Cir. 2006) (pepper spray and diversionary devices properly used in attempt to forestall more violence from man who had fired gun into residential neighborhood and barricaded himself in his home). Even where officers do not have recent information that the suspect is probably armed, if the suspect has a history of violence and armed resistance, the use of diversionary devices will not be likely to lead to civil liability or suppression of evidence. *United States v. Morris,* 349 F.3d 1009 (7th Cir. 2003); *United States v. Myers,* 106 F.3d 936 (10th Cir.), *cert. denied,* 520 U.S. 1270 (1997); *Commonwealth v. Garner,* 772 N.E.2d 510 (Mass. 1996). Caution: Even though the use of a diversionary device may not cause suppression of evidence and a conviction may follow, there still may be a civil suit for the same incident. *Means v. United States,* 176 F.3d 1376 (11th Cir. 1999) (diversionary device burned suspect's leg, fractured small left toe and blew nail off toe).

Alternative force tools

Application of alternative force tools, such as electronic tools, pepper spray, bean bags, or baton rounds, are subject to the *Graham v. Connor* analysis for reasonableness. Though some call such tools "less-lethal" or "less-than-lethal" weapons, such terminology is not entirely accurate. Bean bags and baton rounds, pepper spray, conducted electricity tools (also called electro-muscular disruption tools), and similar tools are specifically designed to be non-lethal. Courts acknowledge the non-lethal quality of such tools. *Ewolski v. City of Brunswick,* 287 F.3d 492 (6th Cir. 2002) (Taser is non-deadly force); *Jolivet v. Cook,* 48 F.3d 1232 (10th Cir.

1995) ("A Taser is a non-lethal weapon that delivers an electric shock."); *Passino v. State,* 689 N.Y.S.2d 258 (N.Y. App. 1999) (pepper spray non-deadly force); *Griffen v. City of Clanton,* 932 F. Supp. 1359 (M.D. Ala. 1996) (pepper spray only a temporarily incapacitating force application). Other non-lethal force options have resulted in death on rare occasions. That does not convert the non-lethal force option into deadly force. *Robinette v. Barnes,* 854 F.2d 909 (6th Cir. 1988) (police dog bite that resulted in death was not "deadly force" when death was not a likely consequence of a dog bite).

These options are often alternatives to deadly force when deadly force might well be lawful under *Graham v. Connor. Russo v. City of Cincinnati,* 953 F.2d 1036 (6th Cir. 1992) (using Taser multiple times on knife-wielding suspect who was no longer an immediate threat deemed proper when use was intended to avoid having to resort to lethal force). Faced with an uncooperative knife-waving suspect who presented no immediate threat to the officers, officers fired two Sage rounds (1.5-inch polyurethane projectiles) and successfully incapacitated the suspect and took him into custody. The court approved the use of the device and acknowledged the potential alternative use of deadly force. *Mercado v. City of Orlando,* 323 F. Supp. 2d 1266 (M.D. Fla. 2004). A similar ruling was reached in a case of a woman who was holding a knife to her own throat and was shot by police with two lead shot–filled bean-bag rounds. *Brown v. City of Bloomington,* 280 F. Supp. 2d 889 (D. Minn. 2003).

Alternative force tools do not need to be limited to circumstances where deadly force could otherwise be used. *Singleton v. City of Newburgh,* 1 F. Supp. 2d 306 (S.D.N.Y. 1998) (no excessive force claim for a single stream of pepper spray to prevent unarmed suspect from destroying evidence of a crime). Even so, other alternative force options should always be considered. One court found the use of wooden baton rounds to be excessive, not because of the injury caused, but because officers failed to consider lesser levels of force prior to shooting the wooden rounds. *Otero v. Wood,* 316 F. Supp. 2d 612 (S.D. Ohio 2004).

The three most common alternative force tool options (other than empty-hand techniques) include handcuffing, baton strikes, and chemical aerosol sprays. Each application of force—even handcuffing—can reach the level of excessive force. *Kostrzewa v. City of Troy,* 247 F.3d 633 (6th Cir. 2001) (too-tight handcuffs on non-violent suspect might be constitutionally excessive force). The application of pepper spray is generally ruled to be reasonable on uncooperative though not yet assaultive suspects. *Passino v. State*, 689 N.Y.S.2d 258 (N.Y. App. 1999) (pepper spray not excessive when DUI suspect refused to be handcuffed). Like any other force, pepper spray cannot be used as a punitive measure and should not be used on controlled suspects. *Vinyard v. Wilson*, 311 F.3d 1340 (11th Cir. 2002) (courts consistently rule "that using pepper spray is excessive force in cases where the arrestee surrenders, is secured, and is not acting violently, and there is no threat to the officers or anyone else"). Officers must adhere to training protocols, such as providing first aid as promptly as possible, or a reasonable application of pepper spray may turn into an excessive force claim. *LaLonde v. County of Riverside*, 204 F.3d 947 (9th Cir. 2000) (use of pepper spray could be excessive when pepper spray left in suspect's eye longer than necessary).

Baton strikes are considered non-deadly force when applied to non-lethal target areas. The application of a baton, or a flashlight used as an impact weapon, is considered under the three factors of *Graham v. Connor*. *Kellough v. Bertrand*, 22 F. Supp. 2d 602 (S.D. Tex. 1998) (no excessive force for flashlight strikes on robbery suspect who refused to follow instructions to go to ground); *Nicholson v. Kent County Sheriff's Dept.*, 839 F. Supp. 508 (W.D. Mich. 1993) (strike with collapsible metal baton was not excessive force when suspect resisted and only two blows to proper target area). When the baton or flashlight strikes are in lethal target zones, they are considered as deadly force. *Nelson v. County of Wright*, 162 F.3d 986 (8th Cir. 1998). Though deadly force, blows to the head may be lawful when justified by the suspect's actions. *Tapp v. Banks*, 72 F. Supp. 2d 739 (E.D. Ky. 1999), *aff'd*, 1 Fed. Appx. 344 (6th Cir. 2001) (striking suspect on head with flashlight reasonable after 50-mile pursuit at speeds of 80 mph, suspect drove through roadblock and flares, used his vehicle to strike police cruiser, and acted in threatening manner toward officer).

Use of force to obtain evidence

Force may be used to obtain evidence from a suspect when the force does not unduly endanger the suspect and there is a significant need for the evidence. Force may be used to retrieve evidence from a suspect in certain circumstances. Generally, these situations fall into two categories: forcing suspects to spit out drugs from the mouth and forced blood draws. The question of whether a blood draw may be forced involves both an analysis of the search and seizure question, discussed in the Warrantless Search and Seizure chapter, and an analysis of how much force is reasonable. The officer's force will be assessed against three factors: (1) whether (and how much) the application of force threatened the suspect's safety or health; (2) the degree of the intrusion upon the suspect's personal privacy and bodily integrity; and (3) the public interest in fairly and accurately determining guilt or innocence. *Winston v. Lee,* 470 U.S. 753 (1985).

When a suspect attempts to swallow evidence, most courts approve applying force to obtain evidence from the suspect's mouth. *State v. Alverez,* 147 P.3d 425 (Utah 2006) (suspect placed in an arm lock, head bent forward, and forced to spit out balloons containing heroin); *Jones v. United States,* 620 A.2d 249 (D.C. 1993) (use of Heimlich maneuver to force contraband from suspect's mouth was not unreasonable); *State v. Harris,* 505 N.W.2d 724 (Neb. 1993) (use of lateral vascular neck restraint to prevent swallowing of drugs was not unreasonable search); *People v. Fulkman,* 235 Cal. App. 3d 555 (1991) (officers pounded suspect on back, placed pressure on Adam's apple to prevent him from swallowing, and pried contraband out of suspect's mouth with pen); *People v. Holloway,* 330 N.W.2d 405 (Mich. 1982) (applying pressure on suspect's jaw and placing fingers in suspect's mouth to recover tinfoil packets containing heroin and cocaine was reasonable), *cert. denied,* 461 U.S. 917 (1983). Suspects are more likely to succeed in suppressing the evidence where the quantity of drugs is negligible, *Locke v. State,* 588 So. 2d 1082 (Fla. App. 1991), or if significant force is used. *State v. Tapp,* 353 So. 2d 265 (La. 1977) (evidence inadmissible where defendant was caused to disgorge the packet from his throat after a struggle lasting 15 to 20 minutes).

The *Winston* factors also apply in forcing a blood draw. *State v. Clary,* 2 P.3d 1255 (Ariz. App. 2000). The majority rule is that substantial force may be used when a suspect refuses a lawful order to submit to a blood draw. *State v. Worthington,* 65 P.3d 211 (Idaho App. 2002). In *Worthington,* the suspect was arrested for DUI and refused a blood test. The suspect promised a fight if officers tried to take his blood. The suspect was handcuffed and belly-chained on a gurney. Three officers and two nurses held the suspect while a blood technician drew blood from the suspect's ankle. The court ruled that the force was reasonable in light of the resistance given by the suspect. Reasonable force may also be used to take other types of physical samples, such as fingernail scrapings, pubic combing, and plucking hair samples. *Roe v. Marcotte,* 193 F.3d 72 (2d Cir. 1999) (force may be used to obtain DNA samples from sex offenders); *Sanders v. Coman,* 864 F. Supp. 496 (E.D.N.C. 1994) (reasonable force may be used to obtain DNA samples required by statute).

Use of force in correctional facilities

Prison and jail officers operate under a unique set of use of force rules. The United States Supreme Court established a two-part test to measure the use of force in a correctional setting. First, did the use of force inflict "unnecessary and wanton pain and suffering"? Only if the particular force supports "a reliable inference of wantonness in the infliction of pain" will the force be constitutionally excessive. Second, the inmate must show that the force was "objectively harmful enough to offend contemporary standards of decency." *Hudson v. McMillian,* 503 U.S. 1 (1993).

Courts have upheld a variety of force options in excessive force claims by inmates. *Michenfelder v. Sumner,* 860 F.2d 328 (9th Cir. 1988) (using Taser on inmate who refuses to submit to a strip search is not cruel and unusual punishment); *Caldwell v. Woodford County,* 968 F.2d 595 (6th Cir. 1992) (use of stun gun and straitjacket on inmate who refused to obey jailers' orders was not excessive); *Soto v. Dickey,* 744 F.2d 1260 (7th Cir. 1984) (using chemical spray on inmate who refused to submit to body cavity search by bending over and spreading buttocks, then permitting a forcibly conducted search, was not considered excessive force), *cert. denied,* 470 U.S. 1085 (1985); *Poindexter v. Woodson,* 510 F.2d 464 (10th Cir.) (permissible to use water hoses on inmates where force was necessary to control prison disruption), *cert. denied,* 423 U.S. 846 (1975). In contrast, the force is generally found excessive when it is ruled to be punitive rather than an attempt to gain compliance and maintain order. *Campbell v. Grammer,* 889 F.2d 797 (8th Cir. 1989) (excessive force to use fire hoses on inmates where there was "absolutely no justification for this application of force," and inmates suffered back pain, blurred vision, and pain in ribs and thighs); *Slakan v. Porter,* 737 F.2d 368 (4th Cir. 1984) (excessive force to use steady blasts of water from two high-pressure water hoses, tear gas, and use of batons to "savagely" beat inmate who had complained about missing his usual morning coffee, where inmate was confined in one-person cell and posed no direct physical threat), *cert. denied*, 470 U.S. 1093 (1985).

Reporting use of force

The use of force factors established in *Graham v. Connors* should guide the reporting of every use of force incident. The report should answer these questions: Did I use force in a good-faith effort to maintain or restore order? What did I believe to be the severity of the crime? Why did I so believe? Was the suspect an immediate threat? To whom? What was the threatening behavior? Was the suspect resisting or fleeing? How?

Use of force will be reviewed on many levels. The department should investigate to answer these questions: Was the force justified at the actual moment of force? Did any action by the officer or others precipitate use of deadly force? Would policy or procedure, additional training or equipment have potentially avoided the necessity for force? There may also be a department internal affairs inquiry to consider whether the officer followed policies. Almost always in cases resulting in death or serious injury, the local prosecutor will look at whether criminal laws were violated by the use of force. The city or county risk management or insurance department will investigate in anticipation of a lawsuit.

Consequences of improper use of force

An officer who unlawfully uses force may face a federal civil rights investigation and federal criminal liability under 18 U.S. Code §§ 241-242. Responding to a burglary call, officers requested canine units. While surrounded by numerous officers and under the glare of a helicopter spotlight, the two suspects surrendered. Perhaps frustrated by the lack of pursuit, a canine handler asked the supervising sergeant for permission to send a dog to bite one of the compliant suspects. Permission was granted, the dog was sent, and the suspect received a lengthy bite. The canine handler was sentenced to 10 years in federal prison for civil rights violations. The sergeant who allowed the bite was sentenced to 15 months. *United States v. Mohr*, 318 F.3d 613 (4th Cir. 2003). A supervisor or other officer who witnesses unlawful force by an officer and who fails to intervene may be charged criminally. *United States v. Reese*, 2 F.3d 870 (9th Cir. 1993).

Either the federal government or the injured party may also file a federal rights civil lawsuit under 42 U.S. Code § 1983. *Priester v. City of Riviera Beach*, 208 F.3d 919 (11th Cir. 2000). There is also the potential of being charged with a state-law crime. Though the officer may be sued in state court, state law does not always provide for attorney fees, so most civil suits against officers are filed in federal court. Plaintiffs also generally believe that the 12-person juries in federal court are more favorable than the six or eight-person juries in many state courts. Of course, the officer may be fired and could even lose peace officer certification in extreme cases.

CHAPTER 5

INTERVIEW AND INTERROGATION

The Fifth Amendment and *Miranda*

- Voluntariness of the confession
- Custody
- Interrogation
- "Question first, *Miranda* second"
- Form of warnings
- What constitutes an effective waiver of *Miranda* rights
- Voluntariness of waiver of *Miranda* rights
- Equivocal answers and requests for counsel
- Repeated attempts at interrogation
- When warnings are not essential
- Jailhouse informants
- *Miranda* for incarcerated persons suspected of new crimes
- *Miranda* issues for probationers/parolees
- Speaking with a formally charged and/or represented suspect
- Non-testimonial evidence
- Exclusionary rule applied to *Miranda* violation
- Use of statements taken without *Miranda* warnings

The Fifth Amendment and *Miranda*

The case of *Miranda v. Arizona* brought a major shift to American criminal procedure. Prior to the *Miranda* decision, the primary issue in the admissibility of confessions was voluntariness. *Brown v. Mississippi*, 297 U.S. 278 (1936). Involuntary statements, generally the result of some form of coercion, were ruled inadmissible because of their inherent unreliability and the notion that coercion violates due process of law. *Rogers v. Richmond*, 365 U.S. 534 (1961). Shortly before the *Miranda* decision, the Supreme Court ruled that an accusatory investigative focus on a particular suspect gave rise to the right to confer with an attorney before questioning. *Escobedo v. Illinois*, 378 U.S. 478 (1964).

The core ruling in the *Miranda* decision states that the "prosecution may not use statements stemming from custodial interrogation of the defendant unless it demonstrates the use of procedural safeguards effective to secure the privilege against self-incrimination." *Miranda v. Arizona*, 384 U.S. 436 (1966). Thus, the *Miranda* rule applies when there is both **custody and interrogation**. The now-famous *Miranda* warning is not actually contained verbatim in the ruling; it was developed to summarize the rights articulated in the Court's decision.

Several criminal procedure issues arise from *Miranda*: Was the statement a product of *interrogation*? Was the interrogation done by a *law enforcement officer*? Was the suspect in *custody*? Were the *warnings* adequate? Was there an explicit *waiver* of rights? Was the suspect *competent* to make a waiver? Each of these issues is discussed in this chapter.

Voluntariness of the confession

The *Miranda* decision is not the only legal doctrine affecting law enforcement interrogation. The issue of voluntariness is still important, although it would be a rare case in which *Miranda* rules were followed and a court still found a confession to be involuntary. If the defendant challenges the voluntariness of the confession, the prosecution has the ultimate burden of showing voluntariness, separate from the questions of whether a *Miranda* warning was given and a waiver was obtained. *Arizona v. Fulminante*, 499 U.S. 279 (1991).

A confession is invalid if circumstances show that the confession resulted from some form of coercion—even if the *Miranda* warning was given and rights were waived. *Jackson v. Denno*, 378 U.S. 368 (1964). Courts consider factors such as the suspect's age, level of education, and low intelligence. *Schneckloth v. Bustamonte*, 412 U.S. 218 (1973). In addition to the suspect's characteristics, courts scrutinize officers' conduct.

Courts also consider the persistence of interrogating officers and trickery or deception. *State v. Werner*, 76 P.3d 304 (Utah App. 2003). Some deception is permissible. *Frazier v. Cupp*, 394 U.S. 731 (1969). Officers may "pressure and cajole, conceal material facts, and actively mislead." *United States v. Rutledge*, 900 F.2d 1127 (7th Cir. 1990). Failure to tell a suspect the subject of the interrogation is allowed. *Colorado v. Spring*, 479 U.S. 564 (1987). The "false friend" technique, or the "good cop, bad cop" technique is not enough—considered alone—to render a confession involuntary, though such techniques come close to the edge of impermissible coercion. *Miller v. Fenton*, 796 F.2d 598 (3d Cir. 1986) (excessive friendliness or good cop approach is valid technique); *Crowe v. County of San Diego*, 303 F. Supp. 2d 1050 (S.D. Cal. 2004) (good cop/bad cop technique is common and is acceptable if not overly coercive); *State v. Bell*, 80 P.3d 367 (Kan. 2003) (good cop/bad cop technique was valid because it was "not so unfair or coercive as to render suspect's statements involuntary"); *Mason v. State*, 116 S.W.3d 248 (Tex. App. 2003) (false friend approach is permissible).

False statements about incriminating evidence, e.g., a false statement that a suspect's fingerprints or DNA were found at a crime scene, are allowed. *Commonwealth v. Edwards*, 651 N.E.2d 398 (Mass. 1995). Other deceptions have been allowed: statement that tire and shoe prints and DNA samples matched the suspect's, *State v. Register*, 476 S.E.2d 153 (S.C. 1996), *cert. denied*, 519 U.S. 1129 (1997); claims that co-defendant implicated the suspect, *Hopkins v. State*, 311 A.2d 483 (Md. App. 1973), *cert. denied*, 271 Md. 738 (1974); claim that the suspect was seen by an eyewitness, *Holland v. McGinnis*, 963 F.2d 1044 (7th Cir. 1992), *cert. denied*, 506 U.S. 1082 (1993); claim that a sexual assault victim contracted the same sexually transmitted disease as the suspect's, *State v. Manning*, 506 So. 2d 1094 (Fla. App. 1987); and suspect father of sex abuse victim told that his victim daughter passed a polygraph, *State v. Boren*, 224 N.W.2d 14 (Iowa 1974), *cert. denied*, 422 U.S. 1008 (1975). Courts generally draw the line of permissible deception when officers actually manufacture false evidence to induce a confession. *State v. Patton*, 826 A.2d 783 (N.J. Super.), *cert. denied*, 834 A.2d 408 (N.J. 2003). However, even false documents may be allowed if they do no more than bolster false statements about evidence that officers claim to hold. *Arthur v. Commonwealth*, 480 S.E.2d 749 (Va. App. 1997) (rejecting argument that "dummy" DNA reports rendered confession involuntary; declining to draw bright-line prohibition because false documents were used).

Tactics such as physical abuse, threats, or deprivation of food, medical treatment, or sleep during an interrogation will invariably render a confession involuntary. *Andersen v. Thieret*, 903 F.2d 526 (7th Cir. 1990); *In re Goins*, 738 N.E.2d 385 (Ohio App. 1999). Any physical torture or beating will render a confession inadmissible. *Brown v. Mississippi*, 297 U.S. 278 (1936). A relaxed environment, the absence of handcuffs, and polite demeanor of officers will strongly support a finding of voluntariness. *Commonwealth v. Edmiston*, 634 A.2d 1078 (Pa. 1993).

Some forms of psychological pressure will also render a confession involuntary. A confession obtained by physical violence is presumptively involuntary; a confession obtained by psychological coercion is generally voluntary. *United States v. Miller*, 984 F.2d 1028 (9th Cir.), *cert. denied*, 510 U.S. 894 (1993). When there is alleged psychological coercion, the question for the court is whether the suspect's will was overborne, resulting in a confession. "Courts allow interrogators in these already coercive custodial settings considerable latitude in playing on the guilt and fears of the person interrogated in order to extract a confession that he will shortly regret having given." *Johnson v. Trigg*, 28 F.3d 639 (7th Cir. 1994).

Courts determine whether a confession is the result of unlawful psychological pressure by examining the totality of the circumstances. *United States v. Sablotny*, 21 F.3d 747 (7th Cir. 1994). Courts consider the officer's conduct, the conditions of the interrogation, and the characteristics of the suspect. The most important question is whether the officer's conduct was coercive. Coercion by the officer is a "necessary predicate to the finding that a confession is not 'voluntary.'" *Colorado v. Connelly*, 479 U.S. 157 (1986). If this first element is met, courts consider a variety of other factors, including:

- Promises of protection from inevitable injury in custody or promises of physical harm; both destroy the voluntariness of a confession. *Arizona v. Fulminante*, 499 U.S. 279 (1991).
- Statements that exercising the right to remain silent will result in harsher treatment. *United States v. Harrison*, 34 F.3d 886 (9th Cir.1994).
- Stating: "You have to talk to me now without a lawyer present." *Smith v. Illinois*, 469 U.S. 91 (1984).
- Threat of a lengthy prison term and separation from family. *Rogers v. Richmond*, 365 U.S. 534 (1961) (confession coerced when police threatened to take suspect's wife into custody if he did not confess); *United States v. Tingle*, 658 F.2d 1332 (9th Cir. 1981).
- Threats of placement in a facility or unit with persons likely to harm the suspect are equally improper. *United States v. McCullah*, 76 F.3d 1087 (10th Cir. 1996).
- Threats of being held and interrogated without the opportunity to contact family or legal counsel. *Haynes v. Washington*, 373 U.S. 503 (1963).
- Threats to remove the suspect's children into state custody. *Lynumn v. Illinois*, 372 U.S. 528 (1963); *People v. Medina*, 25 P.3d 1216 (Colo. 2001).
- Deceptively subjecting suspect to hypnosis. *Leyra v. Denno*, 347 U.S. 556 (1954).
- Whether "the defendant was in custody or free to leave and was aware of his situation; whether *Miranda* warnings were given prior to any interrogation and whether the defendant understood and waived his *Miranda* rights; whether the defendant had the opportunity to confer with counsel." *People v. Gray*, 975 P.2d 1124 (Colo. App. 1997).
- The nature and duration of the questioning used to secure the confession; whether the suspect was prevented from eating or sleeping. *United States v. Sablotny*, 21 F.3d 747 (7th Cir. 1994).
- Suspect's age, intelligence, education, and experience with the criminal justice system. *United States v. Oglesby*, 764 F.2d 1273 (7th Cir. 1985).
- A confession following ingestion of drugs that affect the free will or mental state of a suspect may be suppressed if the level of intoxication sufficiently impairs the free will of the suspect. *Townsend v. Sain*, 372 U.S. 293 (1963); *United States v. Casal*, 915 F.2d 1225 (8th Cir. 1990), *cert. denied*, 499 U.S. 941 (1991) ("intoxication and fatigue do not automatically render a confession involun-

tary; rather, the test is whether these mental impairments caused the defendant's will to be overborne"); *Graves v. United States,* 878 F. Supp. 409 (N.D.N.Y. 1995) ("Even if the court assumes that the petitioner was functioning with a limited capacity due to voluntary consumption of alcohol, in order for the petitioner to prove that the confession was involuntary there must still be some showing of official coercion.").

Promises of leniency by officers or the prosecutor affect voluntariness. *Wilkins v. State,* 104 P.3d 85 (Wyo. 2005). The ultimate question in such cases is whether "the promise was coercive in nature, i.e., whether the accused was so gripped by the hope of leniency that he did not or could not freely and rationally choose among the available courses of action." *United States v. Garot,* 801 F.2d 1241 (10th Cir. 1986). Simply promising the suspect to tell the prosecutor and court of the suspect's cooperation does not render a confession involuntary. However, if the confession is *induced by* the promise of leniency, it will be excluded. *State v. Lobato,* 134 P.3d 122 (N.M. 2006). Promises to recommend release without bail, though significant, will not render a confession involuntary. *Commonwealth v. Templin,* 795 A.2d 959 (Pa. 2002). Promises to make mental health treatment available, which suggested that the crime was committed because the defendant is mentally ill, generally do not make the confession involuntary. *United States v. McClinton,* 982 F.2d 278 (8th Cir. 1992).

As a final note, some courts consider the lack of an audio and/or video recording of the interrogation as a factor in voluntariness. *Commonwealth v. DiGiambattista,* 813 N.E.2d 5165 (Mass. 2004). Some states have imposed recording requirements through the application of the exclusionary rule to unrecorded confessions. *State v. Scales,* 518 N.W.2d 587 (Minn. 1994); *Stephen v. State,* 711 P.2d 1156 (Alaska 1985). The lack, or existence, of the recording obviously does not alter the reality of the circumstances of the interrogation. Such rulings are merely intended to persuade law enforcement agencies to create electronic records. To date, six states require tape-recording in certain cases, generally homicides. Legislation to require recording of confessions is pending in more than a dozen states. There is no federal requirement for tape-recording. In fact, the FBI steadfastly refuses to create taped records of interrogations conducted by its agents. Neither a taped record of the interrogation or

Miranda waiver nor a formal written *Miranda* waiver are constitutional requirements. *United States v. Williams,* 429 F.3d 767 (8th Cir. 2005).

Custody

If a suspect is not in "custody," no *Miranda* rules ever apply. To determine whether a suspect was in custody, courts consider several factors. **First, was there a formal arrest? Second, would a reasonable person have felt that he or she was not free to end the questioning and walk away? Third, was the suspect's movement restrained or curtailed to the degree associated with a formal arrest?** *Thompson v. Keohane,* 516 U.S. 99 (1995). The custody determination is measured objectively by looking at these factors. Neither the officer's nor the suspect's subjective belief about custody figure very significantly in the analysis. *Stansbury v. California,* 511 U.S. 318 (1994).

A number of facts help answer the custody question. The time, length, and location of the interrogation are all important. The number of officers involved in the questioning and the presence of the suspect's attorney or other non-law enforcement persons are also critical factors. **Courts consider four general factors in deciding the custody question**: First, the site of interrogation; second, whether the investigation focused on the suspect; third, whether objective signs of arrest, such as handcuffs, weapons displayed, and statements of arrest, were present; and fourth, the length and form of interrogation. *United States v. Salvo,* 133 F.3d 943 (6th Cir.), *cert. denied,* 523 U.S. 1122 (1998). Additional factors that courts may consider include "whether there was a threatening presence of several officers and a display of weapons or physical force, whether the officers deprived the defendant of documents she needed to continue on her way," *United States v. Yusuff,* 96 F.3d 982 (7th Cir. 1996); "whether strong-arm tactics or deceptive stratagems were employed during questioning," *United States v. Griffin,* 922 F.2d 1343 (8th Cir. 1990); and whether the suspect came to the place of interrogation voluntarily or not, *State v. Gray,* 851 P.2d 1217 (Utah App. 1993). No single factor is determinative. Rather, the court looks at the totality of the circumstances. *State v. Worthington,* 970 P.2d 714 (Utah App. 1998).

Following are examples of factors that may or may not indicate custody:

- **Site of interrogation.** The mere fact that the interrogation takes place at a law enforcement facility does not necessarily create a custodial situation. *Oregon v. Mathiason,* 429 U.S. 492 (1977). In *Mathiason,* the defendant voluntarily came to the police station, was not told that he was under arrest, and was allowed to leave after one-half hour. The Court ruled that he was not in custody, even though he was directly accused of a burglary. However, placing a person in an interrogation room with a locked door or with the door blocked by an officer would likely result in a finding of custody. On the other hand, interrogation at a person's home is generally not considered custodial. *United States v. Howard,* 991 F.2d 195 (5th Cir.) (no custody when questioning occurred at suspect's home and he was told he was not under arrest, although told to "stay put"), *cert. denied,* 510 U.S. 949 (1993); *Devier v. Zant,* 3 F.3d 1445 (11th Cir. 1993) (*Miranda* warnings not required when suspect was questioned at home without warnings and then volunteered to continue questioning at station), *cert. denied,* 513 U.S. 1161 (1995). Sitting in the back of a police car also does not automatically create custody. *United States v. Baker,* 78 F.3d 1241 (7th Cir. 1996) ("there was no need to give suspect *Miranda* warnings" merely because suspect was questioned in a police car), *cert. denied*, 520 U.S. 1222 (1997); *United States v. Boucher,* 909 F.2d 1170 (8th Cir. 1990) ("*Miranda* warnings are not imposed because the questioning is conducted in a certain place, i.e., a patrol car").
- **Investigative focus.** If an officer directly accuses a suspect of a crime, or tells the suspect that he or she is under investigation, the statement may be a factor in creating custody insofar as the statement would affect a reasonable person's belief that he or she was not free to leave. *Stansbury v. California,* 511 U.S. 318 (1994). However, just because an officer focuses the investigation on the suspect does not trigger the need for *Miranda* warnings. *Minnesota v. Murphy,* 465 U.S. 420 (1984).
- **Indications of arrest.** The application of handcuffs, placing a suspect behind locked doors, or displaying drawn guns are indications of arrest but do not necessarily mandate a conclusion of arrest. *United States v. Beard,* 119 Fed. Appx. 462 (4th Cir. 2005); *State v. Levin,* 101 P.3d 846 (Utah App. 2004). Other potential indicators of arrest include: presence of numerous officers, *People v. Herdan,*

42 Cal. App. 3d 300 (1974), showing a badge or uniform, *State v. Brandley*, 972 P.2d 978 (Utah App. 1998), an officer's raised voice, *id.*, requiring a suspect to lie prone on the roadway, *State v. Carver*, 577 N.W.2d 245 (Minn. App. 1998), use of force to detain, *Commonwealth v. Willis*, 616 N.E.2d 62 (Mass. 1993), giving of verbal commands to stop, *People v. Ocasio*, 85 N.Y.2d 982 (1995). No one factor is determinative. Though the application of handcuffs is generally recognized as the "hallmark of a formal arrest," *United States v. Newton*, 369 F.3d 659 (2d Cir. 2004), even that may not always create an arrest. *United States v. Acosta-Colon*, 157 F.3d 9 (1st Cir. 1998).

- **Length of questioning.** Generally, the longer the questioning, the more likely it is that a custodial detention has been created. A detention for questioning as short as 20 minutes has been ruled as custodial. *United States v. Mahar*, 801 F.2d 1477 (6th Cir. 1986). On the other hand, questioning lasting more than one hour was ruled not to be custodial where there were multiple suspects and officers had called for a drug recognition expert. *State v. Levin*, 101 P.3d 846 (Utah App. 2004). Even questioning lasting several hours may not create custody if other factors indicate that the suspect is free to leave. *Davis v. Allsbrooks*, 778 F.2d 168 (4th Cir. 1985). Though important, this factor is always considered in light of additional factors.
- **Form of interrogation.** "Whether the interview was aggressive or, instead, informal and influenced in its contours by the suspect" helps determine whether an interrogation is custodial. *Commonwealth v. Cameron*, 689 N.E.2d 1365 (Mass. App. 1998). Hostile and accusatory questioning suggests custody. *Nova v. Bartlett*, 63 F. Supp. 2d 449 (S.D.N.Y. 1999). Friendly discussions of crimes, on the other hand, suggest that the suspect is not in custody. *United States v. Motti*, 946 F.2d 1366 (8th Cir. 1991).
- **Time of day.** Questioning late at night or early in the morning is more likely to support a finding of custody. *Bond v. State*, 788 A.2d 705 (Md. App. 2002) (questioning suspect late at night while suspect was in his bed, partially unclothed, created custody even though interrogation was in the suspect's home); *Orozco v. Texas*, 394 U.S. 324 (1969). Questioning during business hours will not generally lead to a conclusion of custody. *United States v. Mahan*, 190 F.3d 416 (6th Cir. 1999); *State v. Means*, 547 N.W.2d 615 (Iowa App. 1996).

Interrogation

In the famous *Miranda* decision, the Supreme Court defined "interrogation" as "questioning initiated by law enforcement officers after a person has been taken into custody or otherwise deprived of his freedom of action in any significant way." *Miranda v. Arizona,* 384 U.S. 436 (1966). The Court later refined this statement, noting: "**the definition of interrogation can extend only to words or actions on the part of police officers that they should have known were *reasonably likely to elicit an incriminating response*.**" *Rhode Island v. Innis,* 446 U.S. 291 (1980). The issue of whether there has been interrogation is a subjective question. Courts apply the standard of whether a reasonable person would have believed that the custodial questioning was intended to elicit an incriminating response, not the officer's subjective motive in asking the question. *United States v. Rambo,* 365 F.3d 906 (10th Cir. 2004).

Following are examples of forms of questioning frequently at issue in determining whether there was interrogation:

- **Routine booking questions.** Questions intended to obtain biographical data necessary to complete booking or pretrial services are not considered interrogation. *Pennsylvania v. Muniz,* 469 U.S. 582 (1990). However, even if a question is routinely asked during booking, if it is *intended to elicit an incriminating response,* it constitutes interrogation. *State v. Ketchum,* 34 P.3d 1006 (Haw. 2001). Thus, an officer's questioning of an arrestee about the arrestee's true name, as part of an investigation, may be considered interrogation, while a booking officer's identical question in order to complete a jail roster is not interrogation. Booking questions asking whether the arrestee is currently under the influence of drugs or alcohol have been ruled as interrogation when the arrest is drug- or alcohol-related. *Hughes v. State,* 695 A.2d 132 (Md.), *cert. denied,* 522 U.S. 989 (1997). The question can, and perhaps should, still be asked. Yet the answer may not be admissible in court. On the other hand, if the question is primarily motivated by an obvious medical concern, such as discovering why a lethargic arrestee seems ill or is vomiting, the answer may be admissible. *Colon v. State,* 568 S.E.2d 811 (Ga. App. 2002) (statement that arrestee had ingested GHB admissible when officer was concerned about reason for vomiting). An arrestee's inappropriate or non-responsive answers to routine booking questions may be admitted to show a measure of impairment, again assuming that the purpose was not to elicit an incriminating response. *State v. Geasley*, 619 N.E.2d 1086 (Ohio. App. 1993).

- **Functional equivalent of interrogation.** "Interrogation" does not necessarily require that a question be asked. For example, placing an item of evidence in front of a suspect and staring silently at the suspect can constitute interrogation. *Drury v. State*, 793 A.2d 567 (Md.), *cert. denied*, 537 U.S. 942 (2002). Non-questioning words or actions may constitute interrogation when they go beyond those normally associated with the arrest process, and could be reasonably construed as likely to generate an incriminating response. *United States v. Lovell*, 317 F. Supp. 2d 663 (W.D. Va. 2004). A suspect invoked his right to counsel. Officers then handed him a list of charges, including a death penalty notification, and said "I bet you want to talk now, huh!" Within a half-hour, the suspect provided a statement to the officers. The court found that the statement was the functional equivalent of questioning. *Blake v. State*, 849 A.2d 410 (Md. 2004). The most famous case discussing the "functional equivalent of interrogation" is the "Christian Burial Speech" case. *Brewer v. Williams*, 430 U.S. 387 (1977). Detectives transporting a man suspected of murdering a young girl were instructed to not question the suspect. Knowing of his particular sensitivity to religious issues, the two detectives conversed between themselves about the impending Christmas season and the family's disappointment at not having their daughter's body for a Christian burial. The suspect, sitting in the back seat of the car, "volunteered" the location of the girl's body. The Supreme Court ruled that this conversation was interrogation, "perhaps more effective" than the questioning that had been forbidden to them.
- **Volunteered statements.** Voluntary statements are not subject to *Miranda* warnings, and an officer need not stop a suspect making a voluntary statement. *Miranda v. Arizona*, 384 U.S. 436 (1966). While tracking a shooting suspect, an officer noticed a man running from him. He caught the man, whom he recognized. When the officer asked the man "How you doin'?," the man responded that he was running because he had been trying to buy drugs and he was on parole. The man then asked if officers were looking for his "jacket." The suspect's jacket

matched the clothing description given for the shooting suspect. The court ruled that there was no interrogation. *Youngblood v. Conway*, 426 F. Supp. 2d 107 (W.D.N.Y. 2006). A voluntary statement is not necessarily limited to a statement made completely spontaneously by the suspect. For example, when a suspect stated his age as 11 years old and the officer expressed disbelief, the suspect stated that he had been paid $40 to watch a stolen car on the previous night. Because the statement was entirely non-responsive to the officer's comment, the court ruled it to be voluntary and not subject to a *Miranda* warning. *State v. Dutchie*, 969 P.2d 422 (Utah 1998). Even voluntary statements made following custodial interrogation without *Miranda* warnings may be admitted if the prosecution can show the lack of coercion. Pettigrew was highly intoxicated and was the driver in a fatal traffic crash. Officers interrogated him following his arrest, but failed to give *Miranda* warnings. A short time later, Pettigrew asked why he was arrested. When an officer told him that he might have killed someone, Pettigrew made incriminating statements. The court ruled that allowing Pettigrew's statement to be admitted "would not likely implicate *Miranda*'s central concern—introduction into evidence of a criminal defendant's compelled testimony—and the truth-finding mission of the criminal justice system is best served by its introduction." *United States v. Pettigrew*, 455 F.3d 1164 (10th Cir. 2006).

- **Clarification of volunteered statements.** Ambiguous voluntary statements can be clarified without giving a *Miranda* warning. When a suspect was stopped for speeding and asked about his reason for speeding, he told officers to "go ahead and arrest me." The officer, shocked at the statement, replied "What did you say?" The suspect then stated "I did it. I stabbed David. I'm the one you're looking for. You would have caught me anyway." The court found that the clarifying question did not constitute interrogation. *Stone v. State*, 900 S.W.2d 515 (Ark. 1995). When a suspect interrupted an officer speaking to other people in an apartment about possession of a stolen car and said, "I did it," the officer asked what he had done. The suspect said, "I killed him. I killed a man." The court admitted the suspect's statements, even though the officer had interjected clarifying questions. *State v. Laws*, 481 S.E.2d 641 (N.C. 1997).

- **Questioning by private citizen/informant/security.** The *Miranda* rule applies only to interrogation by a government agent. *Colorado v. Connelly,* 479 U.S. 157 (1986). Questioning by government employees who do not have a primary responsibility of law enforcement will not likely constitute interrogation. *United States v. Eide,* 875 F.2d 1429 (9th Cir. 1989). Thus, information relayed by a schoolteacher, for example, and not obtained at the request of an officer, is not interrogation, no matter how incriminating. *J.D. v. Commonwealth,* 591 S.E.2d 721 (Va. App. 2004). Most courts rule that *Miranda* warnings need not be given by school officials when questioning a student about a violation of law. *In re V.P.,* 55 S.W.3d 25 (Tex. App. 2001); *State v. Tinkham,* 719 A.2d 580 (N.H. 1998). A statement to medical professionals during treatment is not interrogation. *United States v. Romero,* 897 F.2d 47 (2d Cir. 1990). However, statements made during therapy in a correctional facility *may* be the result of interrogation. *Welch v. Commonwealth,* 149 S.W.3d 407 (Ky. 2004) (statements to sex offender therapists should have *Miranda* protection). Questioning by private security officers or bail enforcement officers does not require a *Miranda* warning. *State v. Dorton,* 696 P.2d 1218 (Utah 1985); *Oriji v. State,* 150 S.W.3d 833 (Tex. App. 2004). If the private security officer is acting at the direction of a law enforcement officer, then a custodial interrogation would require appropriate warnings. *Metigoruk v. Anchorage,* 655 P.2d 1317 (Alaska 1982). However, some courts go so far as to not require warnings by private security officers who are off-duty law enforcement officers acting in a purely private capacity. *Owens v. State,* 490 N.E.2d 1130 (Ind. App. 1986).

"Question first, **Miranda** *second"*

In recent years, some investigators have used the technique of asking incriminating questions in a "pre-interrogation" setting. Sometimes the pre-interrogation is forceful and accusatory. Once the suspect makes incriminating statements, the investigator takes a break and leaves the room. A short time later, the investigator returns, gives a *Miranda* warning and obtains further admissions.

This practice was based on a misunderstanding of the decision in *Oregon v. Elstad,* 470 U.S. 298 (1985). In *Elstad,* the Court allowed admission of statements from a non-*Miranda* interrogation, which was followed by a second interrogation with a *Miranda* warning. *See below*. The United States Supreme Court ruled that the intentional "question first, *Miranda* second" technique generally renders a confession inadmissible. *Missouri v. Seibert*, 542 U.S. 600 (2004).

It is possible to conduct a voluntary interrogation after an interrogation where *Miranda* rules applied because the suspect was in custody but officers intentionally omitted the proper warnings. However, the burden of proving that the interrogation responses and the *Miranda* waiver in the second interrogation are voluntary is particularly tough. The second interrogation is *presumed to produce involuntary statements. United States v. Stewart*, 388 F.3d 1079 (7th Cir. 2004). Courts examine: (1) the extent of the first interrogation; (2) the extent to which the first and second interrogations overlap; (3) the timing and setting of both interrogations, including whether the same officers are present; and (4) the extent to which the interrogator's questions treated the second interrogation as a continuation of the first, such as asking questions or seeking admissions that build on statements from the first interrogation. *United States v. Aguilar*, 384 F.3d 520 (8th Cir. 2004).

One court has approved an aggressive and creative variation on the two-step interrogation. Officers "interviewed" Gonzalez-Lauzan for two and one-half hours. However, not only did the officers not question him, they told him several times that they did not want him to say anything. The officers simply laid out the evidence against him of his involvement in a murder. Occasionally, the suspect said things such as "I'm not the guy." The officers would occasionally pause for a few moments of silence to see if the suspect would say anything else. Finally, he said "Okay, you got me." Officers then gave a *Miranda* warning, questioned him, and obtained a confession to his participation in the murder.

Generally, courts agree that confronting a suspect with evidence of a crime is the "functional equivalent" of interrogation. However, the appellate court ruled that Gonzalez-Lauzan's waiver and subsequent confession were voluntary. Several key factors distinguished this case from the improper two-step interrogation disapproved in *Seibert*. First, officers repeatedly told the suspect that they had no questions for him. Second, there was no deliberate misconduct by the officers and no attempt to evade *Miranda* requirements. Third, the entire interrogation was "respectful" and there were no threats, coercion, or hostility by officers. Fourth, the officers did not rely on statements obtained in an improper interrogation to pose questions or obtain statements during a subsequent proper interrogation. *United States v. Gonzalez-Lauzan*, 437 F.3d 1128 (11th Cir. 2006).

Form of warnings

There is no real shortcut to an effective *Miranda* warning. An officer need not use the precise language of the *Miranda* decision. The key issue is whether the warning used "conveys the equivalent essence of the *Miranda* warnings." *California v. Prysock*, 453 U.S. 355 (1981). Even so, courts often advise officers to stick closely to the language of the *Miranda* case, only grudgingly approving deviations. *State v. Schwartz*, 467 N.W.2d 240 (Iowa 1991). Warnings given in another language should follow an approved written translation whenever possible. If an oral translation is made, create an audio recording of the translation for use in court. *United States v. Perez-Lopez*, 348 F.3d 839 (9th Cir. 2003). Remember that the prosecution carries the burden of showing that the *Miranda* waiver was knowing and voluntary. A Spanish-language translation of the *Miranda* warning and waiver form can be found in the appendices of this book.

What constitutes an effective waiver of Miranda *rights?*

An effective waiver is a **voluntary and intentional relinquishment** of the rights addressed in the *Miranda* decision. Ideally, every interrogation would be accompanied by a written, express waiver. *United States v. Gupta*, 183 F.3d 615 (7th Cir. 1999). A written waiver is not the legal requirement, however, and an implied waiver may be sufficient. *North Carolina v. Butler*, 441 U.S. 369 (1979). If the suspect does not give an express waiver, the officer should carefully document all facts that would support a finding of an implied waiver. It is important that there be some evidence that the suspect understands the warning. Non-verbal conduct may also communicate a waiver. If a suspect nods affirmatively and proceeds to answer questions, he may have done enough to demonstrate an implied waiver. *Ragland v. Commonwealth*, 191 S.W.3d 569 (Ky. 2006); *People v. Crane*, 585 N.E.2d 99 (Ill. 1991).

One of the most common circumstances where courts find an implied waiver is the suspect's act of answering questions or making a statement after not specifically responding to a question such as "Do you wish to answer my questions?" *United States v. Frankson*, 83 F.3d 79 (4th Cir. 1996). However, "mere silence is not enough. Silence, coupled with an understanding of his rights and a course of conduct indicating waiver, *may* support a conclusion that a defendant waived his rights." *North Carolina v. Butler,* 441 U.S. 369 (1979). Statements such as "I might as well tell you about it" may constitute a waiver. *United States v. Boykin,* 398 F.2d 483 (3d Cir. 1968), *cert. denied,* 393 U.S. 1032 (1969). This is a tricky area. Another court ruled that a suspect's response of "What do you want to know?" accompanied by an affirmative head nod did not constitute a waiver. *United States v. Gordon,* 895 F.2d 932 (4th Cir. 1990).

The presence of a defense attorney and the attorney's participation in the discussion immediately prior to a custodial interrogation will not excuse officers from giving a *Miranda* warning before questioning. Though the suspect may waive *Miranda* rights, the suspect cannot waive the warning itself. The right to a warning is personal to the suspect and cannot be waived on behalf of the suspect by an attorney. *State v. Joseph,* 128 P.3d 795 (Haw. 2006); *State v. DeWeese,* 582 S.E.2d 786 (W. Va. 2003).

Voluntariness of waiver of Miranda *rights*

A suspect's waiver of *Miranda* rights will be considered voluntary if there is no evidence that the suspect's will was overborne by officers and officers did not use coercive (more than merely persuasive) tactics. *Colorado v. Connelly,* 479 U.S. 157 (1986). In other words, was the suspect's statement a product of the suspect's free and independent will? The burden of showing a voluntary waiver is very heavy and rests with the state. *Tague v. Louisiana,* 444 U.S. 469 (1980). A number of factors are considered by courts, and no one factor is conclusive. *United States v. Benally,* 146 F.3d 1232 (10th Cir. 1998). Though the analysis of voluntariness of a waiver and the ultimate voluntariness of the confession are distinct legal issues, many of the same factors apply, and are discussed below.

Factors that courts consider include:

- "The defendant's age, intelligence, and education; the length of the detention and interrogation; the length and nature of the questioning; whether the defendant was advised of his constitutional rights; and whether the defendant was subjected to or threatened with any physical punishment." *United States v. Lugo,* 170 F.3d 996 (10th Cir. 1999).

- The suspect's background and experience with the criminal justice system. *United States v. Hawthorne,* 316 F.3d 1140 (10th Cir.), *cert. denied,* 540 U.S. 884 (2003).
- Language comprehension. *In re M.W.,* 731 N.E.2d 358 (Ill. App. 2000).
- Ability to read and write. *Johnson v. State,* 158 Ga. App. 333 (1981).
- Familiarity with the United States legal system. *United States v. Robles-Ramirez,* 93 F. Supp. 2d 762 (W.D. Tex. 2000).
- Voluntary intoxication. *Colorado v. Spring,* 479 U.S. 564 (1987).
- "The time interval between the initial *Miranda* advisement and any subsequent interrogation; whether and to what extent the interrogating officer reminded the defendant of his or her rights prior to the interrogation by asking if the defendant recalled his or her rights, understood them, or wanted an attorney; the clarity and form of the defendant's acknowledgment and waiver." *People v. Platt,* 81 P.3d 1060 (Colo. 2004).

Equivocal answers and requests for counsel

If the suspect responds ambiguously or equivocally to a *Miranda* warning, the officer must clarify the suspect's intent. If the officer tries to clarify the suspect's response and the suspect continues to respond ambiguously or equivocally, a valid implied waiver may still be found. *State v. Leyva,* 951 P.2d 738 (Utah 1997). It is essential that the officer proceed with caution and carefully document the suspect's behavior and statements.

An *explicit* request for an attorney requires that all questioning must cease. If the suspect makes an *ambiguous or equivocal* statement concerning the right to legal counsel following an unequivocal waiver of the right to counsel, the officer does not need to stop and ask clarifying questions. *Davis v. United States,* 512 U.S. 452 (1994). When the suspect said, "Maybe I should have a lawyer," the Supreme Court ruled that was not an invocation of the right to counsel, and allowed admission of statements made to officers. Even though officers are not required to stop the questioning and clarify an ambiguous statement regarding counsel, it may be good practice to do so.

Repeated attempts at interrogation

Once the suspect has been advised of and waived *Miranda* rights, a subsequent interrogation generally will not require repetition of the *Miranda* warning. *Wyrick v. Fields,* 459 U.S. 42 (1982). However, if any significant time has passed, repeating the warning is a sensible precaution. Courts consider the following factors: (1) the length of time between the giving of the first warnings and the subsequent interrogation; (2) whether the warnings and the subsequent interrogation were given in the same or different places; (3) whether the warnings were given and the subsequent interrogation conducted by the same or different officers; (4) the extent to which the subsequent statement differed from any previous statements; and (5) the apparent intellectual and emotional state of the suspect. *State v. Tolbert,* 850 A.2d 1192 (Md.), *cert. denied,* 543 U.S. 852 (2004). Various time periods have been permitted: one day, *United States v. Andaverde,* 64 F.3d 1305 (9th Cir. 1995); nine hours, *United States ex rel. Henne v. Fike,* 563 F.2d 809 (7th Cir. 1977); three and one-half hours, *Fagan v. State,* 412 So. 2d 1282 (Ala. App. 1982); two hours, *Commonwealth v. Silanskas,* 746 445 N.E.2d 433 (Mass. 2001); 12 days, *Koger v. State,* 17 P.3d 428 (Nev. 2001).

Rules on repeated attempts at interrogation vary, according to which right, or rights, are invoked by the suspect and at which stage of the investigative process the interrogation is attempted. The right to remain silent, the right to counsel under the *Miranda* decision based on the Fifth Amendment, and the right to counsel under the Sixth Amendment must all be considered separately.

- Attempt to interrogate after the **right to silence** is invoked. When a suspect invokes the right to remain silent, officers may attempt to interrogate the suspect at a later time. In *Michigan v. Mosley,* 423 U.S. 96 (1975), the Supreme Court allowed a second interrogation after the suspect had invoked the right to remain silent. The Court relied on the following factors: first, the interrogation immediately ceased when the defendant said he did not want to talk anymore; second, there was a significant passage of time between the invocation of the right to remain silent and the second interrogation, and a fresh set of *Miranda* warnings preceded the resumption; and third, the renewed interrogation related to a different crime. Later decisions have clarified that the second attempt at interrogation may relate to the same subject as the first attempt. *Kelly v. Lynaugh,* 862 F.2d 1126 (5th Cir. 1988), *cert. denied,* 492 U.S. 925 (1989). An officer wishing to renew an attempt at interrogation should "scrupulously honor" the invocation of the right to remain silent, allow a significant period of time to pass (at least a few hours), provide a full *Miranda* warning again, and avoid any pressure tactics or coercion. *State v. Grant,* 784 S.W.2d 831 (Mo. App. 1990). It may be helpful to show that the suspect has eaten and slept during the interval between invoking the right to remain silent and the second interrogation. Any coercion that might have been presumed from the first interrogation will likely dissipate by the passage of time. *State v. Leger,* 936 So. 2d 108 (La. 2006).

- Attempt to interrogate after the **right to counsel** is invoked. Once the suspect has clearly claimed the right to counsel, all interrogation must immediately stop. *Patterson v. Illinois,* 487 U.S. 285 (1988). Officers cannot question the suspect until the suspect's attorney is present. *Edwards v. Arizona,* 451 U.S. 477 (1981). Even the passage of time will not allow officers to make a second attempt at questioning. *Minnick v. Mississippi,* 498 U.S. 146 (1990). However, an ambiguous request for an attorney that follows an unequivocal waiver of the right to counsel need not stop the interrogation. It is good practice, though not constitutionally mandated, to clarify a suspect's ambiguous request for an attorney.
- Interrogation when the **suspect initiates conversation** after the **right to counsel** is invoked. Though the suspect's invocation of the right to counsel absolutely cuts off interrogation, the suspect may open the door to interrogation by initiating communication with officers. *Minnick v. Mississippi,* 498 U.S. 146 (1990); *Edwards v. Arizona,* 451 U.S. 477 (1981). The court will ask two questions: Did the suspect actually initiate the conversation and indicate a desire to talk about the crime, and was the suspect again given a warning and then voluntarily waived *Miranda* rights, including the right to legal counsel? Since the prosecution bears the heavy burden of showing that the suspect wanted to talk about the crime, officers may need to ask clarifying questions when a suspect indicates a desire to speak with them. Circumstances such as the following, which were preceded by an invocation of the right to counsel, have been held to be invitations to talk: suspect's statement of surprise at learning the nature of

the charge, *Giles v. Commonwealth,* 507 S.E.2d 102 (Va. App. 1998); request to see the arresting officer, *People v. Smith,* 713 N.E.2d 140 (Ill. App. 1999); "Well, I'll talk to you" upon learning that the local officers would turn the suspect over to federal agents, *State v. Wade,* 866 S.W.2d 908 (Mo. App. 1993); request to talk to prosecuting attorney, *State v. Coyle,* 567 A.2d 870 (Del. Super. 1989). Statements made after an invocation of the right to counsel are often challenged in court as being the product of "interrogation" before an expressed willingness to talk and a repeated rights warning. An officer's comments or questions about mundane matters, such as offering food, water, or commenting on the weather and other trivia, do not amount to interrogation. *State v. Kramar,* 440 N.W.2d 317 (Wis. 1989). When officers make statements in the presence of the suspect that are intended to induce a revocation of the invoked right to counsel, subsequent statements will be suppressed. *State v. Earl,* 702 N.W.2d 711 (Minn. 2005).

- After a **custodial interrogation without a *Miranda*** warning. Though the Supreme Court has disapproved of the "question first, warn second" interrogation technique, if officers have not *intentionally* violated the *Miranda* rule, the "fruit of the poisonous tree" doctrine will not necessary bar evidence from a proper second interrogation.

When warnings are not essential

General on-scene questioning, such as asking "What happened here?," does not constitute interrogation (and generally is not "custodial"). *People v. Brand,* 787 N.Y.S.2d 169 (N.Y. App. Div. 2004), *cert. denied,* 797 N.Y.S.2d 425 (N.Y. 2005). Thus, no warning is required. Officers responding to a 911 call asked "What happened?" and were answered with a confession to a double murder. The suspect responded that he had stabbed his sister and his sister's friend. The court ruled that there was no interrogation. *Commonwealth v. Odrick,* 599 A.2d 974 (Pa. Super. 1991), *cert. denied,* 613 A.2d 1209 (Pa. 1992). Similarly, information gathered by emergency dispatchers during a call for police service, even in response to questions, does not constitute interrogation (again, custody would not generally be at issue). *New York v. Moscat,* 777 N.Y.S.2d 875 (2004). Persons who are only witnesses, not suspects, are not entitled to *Miranda* warnings.

Miranda warnings need not be given during **routine traffic stops**. *Clark v. Municipality of Anchorage,* 112 P.3d 676

(Alaska App. 2005). Even though there may be both custody, in some minor degree, and interrogation, the Supreme Court has ruled that roadside questioning is not sufficiently coercive as to require warnings. *Berkemer v. McCarty,* 468 U.S. 420 (1984). Traffic stops are generally brief, and the detained motorist will not have the same fear of police domination as in a circumstance tantamount to a custodial arrest. Because the motorist expects to be detained only long enough to receive a traffic citation, there is no objective reason to believe that the motorist has been deprived of liberty in a significant way.

Questions that are prompted by an **urgent concern for public safety** may constitute interrogation, but are exempt from the general *Miranda* warning rule. *New York v. Quarles,* 467 U.S. 649 (1984). Courts have admitted incriminating responses to questions in situations such as: questioning a wounded man upon arrival at a bank alarm, *Fleming v. Collins,* 954 F.2d 1109 (5th Cir. 1992); asking for the whereabouts of a domestic violence victim believed to be injured, *Commonwealth v. Sepulvida,* 855 A.2d 783 (Pa. 2004), *cert. denied,* ___ U.S. ___, 126 S. Ct. 1330 (2006); questioning a suspect where hostages are being held by accomplices, *Howard v. Garvin,* 844 F. Supp. 173 (S.D.N.Y. 1994); locating one burglar and asking him whether another burglar was in the building, *Joppy v. State,* 719 So. 2d 316 (Fla. App. 1998); and asking an armed robbery suspect for the location of his accomplice, *State v. McKessor,* 785 P.2d 1332 (Kan.), *cert. denied,* 495 U.S. 937 (1990). Though the exception is based on a concern for "public safety," courts include risks to officers as justification for public safety questions. For example, when searching an apartment, an officer asked whether he would find anything "that would hurt" him, and the suspect revealed a gun in the closet. The court allowed the answer under the public safety exception. *United States v. Williams,* 181 F.3d 945 (8th Cir. 1999). Similarly, a court allowed evidence seized when officers arresting a drug dealer asked the same question and the suspect gave up both a gun and his drug stash. *United States v. Reyes,* 353 F.3d 148 (2d Cir. 2003).

The public safety exception will not apply when the questioning is directed at investigatory issues rather than genuine immediate concerns for safety. Nor will the exception apply when the issue is for the suspect's safety alone. *State v. Montoya,* 937 P.2d 145 (Utah App. 1997). Thus, an officer's questions about what drugs a suspect may have consumed cannot be justified under the exception. However, the same question asked by medical staff for purposes of diagnosis and treatment may well be admissible under other rules of evidence.

Jailhouse informants

Officers cannot use informants to do what they themselves must not do. A suspect who has asserted the Sixth Amendment right to counsel cannot be the target of interrogation by an informant inmate at the behest of an officer. Nor can a jailhouse informant stimulate conversation with a defendant to develop trust and confidence in hopes of gaining incriminating evidence against the defendant at the behest of an officer. *United States v. Henry*, 447 U.S. 264 (1980). However, this rule applies only when a defendant has been formally charged. *United States v. Laury*, 49 F.3d 145 (5th Cir. 1995). An informant may be placed in the cell to *passively listen. Kuhlman v. Wilson*, 477 U.S. 436 (1986).

The suspect's Fifth Amendment rights are not at issue when questioning is done by an informant who the suspect believes is a fellow prisoner or, at the very least, not a law enforcement agent. "The essential ingredients of a 'police-dominated atmosphere' are not present when an incarcerated person speaks freely to someone who he believes is a fellow inmate. Coercion is determined from the perspective of the suspect. When a suspect considers himself in the company of cellmates and not officers, the coercive atmosphere is lacking." *Illinois v. Perkins*, 496 U.S. 292 (1990).

Occasionally, an inmate will approach officers with information the inmate has gleaned on his or her own initiative and not at the request of officers. Officers need not ignore the information. As long as the inmate was not directed by officers or placed in a situation where officers reasonably should have known that the inmate would seek incriminating information from another inmate, the information may be used without violating constitutional rights. *United States v. Miller*, 116 F.3d 641 (2d Cir. 1997).

An inmate informant may be placed near a suspect with hope that the suspect will make incriminating statements. Any voluntary statements made by the suspect may be used in court. However, the informant can do nothing more than simply listen or engage in innocuous, normal conversation. *Blackmon v. Scott*, 22 F.3d 560 (2d Cir. 1994). The informant cannot encourage discussion of the suspect's crime in any way, though the informant need not actively discourage such talk. *Bey v. Morton*, 124 F.3d 524 (3d Cir. 1997).

Miranda ***for incarcerated persons suspected of new crimes***

Traditionally, *Miranda* rules apply whenever there is *custody* (deprived of liberty in a significant way) and *interrogation* (questions or statements intended to elicit an incriminating response). Just because an inmate is incarcerated, he or she may not be in *custody* for purposes of *Miranda*. "Where there is no evidence of restraint on the suspect's freedom other than that to which the suspect was already subject by reason of his custody for an unrelated offense, the suspect is not in custody for purposes of *Miranda*." *State v. Tibiatowski*, 590 N.W.2d 305 (Minn. 1999). An inmate may not be in custody until he or she is subject to additional restraints beyond those normally imposed under the terms of incarceration. An additional restraint is "one that places a restriction on the inmate's freedom of action in connection with the interrogation and prevents him from leaving the scene of questioning by placing a further limit on his or her already restricted freedom of movement. *Commonwealth v. Larkin*, 708 N.E.2d 674 (Mass. 1999). Factors determining an additional restraint and, therefore, amounting to custody include: the language used to summon the inmate to the place of interrogation, the physical surroundings of the interrogation, the extent to which the inmate is confronted with evidence of guilt, and the additional pressure exerted to detain the inmate. *People v. Parsons*, 15 P.3d 799 (Colo. App. 2000).

Factors tending to show that an inmate is not "in custody" include asking the inmate whether he or she would like to speak with investigators, interrogating in a day room or other non-lockdown area, lack of pressure from investigators, offering coffee, advising the inmate that there are no adverse consequences for refusing the interview, and telling the inmate that he or she could stop the interrogation by outside investigators at any time by calling for a correctional officer. *United States v. Turner*, 28 F.3d 981 (9th Cir. 1994); *United States v. Lovell*, 317 F. Supp. 2d 663 (W.D. Va. 2004); *Noyakuk v. State*, 127 P.3d 856 (Alaska App. 2006); *Commonwealth v. Larkin*, 708 N.E.2d 674 (Mass. 1999). Don't squelch voluntary and spontaneous statements. "*Miranda* does not protect an accused from a spontaneous admission made under circumstances not induced by the investigating officers or during a conversation not initiated by officers." *United States v. Hayes*, 120 F.3d 739 (8th Cir. 1997).

Aside from *Miranda*, there are Sixth Amendment right to counsel issues to consider. *Miranda* is a Fifth Amendment prophylactic rule designed to protect against compelled self-incrimination. The *Miranda* rule is not charge- or case-specific, and the *Miranda* rights are always implicated by any custodial interrogation. The Sixth Amendment right to counsel attaches only to the specific offense with which a defendant is formally charged. *United States v. Alvarado*, 440 F.3d 191 (4th Cir.), *cert. denied*, ___ U.S. ___, 127 S. Ct. 81 (2006). An inmate in custody awaiting conviction or appeal may not be questioned about the crime for which the inmate is incarcerated without permission of his or her lawyer. However, such inmates may be questioned without counsel about new criminal offenses (assuming *Miranda* concerns are satisfied). *Illinois v. Perkins*, 496 U.S. 292 (1990).

Miranda *issues for probationers/parolees*

A probationer or parolee, though subject to significant restraints on personal freedom, is not in custody for *Miranda* purposes simply by being under supervision. *Minnesota v. Murphy*, 465 U.S. 420 (1984). General supervision interviews conducted with parole or probation officials do not constitute "custodial interrogation." *Dill v. State*, 600 So. 2d 343 (Ala. App. 1991), *cert. denied*, 507 U.S. 924 (1993). Questions asked during probation-revocation hearings generally do not require a *Miranda* warning when directed at the terms and conditions of probation. *United States v. Nieblas*, 115 F.3d 703 (9th Cir. 1997). Questions during pre-sentence interviews or pre-sentence psychosexual examinations relevant to the sentencing process also do not require warnings. *United States v. Rogers*, 921 F.2d 975 (10th Cir. 1990).

An interview with a supervising agent could become custodial interrogation if the probationer or parolee is compelled to attend beyond normal reporting obligations. Whether a new crime is the subject of discussion will also be a factor in the analysis of custodial interrogation. An investigator other than the probationer/parolee's supervising agent must treat a probationer or parolee like any other suspect for purposes of *Miranda*.

In *Minnesota v. Murphy*, the Supreme Court analyzed an interview of a suspect whose probation agreement required that he be "truthful to the probation officer in all matters." The Court held that statements obtained in the probation interview and without a *Miranda* warning were admissible. However, if failure to answer a question would result in probation or parole revocation, the answers would be inadmissible. An officer investigating a gun crime telephoned a parolee's parole officer and said that he wanted to speak to the parolee about the gun. Even though the circumstances of the interview did not amount to custody, the parole officer's order to the parolee that he speak to the officer tipped the balance in favor of custody. Because there was no *Miranda* warning until after the parolee gave the incriminating answers, the statements were suppressed. *United States v. Ollie*, 442 F.3d 1135 (8th Cir. 2006).

Speaking with a formally charged and/or represented suspect

The Sixth Amendment guarantees a defendant the right to legal counsel. Once a defendant claims Sixth Amendment rights to counsel, officers may not attempt interrogation unless and until the defendant initiates communication with officers and waives rights or counsel is present. *Massiah v. United States*, 377 U.S. 201 (1964). The Sixth Amendment right to counsel begins when the suspect is charged or, in other words, the "suspect" becomes the "defendant." *Michigan v. Harvey*, 494 U.S. 344 (1990). The Sixth Amendment right continues through the pendency of the case and does not depend on whether the defendant is incarcerated. In contrast, the Fifth Amendment right to counsel under the *Miranda* rule applies only when the defendant is in custody.

The right to counsel is *case-specific* and applies only to interrogation concerning the case in which the defendant has been charged. *Maine v. Moulton*, 475 U.S. 412 (1985). Thus, a defendant who is awaiting trial on a particular charge but is not in custody may be questioned about an unrelated crime. Normal *Miranda* rules apply, and the defendant may still voluntarily waive the right to counsel during the interrogation on the new crime. Whenever possible, the interrogation should take place in the least-restrictive setting possible, such as a day room or conference room. Demonstrating that the inmate's custody status was effectively relaxed during the interview helps defeat a claim of custodial interrogation. *United States v. Cooper*, 800 F.2d 412 (4th Cir. 1986).

Though likely to occur only infrequently, a suspect who has invoked the right to counsel pertaining to charges from one sovereign, i.e., a particular state or federal government, may be questioned following a proper *Miranda* warning and waiver by an officer of a distinct sovereign. Alvarado was arrested following a joint state and federal drug investigation. He was charged in state court with drug crimes, and the court appointed a public defender, thereby activating his Sixth Amendment right to counsel. Within two months, the state charges were dismissed. Federal agents obtained a federal arrest warrant for charges arising out of the same incident. When Alvarado was released from state custody, he was rearrested by a federal officer. Alvarado told the federal officer (known to him from the initial arrest as an officer who spoke fluent Spanish) that he wanted to tell the officer his side of the story. The officer interrupted, administered a *Miranda* warning and then obtained an incriminating statement from Alvarado.

Even though the state charges had been dismissed, the Sixth Amendment right to counsel would have prohibited state officers from interrogating Alvarado without his attorney being present or having consented to an interrogation. The court followed the dual-sovereign doctrine and found that the interrogation by the federal officer was lawful. Thus, Alvarado's admissions to the federal officer were admissible against him. *United States v. Alvarado*, 440 F.3d 191 (4th Cir. 2006).

Non-testimonial evidence

Certain types of evidence, including some spoken evidence, are not considered "testimonial" in nature and, therefore, are not subject to the Fifth Amendment privilege against self-incrimination. Thus, no *Miranda* warnings are required. For example, when performing field sobriety tests, a verbal alphabet recitation test or verbal finger count is not testimonial. *Commonwealth v. Curry*, 689 N.E.2d 1365 (Mass. App. 1998). Other non-testimonial evidence includes: providing fingerprints, *United States v. Snow*, 82 F.3d 935 (10th Cir. 1996); providing a voice sample, *United States v. Dionisio*, 410 U.S. 1 (1973); drawing a blood sample, *Schmerber v. California*, 384 U.S. 757 (1966); providing a urine sample, *Rawlings v. Police Dept. of Jersey City*, 627 A.2d 602 (N.J. 1993); taking fingernail scrapings, *Cupp v. Murphy* 412 U.S. 291 (1973); and providing a handwriting sample, *Gilbert v. California*, 388 U.S. 263 (1967).

Exclusionary rule applied to Miranda *violation*

Failure to give a *Miranda* warning prior to custodial interrogation results in an irrebuttable presumption of coercion. Even though a confession may not be actually coerced in violation of the Fifth Amendment, the *Miranda* rule requires suppression. *Oregon v. Elstad,* 470 U.S. 298 (1985). There is no "good faith" exception to this bright-line rule. *Arizona v. Roberson,* 486 U.S. 675 (1988).

Use of statements taken without Miranda *warnings*

The United States Supreme Court has permitted very limited use of statements obtained in violation of the *Miranda* rule. An otherwise suppressible statement may be used to impeach a defendant who testifies untruthfully under oath in court. *Harris v. New York,* 401 U.S. 222 (1971). Physical evidence that is seized based on a suspect's unwarned statement may be admitted in court, since the *Miranda* rule applies only to testimonial evidence. *United States v. Patane,* 524 U.S. 630 (2004).

A written confession obtained after *Miranda* warnings but following an unwarned oral confession may be admissible if officers have not used deliberately coercive or improper tactics to obtain the initial confession. *Oregon v. Elstad,* 470 U.S. 298 (1985). A suspect who first responds to unwarned yet uncoercive questioning is still able to waive rights and confess after being given the *Miranda* warnings as long as the second statement is voluntary. The *Elstad* rule was based on the officer's good-faith, mistaken belief that warnings were not required in the first interrogation and the fact that the second interrogation was an effort to salvage the admissions obtained from the suspect. Of course, this does not permit a deliberate *Miranda* violation to be cured by a subsequent warning, waiver, and interrogation. Under the *Elstad* rule, an officer would be wise to administer a fresh *Miranda* warning with each subsequent interrogation. In cases where a second interrogation occurs, there is often time to consult with a prosecutor and obtain guidance on whether the *Elstad* doctrine will apply to a particular case.

Exhibit 5-1
Interrogation Flow Chart

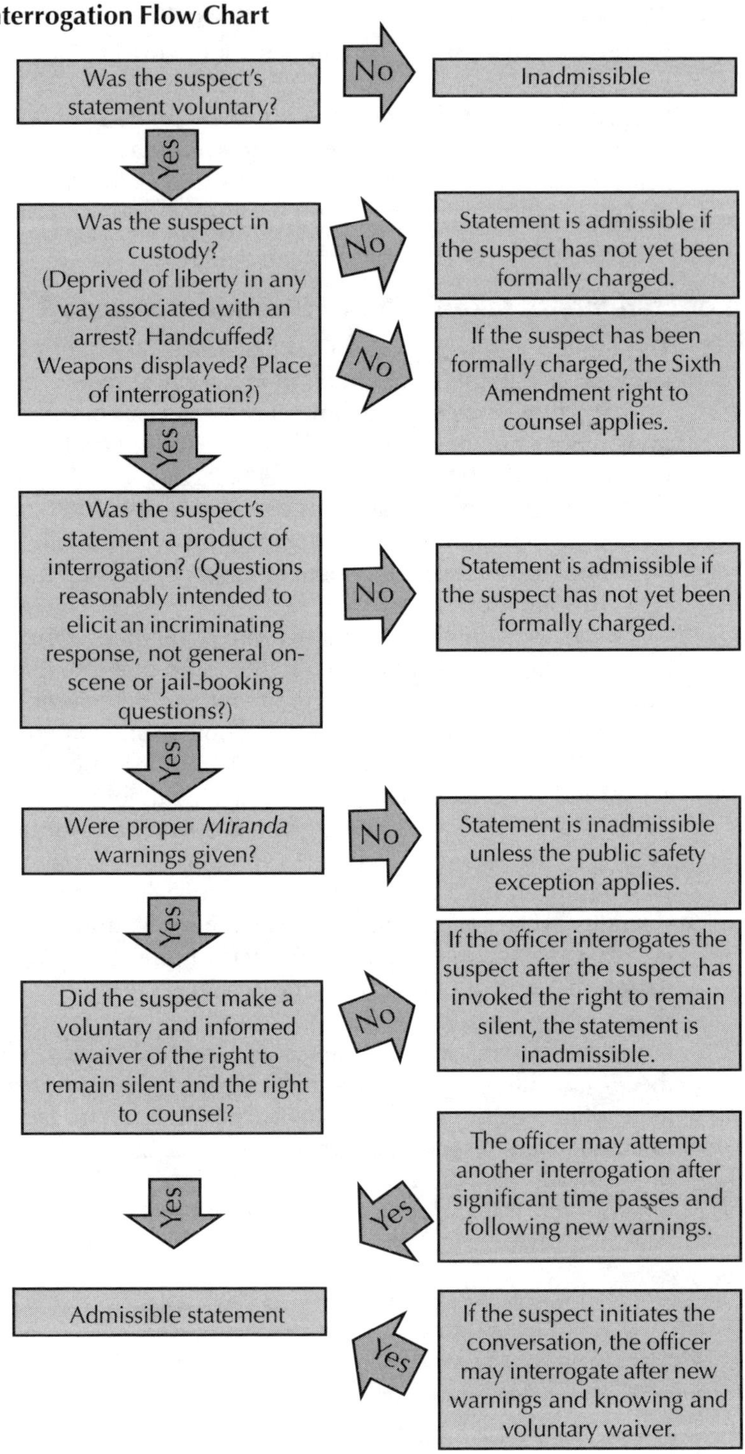

CHAPTER 6

SEARCH AND SEIZURE

Constitutional Parameters of Warrants and Warrantless Searches

- What constitutes a "search" under the Fourth Amendment?
- Activities considered not to be searches
- Abandoned property
- Canine sniff
- Open field
- Aerial surveillance
- Plain view
- Plain smell
- Plain hearing
- Private citizen search
- Field test

Overview of Warrant Clause Exceptions

- Consent
- Automobile
- Plain touch
- Search incident to a lawful arrest
- Administrative searches
- Administrative searches of personal effects, desks, and lockers
- Administrative security screening
- Inventory and community care-taking
- Exigent circumstances
- Evanescent evidence
- Special government needs
- Probation and parole searches
- Inmate and cell searches
- Visitor searches
- Miscellaneous exceptions

Constitutional Parameters of Warrants and Warrantless Searches

> The right of the people to be secure in their persons, houses, papers, and effects, against unreasonable searches and seizures, shall not be violated and no warrants shall issue, but upon probable cause, supported by oath or affirmation, and particularly describing the place to be searched, and the persons or things to be seized.
>
> UNITED STATES CONSTITUTION
> *Fourth Amendment*

The Fourth Amendment is the basic restriction on all searches by police. It applies equally to state and federal officers. *Wolf v. Colorado*, 338 U.S. 25 (1949). There are two distinct clauses in the Fourth Amendment: one contains a prohibition on unreasonable searches and seizures, and the other a requirement of probable cause for all search warrants. **Searches conducted without a warrant are presumed to be unlawful**. *Mincey v. Arizona*, 437 U.S. 385 (1978). This means that the prosecution bears the burden of showing that a warrantless search falls under an established exception to the warrant requirement of the Fourth Amendment. *Welsh v. Wisconsin*, 466 U.S. 740 (1984). This chapter first addresses activities that are not searches under the Fourth Amendment and then activities that are excepted from the warrant requirement of the Fourth Amendment.

What constitutes a "search" under the Fourth Amendment?

Unless a person has a **legitimate expectation of privacy**, there can be no "search" protected by the Fourth Amendment. Items found in plain view or abandoned are not considered products of a search, since the target has not demonstrated an expectation of privacy. A person cannot challenge the legality of a search unless the person has a legitimate expectation of privacy in the area that is searched. *Minnesota v. Carter*, 525 U.S. 83 (1998). Having a legitimate expectation of privacy is often referred to as having "standing" to contest the search.

An expectation of privacy arises in many different contexts. For example, courts have recognized the following as having legitimate expectations of privacy: body fluids, skin, and cell samples, *Skinner v. Railway Labor Executives' Ass'n*, 489 U.S. 602 (1989); containers intended to shield the view of contents, *United States v. Ross*, 456 U.S. 798 (1982); homes, *United States v. U.S. District Court*, 407 U.S. 297 (1972); curtilage of a home, *United States v. Dunn*, 480 U.S. 294 (1987); heat emanating from a home, *Kyllo v. United States*, 553 U.S. 27 (2001); mail contents (not information on the outside of mail), *United States v. Van Leeuwen*, 397 U.S. 249 (1970); a makeshift tent pitched on public lands, *United States v. Sandoval*, 200 F.3d 659 (9th Cir. 2000); and hotel rooms, *Stoner v. California*, 376 U.S. 483 (1964).

The following areas or activities have been found not to hold a legitimate expectation of privacy: two persons standing in a one-person restroom for an extended time, *United States v. Hill*, 393 F.3d 839 (8th Cir. 2005); sound of a person's voice, *United States v. Dionisio*, 410 U.S. 1 (1973); a person on a "banned" list visiting public housing, *State v. Oien*, 717 N.W.2d 593 (N.D. 2006); a squatter in an abandoned residence, *Whiting v. State*, 885 A.2d 785 (Md. 2005); common areas of an apartment complex, *United States v. Barnes*, 399 F. Supp. 2d 169 (W.D.N.Y. Oct. 31, 2005); fingerprints, *Davis v. Mississippi*, 394 U.S. 721 (1969); handwriting, *United States v. Mara*, 410 U.S. 19 (1973); exterior of a car and vehicle identification number, *New York v. Class*, 475 U.S. 106 (1986); portion of a car's interior visible through windows, *Texas v. Brown*, 460 U.S. 730 (1983); trash left at the curb, *California v. Greenwood*, 486 U.S. 35 (1988); and prison cells, *Hudson v. Palmer*, 468 U.S. 517 (1984).

Activities considered not to be searches

Because of the lack of a legitimate expectation of privacy, a number of law enforcement activities that may (or may not) lead to the collection of evidence are not considered searches. These activities include inspection of abandoned property, canine sniff, views of an open field, aerial surveillance, plain view, plain smell, plain hearing, and field tests to determine drug identification. One other activity that is not a search (for purposes of the Fourth Amendment) is a search by a private citizen. The Fourth Amendment applies only to government officers and agents.

Abandoned property

When an owner **voluntarily abandons property**, the owner surrenders any privacy expectation. Property may be abandoned in a variety of manners, including when it is voluntarily dropped during a chase, *Wilson v. State,* 825 N.E.2d 49 (Ind. App. 2005); the ownership of luggage or packages is denied, *United States v. Ojeda-Ramos,* 455 F.3d 1178 (10th Cir. 2006); items are left in a storage unit with rent overdue, *United States v. Poulsen,* 41 F.3d 1330 (9th Cir. 1994); or unshredded papers are put in the garbage and taken out for collection, *Powell v. State,* 776 A.2d 700 (Md. App.), *cert. denied,* 783 A.2d 223 (Md. 2001). Trash at the curb is generally accepted as abandoned. *California v. Greenwood,* 486 U.S. 35 (1988). Trash may be considered abandoned after it is left in the customary pickup location even if it remains within the curtilage of a residence. *United States v. Segura-Baltazar,* 448 F.3d 1231 (11th Cir. 2006). At least one state appellate court has used a state constitutional provision to rule that trash sealed in an opaque bag continues to be subject to an expectation of privacy when discarded. *State v. Granville,* 142 P.3d 933 (N.M. App. 2006), *cert. granted,* 143 P.3d 185 (N.M. 2006).

To determine whether property has been abandoned and therefore may be searched without a warrant, two questions must be answered. First, did the owner (or legitimate possessor) relinquish a legitimate expectation of privacy in the object? Second, was the abandonment voluntary? While the possessor's subjective intent to abandon the item is an important factor in the expectation of privacy analysis, the expectation of privacy must be objectively reasonable. *United States v. Benitez-Arreguin,* 973 F.2d 823 (10th Cir. 1992); *United States v. Thomas,* 864 F.2d 843 (D.C. Cir. 1989). Abandonment may be inferred from words spoken, acts done, and other objective facts. *United States v. Austin,* 66 F.3d 1115 (10th Cir. 1995), *cert. denied,* 516 U.S. 1084 (1996).

An abandonment of property that results from unlawful police conduct cannot be voluntary. *United States v. Garzon,* 119 F.3d 1446 (10th Cir. 1997) (when police issued unlawful order to remove all possessions from bus, property left on the bus was not voluntarily abandoned). For example, police approached a man in an airport terminal. The man repeatedly tried to avoid talking to the police. After a few minutes, he began to run from police and tossed his coat away. The coat was seized, and drugs were found in the pocket. The court found that the man had been seized without reasonable suspicion before he ran. Consequently, the abandonment followed an illegal seizure and could not be voluntary. *United States v. Wilson,* 953 F.2d 116 (4th Cir. 1991).

Drug interdiction officers may seize items bus passengers leave behind when they end their journey or change buses. Luggage that is left behind on a bus or in a terminal, even if left unintentionally, is considered abandoned. *United States v. Tugwell,* 125 F.3d 600 (8th Cir. 1997) (finding abandonment where defendant left luggage at bus station after all passengers were told to claim luggage). When a bus from Los Angeles reached Denver, it was due to be cleaned or replaced with a substitute bus. Accordingly, passengers were required by the bus company to leave the bus with their carry-on items, and their checked bags were removed from the baggage compartment. Interdiction officers boarded the bus and merely requested passengers to debark and take their carry-on luggage with them. The officers told passengers that a drug dog was present and asked passengers not to approach the dog. An officer saw one passenger attempt to replace his carry-on bag in the overhead rack before getting off the bus. A dog sniff indicated the odor of controlled substances, and a kilo of cocaine base was found in the bag. The defendant claimed that the abandonment followed an illegal seizure lacking reasonable suspicion, thus the search of the abandoned bag was tainted. The defendant left the bag on the bus out of fear that the contents would be discovered. The court found that the bag was abandoned and noted that the officers did not compel the debarking or the removal of luggage. Therefore, there was no seizure of the passengers. *United States v. Jones,* 914 F. Supp. 421 (D. Colo. 1996), *aff'd,* 124 F.3d 218 (10th Cir. 1997).

Canine sniff

The Supreme Court has ruled that sniffing of luggage located in a public place "does not constitute a search within the meaning of the Fourth Amendment." *United States v. Place,* 462 U.S. 696 (1983). Canine sniffs of luggage, packages, and vehicle exteriors are not intrusive. A dog's sniff only reveals the presence of the odor of contraband outside the item. A person cannot have a reasonable expectation of privacy in contraband, such as controlled substances. *United States v. Jacobsen,* 466 U.S. 109 (1984). **A positive alert by a trained drug detection dog creates probable cause to search and probable cause to arrest.** *(See Canine Search and Seizure chapter.)*

Open field

The curtilage is "the area into which extends the intimate activity associated with the sanctity of a man's home and the privacies of life." *Oliver v. United States,* 466 U.S. 170 (1984). An area outside of a residence's "curtilage" may be considered an open field and subject to a free peek. An open field may be searched without any suspicion or probable cause. *United States v. Pinter,* 984 F.2d 376 (10th Cir. 1993) ("The open fields doctrine does not require that law enforcement officials have some objective reason—either probable cause or reasonable suspicion—before entering an open field."). An area need not be either "open" or a "field" to qualify as an area not subject to an expectation of privacy under the open fields doctrine. *Oliver v. United States,* 466 U.S. 170 (1984) (even thickly wooded area may be an "open field"). "Curtilage" is treated as part of the home itself for Fourth Amendment purposes, and the curtilage concept is an exception to the open fields doctrine. *Hester v. United States,* 265 U.S. 57 (1924).

The scope of the curtilage is determined by considering the **proximity to the home**, **whether it is fenced** or otherwise enclosed, the **nature of the use of the area**, and the **efforts the resident takes to screen the area** from public view. *United States v. Dunn,* 480 U.S. 294 (1987). Following are examples of applications of these factors:

- **Proximity.** In *Dunn,* the Supreme Court noted that a barn that was 180 feet from the house was not an "adjunct of the house." Other courts have found that distances of 45 to 50 feet are outside the curtilage of a house. *United States v. Brady,* 993 F.2d 177 (9th Cir. 1993) (45 feet is outside the curtilage); *United States v. Calabrese,* 825 F.2d 1342 (9th Cir. 1987) (50 feet is outside the curtilage). But distance alone will not create an open field. *United States v. Depew,* 8 F.3d 1424 (9th Cir. 1993) (60 feet is inside the curtilage).
- **Fencing or enclosures.** Whether the area is fenced, particularly if with a privacy fence, is an important factor in assessing the scope of the curtilage. *California v. Ciraolo,* 476 U.S. 207 (1986) (yard surrounded by high double fences and within close proximity to the house was within the curtilage). However, the presence of a fence is not a conclusive boundary of the curtilage. *United States v. Van Damme,* 48 F.3d 461 (9th Cir. 1995) (high board fence around greenhouse, located 200 feet from home,

did not create curtilage); *United States v. Hatch,* 931 F.2d 1478 (11th Cir. 1991) (perimeter fence around property does not create a constitutionally protected interest in all open fields on the property). Perimeter fences, especially open wire fences, do not necessarily define the curtilage. The fencing factor is best viewed in conjunction with the question of steps taken to obstruct the open view and whether the activities conducted within the fence line are intimately associated with the "immediate domestic establishment of the home." *United States v. Berrong,* 712 F.2d 1370 (11th Cir. 1983).

- **Use of the area.** In *Dunn,* the Supreme Court noted that it was "especially significant" that the barn where drug precursor chemicals were found was not used "for intimate activities of the home." Most courts rule that the driveway and walkways approaching the doors of a home are not within the curtilage unless they are gated or fenced. *United States v. French,* 291 F.3d 945 (7th Cir. 2002) (public drives, sidewalks, or walkways, even those which lead to a rear side door, are not within the curtilage of the home when they are not enclosed by a gate or fence); *Rogers v. Pendleton,* 249 F.3d 279 (4th Cir. 2001) ("officers may enter a person's yard without probable cause if they have a legitimate reason unconnected with a search of the premises"); *United States v. Smith,* 783 F.2d 648 (6th Cir. 1986) (marijuana lawfully observed when detective drove 75 to 100 yards up unobstructed driveway to investigate tip that a large marijuana plant was growing by the house). A garage is typically considered to be within the curtilage. *Los Angeles Police Protective League v. Gates,* 907 F.2d 879 (9th Cir. 1990) (if garage is not long distance from the home, it is part of the curtilage). Business property is generally considered to not have a curtilage except to the extent that the business takes affirmative action to exclude the public from a particular area. *Dow Chemical Co. v. United States,* 476 U.S. 227 (1986).
- **Efforts to conceal.** This factor is closely related to the presence of fencing. Fencing material designed to obstruct view, rather than to exclude persons or corral animals, works in favor of a finding that the area is within the curtilage. *United States v. Breza,* 308 F.3d 430 (4th Cir. 2002); *United States v. Hatfield,* 333 F.3d 1189 (10th Cir. 2003) (officer walking in open field and being told by owner that he was trespassing and to leave could law-

fully observe through the fence the marijuana growing inside the curtilage).

Searching outbuildings located in an open field without a warrant is generally unwise. *United States v. Pennington,* 287 F.3d 739 (8th Cir. 2002) ("very close issue" of warrantless search of underground bunker in open field with visible entryway, ladder, no lock or door). Whether a warrant is required is a fact-intensive question that generates variable results in appellate courts. *United States v. Ramapuram,* 632 F.2d 1149 (4th Cir. 1980) ("far from easy question," upholding warrantless search of open trunk of junk car in open field). The better course is to maintain security of the outbuilding and obtain a warrant. Strictly speaking, the open fields doctrine is unrelated to the concept of exigency. Yet courts have relied on a lack of exigency in overturning searches of outbuildings in open fields. *United States v. Longie,* 370 F. Supp. 2d 941 (D. N.D. 2005) (search of shed disallowed because there was time to obtain a warrant); *United States v. Elder,* 352 F. Supp. 2d 880 (C.D. Ill. 2005) (search of barn allowed because court found exigent circumstances); *People v. Pittman,* 813 N.E.2d 93 (Ill. 2004) (even though doors of unused barn were open, officers had sufficient time to apply for a warrant; court recognized that its view was in conflict with prevailing law).

Aerial surveillance

For reasons similar to those that support the open fields doctrine, observations from aircraft are not searches in most cases. As long as the aircraft is obeying Federal Aviation Administration rules and not creating a hazard to persons or property on the ground, the observation made from a flight is not likely to be considered a search. *United States v. Boyster,* 436 F.3d 986 (8th Cir. 2006) (observation of marijuana field not a search when pilot flew in public airspace and no evidence that flights at 100 feet altitude are so rare as to make aerial surveillance at that height unreasonable); *Doggett v. State,* 791 So. 2d 1043 (Ala. App. 2000). Helicopters and ultralight aircraft are not subject to the same height limitations as fixed-wing craft. 14 C.F.R. §§ 91.119 (helicopters may be operated below the minimums set for aircraft if done without hazard to persons or property below). Observation from a helicopter hovering at 400 feet above a partially open greenhouse where marijuana was growing was not a violation of a legitimate expectation of privacy. *Florida v. Riley*, 488 U.S. 445 (1989). However, the United States Supreme Court has ruled that the warrantless use of a thermal-imaging device to view heat sources in homes from aircraft violates the Fourth Amendment. *Kyllo v. United States*, 533 U.S. 27 (2001).

Plain view

Seizable items that are in "plain view" may be seized without warrant. To satisfy the plain view doctrine, three factors must be satisfied. *Horton v. California*, 496 U.S. 128 (1990). A plainly visible item may be seized when:

- The seizing officer is **lawfully present** and lawfully able to access the item without violating the Fourth Amendment. If an officer is present in a location serving an arrest or search warrant, conducting an inventory (*see below*), conducting a traffic or other investigatory stop, or has been admitted by consent or invitation, the officer is not violating the Fourth Amendment.
- Second, the item is in "**plain view**."
- Third, the **incriminating nature of the item is immediately apparent**.

Evidence is "clearly incriminating" if the officer has probable cause to associate the item with criminal activity. *Minnesota v. Dickerson*, 508 U.S. 366 (1993). The officer must be able to identify the object as an incriminating one without moving or exposing it. *Arizona v. Hicks*, 480 U.S. 321 (1987). Though inadvertent discovery is generally the case, it is not a legal requirement. *Horton v. California*, 496 U.S. 128 (1990). The question of whether the item's incriminating nature was immediately apparent is measured by what the officer knew at the time of viewing. *Coolidge v. New Hampshire*, 403 U.S. 443 (1971). Using a flashlight, inspecting under a car, or peering through a window are permissible. *Texas v. Brown*, 460 U.S. 730 (1983); *United States v. Dunn*, 480 U.S. 294 (1987) ("officers' use of the beam of a flashlight, directed through the essentially open front of respondent's barn, did not transform their observations into an unreasonable search within the meaning of the Fourth Amendment"). Using night-vision scopes or binoculars is also permissible, as long as they do not allow officers to view what would otherwise be impossible to see. In other words, vision-enhancing equipment may be used to clarify that which may be seen by the human eye, but not to extend the field of vision beyond that which could be seen from a closer vantage point. *United States v. Hensel,* 509 F. Supp. 1376 (D. Me. 1981) (use of binoculars to see activities outside buildings across a river was acceptable); *State v. Manly,* 530 P.2d 306 (Wash.) (binocular use is not a particularly intrusive method of viewing as long as the object observed could have been seen with the naked eye had the officer been closer to it), *cert. denied,* 423 U.S. 855 (1975); *Colorado v. Oynes,* 920 P.2d 880 (Colo. App. 1996) (officer's view of interior of defendant's home with binoculars from nearby field was not a search); *State v. Ludvik,* 698 P.2d 1064 (Wash. App. 1985) (use of binoculars and spotting scope did not violate privacy interest because activities were also visible to the unaided eye from the street; enhancement devices merely allowed officers to avoid detection). At least one court has disapproved of observations made possible by a spotting scope aimed at unshuttered windows. *United States v. Lace,* 502 F. Supp. 1021 (D. Vt. 1980) (use of 45-power spotting scope to see inside home constituted a search, not plain view), *aff'd,* 669 F.2d 46 (2d Cir.), *cert. denied,* 549 U.S. 854 (1982). Picking up an item to more closely examine it to determine whether it is contraband likely defeats a claim of plain view. *Commonwealth v. Hatcher,* 199 S.W.3d 124 (Ky. 2006) (pipe was not in plain view because officer did not determine incriminating nature until he picked it up and sniffed it).

An officer may be in a lawful position to observe incriminating items in many contexts. Following are some common situations leading to plain view seizures:

- **Making an arrest or an investigatory detention.** In the course of an arrest, there may be items in plain view in the room or area where the arrest is made that are not within the immediate control of the arrestee. Thus, the search incident to arrest doctrine may not apply, but a plain view seizure may still be possible.
- **Executing a search warrant.** Items in plain view may be seized because the officer's right to be present (where there may otherwise be a legitimate expectation of privacy) is established in the warrant. Items that must be moved in order for their incriminating nature to be apparent, for example, to see a serial number, cannot be seized under the plain view doctrine. *State v. Gallegos,* 712 P.2d 207 (Utah 1985).

- **Controlled deliveries of contraband.** Once an item is identified by lawful means as contraband and is subjected to a controlled delivery, the item may be seized from the possession of the recipient and opened. *Illinois v. Andreas,* 463 U.S. 765 (1983).
- **Hot pursuit of fleeing suspect.** Officers who chase a suspect in hot pursuit and enter a home (or other location where there may be a legitimate expectation of privacy) may seize items seen in plain view. *State v. Lewis,* 573 So. 2d 1282 (La. App. 1991) (officers chased suspect seen selling drugs and armed with gun into home and found cocaine and paraphernalia).
- **Assisting with a medical emergency.** When either serving as first responders or assisting emergency medical personnel and entering a zone of privacy, evidence may be seized. *State v. Bower,* 21 P.3d 491 (Idaho App. 2001) (officers saw drugs in plain view when entering motel behind firefighters called to assist unconscious man).
- **Responding to call for police service.** Officers responding to a burglary in progress call found an open door and entered a home. They discovered that the female resident had shot her husband in the head with an arrow from a crossbow. *State v. Magnano,* 528 A.2d 760 (Conn. 1987).

Seeing obvious contraband inside a residence from a lawful vantage point outside does not necessarily bestow authority to enter. Officers must have an independent right to enter to the home in order to seize the contraband. *Commonwealth v. Mallory,* 775 N.E.2d 764 (Mass. App.), *cert. denied,* 780 N.E.2d 468 (Mass. 2002). It may be that the exigent circumstances doctrine will excuse a warrantless entry and allow seizure of contraband in plain view. Nonetheless, the burden remains on the officer to articulate a genuine exigency to enter without a warrant.

Plain smell

If an officer smells contraband, usually burnt marijuana, from a place where he is legitimately entitled to be, a warrantless search and/or seizure may follow. *United States v. Angelos,* 433 F.3d 738 (10th Cir. 2006) ("plain smell doctrine is merely an extension of plain view"); *State v. Dudley,* 847 P.2d 424 (Utah App. 1993). Similarly, if an officer's training and experience allow the officer to correlate particular smells with unlawful activities, e.g., phenylacetic acid with methamphetamine production, a warrantless search can be conducted. *United States v. Miller,* 812 F.2d 1206 (9th Cir. 1987); *State v. Rowland,* 73 S.W.3d 818 (Mo. App. 2002). Some courts require that smell-related drugs or paraphernalia be found, thus substantiating, after the fact, probable cause to search and before any other found evidence may be admitted into evidence. *State v. Maycock,* 947 P.2d 695 (Utah App. 1997).

The plain smell of contraband may support warrantless entry into a home under the exigent circumstances doctrine. *Holder v. State,* 847 N.E.2d 930 (Ind. 2006) (strong odor of ether justified entry); *United States v. Stafford,* 416 F.3d 1068 (9th Cir. 2005) (odor of decaying flesh in home justified entry and search); *Smock v. State,* 766 N.E.2d 401 (Ind. App. 2002) (warrantless entry proper when officer smelled decaying flesh at the doorway); *Cherry v. Commonwealth,* 605 S.E.2d 297 (Va. App. 2004) (odor of burning marijuana when defendant opened door justified entry). Acting on a citizen tip of juveniles drinking at Parker's house, officers knocked on the door. Parker opened the door and spoke with officers about the alcohol party, but he refused to let them enter. Officers could smell fresh marijuana smoke. When Parker tried to shut the door, one officer stuck his foot in the door and said that he was coming in because of the odor of marijuana. Marijuana was found in plain view on top of a pizza box. The court ruled that the officers had probable cause to enter and distinguished the probable cause to enter the home from probable cause to search and probable cause to arrest. *State v. Parker,* 206 S.W.3d 593 (Tex. App. 2006).

Plain hearing

Some courts have extended the plain view doctrine to "plain sound" when officers have heard discussions of criminal activity in adjoining motel rooms. *United States v. Jackson,* 588 F.2d 1046 (5th Cir.), *cert. denied,* 442 U.S. 941 (1979); *State v. Gil,* 561 N.E.2d 760 (Wis. App. 1997). If an officer inadvertently hears an incriminating statement from a place where the officer has a lawful right to be, the statement is generally admissible as evidence. *United States v. Baranek,* 903 F.2d 1068 (6th Cir. 1990) (officers heard statement when defendant unintentionally left phone off the hook); *United States v. Pace,* 709 F. Supp. 948 (C.D. Cal. 1989) ("Under the 'plain hearing' exception, if police officers overhear statements without the benefit of listening devices while they are stationed at a lawful vantage point, then those statements are admissible.").

Private citizen search

The Fourth Amendment does not restrict private citizens. As long as the citizen is not acting at an officer's invitation or direction, items seized by the citizen may be used as evidence even if they are located during a search that would have been unlawful if it had been conducted by an officer. "Whether a private party should be deemed an agent or instrument of the Government for Fourth Amendment purposes necessarily turns on the degree of the Government's participation in the private party's activities." *Skinner v. Railway Labor Executives' Ass'n*, 489 U.S. 602 (1989). The mere fact that the searching party is employed by a government agency does not mean that the Fourth Amendment applies. An emergency medical technician who found drugs in an injured driver's backpack was not a "government agent." *State v. Amirkhizi*, 100 P.3d 225 (Utah App. 2004); *State v. Ludvik*, 698 P.2d 1064 (Wash. App. 1985) (state game warden acting without peace officer powers was not government agent when he observed drug transaction). If a private person discovers evidence of criminal activity during a private search or during entry allowed by the target's consent, the information may be used to obtain a search warrant. *State v. Koury*, 824 P.2d 474 (Utah App. 1991).

When a private citizen informs an officer about the contents of an area or item that the private citizen has searched, the officer may conduct a search that is strictly limited to the scope of the private citizen's search. *Walter v. United States*, 447 U.S. 649 (1980). When FedEx employees opened a package containing cocaine, left the package unsealed, and notified officers, the officers were entitled to look in the package. The search was upheld because the officers did not exceed the scope of the private search, and the private search had extinguished the expectation of privacy in the package. *United States v. Jacobson*, 446 U.S. 109 (1984). A similar result followed when a briefcase without identifying tags was found in a company truck. The briefcase contained illegal child pornography, and it was searched by three different employees before officers arrived. The employees told the officers about its contents. Officers then searched the briefcase and seized the pornography. The search was allowed because it was identical in scope to the private search and there was little likelihood that any additional evidence would be discovered. *State v. Miller,* 104 P.3d 1272 (Utah App. 2004); *Commonwealth v. Kozak,* 336 A.2d 387 (Pa. Super. 1975) (police search of briefcase lawful after airline lost-and-found worker searched for identification and found drugs).

Field test

A chemical test conducted in the field to identify controlled substances is not a search. *Commonwealth v. Franco,* 646 N.E.2d 749 (Mass. 1995) (field test on lawfully obtained substance believed to be narcotic not a search because there is no legitimate expectation of privacy in chemical composition of substance lawfully obtained by police). A field test merely confirms the composition of a substance believed to be contraband. *State v. Wallace,* 910 P.2d 695 (Haw. 1996) (opening transparent bags of white powder and conducting field test not a search; white powder contraband was in plain view). Opening a suspicious opaque package to identify suspected controlled substances is a search, not merely a field test of a substance lawfully in police possession. *Robles v. State,* 510 N.E.2d 660 (Ind. 1987), *cert. denied,* 487 U.S. 1218 (1988) (field test was a search when duct-taped packages were opened to examine contents; field test was justified because exigent circumstances existed).

Overview of Warrant Clause Exceptions

Warrantless searches are presumptively unreasonable unless an established exception applies to the search. *Katz v. United States,* 389 U.S. 347 (1967). Over many years, the Supreme Court has articulated several exceptions to the general requirement of a search warrant. Familiarity with these exceptions will help the officer know when to seek a warrant. Of course, a warrant may be very helpful even when the search might be justified under an exception. *See discussion of Suppression Burden, below.*

Consent

Even in the course of executing a search warrant, obtaining consent to the search may be a valuable tool when the officer discovers an area or person not included in the warrant. Consent must be both **voluntary and given by one with authority to consent** to be valid. *Schneckloth v. Bustamonte,* 412 U.S. 218 (1973).

- **Voluntariness** is determined by the totality of the circumstances under which it was given. **Consent** must be unequivocal and intelligently given, and must not be the product of duress or coercion. *United States v. McRae,* 81 F.3d 1528 (10th Cir. 1996). Consent may be express or implied, although the state carries a particularly heavy burden when relying on a claim of implied consent. *United States v. Flores,* 48 F.3d 467 (10th Cir.), *cert. denied,* 516 U.S. 839 (1995).
- Consent may occur when a suspect asks an officer to enter a residence for purposes other than searching. For example, a suspect was found to have consented to entry into his home when he was being taken to jail and he asked officers to enter and lock up his apartment. *State v. Grossi,* 72 P.3d 686 (Utah App. 2003).
- One factor addressing voluntariness is knowledge of the right to refuse, though federal and most state laws do not require the officer to inform the target of the right to refuse to consent. *Schneckloth v. Bustamonte,* 412 U.S. 218 (1973).
- If officers use force against a suspect, it will be difficult to show that the suspect's consent to search was voluntary. *United States v. Carbajal,* 956 F.2d 924 (9th Cir. 1992) (consent invalid where officer pointed gun at suspect's head), *cert. denied,* 510 U.S. 900 (1993); *United States v. Rodriguez,* 931 F. Supp. 907 (D. Mass. 1996) (consent valid even though officers had guns drawn when they knocked on door and stated they were looking for drive-by shooting suspects), *aff'd sub nom. United States v. Torres,* 162 F.3d 6 (1st Cir. 1998), *cert. denied,* 526 U.S. 1057 (1999).
- A person who is under arrest may still give a voluntary consent to search, though the court will closely examine the circumstances of the consent. *De Jesus v. State,* 917 S.W.2d 458 (Tex. App. 1996). Other factors are display of force, the extent of the suspect's cooperation with police, the suspect's intelligence and education, the length of the detention and questioning, and the suspect's belief that no incriminating evidence will be found. *Schneckloth v. Bustamante,* 412 U.S. 281 (1973); *United States v. Boone,* 245 F.3d 352 (4th Cir. 2001), *cert. denied,* 541 U.S. 953 (2004). One court noted six factors to be considered in evaluating voluntariness: "the voluntariness of the defendant's custodial status; the presence of coercive police procedures; the extent and level of the

defendant's cooperation; the defendant's awareness of his or her right to refuse to consent; the defendant's education and intelligence; and, the defendant's belief that no incriminating evidence will be found." *United States v. Asibor,* 109 F.3d 1023 (5th Cir.), *cert. denied,* 522 U.S. 902 (1997). The court may also consider the defendant's prior dealings with law enforcement. *Basnueva v. United States,* 874 A.2d 363 (D.C. App. 2005). No single factor is determinative. *United States v. Watson,* 423 U.S. 411 (1976). Though the burden to show voluntariness may be particularly high, a person may even be under the influence of drugs or alcohol and still be able to give valid consent. *Hines v. State,* 514 N.E.2d 296 (Ind. 1987).

- In addition to giving voluntary consent, the target must have **apparent authority over the property or area** in order to consent to a search. *United States v. Morgan,* 435 F.3d 660 (6th Cir. 2006). As long as the officer has a good-faith belief that the person has authority to consent, the consent will be upheld in court. *Illinois v. Rodriguez,* 497 U.S. 177 (1990). Persons who have joint access to an area are deemed to have common authority to consent. *United States v. Matlock,* 415 U.S. 164 (1974). As long as one of the parties who has common authority to consent gives a voluntary consent, another party with authority cannot prevent officers from searching. *United States v. Rith,* 164 F.3d 1323 (10th Cir.), *cert. denied,* 528 U.S. 827 (1999). A third party can consent to a search if (1) the third party had access to the area searched, and (2) either common authority over the area *or* a substantial interest in the area, *or* permission to gain access. A third party can properly consent to a search if the third party has *either* mutual use of the property by virtue of joint access *or* control for most purposes over it. *United States v. Davis,* 967 F.2d 84 (2d Cir.), *cert. denied,* 506 U.S. 928 (1992).
- A spouse is presumed to have common authority to consent to a search of the couple's home. Parents are presumed to have common authority to consent to a search of a child's room. *United States v. Corley,* 342 F. Supp. 2d 776 (N.D. Ind. 2004). The Supreme Court recently ruled that officers cannot search a residence when one physically present resident consents to the search and the other physically present resident objects to the search. However, officers who obtain consent from one resident are not required to seek out other residents and ask their con-

sent. The rule applies only when both the consenting party and the objecting party are physically present at the home. *Georgia v. Randolph*, ___ U.S ___, 126 S. Ct. 1515 (2006).

- Children may have apparent authority to consent to the search of a home. The child's age is merely one factor in assessing the validity of apparent authority to grant consent. *Abdella v. O'Toole*, 343 F. Supp. 2d 129 (D. Conn. 2004); *State v. Butzke*, 584 N.W.2d 449 (Neb. App. 1998) (court must consider whether law enforcement reasonably believed the child had apparent authority); *People v. Jacobs*, 729 P.2d 757 (Cal. 1987) ("As a child advances in age she acquires greater discretion to admit visitors on her own authority.").
- Persons with joint access to a computer are presumed to have authority to consent to a search of computer files. *United States v. Trulock*, 275 F.3d 391 (4th Cir. 2001) (person with joint access to a computer may consent to a general search of the computer in the absence of the other users but could not consent to search the other users' password-protected files). Spouses and cohabitants may consent to searches of computers used by both parties even with passwords and privacy programs installed. *United States v. Morgan*, 435 F.3d 660 (6th Cir. 2006) (wife installed spyware to monitor husband's downloads, and wife could consent to police search of computer even when husband installed eraser program); *United States v. Buckner*, 407 F. Supp. 2d 777 (W.D. Va. 2006) (wife could consent to search of husband's password-protected files due to "sufficient relationship" between spouses; husband should have known that privacy in files was not absolute).
- Landlords cannot typically consent to searches of tenants' apartments. *Chapman v. United States*, 365 U.S. 610 (1961). If a landlord has lawful general access to rented premises, then the landlord can consent to a search of the premises. *United States v. Matlock*, 415 U.S. 164 (1974). If the landlord tells officers that he or she intends to evict the tenant, perhaps for overdue rent, the landlord still does not gain the right to consent to a search. *State v. Earl*, 92 P.3d 167 (Utah App.), *cert. denied*, 106 P.3d 743 (Utah 2004).
- Hoteliers cannot consent to searches of hotel rooms as long as the room rent is paid and the check-out time has not passed. *Stoner v. California*, 376 U.S. 483 (1964).

- Employers may generally consent to search of property belonging to the employer and over which the employer maintains some measure of control. The consent will be more likely to be held valid if employees are given notice that lockers, desks, and other property are subject to search. *Dawson v. State*, 868 S.W.2d 363 (Tex. App. 1993). Public employees enjoy a slightly higher expectation of privacy in desks and lockers than private employees. *O'Connor v. Ortega*, 480 U.S. 709 (1987).
- Consent to search a vehicle may be given by the owner. The driver may also consent to a vehicle search if the driver has a right to possess the vehicle, such as permission from the owner. Passengers generally cannot consent to a vehicle search or object to a vehicle search unless the passengers have some ownership in the vehicle. *Rakas v. Illinois*, 439 U.S. 128 (1978). A passenger does have the right to refuse to consent to a search of the passenger's personal effects, such as coats and purses, in a vehicle. *United States v. Crain*, 33 F.3d 480 (5th Cir. 1994). The passenger may lose that right through the passage of time. For example, if an officer orders all of the occupants of a vehicle to get out of the vehicle during a traffic stop and then obtains consent from the vehicle owner to search the vehicle, a passenger could refuse to consent to a search of his or her personal items left in the car. However, if the same passenger leaves a jacket in the car and the car is stopped a day later while the former passenger is not present and the car's owner consents to a search of the car, any evidence seized from the jacket will likely be admissible against the former passenger.
- There is a wide dispute among courts on the right of a non-renting driver of a rental car to give or deny consent to a search. The question is rooted in a determination of standing to challenge the search. *United States v. Thomas*, 447 F.3d 1191 (9th Cir. 2006) (unauthorized driver of rental car could challenge validity of search only if an authorized driver gave permission to the unauthorized driver to control car); *United States v. Jones*, 44 F.3d 860 (10th Cir. 1995) (unauthorized driver has no expectation of privacy and cannot refuse a search of car); *United States v. Smith*, 263 F.3d 571 (6th Cir. 2001) (unauthorized driver who borrowed rental car from authorized driver had reasonable expectation of privacy and could withhold consent to search); *United States v. Boruff*, 909 F.2d 111 (5th Cir. 1990) (driver of rental car who was not

listed as valid driver on rental agreement had no legitimate expectation of privacy in rental car even though he had permission of actual renter to drive the car), *cert. denied*, 499 U.S. 975 (1991); *Parker v. State*, 182 S.W.3d 923 (Tex. App. 2006) (unauthorized driver held expectation of privacy in rental car). A driver can have no expectation of privacy in a stolen car and thus has no right to deny consent to search the car. *United States v. Hensel*, 672 F.2d 578 (6th Cir. 1982); *Hall v. State*, 820 So. 2d 113 (Ala. App. 1999).

- In general, there is no right to refuse consent to search stolen property because the wrongful possessor can hold no legitimate expectation of privacy in the property. *United States v. Caymen*, 404 F.3d 1196 (9th Cir. 2005) (stolen computer); *United States v. Lyons*, 992 F.2d 1029 (10th Cir.1993) (stolen computer disks); *Pennywell v. State*, 84 S.W.3d 841 (Tex. App. 2002) (stolen bag).

A consent search is **limited to the scope of the consent**. *Florida v. Jimeno*, 500 U.S. 248 (1991). If the target has not specifically limited the consent, the scope of the search is the area that a reasonable person would understand from the target's consent. *United States v. Wacker*, 72 F.3d 1453 (10th Cir.), *cert. denied*, 519 U.S. 848 (1996). Consent **may be revoked** at any time by the person who consented. *United States v. Ibarra*, 731 F. Supp. 1037 (D. Wyo. 1990). The revocation of consent must be clear and unequivocal. *State v. Mattison*, 575 S.E.2d 852 (S.C. App. 2003).

Automobile

An officer may search a vehicle without a warrant if there is **probable cause to believe that it contains evidence or contraband**. The officer **may search anywhere a warrant could have authorized** a search. The courts have adhered to this exception for years; when it was first allowed, the Ford Model T was still in production. *Carroll v. United States*, 267 U.S. 132 (1925). This exception is based both on the lesser expectation of privacy in a vehicle traveling public roads and the ready mobility of a vehicle. *Rakas v. Illinois*, 439 U.S. 128 (1978). The Supreme Court has also noted the reduced expectation of privacy in a vehicle operated on public roads, due to the pervasive regulation of motor vehicle traffic. *Cady v. Dombrowski*, 413 U.S. 433 (1973). Under federal law, there is no separate requirement of exigency for the automobile search doctrine. *Maryland v. Dyson*, 527 U.S. 465

(1999); *Pennsylvania v. Labron*, 518 U.S. 938 (1996). Some states require an element of exigency, which is presumed when the vehicle is capable of mobility, the occupants are alerted to police interest, and the evidence could be destroyed while police seek a warrant. *State v. Snell*, 99 P.3d 191 (Mont. 2004); *State v. Wilson*, 833 A.2d 1087 (N.J. 2003); *Commonwealth v. Perry*, 798 A.2d 697 (Pa. 2002); *State v. Harnisch*, 954 P.2d 1180 (Nev. 1998); *State v. Gomez*, 932 P.2d 1 (N.M. 1997); *State v. Limb*, 581 P.2d 142 (Utah 1978).

The automobile search doctrine does not depend on the suspect being able to control and move the vehicle. *United States v. Brookins*, 345 F.3d 231 (4th Cir. 2003). The exception applies even if the car is seized and impounded. *United States v. Paredes*, 388 F. Supp. 2d 1185 (D. Haw. 2005). When a vehicle is obviously incapable of movement, e.g., is raised on blocks or missing a motor, then the mobility prong of the automobile search exception fails and the doctrine does not apply. *Lavicky v. Burnett*, 758 F.2d 4685 (10th Cir. 1985), *cert. denied*, 474 U.S. 1101 (1986). Although there is no requirement that obtaining a warrant be impracticable, remember that obtaining a warrant may offer strong protection against later suppression.

The **search need not occur contemporaneously with the seizure**. *United States v. Gastiaburo*, 16 F.3d 582 (4th Cir.), *cert. denied*, 513 U.S. 829 (1994). In one case, a warrantless search was upheld when it occurred two months after a car had been impounded. *United States v. Casares-Cardenas*, 14 F.3d 1283 (8th Cir.), *cert. denied*, 513 U.S. 849 (1994). "Not a single published federal case speaks of a 'temporal limit' to the automobile exception. The Supreme Court has repeatedly stated that a warrantless search of a car need not occur contemporaneously with the car's lawful seizure and need not be justified by the existence of exigent circumstances that might have made it impractical to secure a warrant prior to the search." *United States v. Gastiaburo*, 16 F.3d 582 (4th Cir. 1994) (approving a search that followed 38 days after the seizure). The automobile exception may be used to justify a thorough search even if an inventory has already been conducted. *Florida v. Meyers*, 466 U.S. 380 (1984).

The scope of a search under the **automobile exception includes closed containers** in the vehicle, even if there is no distinct probable cause for the container. *California v. Acevedo*, 500 U.S. 565 (1991). The search includes the entire vehicle, bumper to bumper, as long as the item for which there is probable cause to search could be concealed in the location searched. *United States v. Ross*, 456 U.S. 798 (1982). The search may extend to the undercarriage, *United States v. Nicholson*, 17 F.3d 1294 (10th Cir. 1994), and may even go so far as dismantling door panels when there is general probable cause to search for drugs or other easily concealed items. *United States v. Zucco*, 71 F.3d 188 (5th Cir. 1995), *cert. denied*, 519 U.S. 827 (1996). If the probable cause extends to containers, the containers may even be searched at a later time and at another location. *United States v. Oliver*, 363 F.3d 1061 (10th Cir. 2004).

When small objects, such as illegal drugs, are the object of the probable cause, officers may search handbags and personal effects found in the car, regardless of whether such items are claimed by the driver or passengers. "We hold that police officers with probable cause to search a car may inspect passengers' belongings found in the car that are capable of concealing the object of the search." *Wyoming v. Houghton*, 526 U.S. 295 (1999). Otherwise, a drug dealer might commonly escape a lawful search by hiding contraband in a passenger's purse.

Justice Breyer's concurring opinion in *Wyoming v. Houghton* argued that searches of purses and wallets should be treated as extensions of searches of persons because of the heightened expectation of privacy in an item generally carried on one's person. Some state courts have followed Justice Breyer's concurrence and held that an officer may search purses and other articles that unarrested occupants voluntarily leave in the vehicle. *State v. Tognotti*, 663 N.W.2d 642 (N.D. 2003); *State v. Friedel*, 714 N.E.2d 1231 (Ind. App. 1999). The Kansas Supreme Court held that a purse does carry a higher expectation of privacy and that police officers cannot order a passenger to leave a purse behind in a car when the driver gives consent to search the car. *State v. Boyd*, 64 P.3d 419 (Kan. 2003). The same court recently distinguished a case where probable cause existed before a passenger asked to retrieve her purse and held that the officer could require her to leave it in the car. "We hold a law enforcement officer may search a passenger's purse left in the vehicle when the passenger exits, if the passenger makes no effort to retrieve the purse before probable cause to search the vehicle develops." *State v. Groshong*, 135 P.3d 1186 (Kan. 2006).

When a small amount of contraband is located during a search pursuant to the automobile exception, the search may continue to any area capable of concealing contraband. After a Wyoming state trooper stopped a car and smelled burning marijuana, the driver handed the trooper a bag of marijuana and a pipe. The trooper then searched the entire car including the trunk, where he found more marijuana. The driver claimed that the trooper did not have probable cause to search the trunk. The court ruled that the presence of lawfully discovered contraband in the passenger compartment created probable cause to search all places in the entire car where similar contraband could be hidden (including, in this case, the trunk). *United States v. Bradford,* 423 F.3d 1149 (10th Cir. 2005). Note that the mere odor of burnt marijuana would not have given probable cause to search the trunk. *United States v. Parker,* 72 F.3d 1444 (10th Cir. 1995).

There are some limitations on the automobile exception. A car parked in a driveway of a house under surveillance, when there is ample time to obtain a warrant and no suggestion that the car will be driven away, may be searched only under a warrant. *Coolidge v. New Hampshire,* 403 U.S. 443 (1971). A warrant must also be obtained for a car on blocks or otherwise obviously not capable of mobility. *Lavicky v. Burnett,* 758 F.2d 468 (10th Cir. 1985), *cert. denied,* 474 U.S. 1101 (1986). The automobile search exception also does not extend to searches of the vehicle passengers themselves. *Wyoming v. Houghton,* 526 U.S. 295 (1999) (automobile exception "does not extend to the search of a person found in that automobile"); *United States v. Di Re,* 332 U.S. 581 (1948).

Plain touch

The basic requirements of the plain touch doctrine are similar to the requirements for plain smell. The officer must be lawfully in the position from which she touched the item, its incriminating nature must be immediately apparent to the touch, and the officer must be lawfully able to access the item. *Minnesota v. Dickerson,* 508 U.S. 366 (1993). For example, if an officer patted down a suspect during a search warrant and was immediately able to identify a set of lock picks or a package of marijuana, the officer could reach into the pocket and retrieve the item. However, if further manipulation of the object to identify it is necessary, the plain touch doctrine will not apply. *United States v. Bustos-Torres,* 396 F.3d 935 (8th Cir. 2005).

Search incident to a lawful arrest

When an officer makes a lawful custodial arrest, the officer may **search the arrestee and the area within the arrestee's control**. *Chimel v. California,* 395 U.S. 752 (1969). This exception is based on the need to discover weapons that the arrestee might use against the officer and to discover evidence within the arrestee's control. The search extends to containers, luggage, and closets within the arrestee's immediate control. *United States v. Ivy,* 973 F.2d 1184 (5th Cir. 1992), *cert. denied,* 507 U.S. 1022 (1993); *United States v. Lucas,* 898 F.2d 606 (8th Cir.), *cert. denied,* 498 U.S. 838 (1990); *United States v. Herrera,* 810 F.2d 989 (10th Cir. 1987). Incident to the arrest, officers may also conduct a **protective sweep** of the immediate area and "without probable cause or reasonable suspicion, look in closets and other spaces immediately adjoining the place of arrest from which an attack could be immediately launched." *Maryland v. Buie,* 494 U.S. 334 (1990).

When a person is arrested while inside or near a car, the scope of the search incident to arrest extends to the passenger compartment and all closed containers therein. *Knowles v. Iowa,* 525 U.S. 113 (1998). Even locked containers, such as the glove box, may be searched. *United States v. Woody,* 55 F.3d 1257 (7th Cir.), *cert. denied,* 516 U.S. 889 (1995). "Container" means any object capable of holding another object. "It thus includes closed or open glove compartments, consoles, or other receptacles located anywhere within the passenger compartment, as well as luggage, boxes, bags, clothing, and the like. Our holding encompasses only the interior of the passenger compartment of an automobile and does not encompass the trunk." *New York v. Belton,* 453 U.S. 454 (1981).

A search of the passenger compartment incident to arrest may be conducted as long as the arrest occurs within close proximity to the vehicle, although outside of the vehicle. *United States v. Franco,* 981 F.2d 470 (10th Cir. 1992). "The arrest of a suspect who is next to a vehicle presents identical concerns regarding officer safety and the destruction of evidence as the arrest of one who is inside the vehicle. A custodial arrest is fluid and the danger to the police officer flows from the fact of the arrest, and its attendant proximity, stress, and uncertainty. The stress is no less merely because the arrestee exited his or her car before the officer initiated contact, nor is an arrestee less likely to attempt to lunge for a weapon or to destroy evidence if he is outside of, but still in control of, the vehicle." *Thornton v. United States*, 541 U.S. 615 (2004).

The search incident to arrest must be **substantially contemporaneous** with the arrest. *United States v. Edwards*, 415 U.S. 800 (1974). In some cases, the search may actually precede the arrest as long as the officer has probable cause to arrest at the time of the search. *Rawlings v. Kentucky*, 448 U.S. 98 (1980). However, evidence found may not provide the sole basis for the arrest. *Smith v. Ohio*, 494 U.S. 541 (1990). A few courts have required that the search follow a custodial arrest or a detention equivalent to a formal arrest. *United States v. Powell*, 451 F.3d 862 (D.C. Cir. 2006); *Ochana v. Flores*, 347 F.3d 266 (7th Cir. 2003).

As more time passes between the arrest and the search, it becomes less likely that a court will find the search to be proper as "incident to the arrest." *United States v. Smith*, 389 F.3d 944 (9th Cir. 2004) (search need not be "immediately upon the heels of an arrest," but can be "well after" the arrest as long as there has been a continuous sequence of events leading up to the search), *cert. denied*, 544 U.S. 956 (2005); *United States v. $639,558 in U.S. Currency*, 955 F.2d 712 (D.C. Cir. 1992) (30- to 45-minute delay rendered search too "remote in time" to allow as incident to an arrest); *United States v. Vasey*, 834 F.2d 782 (9th Cir. 1987) (search conducted 30 to 45 minutes after arrest and following conversations where officers sought consent to search "did not follow closely on the heels of the arrest" and was too remote in time); *United States v. Scott*, 428 F. Supp. 2d 1126 (E.D. Cal. 2006) (search that followed arrest by 50 minutes was valid because the delay was due to reasonable safety precautions). One court recently approved a search that followed the initial detention by over an hour. While the detention and search were remote in time, the search followed closely on the heels of the formal arrest. *United States v. Hrasky*, 453 F.3d 1099 (8th Cir. 2006).

The search **must be at the place of arrest**. *United States v. Lugo*, 978 F.2d 631 (10th Cir. 1992) (search not incident to arrest when the suspect was in custody and being driven away from the scene of the arrest). Some courts have extended the *Belton* rule to allow searches that immediately follow a formal arrest even after the suspect is taken into custody and removed from the scene, *United States v. Snook*, 88 F.3d 605 (8th Cir. 1996), or handcuffed at the scene but away from the vehicle. *United States v. Barnes*, 374 F.3d 601 (8th Cir. 2004). Once luggage and closed containers have been taken into the control of the police and more than a few minutes have passed following the arrest, their search cannot be justified as incident to arrest. *United States v. Donnes,* 947 F.2d 1430 (10th Cir. 1991). If the search of the arrest scene is commenced before the suspect is removed, the search may continue in the suspect's absence. *United States v. Doward,* 41 F.3d 789 (1st Cir. 1994) ("Nothing in *Belton* even remotely implies that officers must discontinue a passenger compartment search properly initiated as a contemporaneous incident of an occupant's arrest at the instant the arrestee is transported from the scene."), *cert. denied,* 514 U.S. 1074 (1995).

Searches that intrude into body cavities generally require probable cause and exigency. *(See Exigent Circumstances, below.)* One court approved repetitive forced administration of a laxative to a suspect who swallowed packets of illegal drugs as a valid search incident to arrest. The court considered the search under the rule announced in *Winston v. Lee,* 470 U.S. 753 (1985), in which the Supreme Court prescribed the following factors to analyze a search involving a medical procedure: one, the extent to which the procedure may threaten the safety or health of the individual; two, the extent of the intrusion upon the individual's dignitary interests in personal privacy and bodily integrity; and three, the community's interest in fairly and accurately determining guilt or innocence. One of the justifications for the search incident to arrest doctrine is to prevent the destruction of evidence. The court found that factor weighed in favor of the prosecution in this case. One of the officers had seen the suspect swallow the bag of cocaine, and there was clear evidence that the search would likely produce evidence. The court also relied on evidence that a nurse told one of the officers that the laxative would help prevent an overdose that might result from the rupture of the bag. *State v. Payano-Roman,* 714 N.W.2d 548 (Wis. 2006).

Administrative searches

Certain highly regulated businesses may be subject to limited warrantless searches to promote regulatory compliance. "Liquor and firearms are industries of this type; when an entrepreneur embarks upon such a business, he has voluntarily chosen to subject himself to a full arsenal of governmental regulation." *Marshall v. Barlow's, Inc.,* 436 U.S. 307 (1978). Administrative searches will be allowed when there is a substantial government interest in the regulatory scheme, the search is necessary to achieve effective regulation, and the authorizing statute gives notice to the business and effectively limits the discretion of the authorities conducting the search. *New York v. Burger,* 482 U.S. 691 (1987). Administrative searches cannot be used as pretexts to investigate criminal activity. Examples of businesses subject to administrative searches include mining, liquor manufacture and sales, interstate trucking, firearms manufacture and sales, and auto wrecking.

In an auto-wrecking sting operation, officers placed a bait vehicle on a public street. The vehicle was equipped with a global positioning satellite transmitter and audio/visual recorders. Officers watched a suspect steal the truck and arrested him. The suspect worked at an auto-wrecking yard. Officers decided to conduct an administrative search of the wrecking yard. While searching for detached VIN plates, officers located a locked tool box. The officers opened the tool box and found a gun and ammunition. The court reasoned that the search of the tool box was within the scope of the statute authorizing salvage yard inspections and upheld the firearms conviction. The officers' subjective intent in searching the salvage yard was irrelevant. *United States v. Johnson,* 408 F.3d 1313 (10th Cir. 2005).

Administrative searches of personal effects, desks, and lockers

Whether an employee holds a legitimate expectation of privacy in personal effects at the office or in an office desk, filing cabinet, or locker depends on employer search policies and practices. *Schowengerdt v. General Dynamics Corp.,* 823 F.2d 1328 (9th Cir. 1987) (plaintiff had reasonable expectation of privacy in his locked desk and credenza absent notice that items could be searched); *United States v. Speights,* 557 F.2d 362 (3d Cir. 1977) (police officer had reasonable expectation of privacy in his locker where no regulations or practices would have alerted him to expect searches); *United States v. Bunkers,* 521 F.2d 1217 (9th Cir. 1975) (postal worker had no expectation of privacy in locker where Postal Service regulations and collective bargaining agreement stated that lockers were subject to search). Public employees, particularly law enforcement officers, may have their expectation of privacy balanced against the public employer's reasonable interests in control and efficient operation of the workplace. A search of a public employee's possessions at the workplace must be "reasonably related in scope to the circumstances which justified the interference in the first place." *O'Connor v. Ortega*, 480 U.S. 709 (1987). In *O'Connor v. Ortega*, the Supreme Court ruled that a doctor employed in a public hospital had a reasonable expectation of privacy in his desk and file cabinets. Neither a search warrant nor probable cause was needed to search those places, but the search still had to be justified by "reasonableness."

Certain workplace areas hold a higher expectation of privacy and cannot be searched under an administrative search justification. Locker and change rooms are generally protected from a search justified by the administrative search doctrine. *Trujillo v. City of Ontario*, 428 F. Supp. 2d 1094 (C.D. Cal. 2006) (officers held expectation of privacy in police locker room where officers changed and showered). There may be a lesser expectation in a workplace locker itself. *Los Angeles Police Protection League v. Gates*, 579 F. Supp. 36 (C.D. Cal. 1984) (officer has no reasonable expectation of privacy in station locker where regulation provides that locker can be searched under various circumstances).

Courts are less likely to find a reasonable expectation of privacy in areas where the general public is able to enter. *O'Connor v. Ortega*, 480 U.S. 709 (1987). Administrative searches of desks and filing cabinets are highly fact-sensitive and depend largely on the access practices in the office. *Gossmeyer v. McDonald*, 128 F.3d 481 (7th Cir. 1997) (investigator's expectation of privacy in her filing cabinet was not reasonable despite the fact that she locked it because the cabinet was "part of the workplace, not part of her personal domain"); *Sheppard v. Beerman*, 18 F.3d 147 (2d Cir.) (law clerk's expectation of privacy in office desk was not objectively reasonable because the nature of employment relationship calls for free flow of information), *cert. denied*, 513 U.S. 816 (1994). Workplace computers are generally fair game for an administrative search when employees are given notice of policies restricting the computer use to business purposes. *United States v. Simons*, 206 F.3d 392 (4th Cir. 2000), *cert. denied*, 534 U.S. 930 (2001).

Administrative security screening

Courts routinely uphold the validity of warrantless, suspicionless searches at transportation and public building security screening checkpoints as valid administrative searches based on the government's overwhelming public safety interest. Courts have long upheld security searches at international borders. *Carroll v. United States*, 267 U.S. 132 (1925) ("Travelers may be so stopped in crossing an international boundary because of national self-protection reasonably requiring one entering the country to identify himself as entitled to come in, and his belongings as effects which may be lawfully brought in."). Following the administrative search doctrine avoids a Fourth Amendment analysis of reasonableness of the search. In ruling on the validity of a security screening, the court is required to balance between "the gravity of the public concerns served by the seizure, the degree to which the seizure advances the public interest, and the severity of the interference with individual liberty." *United States v. Hartwell*, 436 F.3d 174 (3d Cir. 2006) (court allowed admission of a bag of cocaine from traveler's pocket found when an alarm on the airport metal detector prompted a secondary screening). Another court recently approved random secondary airport searches conducted with ion scanners and handheld magnetometers as valid administrative searches. *United States v. Marquez*, 410 F.3d 612 (9th Cir. 2005).

Security screening checkpoints at the entrances to courthouses and other public buildings are legitimate administrative searches. *State v. Book*, 847 N.E.2d 52 (Ohio App. 2006). A security screening is a valid administrative search when three elements are met. First, the search must have a valid administrative purpose. Second, the method employed must be the least-intrusive means to accomplish the administrative purpose. Third, persons potentially subject to the search must have an available alternative that would enable them to avoid the search by choosing to not enter. For example, the person may decide not to enter. By choosing to enter and, as a consequence, then being subject to a search, the person effectively consents to the administrative search. If the administrative search meets the three-element test, it is valid even if the seizure of weapons or contraband leads to a criminal prosecution. *United States v. Davis*, 482 F.2d 893 (9th Cir. 1973). Security searches that go beyond checking for weapons or explosives are not valid administrative searches. *United States v. Bulacan*, 156 F.3d 963 (9th Cir. 1998). Some courts uphold security screenings because they are consensual, without analysis of the administrative search doctrine, as long as notice is provided that entry to the facility is contingent on submitting to a search. *State v. Kurth*, 981 S.W.2d 410 (Tex. App. 1998).

The Ninth Circuit Court of Appeals made a significant shift in the consent analysis of security searches when they ruled that a traveler who initially submits to an airport search cannot then choose not to fly and thereby avoid a secondary suspicionless search. The court declined to follow prior rulings that allowed passengers, if they did not agree to searches, to simply abandon their intent to fly and leave the airport. In this case, the traveler asked to leave the airport when he was selected for a secondary search but was not allowed to leave. The secondary search revealed a small amount of methamphetamine in his pocket. The court reasoned that "changed circumstances, expectations, and technology involved in modern air travel and airport screening" lead to a new understanding of the scope of an air traveler's implied consent and held that the consent cannot be revoked once it is given by submitting to initial screening measures. *United States v. Aukai*, 440 F.3d 1169 (9th Cir. 2006). Once the traveler places baggage into the inspection process, such as placing carry-on baggage on the x-ray belt, the items may be searched, and the traveler may not choose to leave and avoid the search. *Torbet v. United Airlines, Inc.*, 298 F.3d 1087 (9th Cir. 2002); *People v. Heimel*, 812 P.2d 1177 (Colo. 1991).

The United States Court of Appeals recently upheld security screening conducted at subway entrances. The court relied on the special needs doctrine rather than the administrative search doctrine. *(See discussion of the Special Needs doctrine, below).* The New York Civil Liberties Union claimed that the random checkpoints were unconstitutional intrusions on privacy. The New York City Police Department countered that the checkpoints were reasonable steps to deter and thwart probable terrorist attacks on the transportation system. The appellate court recognized that "in light of the thwarted plots to bomb New York City's subway system, its continued desirability as a target, and the recent bombings of transportation systems in Madrid, Moscow, and London, the risk to public safety is substantial and real." The New York subways were terrorist targets in 1997 (plot to bomb the Atlantic Avenue Station) and 2004 (attempt to blow up the Herald Square Station). The Civil Liberties Union argued that there was no reasonable suspicion to detain passengers at checkpoints.

The court's decision was announced, coincidentally, one day following the discovery of a terrorist plot to blow up commercial airplanes. The court agreed with the plaintiffs' claim that the searches intrude on privacy rights. However, the court noted that the exceedingly brief inspections were limited to bags that could likely hold a bomb. The judges noted that the inspection program "deters both a single-bomb attack and an attack consisting of multiple, synchronized bombings, such as those in London and Madrid." *MacWade v. Kelly*, 460 F.3d 260 (2d Cir. 2006). As the worldwide effort to thwart terrorist attacks continues, more developments are certain to shape the parameters of the law of security searches.

Inventory and community care-taking

Police may conduct inventories of seized property. *Colorado v. Bertine*, 479 U.S. 367 (1987). The justification for inventories rest on three needs: "the protection of the owner's property while it remains in police custody; the protection of the police against claims or disputes over lost or stolen property; and the protection of the police from potential danger." *South Dakota v. Opperman*, 428 U.S. 364 (1976). An inventory may not be used as a ruse to search for evidence.

The **inventory must be conducted in accordance with a standard policy**. *Florida v. Wells*, 495 U.S. 1 (1990). A written policy leaves little room for unlawful discretion. Still, courts have occasionally allowed evidence seized during an impound conducted under an unwritten policy. *United States v. Agofsky*, 20 F.3d 866 (8th Cir. 1994); *Welch v. State*, 955 S.W.2d 181 (Ark. 1997). The policy must define the scope of the inventory. An inventory of a car may extend to the glove compartment, trunk, and closed containers if so directed by the policy. *United States v. Long*, 705 F.2d 1259 (10th Cir. 1983); *United States v. Thompson*, 29 F.3d 62 (2d Cir. 1994). An inventory may also be taken of an arrestee's property during the booking process. *United States v. Edwards*, 415 U.S. 800 (1974).

As long as officers have a valid reason for an impound and inventory of property, it is not significant that there may be alternatives to the impound. Even though another driver may be available to remove the car from an arrest scene, or even if the car may be towed to the owner's home rather than a police impound, the impound and subsequent inventory is permissible. *Colorado v. Bertine*, 479 U.S. 367 (1987) (police need not give driver "an opportunity to make alternative arrangements" that avoid impoundment); *United States v. Cherry*, 436 F.3d 769 (7th Cir. 2006) (police need not offer driver choice of towing services and destinations). Officers need not allow the driver and occupants to remove personal items prior to the inventory. *United States v. Penn,* 233 F.3d 1111 (9th Cir. 2000) (sustaining inventory under policy that allowed occupants to retrieve personal items at the discretion of the officer, but only after non-discretionary inventory was complete), *cert. denied,* 532 U.S. 1033 (2001).

As part of the police community care-taking responsibility, officers may impound and subsequently inventory vehicles that "jeopardize public safety and the efficient movement of vehicular traffic." *South Dakota v. Opperman,* 428 U.S. 364 (1976). Following the arrest of a driver, officers may impound any vehicle that impedes traffic, endangers the public, or may be subject to vandalism. *Hallstrom v. City of Garden City,* 991 F.2d 1473 (9th Cir. 1993). Most states mandate the impoundment of a vehicle used in an impaired-driving crime. Ariz. Rev. Stat. § 28-3511; Utah Code. Ann. § 41-6a-527. An impound may be justified under the community care-taking function when there is no licensed driver in the car or when the car is being operated without liability insurance if agency policy so dictates. *United States v. Skillern,* 947 F.2d 1268 (5th Cir. 1991) (impound reasonable where the driver had no license or insurance; police were not required to offer an alternative to impound), *cert. denied,* 503 U.S. 949 (1992); *United States v. Rodriguez-Morales,* 929 F.2d 780 (1st Cir. 1991) ("Upon ascertaining that neither occupant was properly licensed to drive, the decision not to let the vehicle continue on its journey was quintessentially reasonable."), *cert. denied,* 502 U.S. 1030 (1992).

Exigent circumstances

If public safety or officers' safety is threatened, officers may enter a home or other building and conduct whatever search is necessary to quell the threat. *Warden v. Hayden,* 387 U.S. 294 (1967). There are four general categories of exigent circumstances that justify warrantless entries: first, hot pursuit of a fleeing felon; second, imminent destruction of evidence; third, the need to prevent a suspect's escape; and fourth, a risk of danger to the police or the public. *United States v. Zogmaister,* 90 Fed. Appx. 325 (10th Cir. 2004); *United States v. Williams,* 354 F.3d 497 (6th Cir. 2003); *United States v. Standridge,* 810 F.2d 1034 (11th Cir. 1987), *cert. denied,* 481 U.S. 1072 (1987). If the exigent circumstances do not merit a full search, the property may be temporarily secured for as long as is reasonably necessary to obtain a warrant. *Segura v. United States,* 468 U.S. 796 (1984). There is **no exception to the Fourth Amendment rules for murder scenes** or crime scenes for other serious crimes. *Flippo v. West Virginia,* 528 U.S. 11 (1999). The exigent circumstances search exception is very carefully applied by courts because no probable cause determination is required. *State v. Comer,* 51 P.3d 55 (Utah App.), *cert. denied,* 59 P.3d 603 (Utah 2002).

Exigent circumstances entry is not allowed when police cause the exigency. After a motel manager told officers about drug activity, they conducted an admittedly illegal search of a motel room and found drugs and paraphernalia. When the defendant returned to the room, the officers knocked and claimed to be from room service. That ruse didn't work, so the officers tried again and claimed to be from motel maintenance. Officers then pounded on the door and said, "Open up, this is the police." When the officers heard scurrying footsteps and a flushing toilet, they forced the door open and seized drugs. The court found that the officers had created the exigency to enter, and the evidence was suppressed. There was no evidence that the officers intended to obtain a warrant. Moreover, there was no practical reason not to seek a search warrant. *United States v. Coles,* 437 F. 3d 361 (3d Cir. 2006).

The exigent circumstances doctrine is most often applied in cases where officers perform "community caretaker" functions rather than traditional law enforcement functions. *Michigan v. Tyler,* 436 U.S. 499 (1978) (applying the exigent circumstances exception to a warrantless entry of a burning building). Generally, cases where officers are acting as community caretakers are analyzed as "emergency aid" situations. However, the Supreme Court recently emphasized that whether the officer's motivation for entering is to arrest persons and gather evidence, prevent an injury, or to assist the injured is irrelevant as long as the circumstances objectively justify the entry. *Brigham City v. Stuart,* ___ U.S. ___, 126 S. Ct. 1943 (2006).

In *Brigham City v. Stuart,* officers responding to a complaint of a loud party heard thumping against walls and furniture and shouting inside a home. After walking to the rear of the home, officers saw four adults attempting to restrain a juvenile against a refrigerator. Officers saw the juvenile punch a woman in the face as the juvenile broke one arm free. Officers were yelling loudly through the screen door, though the suspects appeared not to hear them. The officers entered the home without knocking, because they believed that a knock would be futile given the lack of response to the loud shouts from a few feet away through a screen door. The Utah Supreme Court analyzed the officers' decision to enter and intervene under both the exigent circumstances and emergency aid doctrines and ruled that the entry was illegal. The United States Supreme Court rejected both analyses. "The role of a peace officer includes preventing violence and restoring order, not simply rendering first aid to casualties; an officer is not like a boxing (or hockey) referee, poised to stop a bout only if it becomes too one-sided. It would serve no purpose to require them to stand dumbly at the door awaiting their response while those within brawled on, oblivious to their presence." *Brigham City v. Stuart*, ___ U.S. ___, 126 S. Ct. 1943 (2006).

One court recently interpreted *Brigham City v. Stuart* as a reformulation of the emergency aid doctrine and observed that it is no longer necessary to distinguish between an assertion of exigent circumstances or emergency aid. After a 911 hang-up call and several attempts to call the number back, officers went to Najar's trailer. They could see movement in the trailer and they knocked several times with no response. Najar finally answered the door. Officers asked if they could come in and check on other occupants, and Najar claimed that he was alone. Concerned over the unusual series of events, a supervising officer decided that the officers should enter. They found a woman lying face down. She said that she was okay. The officers saw a shotgun, and arrested Najar for being a felon in possession of a firearm. The court of appeals ruled that the emergency aid doctrine allows officers to enter a home without a warrant when "the officers have an objectively reasonable basis to believe there is an immediate need to protect the lives or safety of themselves or others, and the manner and scope of the search is reasonable." The court interpreted *Brigham City v. Stuart* to implicitly reject probable cause as the standard for measuring the emergency. A court should no longer ask whether an objectively reasonable belief in the existence of an emergency approached a level of certainty that would make it comparable to probable cause. The proper "test is now two-fold, whether the officers have an objectively reasonable basis to believe there is an immediate need to protect the lives or safety of themselves or others, and the manner and scope of the search is reasonable." *United States v. Najar,* 451 F.3d 710 (10th Cir. 2006).

A classic example of an exigent circumstances search is presented in the case of officers searching for a missing child. *People v. Panah,* 107 P.3d 790 (Cal. 2005), *cert. denied,* ___ U.S. ___, 126 S. Ct. 1432 (2006). Officers learned that the child's clothes had been discovered in an area near a suspect's apartment balcony. Neighbors told officers of suspicious behavior by the suspect. The suspect gave inconsistent statements to officers; was evasive, uncooperative and unresponsive; and appeared to be very nervous and agitated. Officers entered the suspect's apartment, searched, and found the missing five-year-old girl, who had been sexually assaulted and was tightly bound. *State v. Yoder,* 935 P.2d 534 (Utah App. 1997).

Other examples where courts have found that exigent circumstances justify warrantless entry include to investigate reports of gunshots, *Bing ex rel. Bing v. City of Whitehall, Ohio,* 456 F.3d 555 (6th Cir. 2006); *United States v. Holloway,* 290 F.3d 1331 (11th Cir. 2002); to follow a fresh blood trail, *United States v. Chipps,* 410 F.3d 438 (8th Cir. 2005); *Alspach v. State,* 755 N.E.2d 209 (Ind. App. 2001); to check on the welfare of a domestic violence victim when police learned of credible threats against the victim, *United States v. Davis,* 290 F.3d 1239 (10th Cir. 2002) (entry proper upon a reasonable belief that officers' safety or victim's safety is at risk); *Commonwealth v. Snell,* 705 N.E.2d 236 (Mass.), *cert. denied,* 527 U.S. 1010 (1999); to check on the welfare of a person reported as missing, *State v. Jones,* 947 P.2d 1030 (Kan. App. 1997); to check on the welfare of an unattended child where the child may be at risk, *United States v. Gillespie,* 332 F. Supp. 2d 923 (W.D. Va. 2004) (finding no blanket child-welfare exigency exception); *State v. Peterson,* 543 S.E.2d 692 (Ga.) (entry to check on welfare of young children proper, even though exigency had passed), *cert. denied,* 534 U.S. 955 (2001); to investigate a burglary in progress, *United States v. Tibolt,* 72 F.3d 965 (1st Cir. 1995); to locate a kidnapping victim or find information that would lead to the victim's location, *State v. Matthews,* 665 N.W.2d 28 (N.D. 2003); *Brimage v. State,* 918 S.W.2d 466 (Tex. App. 1994); to investigate odors associated with a dead body, *United States v. Stafford,* 416 F.3d 1068 (9th Cir. 2005); to investigate odors of dangerous chemicals, *Holder v. State,* 847 N.E.2d 930 (Ind. 2006); to investigate an open door or window where circumstances suggest a burglary or other crime in progress, *Murdock v. Stout,* 54 F.3d 1437 (9th Cir. 1995); and to respond to a burglar alarm, *United States v. Dighera,* 2 F. Supp. 2d 1377 (D. Kan. 1998) ("It appears well-settled that responding to a burglary alarm is an exigent circumstance authorizing the police to make a warrantless entry to a home.").

A search may also be conducted when police are in "hot pursuit" of a suspect and there is probable cause to arrest the suspect. *United States v. Dodds,* 946 F.2d 726 (10th Cir. 1991). The search may extend only as far as necessary to apprehend the suspect. The crime involved must be serious, such as felonious drug-trafficking or a crime involving personal injury or threat. *United States v. Aquino,* 836 F.2d 1268 (10th Cir. 1988). The search must be conducted in a reasonable fashion. *United States v. Brown,* 64 F.3d 1083 (7th Cir. 1995). If there is time to obtain a telephonic warrant, the officer must do so. *United States v. Tarazon,* 989 F.2d 1045 (9th Cir.), *cert. denied,* 510 U.S. 853 (1993).

Evanescent evidence

Although really a form of an exigent circumstances search, searches for evanescent evidence (evidence susceptible to rapid deterioration) may be conducted when the search is minimally intrusive and the **evidence is in imminent danger of destruction**. *Cupp v. Murphy,* 412 U.S. 291 (1973); *United States v. Smith,* 470 F.2d 377 (D.C. Cir. 1972). Warrantless seizures of evanescent evidence have been allowed for a variety of physical evidence. *Cupp v. Murphy,* 412 U.S. 291 (1973) (warrantless search of evidence beneath suspect's fingernails reasonable in strangulation murder); *Kimble v. Eugene Police Department,* 114 Fed. Appx. 784 (9th Cir. 2004) (forced pubic hair combing of assault suspect); *United States v. Jones,* 215 F.3d 1322, 2000 WL 690182 (4th Cir. 2000) (gunshot residue swab of suspect's hands); *Hubbert v. State,* 759 So. 2d 504 (Miss. App. 2000) (gunshot residue); *State v. Norman,* 397 S.E.2d 647 (N.C. App. 1990), *cert. denied,* 400 S.E.2d 459 (N.C. 1991) (strip search at crime scene to conduct pubic hair combing); *State v. Burke,* 108 Wash. App.1048, 2001 WL 1265264 (Wash. App. 2001) (swab of suspect's penis and genital area to preserve evidence of child victim's vomit); *State v. Merkt,* 1998 WL 202638 (Minn. App. 1998) (swabbing of penis and groin area of assault suspect); *Franklin v. State,* 308 A.2d 752 (1973) (seizure of rape suspect's underwear to preserve blood, pubic hair, and semen). Even the seizure of hair samples may be allowed if there is enough reason to believe that evidence will be destroyed. *United States v. D'Amico,* 408 F.2d 331 (2d Cir. 1969).

Most states allow the warrantless, non-consensual seizure of blood from a driver suspected of drug or alcohol impairment. *State v. Clary,* 2 P.3d 1255 (Ariz. App. 2000) (officers may use reasonable force to overcome resistance to non-consensual blood draw). The United States Supreme Court recently refused to consider the issue of non-consensual blood draws for impaired drivers. *State v. Faust,* 682 N.W.2d 371 (Wis. 2004), *cert. denied,* 543 U.S. 1089 (2005). Several states, including Alaska, Arizona, Florida, Indiana, Iowa, Michigan, Nevada, and Texas, have all passed legislation authorizing forcible extraction of blood samples. In many states, courts presume exigency when confronted with the need to obtain a blood sample for chemical analysis. *Frensemeier v. State,* 849 N.E.2d 157 (Ind. App. 2006) ("the threat of the 'metabolic destruction of evidence' of a suspect's intoxication, i.e., the bodily absorption of alcohol in the bloodstream," constitutes exigent circumstances); *State v. Aleman,* 109 P.3d 571 (Ariz. App. 2005) ("highly evanescent nature of alcohol in the defendant's blood stream" creates exigent circumstances); *State v. Arakawa,* 2003 WL 22162342 (Haw. 2003) ("exigent circumstances were present because defendant's blood alcohol was dissipating with time"); *State v. Baldwin,* 37 P.3d 1220 (Wash. App. 2001), *cert. denied,* 60 P.3d 92 (Wash. 2002) ("Exigent circumstances exist when a police officer who reasonably believes that a driver is under the influence of alcohol or drugs asks the driver to take a breath or blood test; officers have no way of knowing what drugs were in a defendant's system or how long a particular drug stays in the system of a particular person."); *State v. Carroll,* 2002 WL 1841627 (Tenn. App. 2002) (compulsory breath or blood test, taken with or without the consent of the donor, falls within the exigent circumstances exception to the warrant requirement).

Some states' courts do not presume exigency in impaired driving cases. For example, Wisconsin courts require: (1) that the blood draw is intended to obtain evidence of intoxication from a person lawfully arrested for driving under the influence of drugs or alcohol; (2) there is a clear indication that the blood draw will produce evidence of impairment; (3) the prosecution must show that the method used to take the sample is reasonable and is performed in a reasonable manner; and (4) the arrestee must present no reasonable objection to the blood draw. *State v. Krajewski*, 630 N.W.2d 219 (Wis. 2001), *cert. denied*, 537 U.S. 1089 (2002). Utah courts currently require that four factors exist prior to a warrantless, non-consensual blood draw for chemical analysis. First, the officer must have probable cause to believe that the suspect has committed an alcohol-related offense. Second, the officer must reasonably believe that the blood sample will show the suspect's level of blood alcohol or drug consumption at the time that the crime was committed. Third, the officer must reasonably believe that the delay necessary to obtain a warrant threatens the destruction of the evidence. Fourth, the method used by the officer to obtain the blood sample must be performed in a reasonable manner. *State v. Rodriguez*, 93 P.3d 854 (Utah App.), *cert. granted*, 100 P.3d 220 (Utah 2004). At the time of this book's publication, the widely criticized *Rodriguez* case had already been in the appeals process for two years.

Special government needs

In the past two decades, the Supreme Court has developed several Warrant Clause exceptions based exclusively on special needs of the government. The special needs doctrine applies when government needs beyond the normal need for law enforcement make the Fourth Amendment's warrant and probable cause requirement impracticable. *Griffin v. Wisconsin*, 483 U.S. 868 (1987). The special needs analysis uses "a balancing test that weighs the intrusion of the individual's interest in privacy against the special needs" of the government. *Ferguson v. City of Charleston*, 532 U.S. 67 (2001).

Under the special needs doctrine, warrantless drug testing of public school student athletes was justified by the school's interests in deterring drug use and maintaining discipline. *Vernonia School District 47J v. Acton*, 515 U.S. 646 (1995). Subjecting students to metal detector searches is also allowed. *C.N.H. v. State*, 927 So. 2d 1 (Fla. App. 2006); *In re Latasha W.*, 70 Cal. Rptr. 2d 886 (Cal. App. 1998). Random warrantless drug testing has also been allowed for railway operators and law enforcement officers. *Skinner v. Railway Labor Executives' Association*, 489 U.S. 602 (1989); *National Treasury Employees Union v. Von Raab*, 489 U.S. 656 (1989). Courts have also upheld warrantless entries into residences to enforce the provisions of domestic violence orders. *Parkes v. County of San Diego*, 345 F. Supp. 2d 1071 (S.D. Cal. 2004). Probationers and parolees subject to the

DNA Analysis Backlog Elimination Act of 2000 may be compelled to submit to DNA testing without a warrant and without individualized suspicion of the commission of a new crime as part of the special need to create an accurate DNA database. *United States v. Kincaid,* 379 F.3d 813 (9th Cir. 2004), *cert. denied,* 544 U.S. 924 (2005).

Probation and parole searches

Probationers and parolees enjoy only conditional liberty and thus do not have the same expectation of privacy in their homes, possessions, and vehicles. *Griffin v. Wisconsin,* 483 U.S. 868 (1987). It follows that reasonable suspicion, and not probable cause, is the standard for evaluating a probation or parole search. To constitute a valid warrantless search, the probation officer must have reasonable suspicion that the probationer has committed a probation violation or crime and that the search is reasonably related to the probation officer's duty to supervise the probationer or parolee. *Griffin v. Wisconsin,* 483 U.S. 868 (1987). The purpose of the second part of the test (reasonable connection to probation or parole supervision) is to deter officers from using probation and parole agents to perform general warrantless searches. *United States v. Lewis,* 71 F.3d 358 (10th Cir. 1995). That does not mean that probation and parole agents cannot, or should not, cooperate and work in tandem with other officers. *United States v. Watts,* 67 F.3d 790 (9th Cir. 1995), *rev'd on other grounds,* 519 U.S. 148 (1997) (collaboration between a probation officer and police does not, in itself, render a probation search unlawful). A custodial arrest of the probationer or parolee does not extinguish probation and parole search rules. *United States v. Trujillo,* 404 F.3d 1238 (10th Cir. 2005).

The Supreme Court recently upheld a California statute allowing law enforcement officers (not only probation and parole officers) to conduct suspicionless investigatory searches and seizures of parolees at any time. *Sampson v. California,* ___ U.S.___, 126 S. Ct. 2193 (2006). The Court ruled that parolees are like prisoners and have substantially diminished privacy interests. In *United States v. Knights,* 534 U.S. 112 (2001), the Court ruled that officers could search the home of a California probationer based on reasonable suspicion because he was subject to a probation condition that allowed suspicionless searches and seizures by any law enforcement officer at any time. In *Knights,* the Court did not answer the question of suspicionless searches authorized by a waiver of privacy rights contained in a parole condition. Sampson argued that officers should be required to have at least reasonable suspicion before searching. The Court disagreed: "Imposing a reasonable suspicion requirement, as urged by Sampson, would give parolees greater opportunity to anticipate searches and conceal criminality." Most states' parole schemes and the federal system do not authorize suspicionless searches and seizures of parolees; therefore, the applicability of this decision is limited.

The reasonable suspicion standard applies only to searches of parolees or probationers that are conducted by probation and parole agents. Other officers dealing with parolees and probationers must follow general search and seizure rules. However, an officer who lawfully contacts a probationer or parolee may search upon the express direction of the probation or parole agent to do so. *United States v. Dally*, 606 F.2d 861 (9th Cir. 1979). States may choose to adopt statutes similar to the California Code sections and probation/parole supervision agreements reviewed in *United States v. Knights* and *Sampson v. California,* which will offer greater search authority over probationers and parolees. Though an officer may request a probation or parole agent to determine that the search should be made, and the officer's primary motive may be to find evidence of a new crime, there must be a legitimate probation or parole reason to authorize the search. *United States v. McFarland,* 116 F.3d 316 (8th Cir.), *cert. denied,* 522 U.S. 961 (1997).

Inmate and cell searches

The United States Supreme Court has consistently ruled that there is no expectation of privacy in a prison cell or common area, such as a day room. "A right of privacy in traditional Fourth Amendment terms is fundamentally incompatible with the close and continual surveillance of inmates and their cells required to ensure institutional security and internal order. We believe that it is accepted by our society that loss of freedom of choice and privacy are inherent incidents of confinement." *Hudson v. Palmer,* 468 U.S. 517 (1984). The same doctrine applies to pretrial detainees in county jail custody. *Bell v. Wolfish,* 441 U.S. 520 (1979).

Corrections authorities have a general right to strip-search inmates (though not pretrial detainees) that includes non-invasive body cavity inspections. *Bell v. Wolfish,* 441 U.S. 520 (1979). Body cavities may be searched by appropriate medical personnel upon reasonable suspicion, although an x-ray may be just as effective and can be conducted with little articulated suspicion. *Moore v. Carwell,* 168 F.3d 234 (5th Cir. 1999). Inmates have no protection against blood extraction for purposes of DNA testing. *Shaffer v. Saffle,* 148 F.3d 1180 (10th Cir.), *cert. denied,* 525 U.S. 1005 (1998). Even so, consider obtaining a warrant if the blood extraction is for any purpose other than routine contribution of information to a DNA database. The DNA evidence won't change, and a warrant shifts the burden of a suppression hearing to the criminal defendant.

Most courts require at least reasonable suspicion before allowing a strip-search of a newly booked misdemeanor prisoner. Though strip-searches are generally allowed for convicted inmates, much more stringent rules apply to pretrial detainees. Several courts have found strip-searches of misdemeanor arrestees to be unconstitutional. *Foote v. Spiegel,* 118 F.3d 1416 (10th Cir. 1997) (noting that strip-searches are not reasonable in cases of DUI drug arrests); *Stewart v. County of Lubbock,* 767 F.2d 153 (5th Cir. 1985); *Mary Beth G. v. City of Chicago,* 723 F.2d 1263 (7th Cir. 1983); *Logan v. Shealy,* 660 F.2d 1007 (4th Cir. 1981). In a recent case where a DUI suspect was strip-searched and subjected to a body cavity search, the court ruled that the misdemeanor charge of being under the influence of drugs was not a sufficient reason for a strip-search and that the jail's blanket drug arrest strip-search policy was unconstitutional. *Way v. Ventura County,* 445 F.3d 1157 (9th Cir. 2006).

Visitor searches

Those who voluntarily go to correctional institutions surrender significant privacy expectations. Visitors may be searched upon reasonable suspicion of complicity in criminal activity. A strip-search of even a visitor may be premised upon reasonable suspicion. *Burgess v. Lowery,* 201 F.3d 942 (7th Cir.), *cert. denied,* 531 U.S. 817 (2000); *Romo v. Champion,* 46 F.3d 1013 (10th Cir.), *cert. denied,* 516 U.S. 947 (1995). With appropriate same-gender staff and personal privacy concerns met, even a body cavity search of a visitor may be based on the lower standard of reasonable suspicion. *Spear v. Sowders,* 71 F.3d 626 (6th Cir. 1995). Remember that although the legal right may exist, strip-searches and body cavity intrusions should be limited to times of true need and be accompanied by steps to preserve as much personal dignity as possible.

Once a visitor enters a facility and becomes subject to search, officers may prevent the visitor from leaving without first being searched. A prison visitor drove past several warning signs telling her that all vehicles entering prison property would be searched. An officer approached her and asked if she had drugs or weapons in her car. The visitor did not want to reply and asked to leave. The officer did not allow her to leave, searched her car, and found a gun, drugs, and nearly $23,000 in cash. The visitor claimed that the search was unreasonable because allowing her to turn and leave would have accomplished the goal of keeping drugs and guns out of the prison. The court disagreed and found that her expectation of privacy became "negligible" once she drove past the warning signs and onto prison grounds. *United States v. Prevo,* 435 F.3d 1343 (11th Cir. 2006).

Miscellaneous exceptions

Other exceptions to the warrant requirement include searches on the high seas, border and immigration searches, and searches upon entering military property closed to the public.

Exhibit 6-1
Warrantless Search Flow Chart

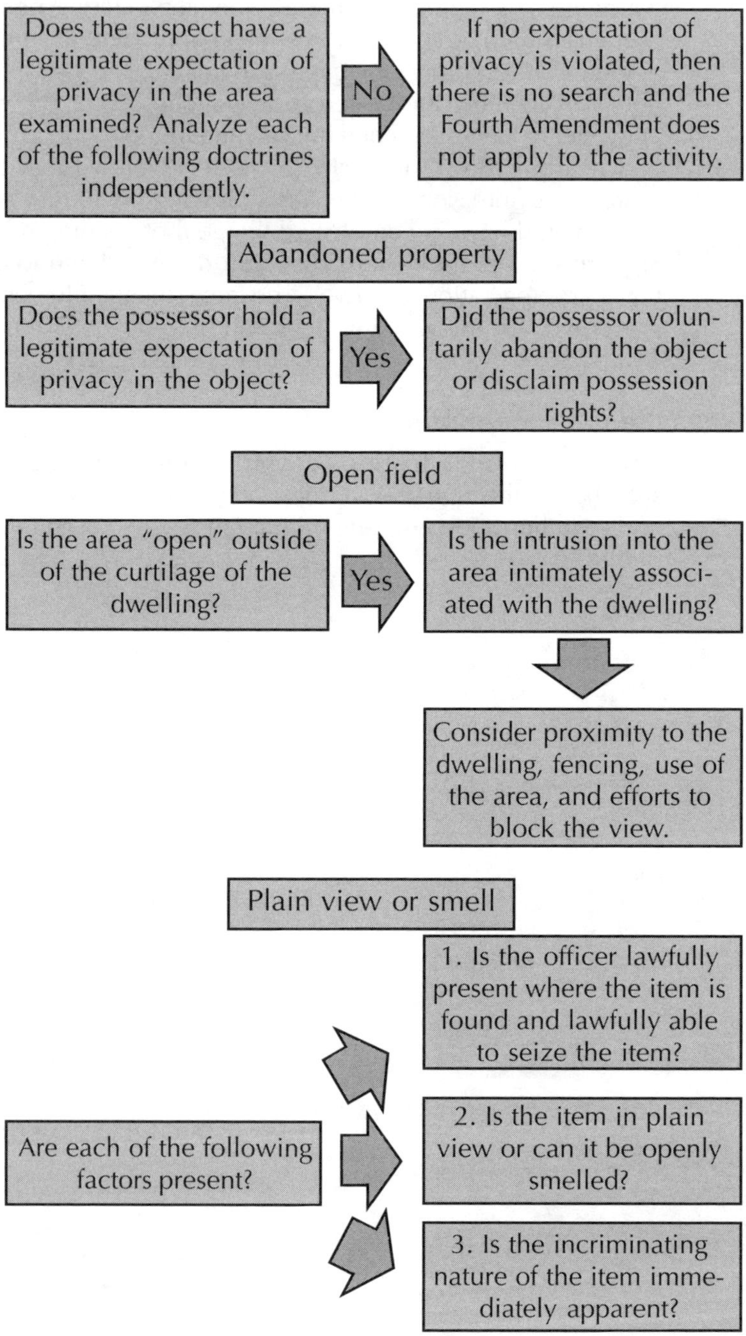

Exhibit 6-1
Warrantless Search Flow Chart (continued)

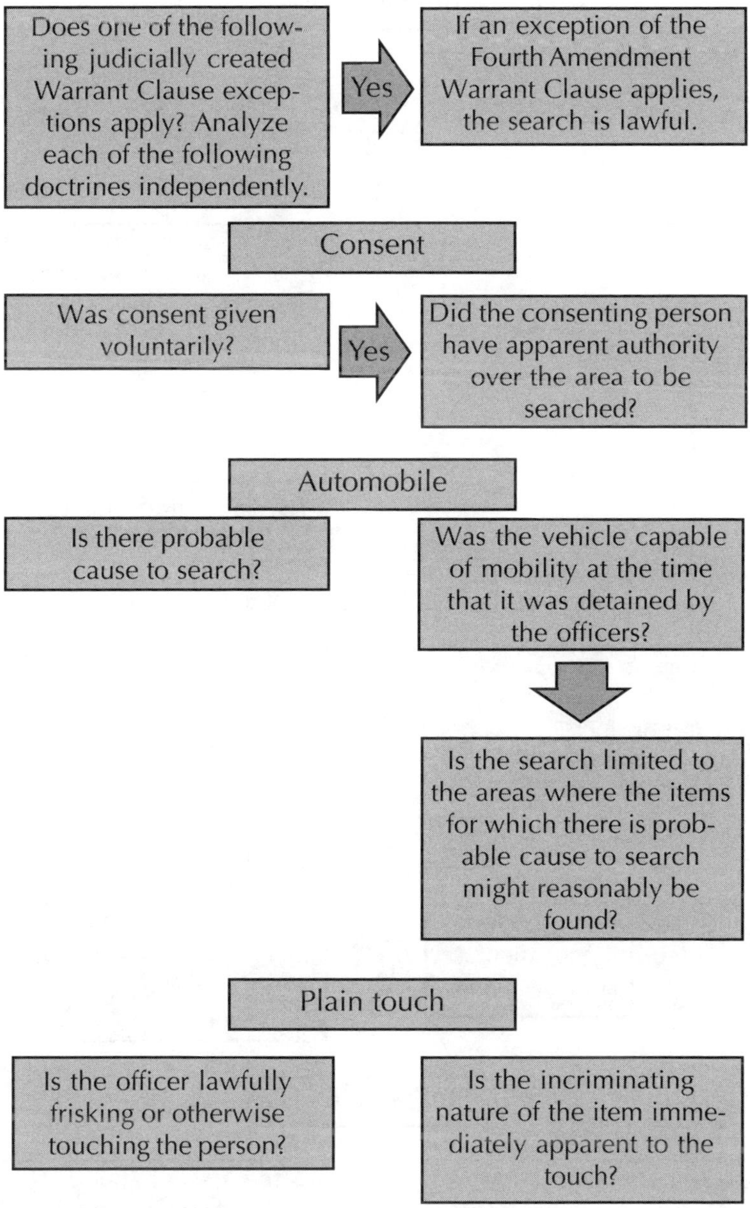

Exhibit 6-1
Warrantless Search Flow Chart (continued)

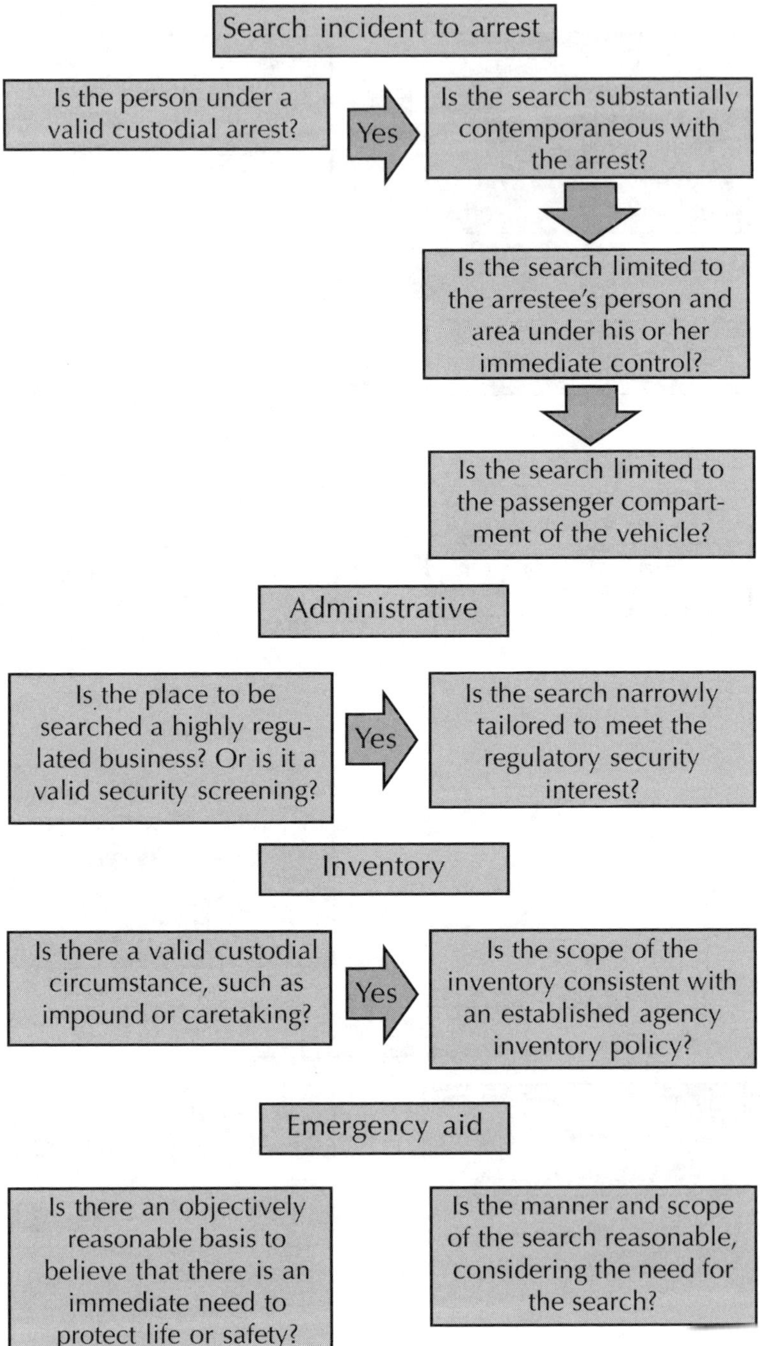

Exhibit 6-1
Warrantless Search Flow Chart (continued)

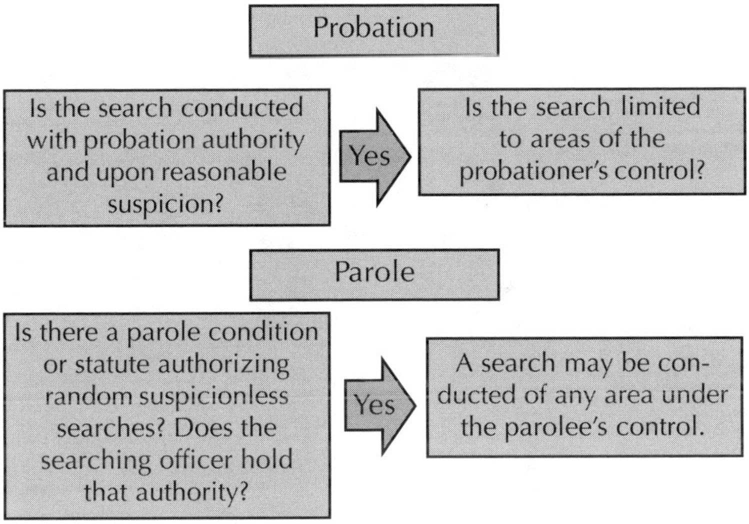

CHAPTER 7

SEARCH WARRANTS

Execution Concerns

Scope of the search warrant defining the warrant search
The area of the search
The extent of the search
Nighttime warrants
Notice and no-knock warrants
Remotely communicated warrant procedure
Protective sweep of the premises
Searches of persons present, leaving and arriving
Plain view discoveries during execution
Strip-searches and body cavity searches
Computer searches
Surreptitious entry warrants
Who may assist in executing the warrant
Service of the warrant document
Receipt required for all seized goods
Return of service

Search warrant terminology

A *search warrant* is a document that judicially authorizes police officers to search the places or persons described in the warrant. A search warrant must be based on a written *affidavit* that establishes probable cause to search. The affidavit is sworn to by an officer known as the *affiant*.

Generally, the warrant will be prepared by the officer or prosecuting attorney, but it is a court *order* after it is signed by a magistrate. The warrant and the affidavit are separate and distinct documents, but each should conform to the other. The warrant cannot be broader in scope than the affidavit.

A third document, the *return*, completes the court's warrant. The return informs the magistrate who issued the warrant about the property that was seized during the search. The return may be as simple as a photocopy of the property report or a search inventory form submitted with a cover letter.

Burden of proof for warrantless searches versus warrant searches

All searches conducted without a warrant are presumptively unreasonable, and hence illegal, unless the prosecution can establish that one of the Warrant Clause exceptions fits the circumstances. *Katz v. United States*, 389 U.S. 347 (1967). There is a strong judicial preference for warrants, "which underlies the rule that a search with a warrant has a stronger claim to justification on later judicial review than a search without one." *Illinois v. McArthur*, 531 U.S. 326 (2001). However, when officers have obtained a search warrant and the defendant challenges the lawfulness of the search, the burden is on the defendant to show that the search violated the Fourth Amendment. *Illinois v. Gates*, 462 U.S. 213 (1983).

Defendant's burden to show material false statements or reckless disregard for the truth by the officer

The defendant has a limited ability to challenge the affidavit "where the defendant makes a substantial preliminary showing that a false statement knowingly or intentionally, or with reckless disregard for the truth, was included in the warrant affidavit." *Franks v. Delaware*, 438 U.S. 154 (1978). Omitted statements that cause a misrepresentation may also be raised in the defendant's challenge to the affidavit. *United States v. Hoyt*, 47 Fed. Appx. 834 (9th Cir. 2002), *cert. denied*, 537 U.S. 1212 (2003). The defendant must show, by a preponderance of the evidence, that the false statement was essential to the finding of probable cause. *United States v. Tzannos*, 460 F.3d 128 (1st Cir. 2006). If the false statement can be disregarded and probable cause still found, the warrant will stand. *United States v. Gladney*, 48 F.3d 309 (8th Cir. 1995). Negligent mistakes or good-faith mistakes will not invalidate an affidavit that on its face establishes probable cause. *United States v. Hammett*, 236 F.3d 1054 (9th Cir.), *cert. denied*, 534 U.S. 866 (2001).

Material omissions of fact may also lead to suppression of evidence seized under the warrant. For example, an officer may neglect to inform the court that a user quantity of drugs was seen at the suspect's home more than two weeks before the affidavit was submitted. Because a user quantity would likely be consumed within the two weeks, the failure to inform the court of the passage of time renders the information stale and results in a material omission. Material omissions known to the affiant officer give the court a basis for questioning or rejecting the credibility of the officer. Omissions are made with reckless disregard if an officer withholds pertinent information that any reasonable person would convey to a reviewing judge. *Wilson v. Russo*, 212 F.3d 781 (3d Cir. 2000). When an affidavit is challenged due to a material omission, the appellate court looks at the affidavit with a sharp eye, asking whether the omitted information materially affected the issuance of the search warrant. *United States v. Runyan*, 290 F.3d 223 (5th Cir.), *cert. denied*, 537 U.S. 888 (2002).

Challenges to the warrant

The defendant may ask the trial court, or ultimately an appellate court, to consider whether the affidavit contained enough information to support the finding of probable cause. Due to the courts' strong preference for search warrants, the standard of review is very deferential to the issuing court. The reviewing court applies a common-sense standard as to whether there was a "substantial basis" in the affidavit for a finding of probable cause. *Illinois v. Gates*, 462 U.S. 213 (1983). Given this highly deferential standard, few search warrants are ever invalidated on the basis that the issuing magistrate could not have found probable cause in the affidavit. "Searches pursuant to a warrant will rarely require any deep inquiry into reasonableness, for a warrant issued by a magistrate normally suffices to establish that a law enforcement officer has acted in good faith in conducting the search." *United States v. Leon,* 468 U.S. 897 (1984); *United States v. Ventresca,* 380 U.S. 102 (1965) ("A search under a warrant may be sustainable where one without it would fail.").

The Fourth Amendment exclusionary rule

Evidence seized during an unlawful search is generally excluded in order to deter officers from willful or negligent violation of the Fourth Amendment. *Michigan v. Tucker,* 417 U.S. 433 (1974). A search may be found unlawful in many circumstances, including when the warrant is rejected, when officers exceed the proper scope of the search, and when officers violate procedural rules (such as knock-and-announce statutes). In order to claim the benefit of the exclusionary rule, a defendant must show a violation of a personal and legitimate expectation of privacy in the place searched. *Minnesota v. Carter,* 525 U.S. 83 (1998). Several exceptions may apply, principally the "good faith" exception, discussed below. Other exceptions include the inevitable discovery and independent source doctrines, the inapplicability of the exclusionary rule to civil proceedings or probation hearings, and use of the evidence to impeach a defendant. *Immigration & Naturalization Service v. Lopez-Mendoza,* 468 U.S. 1032 (1984); *Nix v. Williams,* 467 U.S. 431 (1984); *United States v. Hill,* 60 F.3d 672 (10th Cir. 1995); *United States v. Montez,* 952 F.2d 854 (5th Cir. 1992).

The "good faith" exception to the exclusionary rule

Even when a reviewing court rules that the issuing magistrate did not have a substantial basis for finding probable cause and that the warrant should be invalidated, evidence may still be admissible under the "good faith" doctrine. When an officer objectively and reasonably relies on a search warrant, the evidence will be admitted despite the warrant's failings. *United States v. Leon,* 468 U.S. 897 (1984). Only if an officer's reliance on the search warrant was "wholly unwarranted" will the evidence be suppressed. *United States v. McKneely,* 6 F.3d 1447 (10th Cir. 1993).

The good-faith doctrine will not apply when the affiant makes deliberately false statements or omissions or acts in reckless disregard of the truth. *United States v. Gonzales,* 399 F.3d 1225 (10th Cir. 2005). A court cannot give the benefit of the good-faith exception to the exclusionary rule in any of the following circumstances: first, if the issuing court was misled by information in or omissions from the affidavit that the affiant knew was false or the affiant would have known was false but for his or her reckless disregard of the truth; second, where the issuing court wholly abandoned judicial neutrality; third, where the warrant is based on an affidavit so lacking in probable cause as to render a probable cause finding entirely unreasonable; and fourth, where the warrant so poorly describes the place to be searched or the things to be seized that executing officers are unable to rely on the descriptions. *United States v. Rojas-Alvarez,* 451 F.3d 320 (5th Cir. 2006). The exclusionary rule will not generally bar admission of evidence in *civil* proceedings. *United States v. Janis,* 428 U.S. 433 (1976).

Constitutional definition of probable cause

"Probable cause is a fluid concept—turning on the assessment of probabilities in particular factual contexts—not readily, or even usefully, reduced to some neat set of legal rules." *Illinois v. Gates,* 462 U.S. 213 (1983). "Probable cause is a flexible, common-sense standard. It merely requires that the facts available to the officer would warrant a man of reasonable caution [to believe] that certain items may be contraband or stolen property or useful as evidence of a crime; it does not demand any showing that such belief be correct or more likely true than false." *Texas v. Brown,* 460 U.S. 730 (1983). "Articulating precisely what probable cause means is not possible." *Ornelas v. United States,* 517 U.S. 690 (1996).

For many years, the United States Supreme Court adhered to a two-part test for evaluating probable cause based on an informant's statement, known as the "*Aguilar-Spinelli*" test. *Spinelli v. United States,* 393 U.S. 410 (1969); *Aguilar v. Texas,* 378 U.S. 108 (1969). Under this test, the magistrate would first have to find that the source of information was credible (the veracity and reliability prong). The magistrate would next examine the basis of the information (the basis of knowledge prong). The Court later shifted to a "totality of the circumstances" test. *Illinois v. Gates,* 462 U.S. 213 (1983).

The affidavit must begin establishing probable cause to search by stating the type of criminal conduct under investigation. This is both a logical step to help the officer draft the affidavit properly and to assist the court in determining what inferences a magistrate could properly draw from the facts stated in the affidavit. For example, an affidavit that relates multiple brief visits by different persons to a certain location may not create much of an inference of criminal activity. However, if the affidavit initially states that drug trafficking is the object of the warrant, there may be a fair inference that the target is a drug-selling hub.

Sources of probable cause information and reliability

Various sources of information can help establish probable cause to search. Some are more reliable than others and need little corroboration. The main sources of probable cause include:

- **Personal observations of officers,** which provide a firm basis upon which to build probable cause. *United States v. Sparks,* 291 F.3d 683 (10th Cir. 2002). It makes little difference whether the affiant personally observed a fact or learned of the fact from another officer as long as the basis of knowledge is clearly stated in the affidavit. *Pennsylvania v. Labron,* 518 U.S. 938 (1996). The officer may either directly observe a crime or infer criminal conduct from his or her observations. *United States v. Naugle,* 997 F.2d 819 (10th Cir.), *cert. denied,* 510 U.S. 997 (1993).
- **Officer's training and experience.** The officer may reach conclusions based on prior experience or training that would not be readily apparent to a citizen. A court may rely on the training and experience of officers. *United States v. Gil,* 58 F.3d 1414 (9th Cir.), *cert. denied,* 516 U.S. 969 (1995).
- **Good-citizen informants.** Courts presume that good-citizen informants are truthful when they offer information to officers. *Commonwealth v. Kelly,* 180 S.W.2d 274 (Ky. 2005). In most cases, information provided by a citizen informant establishing the probability of criminal activity, coupled with any available corroboration, will be sufficient probable cause for a warrant. *United States v. Scalia,* 993 F.2d 984 (1st Cir. 1993). Even so, most tips can be corroborated to some degree with minimal effort, and no affidavit was ever rejected due to an excess of probable cause. Citizen informants who have provided information on prior occasions are deemed reliable. *State v. Chansamone,* 69 P.3d 293 (Utah App. 2003). Citizen informants should be named in the affidavit, yet this may be a cause for concern. An officer has an ethical obligation to explain this to the citizen and seek permission to name him in the affidavit. In addition to naming the citi-

zen informant, the affidavit should affirmatively state that the informant voluntarily came forward, is not known to be involved in the criminal activity, has no criminal record, has no known motive to lie about the information, and is not being paid for the information.

- **Anonymous tipsters.** The least reliable kind of informant is the one who declines to be identified. Thus, this informant is the least helpful in establishing probable cause. In assessing the reliability of an anonymous informant, courts consider whether the informant gave enough detail about the observed criminal activity to support a seizure. If the informant observed the details personally (and is not relaying third-party observations), the tip is considered to be more reliable. Courts also ask whether officers can corroborate the information from the anonymous informant, "either by observing the illegal activity or by finding the person, and the other material facts substantially as described by the informant. Moreover, where the reliability of the information is increased, less corroboration is necessary. Absent a risk to public safety, we expect police officers to make significant independent corroborative efforts to confirm the information." *State v. Valenzuela*, 37 P.3d 260 (Utah App. 2001); *Landon v. State*, 941 P.2d 186 (Alaska App. 1997) (even when anonymous informant has no apparent improper motivation for informing, police must make efforts to corroborate the information supplied).
- **Confidential informants: paid and twists.** Confidential informants (CIs) are either working to gain favorable treatment for their own criminal conduct (twists) or are being paid. While good-citizen informants enjoy a presumption of reliability, CIs are subject to careful scrutiny. *United States v. Levenite*, 277 F.3d 454 (4th Cir. 2002) (FBI salaried informant eligible for bonus of up to $100,000 subject to additional scrutiny); *United States v. Holmes*, 229 F.3d 782 (9th Cir. 2000). The reliability of the CI's information is assessed by the totality of the circumstances. *United States v. Smith*, 182 F.3d 473 (6th Cir. 1999). Whenever practicable, the CI should be named in the affidavit. However, keeping the CI's name confidential due to endangerment, continuing operations, or other valid reasons will not necessarily diminish the reliability of the CI's information. A variety of situations arise with CIs, and a number of methods are

used to boost the CI's credibility. Officers should use each and every method available in the affidavit.

- **Prior cases and past reliability.** One of the most common methods of showing reliability and enhancing the strength of the probable cause is to state the CI's track record. *United States v. Allen*, 211 F.3d 970 (6th Cir. 2000); *United States v. Schaefer*, 87 F.3d 562 (1st Cir. 1996). The affidavit need not specify each event where the CI has provided reliable information. However, the affidavit should contain examples of those occasions where the CI provided information and arrests or seizures have followed. The more recent the circumstances, the greater effect they will have on reliability.
- **Information provided by multiple, independent informants** about the same criminal act bolsters the reliability of the individual informants and adds to probable cause. *United States v. Artez*, 389 F.3d 1106 (10th Cir. 2004); *United States v. Spry*, 190 F.3d 829 (7th Cir. 1999).
- **Declarations against penal interest.** An informant who provides information that incriminates him or her is presumed to be truthful, for the simple reason that most criminals will hold back such information. *United States v. Harris*, 403 U.S. 573 (1971); *United States v. McWaine*, 243 F.3d 871 (5th Cir. 2001), *cert. denied*, 537 U.S. 921 (2002). Such information is also likely to be more detailed—for example, revealing the precise location of drugs or other contraband. *United States v. Lloyd*, 71 F.3d 1256 (7th Cir. 1995), *cert. denied*, 516 U.S. 1153 (1996). This kind of information is particularly helpful when accompanied by physical evidence, such as drugs from a CI who recently purchased them from a target and gave them to the officers. *United States v. Stiver*, 9 F.3d 298 (3d Cir. 1993). The fact that a CI participates in a crime—for instance, by consuming illegal drugs—will not render the CI unreliable. *United States v. Strifler*, 851 F.2d 1197 (9th Cir. 1988), *cert. denied*, 489 U.S. 1032 (1989).
- **Corroboration by investigation**. Almost any piece of information can be corroborated at some level. For example, if an informant describes the types of stolen vehicles possessed by the target, a quick drive past the residence will corroborate that the informant has a basis of knowledge concerning the vehicles. Perhaps the drive by the house will also reveal someone dismantling one of the vehicles with a cutting torch, which will provide suffi-

cient probable cause for a search warrant. *United States v. Brown*, 984 F.2d 1074 (10th Cir. 1993).

- **Surveillance.** If the information concerns continuing criminal activity, periodic surveillance may be helpful. *State v. Singleton*, 854 P.2d 1017 (Utah 1993). Similarly, corroboration may take the form of a target repeating conduct that previously involved criminal activity. *United States v. Wright*, 16 F.3d 1429 (6th Cir.), *cert. denied*, 512 U.S. 1243 (1994).
- In drug cases, an excellent method of corroboration is **the controlled purchase of drugs.** *United States v. Sidwell*, 440 F.3d 865 (7th Cir. 2006); *United States v. Richardson*, 86 F.3d 1537 (10th Cir.), *cert. denied*, 519 U.S. 1030 (1996); *United States v. Clyburn*, 24 F.3d 613 (4th Cir.), *cert. denied*, 513 U.S. 907 (1994).
- **Specificity and detail.** The CI's reliability is enhanced by the provision of specific and detailed information. *United States v. Taylor*, 985 F.2d 3 (1st Cir. 1993). The CI's personal observations also strengthen reliability. *State v. Romero*, 660 P.2d 715 (Utah 1983). If a CI provides details concerning the target's habits and criminal operations, it is likely that the CI has firsthand knowledge and has provided reliable information. *United States v. Laury*, 985 F.2d 1293 (5th Cir. 1993). It is particularly helpful when the CI provides details of unusual conduct, such as special security measures taken to protect drugs. *United States v. Sonagere*, 30 F.3d 51 (6th Cir.), *cert. denied*, 513 U.S. 1009 (1994). Information about innocent details that may be corroborated will also boost the CI's reliability. *United States v. Lalor*, 996 F.2d 1578 (4th Cir. 1993) ("Corroboration of apparently innocent details of an informant's report tends to indicate that other aspects of the report are also correct."); *United States v. Phillips*, 727 F.2d 392 (5th Cir. 1984).
- **Unwitting informants.** An unwitting informant is one who is used in tandem with a CI or undercover officer and is unaware of the investigation. *United States v. Artez*, 389 F.3d 1106 (10th Cir. 2004) (upholding probable cause for warrant based upon purchases made by "unwitting informant" whose reliability was not established); *United States v. Jordan*, 999 F.2d 11 (1st Cir. 1993) (upholding probable cause for warrant based upon purchases made by two identified unwitting individuals, whose reliability was not established, at the behest of a reliable informant). A CI may wear a wire and record or broadcast the

unwitting informant's statements establishing probable cause. The unwitting informant may be an intermediary in arranging a drug buy or in contacting a fence. The unwitting informant does not present the same credibility problems as the paid CI because the unwitting informant has no motive or opportunity for misconduct. A CI might plant narcotics in order to ensure an arrest, thereby fulfilling her part of the bargain to gain favored treatment, while an unwitting informant can have no such motivation.

- **Knowledge that a computer's owner subscribes to an unlawful child pornography site** establishes probable cause that the computer will contain illegal images. *United States v. Wagers,* 452 F.3d 534 (6th Cir. 2006); *United States v. Irving,* 452 F.3d 110 (2d Cir. 2006); *United States v. Martin,* 418 F.3d 148 (2d Cir. 2005); *United States v. Froman,* 355 F.3d 882 (5th Cir. 2004). After agents shut down the Lolita Girls child pornography Web site, agents obtained a list of subscribers. An agent relied on a multi-month subscription to Lolita Girls to create probable cause that the suspect wanted to have and intended to have child pornography images and prepared a search warrant for a suspect's computer. The agent also relayed knowledge that child pornography consumers tend to be collectors and keepers of child pornography and that the illegal images were still likely to be stored in the computer even if the suspect tried to delete them. *United States v. Gourde,* 440 F.3d 1065 (9th Cir. 2006).

Staleness of information

Fish, house guests and informants' tips begin to stink after a few days. Staleness must be considered in light of the likelihood of repetition of the criminal conduct (such as ongoing drug sales), the residential stability of the target, the character of the evidence (durable or perishable), and the type of premises to be searched. *United States v. Mathis,* 357 F.3d 1200 (10th Cir. 2004); *United States v. Bucuvalas,* 970 F.2d 937 (10th Cir. 1992), *cert. denied,* 507 U.S. 959 (1993). Other factors that guide the staleness calculation include "the character of the crime [chance encounter in the night or regenerating conspiracy?], the criminal [nomadic or entrenched?], and the place to be searched [mere criminal forum of convenience or secure operational base?]." *United States v. Hython,* 443 F.3d 480 (6th Cir. 2006). "The target's ownership of the real estate to be searched influences the staleness calculus." *United States v. Schaefer,* 87 F.3d 562 (1st Cir. 1996).

Information that the target sold drugs out of her house three weeks ago would be considered stale, while the passage of three weeks is of little concern when the target is attempting to sell a stolen Impressionist painting. Six or seven days is the outer limit for staleness of information of drug sales. *State v. Gogg,* 561 N.W.2d 360 (Iowa 1997); *People v. Mesa,* 121 Cal. Rptr. 473 (Cal. 1975). The longer the criminal activity has been continuously committed, the less concern there is for staleness. *People v. Miller,* 75 P.3d 1108 (Colo. 2003), *cert. denied,* 531 U.S. 1082 (2004).

If the warrant is later challenged on the basis of stale probable cause, an expert witness familiar with the particular type of crime may assist with testimony that the evidence is of a sort not quickly transferred or dissipated. *United States v. Laury,* 985 F.2d 1293 (5th Cir. 1993). For example, pedophiles often keep pornography indefinitely, and an expert's affidavit may be used to establish that fact and defeat a staleness concern. *United States v. Shields,* 458 F.3d 269 (3d Cir. 2006) ("collectors of child pornography rarely, if ever, dispose of their collections"); *State v. Sisson,* 903 A.2d 288 (Del. Super. 2006). Information about possession of stolen items of permanent character and enduring value, such as objects of art, is less likely to become stale than information about possession of consumable contraband (drugs). *United States v. Singer,* 943 F.2d 758 (7th Cir. 1991) (guns, unlike drugs, are durable goods useful to their owners for long periods of time; information that a suspect possessed a gun six months earlier was not too stale to support a no-knock warrant); *United States v. Waxman,* 572 F. Supp. 1136 (E.D. Pa. 1983) (stolen art), *aff'd,* 745 F.2d 49 (3d Cir. 1984).

Many courts allow a target's prior convictions to aid in building probable cause, but little weight is afforded to them. *United States v. Vinson,* 414 F.3d 924 (8th Cir. 2005) (defendant's prior conviction for drug offenses was a relevant factor in evaluating sufficiency of search warrant in drug case); *United States v. Artez,* 389 F.3d 1106 (10th Cir. 2004); *West v. State,* 768 A.2d 150 (Md. App.), *cert. denied,* 774 A.2d 409 (Md. 2001) (numerous arrests within 10 years of the issuance of the warrant are not too stale to be relevant to the probable cause determination); *State v. Clark,* 24 P.3d 1006 (Wash.), *cert. denied,* 534 U.S. 1000 (2001). Prior-conviction information should be included in the affidavit, particularly if the convictions are for crimes similar to that under investigation or they show a similar pattern of conduct. *United States v. Wilhelm,* 80 F.3d 116 (4th Cir. 1996). Even very old convictions may not be too stale to be relevant to probable cause when the prior crimes bear great similarity to the crime under investigation. *State v. Bar-Jonah,* 102 P.3d 1229 (Mont. 2004) (22-year-old conviction not too stale), *cert. denied,* 544 U.S. 1053 (2005).

A related issue is the promptness of service of the warrant. The affidavit must establish probable cause at the time the warrant is issued, and many courts express concern about the dissipation of probable cause when there is a substantial period between the issuance and execution of the warrant. *United States v. Wagner,* 989 F.2d 69 (2d Cir. 1993). The critical issue is whether probable cause existed at the time of the search. *United States v. Shegog,* 787 F.2d 420 (8th Cir. 1986) (reasonableness of search "should be functionally measured in terms of whether probable cause still existed at the time the warrant was executed"). Federal warrants must be served within 10 days of issuance but should be executed as soon as possible after issuance. *Sgro v. United States,* 287 U.S. 206 (1932), Fed. R. Crim. P. 41(d). Some states impose similar or even shorter time limits. Ariz. Rev. Stat. § 13-3918(A) (five days); Neb. Rev. Stat. § 29-815 (10 days); S.D. Codified L. § 25A-35-4 (10 days); Va. Code. § 19.2-56 (15 days). If the information supporting probable cause has become stale in the time between the issuance and execution of the warrant, the search may be ruled unreasonable and the evidence found may be suppressed. *People v. Russom,* 107 P.3d 986 (Colo. App. 2004); *State v. Peters,* 622 N.W.2d 918 (Neb.), *cert. denied,* 533 U.S. 962 (2001).

Basis of knowledge for the information

The unmistakably pungent odor of large-scale methamphetamine production may mean nothing but a noxious annoyance to the average person. To a trained and experienced officer, however, the smell surely indicates illegal activity. Officers can—and should—cite in the affidavit their training and experience relevant to the crime under investigation as a basis for their knowledge. Activity that may not be facially criminal may often form the basis for probable cause when the observing officer's experience and training are considered. *United States v. Jenkins,* 901 F.2d 1075 (11th Cir.), *cert. denied,* 498 U.S. 901 (1990).

Hearsay information may freely be used and may form the sole basis for establishing probable cause. To give the hearsay information a solid basis, corroboration is required. *Draper v. United States,* 358 U.S. 307 (1959). The interplay of the *Aguilar-Spinelli* factors (veracity and reliability of the informant and the basis of the informant's knowledge) is especially important when using hearsay information in the affidavit. The veracity prong must be bolstered by all available corroborating facts.

Physical evidence

In the course of an investigatory detention, consent search, search incident to arrest, or plain view seizure, items may be seized that lead to probable cause to search for additional evidence or contraband. For example, a recipe for methamphetamine production found in a car or on a suspect's person may be connected to a laboratory operation at some other location. *United States v. Martinez,* 808 F.2d 1050 (5th Cir.), *cert. denied,* 481 U.S. 1032 (1987). Marijuana stems and seeds found in the trash can support probable cause. Remember, there is no expectation of privacy in trash taken to the curb for collection. *People v. Thuss,* 133 Cal. Rptr. 149 (Cal. App. 2003). Depending on the quantity and packaging and connecting information, marijuana or other drugs found during a pat-down might be used to establish probable cause of drug sales at another location or, perhaps, a search of a vehicle. *United States v. Parker,* 72 F.3d 1444 (10th Cir. 1995). Officers should always consider every probable implication of physical evidence seized in the course of an investigation.

Anticipatory Search Warrants

Although search warrants normally take effect upon issuance, it is not a constitutional requirement that they do so. In the past few years, anticipatory search warrants have been used in narrow circumstances, usually in connection with controlled delivery of contraband in interstate drug and child pornography cases. Anticipatory warrants resolve the dilemma of seizing contraband or evidence before there is sufficient evidence to obtain a search warrant for a particular target location or seizing the property without a warrant upon delivery and risking exclusion of the evidence. Because the anticipatory warrant often defies the requirement of a particular description of the place to be searched, special care must be taken in the preparation of the affidavit. Generally, an anticipatory warrant should involve participation of a prosecutor.

The Supreme Court recently established a standard for consideration of probable cause to support anticipatory warrants. "Anticipatory warrants are, therefore, no different in principle from ordinary warrants. They require the magistrate to determine that it is now probable that contraband, evidence of a crime, or a fugitive will be on the described premises when the warrant is executed." All warrants are necessarily anticipatory in the context that the warrant is based on a belief that evidence will be found at the time of the search and not necessarily at the time of the affidavit preparation. Accordingly, as long as there is probable cause to believe that evidence of a crime will be at the place to be searched at the time that the warrant is lawfully executed, the warrant is valid. The Court also ruled that an anticipatory warrant does not need to plainly state the triggering condition in the warrant (though that remains a sensible practical step for officers). The warrant is valid if there is probable cause to believe that evidence will be found and that the triggering event will actually occur. Controlled delivery of known contraband meets the test. *United States v. Grubbs*, ___ U.S. ___, 126 S. Ct. 1494 (2006).

There is no requirement of exigent circumstances to obtain an anticipatory warrant. *United States v. Bieri*, 21 F.3d 811 (8th Cir. 1994). Nonetheless, take particular care to articulate how the probable cause will be established and the connection with the event triggering service of the warrant. The search should occur reasonably contemporaneously with the arrival of the contraband at the target location.

Particularity Requirements in Drafting Warrants

"Particularly describing the place to be searched"

The federal constitution and most state constitutions require that the place to be searched be particularly described. The particularity requirement is met if the officer executing the warrant can identify the place to be searched with reasonable effort. *United States v. Hang Le-Thy Tran*, 433 F.3d 472 (6th Cir. 2006); *State v. Young*, 39 P.3d 651 (Idaho App. 2002). "The test for determining the adequacy of the description of the location to be searched is whether the description is sufficient to enable the executing officer to locate and identify the premises with reasonable effort and whether there is any reasonable probability that another premise might be mistakenly searched." *United States v. Bonner*, 808 F.2d 864 (1st Cir. 1986), *cert. denied*, 481 U.S. 1006 (1987). The Supreme Court has expressed the proper standard in terms of whether a third party, unfamiliar with the premises, could locate the place to be searched from the description in the warrant. *Steele v. United States*, 267 U.S. 498 (1925).

The particularity requirement prevents general, exploratory searches. A valid warrant authorizes officers to search when and where they otherwise would have no right; consequently, the terms of the warrant dictate the scope of the officers' authority. *Maryland v. Garrison*, 480 U.S. 79 (1987). General search warrants were repugnant to the Founding Fathers; they were, in fact, one of the root causes of the American Revolution and impetus behind the inclusion of the Fourth Amendment in the Bill of Rights. *United States v. Hunt*, 505 F.2d 931 (5th Cir. 1974), *cert. denied*, 421 U.S. 975 (1975).

Technical deficiencies in the description of the place to be searched will not necessarily invalidate the warrant. *United States v. Lora-Solano*, 330 F.3d 1288 (10th Cir. 2003), *cert. denied sub nom. Cortez-Cruz v. United States*, 541 U.S. 940 (2004). With just a little effort in the drafting stage, no affidavit and warrant should ever fail the particularity test. When dealing with a single-family dwelling or a discrete business location, a street address is generally sufficient to particularly describe the premises. *United States v. Dancy*, 947 F.2d 1232 (5th Cir. 1991). Even so, going beyond a recitation of the address is the best approach. When the address proves to be incorrect, perhaps due to a simple typing error, a description of the location and physical appearance may save the warrant. *United States v. Turner*, 770 F.2d 1508 (9th Cir. 1985). In any case, the officer cannot change the warrant after it is issued even to make simple corrections. *Brown v. Byer*, 870 F.2d 975 (5th Cir. 1989).

Even if the location has a definite and well-marked address, it is helpful to describe the type of construction, main colors, and general landscaping. If there are garages, barns, or sheds, these should be described as identifying factors. The warrant will be more defensible if outbuildings are specifically listed and described. *See Extent of the Search, below.* Only those areas that could reasonably be identified as part of the described area may be searched. *State v. Young,* 39 P.3d 651 (Idaho App. 2002); *In Interest of Wilks,* 613 A.2d 577 (Pa. Super. 1992). The following description leaves little doubt about the target location:

> A single family residence, located at 123 Warren Avenue, Jeffsburg, Steed County, with forest green siding and a black shingle roof. There is a small wooden porch at the front (east approach) of the house by the main door. On the porch is a large planter with various flowers. To the left of the main (east) door is a number "123" approximately four feet above the porch. There is a detached two-car garage of the same color siding and roof to the south of the residence, parallel to the residence and approximately 20 feet from the south side of the residence. The house is fenced with a white wooden picket fence and a gate directly in front of the main (east) door.

It may be important to have the affiant officer assist in serving the warrant if there is a weakness in the description of the target location. If the officer providing the description directs officers to the target location, there is less likelihood of searching beyond the intended scope of the warrant or searching the wrong location. *United States v. Occhipinti,* 998 F.2d 791 (10th Cir. 1993). However, if the sole basis for locating the target is the affiant's knowledge, the warrant description is fatally insufficient. *United States v. Williamson,* 1 F.3d 1134 (10th Cir. 1993).

Harmony of affidavit and warrant

The description of the place to be searched should be identical in the affidavit and the warrant. If the warrant incorporates the language of the affidavit by reference to the affidavit, and the affidavit contains a sufficient description, then the particularity requirement is met. *United States v. Williamson,* 1 F.3d 1134 (10th Cir. 1993). With modern word-processing computers, this is generally an easy task. Slight deviance may be forgiven by a reviewing court, as long as the premises could be identified with reasonable effort. Some cases have upheld warrants with errors in the description when the affidavit clarified any deficiency or ambiguity. *United States v. Beaumont,* 972 F.2d 553 (5th Cir. 1991), *cert. denied,* 507 U.S. 1054 (1993); *State v. Davis,* 809 P.2d

125 (Or. App. 1991). This is particularly true if the affiant is also the officer executing the warrant or the affidavit is attached to the warrant at the time of execution. *State v. Bonynge*, 450 N.W.2d 331 (Minn. App. 1990); *State v. Anderson*, 701 P.2d 1099 (Utah 1985).

Use of diagrams and photographs

When a photograph of the building or residence can be obtained with little effort and no danger to officers and minimal likelihood of compromising the investigation, consider attaching the photograph as an exhibit to the affidavit and warrant. A simple diagram may be invaluable in the case of homes converted to apartments with no numbering identification, or in an area where a building is located in a complex with other buildings. *State v. Lutz*, 553 A.2d 657 (Me. 1989). In some cases involving rural locations with several outbuildings or remote areas with no address references, aerial photographs may be helpful. *United States v. Bieri*, 21 F.3d 811 (8th Cir.), *cert. denied*, 513 U.S. 878 (1994); *State v. Mehner*, 480 N.W.2d 872 (Iowa 1992).

Obtaining a description without committing criminal trespass

Although it is unlikely that a court would invalidate a search warrant due to the method of gathering descriptive information, whenever possible, officers should restrict their pre-warrant approach to the location to an area where they may lawfully be. *Oliver v. United States*, 466 U.S. 170 (1984) (trespass alone will not render a search invalid); *Giacona v. United States*, 257 F.2d 450 (5th Cir.) (when officers merely commit a technical trespass and not a general exploratory search, suppression is not appropriate), *cert. denied*, 358 U.S. 873 (1958). Generally, the area outside of the curtilage may be freely accessed. *See discussion of open field doctrine, above.* Even if there are "no trespassing" signs, an area or zone of approach commonly traveled by delivery persons, mail carriers and visitors may be entered.

Special concerns of rural addresses, apartments, multi-story buildings, businesses, automobiles

Describing premises within apartment complexes poses a minor challenge but one that may be a fruitful ground for suppression motions. Most buildings or complexes will have established designations, often affixed on the individual unit's main door. There may even be a building number in larger complexes. At a minimum, these identifying marks should be recited in the affidavit. Consider the use of a diagram and check the door for identifying information, such as a nameplate on the doorbell or mailbox.

The particularity requirement applies to rural locations, although the standards of description may be modified. *United States v. Bieri*, 21 F.3d 811 (8th Cir. 1994). The ultimate test is still whether an officer could locate the target with reasonable efforts. A variety of description methods may work, and it is best to use as many descriptive factors as possible. Some rural homes may be identified by rural route delivery numbers. Others can be located with utility pole numbers, global positioning satellite plots, odometer measurements from a known intersection or landmark, or distance from a state road mile marker. *See the Appendix for a description worksheet.*

Search Warrant for "All Persons Present"

A search warrant for premises does not include persons present at the target premises. *Ybarra v. Illinois*, 444 U.S. 85 (1979). In many circumstances, persons present may be detained. *See Execution Concerns, below.* However, in order to search all persons present at the target location, the warrant must so authorize. Obviously, a person who is lawfully arrested may be subject to a search incident to the arrest.

The standard for issuing a warrant to search "all persons present" at the target location is particularly stringent. *Owens ex rel. Owens v. Lott*, 372 F.3d 267 (4th Cir. 2004), *cert. denied*, 543 U.S. 1050 (2005). A minority of courts follow a blanket rule that "all persons present" warrants are unlawful. *United States v. Guadarrama*, 128 F. Supp. 2d 1202 (E.D. Wis. 2001) (acknowledging that the blanket prohibition is the clear minority rule); *State v. Cochran*, 217 S.E.2d 181 (Ga. App. 1975) (all-persons warrant is an impermissible general warrant). Where an "all persons present" warrant is allowable, the affidavit must establish probable cause to believe that all persons at the location would be involved in criminal activity. *Baker v. Monroe Township*, 50 F.3d 1186 (3d Cir. 1995). Requests to search all occupants should generally be limited to circumstances where criminal activity is open and obvious at the target location, such as production and active distribution of controlled substances. *State*

v. Babcock*, 718 N.W.2d 624 (S.D. 2006) (all-persons warrant proper where informant reported short-term traffic at all hours, children being locked out of the house during such times, and needles and drugs lying around the house).

Several factors should be articulated in the affidavit requesting authority to search all occupants. First, the target location should be a "small, confined and private" area such as a single-family residence. Second, the type of criminal activity is such that the suspects constantly shift (such as in drug sales customers) so that officers cannot practically predict who will be at the target location at any given time. Third, the items sought in the search are small enough to easily conceal on a person. *State v. Doyle*, 918 P.2d 141 (Utah 1996).

"Particularly describing the persons or things to be seized"

A second particularity requirement applies to the description of the property sought in the warrant. **Failing to particularly describe the things to be seized is fatal to the warrant**. *Groh v. Ramirez*, 540 U.S. 551 (2004). This requirement prevents the issuance of general warrants and restrains the discretion of the officer serving the warrant. *Marron v. United States*, 275 U.S. 192 (1927). Just as in the first particularity requirement, the question is whether an officer could reasonably determine what property is to be seized. *United States v. Kimbrough*, 69 F.3d 723 (5th Cir.), *cert. denied*, 517 U.S. 1157 (1995). "The particularity requirement also ensures that a search is confined in scope to particularly described evidence relating to a specific crime for which there is demonstrated probable cause." *United States v. Janus Industries*, 48 F.3d 1548 (10th Cir.), *cert. denied*, 516 U.S. 824 (1995).

Some items may be readily described with great particularity—for example, a stolen firearm with a model number, finish type, and serial number. Courts have held that a warrant referring to stolen property of a general kind is insufficient if that property is common. *United States v. Spilotro*, 800 F.2d 959 (9th Cir. 1986) (description of "gemstones and other items of jewelry" not sufficiently particular in search of jewelry store). Other items, like quantities of drugs, may not lend themselves to a highly particular description. More generic descriptive language is permitted for such items. *United States v. Layne*, 43 F.3d 127 (5th Cir.), *cert. denied*,

514 U.S. 1077 (1995). **Three factors help determine whether a description is sufficiently particular**. First, whether there is probable cause stated in the affidavit to seize all items of the particular kind. Second, whether the warrant articulates a basis for officers to distinguish the property to be seized from other property. Third, whether the items are reasonably capable of a more precise description than that listed in the warrant. *United States v. Mann*, 389 F.3d 869 (9th Cir. 2004), *cert. denied*, 544 U.S. 955 (2005).

Many officers have acquired the habit of including a phrase authorizing seizure of "evidence, fruits, contraband and instrumentalities of crimes not presently known." Such a phrase will not necessarily invalidate the warrant, but it is a magnet for suppression challenges on the basis of particularity. This is even true when the warrant describes a general class of items, such as "all stolen property." *United States v. Brown*, 984 F.2d 1074 (10th Cir.), *cert. denied*, 510 U.S. 873 (1993). If the catch-all phrase is improper, the court may sever the overbroad language and consider the remainder of the warrant. *United States v. Greene*, 250 F.3d 471 (6th Cir. 2001). A successful challenge to such catch-all phrases will not necessarily invalidate the entire warrant. If there is evidence seized that was described in a more particular portion of the warrant, that evidence will likely be admissible. *United States v. Yusuf*, 461 F.3d 374 (3d Cir. 2006); *United States v. Morris*, 977 F.2d 677 (1st Cir. 1992), *cert. denied*, 507 U.S. 988 (1993).

If it is impossible for officers to particularly describe the property sought due to the circumstances of the investigation, a catch-all description relating to a particular crime may be acceptable. *United States v. Robertson*, 21 F.3d 1030 (10th Cir.), *cert. denied*, 513 U.S. 891 (1994). A catch-all description may also be sufficient when the nature of the crime, such as drug production, does not lend itself to a highly-particularized description. *United States v. Richardson*, 86 F.3d 1537 (10th Cir.), *cert. denied*, 519 U.S. 1030 (1996). A warrant for a general class of goods may also withstand a challenge if the goods are not easily distinguishable, such as "cartons of stolen clothing" and their bills of lading. *United States v. Fucillo*, 808 F.2d 173 (1st Cir.), *cert. denied*, 482 U.S. 905 (1987).

Evidence of other crimes found in the course of executing a search warrant may be seized pursuant to the plain view doctrine. *United States v. Waldrop*, 404 F.3d 365 (5th Cir. 2005). The plain view doctrine will permit seizure of such evidence if: (1) the officers lawfully entered the area where the items could be plainly viewed; (2) the incriminating nature of the items was immediately apparent; and (3) the officers had a lawful right of access to the items. *Horton v. California,* 496 U.S. 128 (1990). In many cases, the more prudent course is to seek a second warrant. A deputy searching a computer for evidence of harassing e-mail messages saw a computer video of an adult male engaged in a sexual act with a three-year-old child. The victim of the alleged harassment became hysterical and screamed that the child being sodomized was her daughter. The deputy stopped the search and obtained a second warrant to search for evidence of child pornography. Responding to a suppression motion, the court noted that the deputy had "acted prudently" in obtaining a second warrant and admitted the evidence found. *United States v. Testerman,* 2005 WL 1047556 (W.D. W. Va. 2005).

Targets: Evidence, Contraband, Instrumentalities, and Fruits

Even if there is no question of propriety of the search, an officer may *seize* only property that constitutes an instrumentality, fruit or evidence of a crime, contraband, and property secured for safekeeping. *Soldal v. Cook County,* 506 U.S. 56 (1992). This is the critical reason for establishing a connection with criminal activity in the affidavit. The affidavit should state why an otherwise lawfully held item should be subject to seizure as an instrumentality, fruit, or evidence of a crime.

Concerns with documentary evidence

When seeking documents, books, films, recordings and other media, First Amendment free speech rights may be implicated. A high degree of specificity is required for the description of items intended to be seized on the basis of the ideas they express or images they portray. *Standford v. Texas,* 379 U.S. 476 (1965). However, there is no blanket prohibition against seizure of expressive materials. For example, documents that advocate tax protesting or extremist views may be seized when they are used to further criminal activity. *Frisby v. United States,* 79 F.3d 29 (6th Cir. 1996). Because of both First Amendment concerns and potential overbreadth of warrants seeking business records, officers would do well to involve a prosecutor to draft the affidavit and narrowly define the scope of the intended search.

Warrants seeking pornographic material must carefully describe the material in detail, or the magistrate issuing the warrant must make a determination that the material is obscene before seizure may be authorized. *Lo-Ji Sales, Inc. v. New York,* 442 U.S. 319 (1979). A warrant that leaves officers to decide whether publications or images are obscene will be invalidated. *Marcus v. Search Warrant,* 367 U.S. 717 (1961). However, warrants involving child pornography, which is not generally protected under the First Amendment, have been upheld when they contained descriptions like "films depicting sexual acts with pre-pubescent children" and material depicting "minors engaged in sexually explicit conduct as defined by statute." *United States v. Koelling,* 992 F.2d 817 (8th Cir. 1993).

When business records are sought, the description must be as specific as possible. *United States v. Le,* 173 F.3d 1258 (10th Cir. 1999). Warrants that authorize seizure of virtually all of the records of a business will usually lead to suppression. *United States v. Dale,* 991 F.2d 819 (D.C. Cir), *cert. denied,* 510 U.S. 1030 (1993). Only when the business is "fraudulent through and through" might such a broad sweep be allowed. *United States v. Bentley,* 825 F.2d 1104 (7th Cir. 1987); *United States v. Kail,* 804 F.2d 441 (8th Cir. 1986). Warrants may seek extensive and voluminous records when the description is sufficient to connect the records to the criminal scheme. *United States v. London,* 66 F.3d 1227 (1st Cir. 1995). Business records of a patently illegal operation, such as drug trafficking, may properly be sought in a warrant to search all documents, ledgers, transaction sheets, and the like. *United States v. Wicks,* 995 F.2d 964 (10th Cir. 1993).

The Affidavit

The affiant's professional resumé

The affidavit should begin with a brief recitation of professional training and experience. This is no time for modesty! This section helps establish the officer's credibility and experience, both for the issuing magistrate and, ultimately, for the reviewing courts if the warrant is challenged.

The resumé section connects an officer's experience to his or her capability to conclude that enough evidence of criminal activity will be found from the information recited in the affidavit. For example, perhaps a particular methamphetamine packaging method—such as heat-sealed drinking straws—is used in a local jurisdiction and the affidavit states that he or she recognized the package as probably containing methamphetamine. The description of the officer's five-year assignment to the narcotics enforcement team, coupled with completion of the specialized drug investigation training, provides a basis for the court to include the officer's opinions in the probable cause calculation.

Newer officers face the challenge of inexperience. A rookie who has worked traffic collision investigation and general patrol will not be able to claim experience that would allow the rookie to give opinions on complex drug trafficking arrangements. The solution is to draw on the experience of other officers by presenting the known facts, solicit their conclusions based on those facts, and articulate their relevant training and experience. This way the rookie "piggybacks" on their experiences and gradually adds to his or her own experience.

The appendices include a worksheet to assist in preparing a narrative resumé for search warrant affidavits. An officer should frequently update this resumé to include additional relevant training and experience. It may be helpful to maintain it in the body of a form affidavit. The officer may need to tailor the resumé after considering the type of crime being investigated.

Describing the crime and connecting the crime to the items sought

The affidavit must refer to criminal activity and the property sought. Probable cause requires a nexus between suspected criminal activity and the place to be searched. *United States v. Danhauer,* 229 F.3d 1002 (10th Cir. 2000). This may be as simple as stating that a burglary was reported last Wednesday. In other cases, the officer may need to describe a series of events, relate the events to the officer's experience, and offer an opinion that criminal activity is under way. This section is often referred to as establishing a "nexus" or connection to criminal activity. *Bouch v. State,* 143 P.3d 643 (Wyo. 2006); *State v. McGovern,* 45 P.3d 624 (Wash. App. 2002).

For example, assume that a confidential informant provides information about drug trafficking at a house. An officer who has other information that corroborates the informant's statements concludes that there is sufficient probable cause to obtain a search warrant. Officers want to search for not only the drugs, but also for cash, records, paraphernalia, packaging material, cellular phones, and weapons. The magistrate probably knows that a search for drugs is likely to turn up all of this and maybe more. Yet the magistrate must rely only on the facts stated in the affidavit to establish a nexus between the cash, records, etc., and not on assumptions suggested by the magistrate's experience.

An officer's conclusions must be supported by facts that create a nexus between a crime and the probable discovery of evidence in the place to be searched. For example, if a suspect is known to have purchased illegal drugs and to have then stopped by a home for a cup of coffee, there are insufficient facts to conclude that drugs will be found in the home. Though it may be possible that the suspect used the drugs at the home and left residue or paraphernalia or that the suspect even left drugs behind at the home, both are mere speculation. Thus, an affidavit claiming a nexus between the home and the drugs would fail. *State v. Dable*, 81 P.3d 783 (Utah App. 2003).

The nexus section may often include statements based on the training and experience described in the resumé section. For example:

> Based on my training and experience in narcotics enforcement, I know that drug dealers commonly possess items of paraphernalia to smoke, ingest, inhale, test, package and store their controlled substances. I have known many drug dealers, in the recent past, to keep firearms near their controlled substances, and have seen weapons present on three of the last five controlled substance search warrants that I have executed. I have found that it is common for drug dealers to keep large sums of cash that are either the profits of drug dealing or the capital to purchase additional stocks of controlled substance or both. Drug dealers keep their profits in cash because of the cash-reporting requirements imposed on banks and the dealers' mistrust of banks.

A short course in grammar and power writing

- Avoid conclusory sentences that invite suppression. Conclusory sentences are an opportunity for the court to suppress the warrant. A conclusory statement is one that presents your conclusion without the basis for the conclusion. For example, "When I opened the car door, I saw tar heroin in a foil packet on the driver's-side floor." The same information, without the conclusion, can be related just as forcefully: "When I opened the car door, I saw what I believed to be tar heroin in a foil packet. The packaging, texture, and color of the substance were consistent with tar heroin that I have seized on other occasions." Instead of describing the suspect as appearing "nervous," tell the court that the "suspect's palms were sweaty, he had a tick at the corner of his mouth, his eyes darted around the room, he licked his lips often, he was swallowing hard and his hands trembled."

- In DUI enforcement training, officers are taught to state their observations, not their conclusions. Instead of reporting that the suspect staggered as he performed the 9-step walk-and-turn test, a conscientious officer states that the suspect missed the line on steps 3, 4, 6, 7, and 9, and missed touching heel-to-toe on the same steps. Similarly, instead of stating that the suspect had poor balance, tell how many inches from center that the suspect swayed from side to side.
- It will be easier to establish the basis for your knowledge as you draft the affidavit if you return to the "who, what, where, when, how and why" questions. First, ask yourself how you know. Did you see it? Did an informant see it and tell you about it firsthand? Did you hear it? Did you smell it? What training or experience helped you to recognize it when you smelled it? What exactly do you know? When did you learn it? These questions are critical to your effort to avoid a challenge based on stale information.
- Avoid police jargon. One federal judge noted: "The agents speak in an almost impenetrable jargon. The agents involved do not get in their cars; they enter official government vehicles. They do not get out of or leave their cars; they exit them. They do not go somewhere; they proceed. They do not go to a particular place; they proceed to its vicinity. They do not watch or look; they surveille. They never see anything; they observe it. No one tells them anything; they are advised. A person does not tell them his name; he identifies himself. A person does not do something; he indicates. They do not listen to a telephone conversation; they monitor it. An agent does not hand money to an informer to make a buy; he

advances previously recorded official government funds. The agents preface answers to simple and direct questions with 'to my knowledge.' They speak in conclusions." *United States v. Marshall*, 488 F.2d 1169 (9th Cir. 1973). "Cop-speak" is not plain or simple. The officer should want the magistrate to understand the facts and conclusions. An excellent way to confuse and irritate the magistrate is to pour as much cop-speak into the affidavit as possible. Remember, too, that a reviewing judge or panel of judges may someday be reading the affidavit without an officer there to translate.

- Use the first-person active voice. Many officers seem to adopt the passive voice as the style of choice in reports and affidavits. Passive voice states that something is done to someone or something. Passive voice uses more words and is less personal than the active voice. Passive voice is weak and generally is more complex, and it often leads to confusion in the reader. Sentences written in the active voice are simpler and shorter. Responsibility for the action described is more clearly defined. The active voice is more forceful and persuasive. Consider which of the following sentences best communicates the concept: The bindle of methamphetamine was handed to the reporting officer by Dope Dealer, and it was observed and recognized by the reporting officer. Or: I saw and recognized the bindle of methamphetamine as it was handed to me by Dope Dealer. The second sentence conveys the same meaning with greater clarity and force and with fewer words. The reader, likely a busy magistrate, does not have to mentally "decode" what is said as he or she does when the passive third-person voice is used.
- Try these helps to write in active voice. Begin the sentence with the actor. Example: The arresting officer completed the property report, instead of: The property report was completed by the arresting officer. Begin the sentence with the verb when the subject is implied. Example: Complete the property report, instead of: You should complete the form. The following passive voice phrases signal poor and confusing writing and should be avoided: it has been found that, it has long been known that, it is a fact that, it is evident that, it is well known that, it may be said that. Other tired and worn phrases that signal passive voice, word clutter, and redundancy may be found in the appendices, along with suggestions for clarity.

- Don't run amok with pronouns. "When the body fell from the airplane into the Volvo station wagon carrying the pizza, it caused real trouble." What caused real trouble? The pizza? The body? The plane? Or the Volvo station wagon? Pronouns are helpful words that help avoid repetition of nouns. Yet pronouns can also confuse the reader.

Third-person pronouns pose a particular problem in affidavits. In the following paragraph, drawn from an example where the affiant is relying on an informant's conversation with a drug dealer, try to identify who did what and who said what to whom. The names of the persons who provided the information have been replaced with third-person pronouns.

> On November 30, 2006, I met with Confidential Informant 10-35 of the Metropolitan Narcotics Task Force, who told me that two days prior, he had spoken to another informant, Confidential Informant 10-96, who told him that he had recently been able to obtain methamphetamine in multiple-gram quantity from Mike Curry. He said that he also can get marijuana in large amounts.

The last sentence leaves the reader in doubt as to who can get marijuana. Is it Confidential Informant 10-35 or the other informant or Mike Curry? Revising the paragraph using the first person voice and omitting pronouns, the passage reads as follows:

> On November 30, 2006, I met with Confidential Informant 10-35 (CI 10-35), of the Metropolitan Narcotics Task Force, who told me that, two days earlier, CI 10-35 spoke to another informant, Confidential Informant 10-96 (CI 10-96). CI 10-96 told CI 10-35 that CI 10-96 had recently been able to obtain methamphetamine in multiple-gram quantity from Mike Curry. CI 10-96 also told CI 10-35 that Curry also can get marijuana in large amounts.

Execution Concerns

Scope of the search warrant defining the warrant search

The particularity requirement relating to the description of the items to be seized governs the scope of the search under the warrant. *United States v. Janus Industries,* 48 F.3d 1548 (10th Cir.), *cert. denied,* 516 U.S. 824 (1995). Seized evidence that is not described in the warrant may be suppressed if the plain view doctrine does not apply. A gross deviation from the scope of the warrant may result in suppression of all seized evidence, even the items described in the warrant. *United States v. Medlin,* 842 F.2d 1194 (10th Cir. 1988). Officers executing the warrant are responsible for ensuring that the warrant adequately describes the place to be searched and the persons or things to be seized, and they may face civil liability if they fail to do so. *Groh v. Ramirez,* 540 U.S. 551 (2004).

There are two main issues that arise from the scope of the warrant search. These questions arise most frequently when the warrant's description of the place to be searched is inadequate. The first issue is the area of the search itself and the question of whether vehicles, outbuildings and yards are to be searched. The second issue involves the scope of the search into locked cupboards and containers, damage done to them, and the size of the particular cupboards, drawers, and containers examined.

The area of the search

A general description of the building, accompanied by terms such as "premises" or "curtilage," in the warrant will allow a search of the building itself, the surrounding yard, garage, and unattached sheds. *United States v. Griffin,* 827 F.2d 1108 (7th Cir. 1987), *cert. denied,* 485 U.S. 909 (1988); *United States v. Bonner,* 808 F.2d 864 (1st Cir. 1986), *cert. denied,* 481 U.S. 1006 (1987); *Brown v. State,* 425 S.E.2d 856 (Ga.), *cert. denied,* 510 U.S. 998 (1993). Even so, officers should include the description of all outbuildings in the affidavit and warrant. Far better to do it right than to invite a suppression hearing roll of the dice.

Vehicles on the premises that appear to be under the control of the occupant of the target location may be searched under the authority of a warrant for building and premises. *United States v. Duque,* 62 F.3d 1146 (9th Cir. 1995), *cert. denied,* 519 U.S. 819 (1996); *United States v. Gottschalk,* 915 F.2d 1459 (10th Cir. 1990); *United States v. Percival,* 756 F.2d 600 (7th Cir. 1985). Many courts decline to allow searches of visitors' vehicles. *State v. Leathers,* 806 P.2d 718 (Or. App. 1991). A truck with a camper may be searched and the camper can too. *United States v. Napoli,* 530 F.2d 1198 (5th Cir.), *cert. denied,* 429 U.S. 920 (1976). A warrant to search a motel room may include authority to search the renter's car in the motel parking lot. *Menendez v. State,* 521 So. 2d 210

(Fla. App. 1988), *rev'd in part,* 562 So. 2d 858 (Fla. 1990). Even so, the best practice is to include a description of the vehicles in the affidavit and warrant.

Some courts allow searches of any vehicles that enter the premises during the search. As officers searched a residence, a suspect drove onto the property. He made inconsistent claims about ownership of the Hummer that he was driving and he had no registration for it. The warrant authorized searches of all vehicles found at the residence. A large truck had already been searched, and officers found 13 kilos of cocaine and over a half-million dollars in cash. Officers searched the Hummer and found $45,000 in cash, identification documents, and a key to the truck where the large quantity of cash and drugs were hidden.

The suspect challenged the search on the grounds that the Hummer was not on the premises when the warrant service began. The court found that the Hummer was properly searched under the search warrant. The fact that it arrived after the warrant service began was not critical and did not trump the warrant provision allowing searches of all vehicles on the premises. The court recognized that sometimes searches take hours and that the warrant was not limited in "temporal authority" to the vehicles at the premises at the start of the warrant execution. As long as the type of contraband sought in the warrant (drugs) could be hidden in the vehicle, it could be searched. *United States v. Tamari,* 454 F.3d 1259 (11th Cir. 2006); *United States v. Alva,* 885 F.2d 250 (5th Cir. 1989).

The extent of the search

"If officers are searching for a canary's corpse, they can search a cupboard, but not a locket. If they are looking for an adolescent hippopotamus, they can search the living room or the garage but not the microwave oven." *United States v. Evans,* 92 F.3d 540 (7th Cir.), *cert. denied,* 519 U.S. 1020 (1996). The general rule governing the extent of **a warrant search allows officers to open any area or container that could possibly conceal the items particularly described and authorized for seizure** by the warrant. *United States v. Ross,* 456 U.S. 798 (1982). Officers may force cabinets, drawers, cupboards, and other containers as necessary to complete the search. *United States v. Canestri,* 518 F.2d 269 (2d Cir. 1975). Obviously, no property may be unnecessarily destroyed or damaged. *Ginter v. Stallcup,* 869 F.2d 384 (8th Cir. 1989). A search that goes beyond the extent necessary to locate the items sought will result in suppression of evidence. *Arizona v. Hicks,* 480 U.S. 321 (1987).

A warrant to search a residence includes authority to search the surrounding yard. *United States v. Pennington,* 287 F.3d 739 (8th Cir.), *cert. denied,* 537 U.S. 1022 (2002). Generally, a warrant to search a residence includes authority to search all outbuildings within the curtilage. *United States v. Bennett,* 170 F.3d 632 (6th Cir. 1999) (search of multiple buildings on property was proper because "there is no need to search for evidence to link the outbuilding to the allegations in the affidavit; the shop building and the residence are sufficiently connected because they are both within the curtilage of the property"); *United States v. Alexander,* 761 F.2d 1294 (9th Cir. 1985) (a warrant to search "all buildings, outbuildings, garages, yard areas, trash containers, storage areas and containers used in connection with or within the curtilage of said premises and buildings" could include every structure on a 40-acre ranch). The preferable course is to include a description of the outbuildings in the affidavit and warrant and, where possible, state particular probable cause for each outbuilding.

The description of the things to be seized should be drafted not only to meet the constitutional particularity requirement but also to permit a reasonably extensive search. For example, in an assault or homicide case, the affidavit and warrant should describe hair and fiber evidence, and thus the search could extend even into envelopes and papers found. *United States v. Doherty,* 867 F.2d 47 (1st Cir.), *cert. denied,* 492 U.S. 918 (1989). A warrant describing keys allows a search of the pockets of clothing in a closet. *United States v. Tolerton,* 669 F.2d 654 (10th Cir.), *cert. denied,* 456 U.S. 949 (1982). A warrant authorizing a search for drug couriers' and customers' addresses and phone numbers permits retrieval of numbers from an electronic pager or cellular telephone. *United States v. Meriwether,* 917 F.2d 955 (6th Cir. 1990). A warrant for business documents authorizes search of the shelves and containers in the garage and cars. *State v. Romero,* 660 P.2d 715 (Utah 1983).

Once the items described in the warrant are located, the search must stop. *United States v. Gagnon,* 635 F.2d 766 (10th Cir. 1980), *cert. denied,* 451 U.S. 1018 (1981). Again, the prosecutor or officer drafting the warrant may have considerable influence over the extent of the search through proper description of the things to be seized. Searches withstand challenges based on the extent of the search when the affidavit and warrant have described a broad class of documents. *State v. Romero,* 660 P.2d 715 (Utah 1983). Similarly, when a warrant describes "any and all marijuana," officers have been allowed to search beyond the initial discovery of drugs, because they could not know if all marijuana had been found. *United States v. Corbett,* 518 F.2d 113 (8th Cir. 1975).

Execution of the search may not extend beyond a reasonable time. Many courts have approved of residential searches lasting several hours. *United States v. Carter,* 854 F.2d 1102 (8th Cir. 1988). Officers may also remain on the premises for a reasonable time after the search in order to wait for transportation or for the security of bulky or large items. *United States v. Gagnon,* 635 F.2d 766 (10th Cir. 1980), *cert. denied,* 451 U.S. 1018 (1981). However, the search cannot be dragged out in hopes that the occupants will return and then be subject to arrest. *United States v. Corrado,* 803 F. Supp. 1280 (M.D. Tenn. 1992).

Nighttime warrants

Federal law dictates that search warrants be executed during the daytime unless there is good cause for a nighttime search or unless controlled substances are the subject of the warrant and nighttime execution is authorized. Fed. R. Crim. P. 41(e)(2)(B) ("The warrant must command the officer to execute the warrant during the daytime, unless the magistrate for good cause expressly authorizes execution at another time."); 21 U.S. Code § 879 ("Search warrant relating to offenses involving controlled substances may be served at any time of the day or night if the judge or United States magistrate issuing the warrant is satisfied that there is probable cause to believe that grounds exist for the warrant and for its service at such time."). Many states have limited nighttime search warrants to searches with reasonable cause to believe that evidence will be concealed, destroyed, damaged, or altered if the search is delayed or if there is other good cause for the nighttime search. Ark. R. Crim. P. 13.2(c) (warrants may only be executed after 8:00 p.m. upon a finding of exigent circumstances); Del. Code Ann. tit. 11, § 2308 (permitting nighttime warrant issuance only when it is "necessary in order to prevent the escape or removal of the person or thing to be searched for"); Me. R. Crim. P. 41(c) (requiring that the warrant affirmatively authorize execution at a time other than between the hours of 7:00 a.m. and 7:00 p.m.); Neb. Rev. Stat. § 29-814.04 (warrant service limited to 7:00 a.m. to 8:00 p.m.). A few have no such restrictions. Kan. Stat. Ann. § 22-2510 ("A search warrant may be executed at any time of any day or night.").

Good cause for nighttime execution might include the suspect's use of surveillance devices effective during the daytime, the imminent consumption or movement of drugs, or where the cover of darkness is essential to officer safety. *McCormick v. State*, 48 S.W.3d 549 (Ark. App. 2001); *State v. Purser*, 828 P.2d 515 (Utah App. 1992). It may also be sufficient that there is information that the drug trafficking occurs only at night and therefore drugs are not likely to be found at the target location during the day. *State v. Ruiz*, 843 P.2d 1044 (Utah App. 1992). As long as the search is properly initiated in the daytime, the search will not be invalidated if it continues into the night. *United States v. Young*, 877 F.2d 1099 (1st Cir. 1989).

If safety reasons are cited, the affidavit should state how a nighttime search would enhance officer safety and not unduly endanger civilians. For example, the terrain surrounding the target location and the need for surreptitious approach may warrant a nighttime search. Nighttime service might also be appropriate where the suspects use guards or look-outs and nighttime service would prevent the alerting of the suspects. Similarly, if small children are present at the target location during the day but not at night, public safety could be enhanced with a nighttime search. In some circumstances, there may be a valid argument that a nighttime search would be less intrusive than a daytime search—for example, when a business is open to the public during the day. Merely stating that the suspect will not be home during the day will not justify a nighttime search.

Notice and no-knock warrants

The knock-and-announce rule is not a constitutional provision, but it is a well-established part of the common law and applies to the execution of search warrants. *Miller v. United States*, 357 U.S. 301 (1958). Most states and the federal government prohibit or regulate no-knock warrant authorization. Even though it is not a constitutional doctrine, failure to obey the knock-and-announce rule may render a search constitutionally unreasonable. *Wilson v. Arkansas*, 514 U.S. 927 (1995).

Officers executing federal search warrants must knock and announce their authority and purpose unless there are exigent circumstances. 18 U.S. Code § 3109 (officer may use force to enter if "after notice of his authority and purpose, he is refused admittance or when necessary to liberate himself or a person aiding him in the execution of the warrant"). "Section 3109 includes an exigent circumstances exception and the exception's applicability in a given instance is measured by the same standard we articulated in *Richards." United States v. Ramirez,* 523 U.S. 65 (1998). In *Richards v. Wisconsin,* 520 U.S. 385 (1997), the Supreme Court disapproved of a blanket exception to the knock-and-announce requirement for felony drug cases. The Court ruled that entry without notice would be reasonable when officers have "reasonable suspicion that knocking and announcing their presence, under the particular circumstances, would be dangerous or futile, or that it would inhibit the effective investigation of the crime by, for example, allowing the destruction of evidence."

When officers observe obvious signs that the occupants of the target location are aware of the officers' presence and are taking steps to prevent or delay the officers' entry or destroy evidence, officers may enter without waiting for a response. *United States v. Stiver,* 9 F.3d 298 (3d Cir. 1993). The officers should still announce their presence and possession of a search warrant as they enter. If notice is not feasible in such circumstances, the warrant will not be invalidated for lack of notice. *United States v. Tracy,* 835 F.2d 1267 (8th Cir.), *cert. denied,* 486 U.S. 1014 (1988).

Without a no-knock warrant or a proper exigency, officers must knock and announce themselves, state that they have a search warrant, and wait for a reasonably prompt response. If there is no response, officers may use whatever force is necessary for them to enter. The Tenth Circuit Court of Appeals has ruled that a 5- to 10-second wait, in the morning when people may still be in bed, is unreasonably short. *United States v. Gallegos,* 314 F.3d 456 (10th Cir. 2002). On the other hand, the U.S. Supreme Court held that waiting 15 to 20 seconds after a knock before forcing entry was reasonable where the evidence sought could be easily destroyed. *United States v. Banks,* 540 U.S. 31 (2003). The reasonableness of the wait for a response is evaluated on a case-by-case basis.

Despite the Supreme Court's rejection of blanket approval for no-knock warrants when searching for controlled substances in *Richards v. Wisconsin,* many courts have been quick to issue no-knock warrants when small amounts of drugs, paraphernalia, or manufacturing equipment or chemicals are sought. *Doran v. Eckold,* 409 F.3d 958 (8th Cir.) (no-knock entry appropriate due to unique dangers of clandestine methamphetamine labs), *cert. denied,* ___ U.S. ___, 126 S. Ct. 736 (2005); *Commonwealth v. Rodriguez,* 614 N.E.2d 649 (Mass. 1993) (no-knock entry lawful in search where large quantities of cocaine held and the affidavit included evidence that drug dealers often carry handguns to protect themselves); *State v. Purser,* 828 P.2d 515 (Utah App. 1992). If officers have information that suspects follow special security precautions or store drugs near sinks or toilets, that information should be stated in the affidavit. *State v. Trujillo,* 854 P.2d 603 (Utah App. 1993).

A variety of other circumstances have been found sufficient to excuse the knock-and-announce requirement. *United States v. Segura-Baltazar,* 448 F.3d 1281 (11th Cir. 2006) (pre-warrant inspection of suspect's trash revealed surveillance device, packaging containers and discarded ammunition boxes); *United States v. Stevens,* 439 F.3d 983 (8th Cir. 2006) (sawed-off shotgun was kept readily accessible in the house to be searched); *United States v. Musa,* 401 F.3d 1208 (10th Cir.) (suspect had criminal record of violent crimes and assault on law enforcement officer), *cert. denied,* ___ U.S. ___, 126 S. Ct. 295 (2005). One court summarized the general circumstances excusing notice as: (1) occupants at the place to be searched are already aware of the officers' authority and purpose; (2) officers have reasonable belief that an occupant is in imminent peril of bodily harm; or (3) officers have a reasonable belief that the occupants are aware of their presence and are attempting to flee or destroy evidence. *United States v. Bates,* 84 F.3d 790 (6th Cir. 1996). Officers may also be excused from knocking and announcing when the door is open, but in that situation, giving notice to those inside will provide additional protection against an effort to suppress evidence found in the search. *United States v. Mendoza,* 281 F.3d 712 (8th Cir.), *cert. denied,* 537 U.S. 1004 (2002); *United States v. Remigio,* 767 F.2d 730 (10th Cir.), *cert. denied,* 474 U.S. 1009 (1985). A few courts have held to the formal requirement of knocking on an open door. *Commonwealth v. Martinelli,* 729 A.2d 628 (Pa. Super.), *cert. denied,* 743 A.2d 917 (Pa. 1999) (acknowledging minority rule and applying state constitution).

Until recently, federal courts disagreed on the proper remedy for a violation of the knock-and-announce rule. The Supreme Court recently ruled that failure by police to knock and announce their authority and their intent to enter prior to execution of a search warrant does not require the remedy of suppression of the evidence seized. Several Detroit police officers served a search warrant for drugs and guns on the home of Booker Hudson. The first officer approached the door and yelled "Police, Search Warrant!" but did not actually knock. The officers entered approximately three to five seconds later and found both cocaine and a loaded gun.

The Supreme Court affirmed the validity of the knock-and-announce rule, but held that the rule has nothing to do with the propriety of the actual seizure of evidence. Rejecting suppression of evidence as a proper remedy for failure to knock and announce, the Court noted that there are still remedies available to aggrieved citizens through filing a civil suit for money damages. Significantly, the justices also cited improved police training and internal discipline systems as a deterrent to civil liberties errors. *Hudson v. Michigan*, ___ U.S. ___, 126 S. Ct. 2159 (2006).

Obtaining a no-knock warrant may not be the only way to enter the target location without alerting the occupants. Officers may use trickery to entice the occupants into opening the door. Entry by deception should be reserved for those situations where giving notice or entering rapidly by force would endanger safety or likely result in destroyed evidence. One effective method is to knock on the door while announcing "Federal Express" or the name of some other delivery service. *United States v. Contreras-Ceballos*, 999 F.2d 432 (9th Cir. 1993). Most criminals will respond eagerly to a pizza delivery. *Adcock v. Commonwealth*, 967 S.W.2d 6 (Ky. 1998) (lawful entry when one officer knocked, called out "Pizza delivery," then officers announced "Police, Search Warrant!" before crossing the threshold); *State v. Moss*, 492 N.W.2d 627 (Wis. 1992), *cert. denied*, 507 U.S. 977 (1993). It helps to order a pizza prior to the warrant execution. (The officers, not the criminals, should enjoy the pizza.) Officers may pretend to be a United States postal carrier. *Hrubec v. United States*, 734 F. Supp. 60 (E.D.N.Y. 1990). Courts have even approved novel tactics such as luring an occupant outside by setting off his car alarm. *People v. Witherspoon*, 576 N.E.2d 1030 (Ill. App. 1991). An officer convinced one person to open the door by knocking and announcing that the officer had just accidentally struck the occupant's car. *State v. Mastracchio*, 721 A.2d 844 (R.I. 1998). One creative officer successfully lured an occupant to the door by pretending to be a prostitute's customer. *Criales v. United States*, 621 A.2d 374 (D.C. Ct. App. 1993).

Remotely communicated warrant procedure

A number of states and federal rules provide procedures for remotely communicated search warrants, generally by telephone, radio, or facsimile, though e-mail warrants are possible. Fed. R. Crim. P. 41(d)(3); Ala. R. Crim. P. 3.8(b); Alaska Stat. §§ 12.35.010; 12.35.015; Ariz. Rev. Stat. § 13-3914; Cal. Penal Code § 1526; Idaho Code § 19-4404; Ind. Code § 35-33-5-8; Iowa Code § 321J.10; § 462A.14D (telephonic warrants for blood samples in cases of impaired driving or boating only); Kan. Stat. Ann. §§ 22-2502; La. Code Crim. Proc. Ann. art. 162.1; Mich. Comp. Laws Ann. § 780.651; Minn. R. Crim. P. 36.08; Mont. Code Ann. § 46-5-221; Neb. Rev. Stat. §§ 29-814.03 & 29-814.05; Nev. Rev. Stat. 179.045(2); N.J. Rules of Court 3:5-3; N.Y. Crim. Proc. Law §§ 690.35 & 690.36; N.C. Gen. Stat. Ann. § 15A-244, 245; N.D. R. Crim. P. 41(c)(2); Or. Rev. Stat. § 133.545(5); S.D. Codified Laws § 23a-35-5; Wash. Sup. Ct. Crim. R. 2.3(c); Wis. Stat. Ann. § 968.12(3). Mississippi courts have specifically rejected telephonic warrants. *White v. State,* 842 So. 2d 565 (Miss. 2003). A few states without applicable statutes have allowed telephonic warrants under the exigent circumstances approach. *State v. Speid,* 605 A.2d 297 (N.J. Super. 1992) (when exigent circumstances are present, the court may issue a telephonically authorized search warrant). One state has adopted a broad scheme that allows for the high-tech communication of affidavits and warrants by e-mail and other computer-based communication techniques. Utah Code Ann. § 77-23-204(2); Utah R. Crim. P. 40.

A remotely communicated warrant must meet the same probable cause standards as any other search warrant. The requesting officer should prepare the warrant prior to calling the magistrate. The officer should prepare a complete warrant. The following procedure provides a general guide to compliance with state remotely communicated warrant procedures. Officers should become familiar with local rules and procedures before seeking a remotely communicated warrant.

The entire warrant application must be recorded and later transcribed, so the affiant must have a tape-recording of the conversation with the magistrate. In the case of an application by facsimile or e-mail, the officer should preserve a copy of the written communication. The affiant first should ask the magistrate to administer an oath of truthfulness to the affiant before the affiant reads the warrant to the magistrate. It is helpful, but not necessary, to have another officer present to witness the application process and the administration of the oath.

After taking the oath, the affiant reads the entire affidavit to the magistrate. The magistrate may then decide that the affidavit contains sufficient probable cause to issue the warrant, or the magistrate may inquire further into probable cause. The magistrate may order modification of the affidavit. The affiant should note these modifications on the affidavit.

Once the magistrate has determined that there is sufficient probable cause contained in the affidavit, the affiant should read the proposed warrant to the magistrate. The affiant should discuss specific authorization for a no-knock warrant if it is needed. The officer must also ask for authorization to serve the warrant in the nighttime, if appropriate. If the magistrate authorizes the warrant, the magistrate will direct the affiant to sign his or her name to the warrant. Once the warrant is approved, the officer should serve and execute it as he or she would any other warrant. A telephonic warrant may be valid for several days from the time of issuance, depending on local rules; however, if the warrant is not served promptly, a regular written warrant should be obtained if possible.

Protective sweep of the premises

Officers executing a warrant may conduct a limited protective sweep of the premises to discover persons who might present a danger to the officers if there is a reasonable belief that the premises conceal such a person. *Maryland v. Buie,* 494 U.S. 325 (1990). There is no general right to conduct a protective sweep; there must be specific, articulable facts that there may be persons hiding who present a danger to officers. *United States v. Cunningham,* 133 F.3d 1070 (8th Cir.), *cert. denied,* 523 U.S. 1131 (1998). This rule applies even if the sweep would exceed the scope of the search warrant or area that may be searched incident to arrest. *United States v. Cavely,* 318 F.3d 987 (10th Cir. 2003). However, officers need not limit protective sweeps to circumstances where they hear movement or perceive other physical signs that persons may be hiding. *United States v. Winston,* 444 F.3d 115 (1st Cir. 2006) (suspect's violent history, girlfriend's misleading statements during warrant execution, and suspect's suspiciously prompt surrender combined to allow a full protective sweep of the home even without evidence that some other person who presented a danger to officers was in the home). The sweep may last only long enough to dispel the reasonable suspicion of danger and no longer than it takes to complete the arrest and depart the area. *Maryland v. Buie,* 494 U.S. 325 (1990).

A typical protective sweep involves the inspection of other areas of a building where officers have already entered. However, when a person is arrested just outside of a residence, a protective sweep of the residence may be justified. *United States v. Wilson,* 306 F.3d 231 (5th Cir. 2002), *cert. denied,* 537 U.S. 1240 (2003). Officers may even be justified in "sweeping" a nearby business when arresting persons are believed to have used the business as a base to commit crimes or where other suspects may be found. *United States v. Soria,* 959 F.2d 855 (10th Cir.), *cert. denied,* 506 U.S. 882 (1992). The issue is always whether there is a reasonable belief that persons who could harm officers are concealed on the premises. If the officers cannot state why they believe that other suspects may be hiding in a nearby home or business, then no protective sweep can happen.

A protective sweep may also be conducted for the protection of potential injured victims. *United States v. Tisdale,* 248 F.3d 964 (10th Cir. 2001), *cert. denied,* 534 U.S. 1153 (2002); *United States v. Arch,* 7 F.3d 1300 (7th Cir. 1993), *cert. denied,* 510 U.S. 1139 (1994). Officers may conduct a protective sweep when searching an area for fleeing suspects. *United States v. Arcobasso,* 882 F.2d 1304 (8th Cir. 1989). This is, essentially, an exigent circumstances search. All persons entering, present, or leaving may be searched when the warrant authorizes search of "all persons present." *See above for probable cause requirements for warrants authorizing a search of all persons present.*

Searches of persons present, leaving, and arriving

When persons are found at the target location, they may not be searched without probable cause—not mere reasonable suspicion—to believe that they may be holding the items sought in the warrant. Normal rules for *Terry* frisks apply. *Denver Peace & Justice Committee v. City of Golden,* 405 F.3d 923 (10th Cir. 2005). If persons are arrested, either on the basis of evidence located during the search or for some other reason, such as an outstanding warrant, they may be searched incident to arrest. Persons present should be asked to voluntarily provide identification so that they may be listed as witnesses in the appropriate reports. Mere presence at the site of warrant execution is not a basis to command identification.

A search warrant for a residence carries the implicit authority to detain persons at the target location during the search. *Michigan v. Summers,* 452 U.S. 692 (1981). Persons either leaving or arriving at the premises may be detained only if there is reasonable suspicion that they are involved in criminal activity. *United States v. Taylor,* 716 F.2d 701 (9th Cir. 1983). Patrons of a business where a search warrant is served should be detained only upon reasonable suspicion of their involvement in criminal activity. *People v. Ingram,* 21 Cal. Rptr. 2d 33 (Cal. App. 1993). The duration of the detention must not be excessive, or it may later be found unconstitutional based on the scope. *Franklin v. Foxworth,* 31 F.3d 873 (9th Cir. 1994). Persons who disrupt the search, whether occupants of the premises or mere visitors, may be required to leave. *United States v. Gantt,* 194 F.3d 873 (9th Cir. 1999).

If the affidavit has established probable cause that persons at the scene are likely to be involved in criminal activity, it is more likely that persons arriving or leaving may be lawfully searched. For example, if the affidavit established that a location was the scene of frequent drug deliveries and sales, it would be proper to search a person driving into the driveway of the residence. *United States v. Barrett,* 890 F.2d 855 (6th Cir. 1989). Specific information in the affidavit as to the identity of persons involved in criminal activity, such as a description of the persons selling drugs, would also justify a search of persons at the scene and who meet that description. *Louis v. State,* 373 S.E.2d 231 (Ga. App. 1988).

Many courts have approved limited frisks of persons present during the execution of search warrants where the underlying crimes suggested a reasonable likelihood of violence or resistance. *State v. Trine,* 673 A.2d 1098 (Conn. 1996) (allowing a *Terry* frisk at scene of a search warrant execution when probable cause affidavit related a high probability that weapons would be at the scene even though the suspect followed officer's orders and was handcuffed prior to the frisk); *People v. Thurman,* 257 Cal. Rptr. 517 (Cal. App. 1989) (*Terry* frisk allowed during the execution of a search warrant for drugs because officers "were engaged in an undertaking fraught with the potential for sudden violence"). A number of courts have allowed weapons frisks of all persons present or arriving at the scene of the warrant execution based solely or primarily on the implicit connection between drug manufacturing and trafficking (not necessarily drug possession alone) and the possession of weapons. *United States v. Proctor*, 148 F.3d 39 (1st Cir. 1998); *United States v. Reid*, 997 F.2d 1576 (D.C. Cir. 1993); *Dashiell v. State*, 821 A.2d 372 (Md. 2003); *State v. Kester*, 51 P.3d 457 (Idaho 2002); *State v. Dawson*, 983 P.2d 916 (Mont. 1999); *Condon v. State*, 416 S.E.2d 802 (Ga. App. 1992); *State v. Curtis*, 964 S.W.2d 604 (Tenn. App. 1997); *State v. Taylor*, 612 N.E.2d 728 (Ohio App. 1992); *State v. Guy*, 492 N.W.2d 311 (Wis. 1992); *Commonwealth v. Patterson*, 591 A.2d 1075 (Pa. Super. 1991).

Plain view discoveries during execution

The plain view doctrine applies to fruits and evidence of a crime and to contraband discovered during the execution of a search warrant. *Horton v. California*, 496 U.S. 128 (1990). However, officers must remember that the incriminating nature of evidence must be "immediately apparent." Thus, if officers locate property that might be stolen, but they must move the item in order to view identifying marks or a serial number, the item is not "immediately apparent" as incriminating evidence. *State v. Gallegos*, 712 P.2d 207 (Utah 1985). If, however, mere vision enhancement devices such as a flashlight or mirror were used, the plain view doctrine would still apply.

Strip-searches and body cavity searches

Ordinarily, there is no real need or legal justification for a strip-search outside of a jail or detention facility. Warrantless strip-searches of arrested persons are permissible when officers have a reasonable belief that the arrestee is concealing a weapon or contraband. *Swain v. Spinney*, 117 F.3d 1 (1st Cir. 1997). Such a reasonable belief might be based on an arrest for a violent crime, or a history of violent crime, a positive indication from a metal detector, or a reputation for carrying drugs concealed under clothing or in body orifices. *Thompson v. City of Los Angeles*, 885 F.2d 1439 (9th Cir. 1989); *United States v. Barnes*, 443 F. Supp. 2d 248 (D. R.I. 2006); *Beasley v. City of Sugar Land*, 410 F. Supp. 2d 524 (S.D. Tex. 2006). Strip-searches must be conducted by a member of the same sex. *Hayes v. Marriott*, 70 F.3d 1144 (10th Cir. 1995). An unjustified strip-search may lead to both evidentiary suppression and civil liability. *Flores v. City of Mt. Vernon*, 41 F. Supp. 2d 439 (S.D.N.Y. 1999).

Evidence may also be obtained, or at least located, through radiological (x-ray) examination. Absent exigent circumstances, a warrant must be obtained. *People v. Thompson,* 820 P.2d 1160 (Colo. App. 1991); *State v. Palmer,* 803 P.2d 1249 (Utah App. 1990), *cert. denied,* 815 P.2d 241 (Utah 1991). Warrantless body intrusions are permitted only when there is clear indication that evidence will be found, there are exigent circumstances, and the method of intrusion is reasonable. *United States v. Holloway,* 906 F. Supp. 1437 (D. Kan. 1995). For example, holding a suspect by the neck to prevent swallowing of drugs, as long as the suspect is not unduly choked, is reasonable in many jurisdictions. *State v. Montgomery,* 665 So. 2d 101 (La. App. 1995), *cert. denied,* 667 So. 2d 538 (La. 1996); *State v. Victor,* 601 N.E.2d 648 (Ohio App. 1991), *cert. denied,* 506 U.S. 902 (1992); *Hernandez v. State,* 548 S.W.2d 904 (Tex. App. 1977). California courts reject any choking. *People v. Johnson,* 282 Cal. Rptr. 114 (Cal. App. 1991). However, stopping a person from swallowing does not necessarily require choking. *People v. Johnson,* 282 Cal. Rptr. 114 (Cal. App. 1991). One court has approved of pepper spray in the mouth to keep a person from swallowing evidence. *United States v. Holloway,* 906 F. Supp. 1437 (D. Kan. 1995). Obviously, such circumstances require quick decisions. However, if evidence is swallowed and no exigent circumstances are present, consider an x-ray examination or the use of a special toilet that captures bodily waste.

On rare occasions, a search warrant may be used to obtain evidence from a suspect through surgical means. Typically, a bullet is the target of the search. Such searches are restricted by the severe test of weighing the medical dangers of the surgery, the degree of intrusion into the suspect's interests in privacy and bodily dignity, and the societal interest in determining guilt or innocence. *Winston v. Lee,* 470 U.S. 753 (1978). Other internally intrusive searches also require a warrant. *People v. Scott,* 145 Cal. Rptr. 876 (Cal. 1984) (approving warrant to allow physician to massage the prostate gland in order to produce a semen sample). No such warrant should ever be sought without the prior approval of the prosecutor.

Computer searches

Computers are increasingly popular with American households, and criminal households are no exception. Computers present two main concerns: computer crime and crime facilitated through computers. The first concern, computer crime, includes situations where the computer is a direct instrumentality of a crime, such as theft of confidential data or embezzlement of funds through electronic transfer. The second concern is where computer use is incidental to the crime, such as transmission of child pornography or a customer database for a drug distributor or fraud perpetrator. Computers have been used for such varied schemes as creating forged securities, transmitting kidnapping ransom demands, laundering narcotics profits, tracking prostitutes' customers preferences and fee schedules, and to display suicide notes.

Computer searches and seizures present peculiar technical challenges, but they are subject to the same constitutional principles that apply to any other type of evidence sought by a search warrant. *United States v. Upham,* 168 F.3d 532 (1st Cir.), *cert. denied,* 527 U.S. 1011 (1999). When attempting to draft a search warrant for a computer, consider securing the services of an expert. For major offenses, there are numerous resources available. These include the Electronic Crimes Special Agent program of the Secret Service, the Computer Analysis and Response Team of the FBI, and the seized evidence recovery specialists of the Internal Revenue Service. Some computer manufacturers, such as IBM and Data General, employ computer experts assigned to assist law enforcement officers with search warrant drafting and execution. Microsoft maintains a comprehensive and free law enforcement training and technical assistance service. Other available resources include state universities and computer service providers. Be wary of using victims of computer crimes for assistance due to their inherent bias.

In most cases, the warrant should specifically authorize officers to remove the computer and all supporting peripherals for a further search in a controlled environment. *United States v. Hunter,* 13 F. Supp. 2d 574 (D. Vt. 1998). The supporting peripherals, the keyboard, mouse, modem, external storage devices, etc., should be seized because other peripherals may or may not be compatible. Also consider requesting seizure authority for supporting documentation and manuals.

A computer expert should be consulted in the execution of the warrant. The local field office of the Federal Bureau of Investigation or the U.S. Attorney's Office can provide access to the *Federal Guidelines for Searching and Seizing Computers.* The guidelines provide an overview of searches and seizures of computer systems and electronic information in criminal cases. The ease of destroying data is not sufficient justification for a "no-knock" warrant. The Guidelines counsel application of the "independent component doctrine," which requires a distinct reason to seize each hardware component. Officers should "seize only those pieces of equipment necessary for basic input/output so that the government can successfully execute the warrant." "Once the analyst has examined the computer system and data and decided that some items or information need not be kept, the government should return this property as soon as possible." Consider making exact copies of the information on the storage devices and returning the computers and data to the targets if they will stipulate that the copy is an exact replica of the original data. Be particularly cautious about the application of the plain view doctrine; evidence not sought in the warrant but inadvertently discovered should generally not be seized without a supplemental warrant. *United States v. Carey*, 172 F.3d 1268 (10th Cir. 1999).

One of the most compelling reasons to consult with computer search and seizure experts is the federal Privacy Protection Act, 42 U.S. Code § 2000aa. The Act contains a "subpoena first rule" when seeking information held by the news media. The Act holds state and local law enforcement officers personally liable for violations of the Act. 42 U.S. Code § 2000aa-6(a)(2). At least one court has held that the Act applies only to state officers and not to municipal officers. *Davis v. Gracey*, 111 F.3d 1472 (10th Cir. 1997).

Developing probable cause to search a computer for records, images, and documents does not legally differ from developing probable cause to search a desk or filing cabinet for the printed version of such items. However, there are a few probable cause issues that are unique to computer searches. For example, evidence that a person subscribed to a Web site containing child pornography can create probable cause to believe the person has downloaded, kept, and otherwise possessed illegal child pornography in his computer. *United States v. Wagers*, 452 F.3d 534 (6th Cir. 2006) ("The evidence connecting the defendant, his computer, his IP address, and his home to the offense is considerably stronger, particularly where the criminal activity (viewing child pornography) is much more tied to a place of privacy, seclusion, and high-speed Internet connectivity, e.g., a home or office, than the storing of drugs (which can take place in a car, a ditch, a hole in the ground, etc.").); *United States v.*

Martin, 418 F.3d 148 (2d Cir. 2005); *United States v. Froman*, 355 F.3d 882 (5th Cir. 2004).

Because a computer invariably holds numerous types of files with different categories of information and images, questions often arise about the scope of a computer search. After finding a computer-printed child pornography image in Brooks's trash during the course of executing a search warrant, officers obtained Brooks's consent to "pre-search" his computer for child pornography. Though officers encountered some technical difficulties during the pre-search, they saw probable illegal images and obtained a warrant for a more detailed search. Brooks claimed that the subsequent warrant search was improper because the warrant did not specify the search methodology to be used and because agents opened and examined non-pornographic files. The critical issue is not how a computer is searched, but rather whether the scope of the search exceeds the scope authorized by the warrant. To determine whether officers have exceeded the scope of a computer search warrant, courts consider: (1) the object of the search; (2) the types of files that may reasonably contain those objects; and (3) whether officers actually expand the scope of the search upon locating evidence of a different crime. *United States v. Brooks*, 427 F.3d 1246 (10th Cir. 2005).

Once illegal images are discovered on a computer during a lawful search, a warrant is not required for a more extensive forensic examination of the computer aimed at finding other illegal images. However, a second warrant should be sought to seize evidence of other crimes. After they received reports that Grimmett had sought out a prostitute and asked her to bring children for their sexual encounter, officers obtained a warrant for Grimmett's home that authorized a search of the home and any electronic media for child pornography. When they served the warrant, the officers found clearly unlawful images of child pornography on Grimmett's computer. They seized the computer, created a mirror image of the hard drive, and enlisted an agent from Immigrations and Customs Enforcement (ICE) to conduct a complete analysis of the hard drive. The ICE agent found over 1,500 child pornography images and over 140 child pornography videos.

Grimmett claimed that the examination of his computer by the ICE agent was unlawful because the officers should have obtained a second search warrant. Grimmett asserted that the first warrant may have justified the initial on-scene examination and seizure, but a second warrant was necessary for an in-depth analysis of the hard drive. He relied on a decision that suppressed child pornography evidence that was inadvertently located and subsequently seized during a search for drug transaction records on a drug dealer's computer. *United States v. Carey*, 172 F.3d 1268 (10th Cir. 1999). That decision held that officers should have obtained a second warrant to examine the computer for illegal pornography. In Grimmett's case, the court ruled that no second warrant was necessary. Even though the complete analysis and extraction of the child pornography files followed the seizure of the hard drive by some time, the warrant clearly contemplated off-site laboratory analysis. *United States v. Grimmett*, 439 F.3d 1263 (10th Cir. 2006).

The federal Electronic Communications Privacy Act prohibits the interception of electronic mail (e-mail) transmissions by private persons or law enforcement officers without a search warrant. A search warrant is required for e-mail that is stored for less than 180 days. If the mail is stored for more than 180 days, officers can obtain it by subpoena or warrant. Obviously, a subpoena may entail the risk that a target will learn about the request and may alter or destroy data. The prohibition includes employers. Officers should be careful not to create an agency relationship with employers who monitor e-mail. The statute allows exceptions for consent, service provider monitoring, and monitoring done in the ordinary course of business. *See Electronic Media Issues chapter.*

Consent to intercept e-mail may be express or implied. Implied consent is not created when a person simply knows that the employer or e-mail host has the technical capability to monitor. However, consent may be present where actual notice of monitoring is given. If e-mail users have taken steps to protect their privacy, such as encryption or user passwords, consent cannot be implied. An employer who does not give notice may still monitor business-related e-mail. Because the Fourth Amendment does not apply to private persons and private searches, an employer or service provider could provide information that was obtained through e-mail monitoring to an officer. However, an officer may not encourage or solicit e-mail monitoring and then use the information obtained.

Execution of a computer search warrant requires forensic technology expertise. It is not difficult to booby-trap a computer to destroy data upon unauthorized access. The device may be as simple as an electromagnet that is powered up when the computer is turned off, or a degauzing loop around a doorway that destroys data when the computer is removed from the room. There are several law enforcement-oriented software packages, such as Micro-Park™, that will "freeze" data on a hard drive to prevent its automatic destruction. Photograph the computer equipment to assist in its reassembly, and disassemble it only to the point necessary to transport it. The entire system, including all peripherals, may be seized, if necessary. *Guest v. Leis*, 255 F.3d 325 (6th Cir. 2001); *Mahlberg v. Mentzer*, 968 F.2d 772 (8th Cir. 1992). However, many technicians prefer that officers seize only the computer itself. Officers should follow the direction of the technicians who perform computer forensic examinations for the agency.

Surreptitious entry warrants

In rare circumstances, officers may wish to pursue a "sneak and peek" warrant that circumvents normal notice requirements and allows surreptitious entry to observe contraband. *United States v. Freitas*, 800 F.2d 1451 (9th Cir. 1986). Sneak and peek warrants are authorized under 18 U.S. Code § 3103a. An affiant must show why providing notice of entry and execution would have an adverse effect. Generally, notice of execution must be given within 30 days after the search. The affidavit must establish a need for covert entry, not merely a statement of convenience or expediency. Necessity for surreptitious entry may be shown when the covert entry would assist in protecting a confidential informant's safety that would likely otherwise be threatened, or there is a need to identify multiple suspects in a large drug distribution or manufacturing operation.

The warrant must contain a provision for notice of the search. *United States v. Villegas*, 899 F.2d 1324 (2d Cir. 1990). This type of warrant can be particularly valuable in controlled substance manufacturing investigations. Any delay beyond the initial period must be justified by developing circumstances and should be approved by the issuing court. Prosecutorial review and approval should be obtained before an affidavit seeking a surreptitious entry search warrant is filed. *United States v. Pangburn*, 983 F.2d 449 (2d Cir. 1993).

Who may assist in executing the warrant

Any police officer may execute a valid warrant. The officer who drafts the affidavit need not be the executing officer. If necessary, the executing officer may request assistance from other law enforcement agencies, either state or federal. *United States v. Medlin*, 842 F.2d 1194 (10th Cir. 1988). The use of civilians to assist in federal search warrant execution is allowed by statute. 18 U.S. Code § 3105 ("A search warrant may in all cases be served by any of the officers mentioned in its direction or by an officer authorized by law to serve such a warrant, but by no other person, except in aid of the officer on his requiring it, he being present and acting in its execution."). A civilian may properly assist with search warrant execution when the purpose is to assist officers and not advance the assisting civilian's interests, the assistance is necessary, and the civilian is limited to those actions that would be proper for the searching officer. *United States v. Sparks*, 265 F.3d 825 (9th Cir. 2001).

Civilian experts may assist in computer searches as necessary. *United States v. Schwimmer*, 692 F. Supp. 119 (E.D.N.Y. 1988) (evidence not suppressed where computer expert seized computer records for officers); *Schalk v. State*, 767 S.W.2d 441 (Tex. App. 1988), *cert. denied*, 503 U.S. 1006 (1992) (officer properly enlisted civilian to assist with search for trade secret in computer software). If the search is for technical material or unique documents that may not be familiar to the officer, civilian experts may be used. *Drill Parts and Service Co., Inc. v. Joy Mfg. Co.*, 619 So. 2d 1280 (Ala. 1993) (civilians assisted with search for stolen engineering drawings); *State v. Wade*, 544 So. 2d 1028 (Fla. App. 1989). Civilians may also be used to perform medical or dental searches. *Harris v. State*, 401 S.E.2d 263 (Ga. 1991) (dentist assisted officers by creating impressions, x-rays and photographs of suspect's teeth); *Rodriques v. Furtado*, 575 N.E.2d 1124 (Mass. 1991) (physician assisted with warrant for a body cavity search). A crime victim may help to identify stolen property. *State v. Ricci*, 472 A.2d 291 (R.I. 1984) (crime victim allowed to be present during search to confirm identity of stolen jewelry). When officers intend to use civilian assistance, the best practice is to seek specific authorization for civilian assistance in the warrant. *Commonwealth v. Sbordone*, 678 N.E.2d 1184 (Mass. 1997).

News media personnel should not be allowed to observe execution of a search warrant, except in the rare case where their presence may be truly described as "assisting" the officers performing the search. *Ayeni v. Mottola,* 35 F.3d 680 (2d Cir. 1994), *cert. denied,* 514 U.S. 1062 (1995). Bringing news media to the scene of a residential search warrant execution violates the target's Fourth Amendment rights. *Wilson v. Layne,* 526 U.S. 603 (1999); *Hanlon v. Berger,* 526 U.S. 808 (1999). Nor should private security personnel be allowed to observe, unless their assistance is required to identify property, provide access, or for some other legitimate purpose. *Bills v. Aseltine,* 958 F.2d 697 (6th Cir. 1992), *cert. denied,* 516 U.S. 865 (1995).

Service of the warrant document

Once the premises have been entered and secured, the officer should serve a copy of the warrant itself (not necessarily the affidavit) on the owner or lawful occupant of the premises. *United States v. Hector,* 361 F. Supp. 2d 1145 (C.D. Cal. 2005) (officers must serve a copy of warrant before, during, or immediately after search). The occupant is entitled to see that a magistrate has issued a command to search, the description of the area to be searched, and the items sought under the warrant. *United States v. Celestine,* 324 F.3d 1095 (9th Cir. 2003). Unless the failure to serve the warrant prejudices the defendant in court, suppression is not the appropriate remedy. *United States v. Ridgway,* 300 F.3d 1153 (9th Cir. 2002).

Receipt required for all seized goods

The officer acting as evidence recorder or property manager must record all property seized and leave a receipt at the time of seizure. If no responsible person is at the location searched, then the receipt should be left in plain view or taped to the front door. Generally, logging all evidence on a multi-part property report and leaving the back copy is the most efficient method of preparing a receipt.

Return of service

The return completes the warrant process in the court. The return informs the magistrate who issued the warrant about the property that was seized. The return may be as simple as a photocopy of the property report or search inventory form with a cover sheet. Most warrants are prepared with the return form attached. Complete the return of service and execute it before the magistrate who issued the warrant.

This must be done as soon as is practicable, but at least within 10 days. Completion of the return is the legal responsibility of the officer who prepared and served the warrant. Failure to make a proper return may not invalidate the warrant, but it will make the court less receptive to future requests. Most courts decline requests to suppress evidence as a remedy for the officer's failure to return the warrant and inventory to the court after the warrant is executed. *United States v. Dauphinee*, 538 F.2d 1 (1st Cir. 1976); *United States v. Primo*, 369 F. Supp. 2d 607 (W.D. Pa. 2005); *State v. Pearson*, 566 S.E.2d 50 (N.C. 2002), *cert. denied*, 537 U.S. 1121 (2003); *State v. Mollison*, 459 S.E.2d 88 (S.C. App. 1995).

Exhibit 7-1
Search Warrant Flow Chart

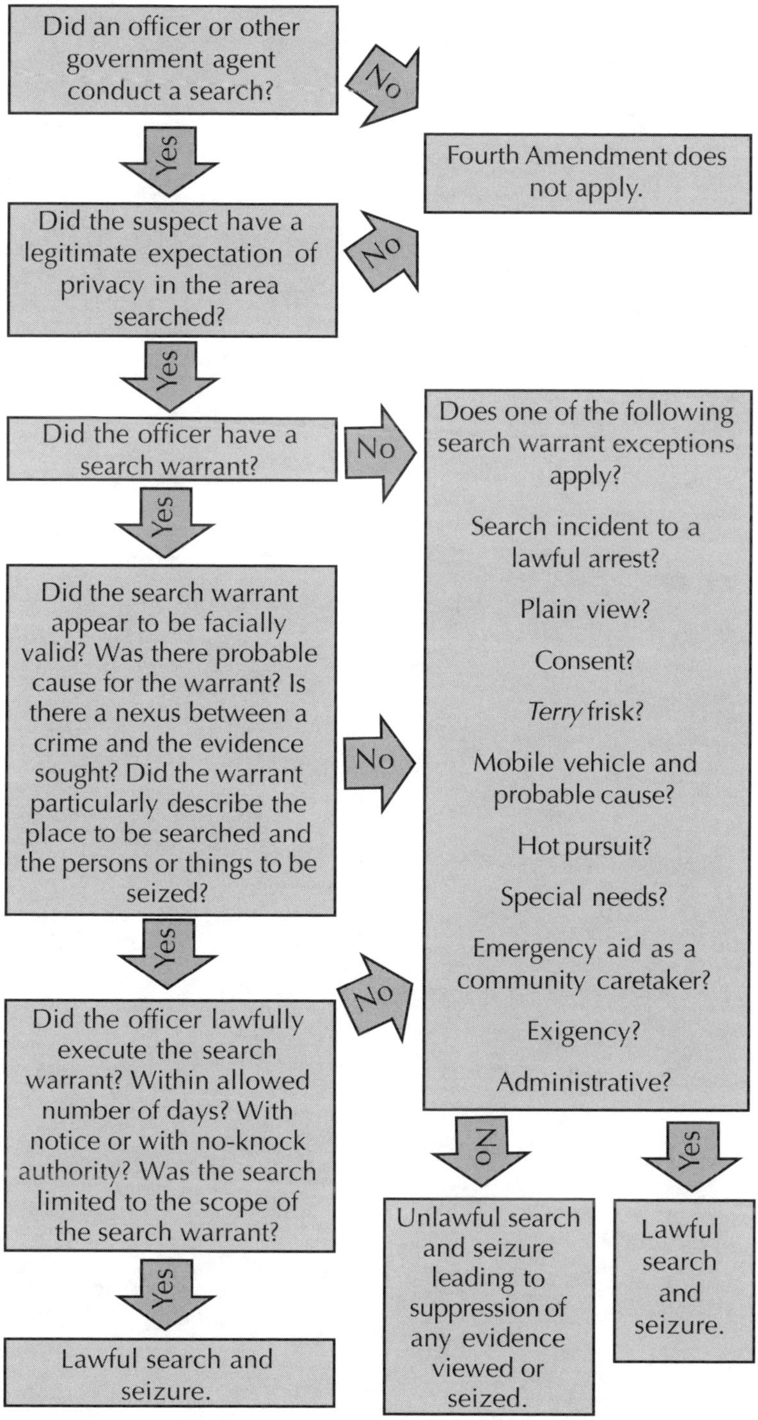

CHAPTER 8

ELECTRONIC MEDIA CONCERNS

Wiretap requirements
Minimization
Pen registers
Stored voice mail and e-mail
One-party consensual monitoring
Computer keyboard key logging
Silent video monitoring
Interception of cellular phone calls
Viewing pager and cell phone memories
Body wires and video cameras
Undisclosed audiotaping while sitting in a patrol car
Bumper beepers
Global positioning satellite tracking devices
Parcel tracking devices
Cell phone tracking
Pole cameras

For many years, the government could intercept and monitor electronic communications without a warrant or other legal process. In 1928, the Supreme Court held that wiretapping should be viewed under trespass laws. If the interception could be accomplished without trespassing, then no legal violation occurred. *Olmstead v. United States*, 277 U.S. 438 (1928). Not until 1967 did the Supreme Court recognize a legitimate expectation of privacy in electronic communications, without regard to whether a trespass occurred. *Katz v. United States*, 389 U.S. 347 (1967). The Court noted that the Fourth Amendment protects "people, not places." In response, Congress passed the Omnibus Crime Control and Safe Streets Act in 1968. The act is often referred to as "Title III," after the significant section of the law.

Another major development in wiretap law came in 1978 when Congress passed the Foreign Intelligence Surveillance Act (FISA). Foreign Intelligence Surveillance Act of 1978, Pub. L. No. 95-511, 92 Stat. 1783 (codified at 50 U.S. Code §§ 1801-1811; 8 U.S. Code § 1101; 47 U.S. Code §§ 605-606). FISA allows the government to intercept communications of aliens and citizens in the United States when there is probable cause to believe that the target of the wiretap is an agent of a foreign power or a member of a foreign terrorist group. There are relaxed standards of probable cause that apply to aliens not lawfully present in the United States and to non-permanent alien residents. State and local law enforcement officers rarely, if ever, will be involved in an investigation conducted under the authority of FISA. However, passage of the USA PATRIOT Act includes a provision that allows federal officials to use FISA warrants to gather evidence in domestic criminal investigations of crimes against national security.

Title III of the Omnibus Crime Control and Safe Streets Act addresses law enforcement investigative wiretaps. In 1986, Congress amended the Omnibus Crime Control and Safe Streets Act with the passage of the Electronic Communications Privacy Act (ECPA). Title I of the ECPA deals with "electronic communications" intercepted in transit. 18 U.S. Code §§ 2510-2522. Title II of the ECPA is the Stored Communications Act, which deals with stored electronic records and communications. 18 U.S. Code §§ 2701-2711. Title III of the ECPA is the Pen Register Statute, which applies to pen registers and trap-and-trace devices. 18 U.S. Code §§ 3121-2127. Even more sweeping changes to electronic surveillance law came with the USA PATRIOT Act (full title: Uniting and Strengthening America by Providing Appropriate Tools Required to Intercept and Obstruct Terrorism Act) passed shortly after the terrorist attacks of September 11, 2001.

Many states have their own electronic interception statutes that impose restrictions on state and local officers who wish to operate a wiretap. In *Berger v. New York*, 388 U.S. 41 (1967), the Supreme Court ruled that the Fourth Amendment applies to states' wiretapping activities and that state law must provide judicial oversight of electronic communication interception.

The law of electronic surveillance is very complex. Electronic interceptions (wiretaps) are usually an investigative tool of last resort and, generally, require the involvement of prosecutors. The Administrative Office of the United States Courts estimates the average cost of a judicially approved wiretap to be approximately $60,000. One particular wiretap cost over $1 million to staff and operate. This chapter provides only a brief overview to acquaint investigators with the potential tool of electronic surveillance.

Title III controlled only electronic interception of voice communications occurring face-to-face or over a wire. Title I of the ECPA extends surveillance controls to non-oral or wire communications that occur over computers, digital-display pagers, and facsimile machines. Any law enforcement agent may apply for a communications-intercept warrant under Title III or Title I of the ECPA. 18 U.S. Code § 2510(7). Only certain crimes may be the predicates for communications intercept warrants, including virtually any federal felony. 18 U.S. Code § 2516(2). One of the significant features of the USA PATRIOT Act was the expansion of the list of crimes that may be investigated by a wiretap.

Wiretap requirements

Though most interceptions are performed by federal agents under the authority of federal court warrants, Title III also gives state public safety agencies the ability to secure interception warrants. 18 U.S. Code § 2516(2). Pursuant to an appropriate state statute, a state court judge may authorize a wiretap in the investigation of the following crimes: "murder, kidnapping, gambling, robbery, bribery, extortion, or dealing in narcotic drugs, marijuana or other dangerous drugs, or other crimes dangerous to life, limb, or property, and punishable by imprisonment for more than one year, or any conspiracy to commit any of the foregoing offenses," or any crime that carries a penalty of at least one year imprisonment. 18 U.S. Code § 2516(2).

Before a court can authorize a wiretap, officers must show probable cause to believe that the target is committing a crime for which a wiretap is authorized, as well as probable cause to believe that the wiretap will produce evidence of that crime. *United States v. Macklin*, 902 F.2d 1320 (8th Cir. 1990), *cert. denied sub nom. Woods v. United States*, 498 U.S. 1031 (1991). In the wiretap context, "probable cause" is measured by "the same standard as the standard for a regular search warrant." *United States v. Fury*, 554 F.2d 522 (2d Cir. 1977). Despite that, wiretap applications must be approved for submission to a court by designated senior officers of the Department of Justice or, in cases of state court applications, by the state attorney general, and in some cases by county or district attorneys. 18 U.S. Code § 2516(1). The probable cause affidavit must contain six distinct elements:

- The affidavit must identify the law enforcement officer who made the application and the authorizing official. 18 U.S. Code § 2518(1)(a).
- The affidavit must list facts such as the nature of the crime under investigation, the location of the intended communications interception, the type of communications to be intercepted, and the name of the wiretap target. 18 U.S. Code § 2518(1)(b); *United States v. Lopez*, 300 F.3d 46 (1st Cir. 2002) (affidavit must include details about the particular offense, a description of the nature and facilities from which the communication is to be intercepted, the kind of communication to be intercepted, and the identity of the suspects or offenders). The officer must list the facts that justify the officer's belief that a wiretap warrant should be issued. 18 U.S. Code § 2518(1)(b). The affidavit should list the names of all known targets. *United States v. Matthews*, 213 F.3d 966 (7th Cir. 2000).
- A wiretap affidavit must include "a full and complete statement as to whether or not other investigative procedures have been tried and failed or why they reasonably appear to be unlikely to succeed if tried or to be too dangerous." 18 U.S. Code § 2518(1)(c); *United States v. Ramirez-Encarnacion*, 291 F.3d 1219 (10th Cir. 2002). This is referred to as the "exhaustion" or "necessity" re-

quirement. Similar requirements are generally imposed under state law. The exhaustion requirement does not mean that every possible investigative technique has been unsuccessfully tried. It is sufficient to show the reasons that traditional means of investigation would not likely be successful. *United States v. Moran*, 349 F. Supp. 2d 425 (N.D.N.Y. 2005); *United States v. Gutierrez-Santiman*, 988 F. Supp. 1410 (D. Utah 1997). "The issue of whether a normal investigative method has been exhausted must be tested in a practical and common sense manner." *United States v. Diaz*, 176 F.3d 52 (2d Cir. 1999).

- Any previous wiretap applications known to the officer and the authorizing individual involving any of the same persons, facilities, or places targeted in the current application must be listed. 18 U.S. Code § 2518(1)(e); *United States v. Bianco*, 998 F.2d 1112 (2d Cir. 1993).
- The affidavit must state the period of time for which the interception will be maintained. 18 U.S. Code § 2518(1)(d). The authorization may not extend more than 30 days without an application for an extension and new findings similar to that required for the original authorization. 18 U.S. Code § 2518(5)-(6); *United States v. Gambino*, 734 F. Supp. 1084 (S.D.N.Y. 1990).
- If the application is for an extension of a wiretap warrant, the affidavit must set forth in detail the results obtained to date from the wiretap. 18 U.S. Code § 2518(1)(f).

Minimization

Any monitoring of intercepted communications pursuant to a warrant must be "minimized." Minimization is the process of listening briefly to each conversation and periodically listening throughout each conversation to determine whether the subject of the conversation is related to the probable cause for the warrant. Officers cannot listen (beyond a brief moment to determine the subject) to conversations not discussing criminal actions. Courts evaluate minimization by analyzing four factors: first, the nature and complexity of the suspected crimes; second, the number of target individuals; third, the ambiguity of the intercepted conversations; fourth, the thoroughness of the government precautions to bring about minimization; and fifth, the degree of judicial supervision over the surveillance practices. *United States v. London*, 66 F.3d 1227 (1st Cir. 1995), *cert. denied*, 517 U.S. 1155 (1996).

Pen registers

Pen registers and trap-and-trace devices do not intercept the content of telephone conversations and are not considered wiretaps under Title III. A pen register is a device that captures all outgoing numbers dialed. A trap-and-trace device captures all incoming numbers. Since the telephone number dialed is automatically revealed to the telephone company in order to place the call, there is no reasonable expectation of privacy, and the Fourth Amendment is not implicated. *Smith v. Maryland,* 442 U.S. 735 (1979). However, state and federal officers are required by statute to obtain a warrant to use pen registers or trap-and-trace devices.

The USA PATRIOT Act added e-mail address information and Internet Protocol (IP) information to the scope of the Pen Register Statute. 18 U.S. Code § 3127(3)-(4). E-mail headers (e-mail addressing information), Uniform Resource Locators (URLs), and IP addresses are all subject to disclosure under the Pen Register Statute. 18 U.S. Code § 3127(3); *In the Matter of Application of the United States of America for an Order Authorizing the Installation and Use of a Pen Register and a Trap & Trace Device on E-mail Account,* 416 F. Supp. 2d 13 (D.D.C. 2006). The subject line of the e-mail header may not be provided to law enforcement under a pen register order because it may disclose a portion of the communication. *In re Application of U.S. for an Order Authorizing Use of a Pen Register and Trap on (XXX),* 396 F. Supp. 2d 45 (D. Mass. 2005).

A warrant for the installation and use of a pen register or a trap-and-trace device may be issued only when officers have certified to the court that the information likely to be obtained is relevant to an ongoing criminal investigation. *In the Matter of Application of the United States of America for an Order Authorizing the Installation and Use of a Pen Register and a Trap & Trace Device on e-mail Account,* 416 F. Supp. 2d 13 (D.D.C. 2006) (as long as an attorney for the government "certified that the information obtained using the devices is relevant to an ongoing criminal investigation, the court is mandated to enter an *ex parte* order authorizing the use of the devices"). An application for a pen register order must contain: the identity, if known, of the person to whom it is leased or in whose name is listed the telephone line to which the pen register or trap-and-trace device is to be attached; the identity, if known, of the person who is the subject of the criminal investigation; the number and, if known, physical location of the telephone line to which the pen register or trap-and-trace device is to be attached and, in the case of a trap-and-trace device, the geographic limits of the trap-and-trace order; and, a statement of the offense to which the information likely to be obtained by the pen register or trap-and-trace device relates. 18 U.S. Code § 3123(a). The warrant may authorize use of the device for 60 days with extensions of 60 days. 18 U.S. Code § 3123(c).

Stored voice mail and e-mail

The Stored Communications Act (Title II of ECPA) generally prohibits intentional unauthorized access to obtain a stored e-mail message. Federal law requires the government to obtain a search warrant in order to compel an Internet service provider to disclose the contents of an e-mail message held in electronic storage for 180 days or less. 18 U.S. Code § 2703(a). Basic subscriber information and messages in storage for more than 180 days may generally be obtained by subpoena or court order. 18 U.S. Code § 2703(b). Probable cause is not the standard to obtain messages stored for 180 days or more; it is sufficient to show that there are "specific and articulable facts showing that there are reasonable grounds" to believe that the information is relevant to a criminal investigation. 18 U.S. Code § 2703(d). A search warrant may be used in lieu of a subpoena if the officer wishes to require that disclosure of the information be kept confidential. 18 U.S. Code § 2703(b). Stored text messages fall within the scope of the Stored Communications Act. *United States v. Jones*, 451 F. Supp. 2d 71 (D.D.C. 2006).

The USA PATRIOT Act amends provisions of Title III and the Stored Communications Act to clear up the ambiguity about which statute governs law enforcement access to voice mail. Officers may obtain a court order for access to voice mail under the Stored Communications Act. Officers need only meet the standard of "relevant to a criminal investigation" rather than the more challenging probable cause standard.

One-party consensual monitoring

Under federal law, officers can monitor and record conversations with the consent of any one party to the conversation. 18 U.S. Code § 2511(2)(c). The majority of states require only "one-party consent," meaning that any one party can give consent to monitoring. A minority of states, including California, Connecticut, Florida, Illinois, Maryland, Massachusetts, Michigan, Montana, Nevada, New Hampshire, Pennsylvania, and Washington, require that all parties to a conversation consent to monitoring. A listening device placed in a fixed location may be monitored only when the consenting party is present at that location.

In one-party consent jurisdictions, the non-consenting party runs the risk that the other party will record or disclose the content of the communication. An officer arresting a heroin dealer picked up the dealer's cell phone and answered it when it rang. The call was a request from the dealer's wholesaler to meet and pick up more heroin. The officer, who spoke Spanish fluently and was street-savvy, played along and set up a meeting. The wholesaler showed up for the arranged meeting and was arrested. The wholesaler claimed that he had an expectation of privacy in his phone call to set up the heroin delivery. The court disagreed, ruling that a person who makes no attempt to verify the identity on the other end of the phone call has no expectation that his statements will remain private. The court ruled that the dealer simply ran the risk of mistaken identity. "The fact that the party to whom the defendant had spoken was not his intended listener, but a police officer who had answered the telephone for the purpose of obtaining incriminating information, is of no consequence." *State v. Gonzalez,* 898 A.2d 149 (Conn. 2006).

Computer keyboard key-logging

Various software programs allow remote monitoring of the keystrokes typed on a computer. Some programs will even e-mail reports of keystrokes entered and Web sites visited. Australia has passed laws specifically allowing police to use keystroke monitoring in serious cases. Though no appellate court has yet ruled on the issue, the concept of keystroke monitoring by law enforcement fits (though none too neatly) into the provisions of Title III. One trial court wrestled with the question and determined that passive key-logging that does not track keystrokes while the computer is "online" does not violate wiretap laws. *United States v. Scarfo,* 180 F. Supp. 2d 572 (D. N.J. 2001). One of the FBI responses to terrorism is the development of the Magic Lantern virus that allows the Bureau to monitor keystrokes remotely by e-mailing a Trojan program to the targeted computer. One court has ruled that non-consensual keystroke monitoring constitutes illegal wiretapping and has awarded damages following a civil trial. *Garfinkel v. Garfinkel,* 2006 WL 1549756 (N.J. Super. A.D. 2006).

Silent video monitoring

Silent video monitoring (without audio monitoring) is not regulated by federal wiretap statutes. *United States v. Falls,* 34 F.3d 674 (8th Cir. 1994). Nonetheless, traditional Fourth Amendment privacy analysis applies to silent video monitoring. *United States v. Corona-Chavez,* 328 F.3d 974 (8th Cir. 2003) (video monitor allowed in hotel room when police informant was in the room and was aware of the camera); *United States v. Nerber,* 222 F.3d 597 (9th Cir. 2000) (video monitoring of hotel room improper once police informant left the room and suspects were unaware of the camera).

Approximately a dozen states have statutes that restrict the use of hidden silent video cameras in places like restrooms and locker rooms. Common work areas and offices where the public enters or passes through are fair game for silent video surveillance. *Vega-Rodriguez v. Puerto Rico Tel. Co.,* 110 F.3d 174 (1st Cir. 1997). On the other hand, if a private work area is controlled by a single individual, that fact may well carry an expectation of privacy that makes monitoring unreasonable. *United States v. Taketa,* 923 F.2d 665 (9th Cir. 1991) (officer had expectation of privacy in private office in airport police facility and monitoring found illegal); *People v. Galvadon,* 103 P.3d 923 (Colo. 2005) (liquor store manager had expectation of privacy in liquor storeroom; police viewing of store tape improper). As a general rule, whatever lawfully can be observed by the naked eye may also be the subject of silent video monitoring. *United States v. McIver,* 186 F.3d 1119 (9th Cir. 1999).

Interception of cellular phone calls

Interception of cellular phone calls is unlawful under ECPA. A cell phone is treated the same as a land-line for purposes of requiring a warrant for interception. A warrant may grant authority to tap a particular cell phone number or any number assigned to a particular person. *United States v. Otibu,* 2002 WL 1033876 (S.D.N.Y. 2002). Nonetheless, early models use an omnidirectional analog radio signal that can be fairly easily intercepted by an unsophisticated scanner. In 1994, Congress passed the Communications Assistance for Law Enforcement Act (CALEA). The law requires cell phone companies to provide technology that allows law enforcement officers to wiretap cell phones with the appropriate warrants.

Viewing pager and cell phone memories

The numbers stored in a cell phone or pager memory are analogous to a written phone directory. When a suspect carrying a pager or cell phone is arrested, the numbers in the memory may be viewed and recorded. Some courts have allowed this under the exigent circumstances doctrine, reasoning that new incoming phone calls or pages, or turning the device on and off, may destroy electronically recorded evidence. *United States v. Ortiz,* 84 F.3d 977 (7th Cir. 1996) (warrantless search of pager to preserve electronic evidence allowed); *State v. DeLuca,* 739 A.2d 455 (N.J. Super. 1999), *aff'd,* 775 A.2d 1284 (2001). Other courts equate the electronic memory to numbers written on paper that might be seized incident to the arrest. *United States v. Mendoza,* 421 F.3d 663 (8th Cir. 2005) (seizure of cell phone valid as a search incident to a lawful arrest), *cert. denied,* ___ U.S. ___, 126 S. Ct. 1804 (2006); *United States v. Parada,* 289 F. Supp. 2d 1291 (D. Kan. 2003); *United States v. Meriwether,* 917 F.2d 955 (6th Cir. 1990) (officers seized pager; later activation of pager ruled no more intrusive than the later opening of a personal telephone book to obtain what might be incriminating evidence); *United States v. Reyes,* 922 F. Supp. 818 (S.D.N.Y. 1996) (pager seized incident to arrest; access of memory data soon after seizure was not too remote in time and was a proper search incident to arrest).

Body wires and video cameras

There is no expectation of privacy in voice or actions knowingly revealed to a government agent. This rule includes a confidential informant who is not known to the suspect as a government agent. *United States v. Longoria,* 177 F.3d 1179 (10th Cir.), *cert. denied,* 528 U.S. 892 (1999). There is also no privacy interest that prevents recording statements made to a government agent. *United States v. White,* 401 U.S. 745 (1971).

Undisclosed audiotaping while sitting in a patrol car

Many officers place suspects in the rear of patrol cars while either activating a tape recorder or allowing the audio recording capacity of an in-car video recorder to record the statements of the suspects in the patrol car. There is no expectation of privacy for a suspect or witness in a patrol car, and tape-recording suspects and witnesses while they are in the patrol car without notice is permissible. *United States v. Gilley*, 43 F.3d 1440 (11th Cir. 1995); *State v. W.E.*, 814 So. 2d 1232 (Fla. App. 2002); *State v. Ramirez*, 535 N.W.2d 847 (S.D. 1995).

Bumper beepers

Federal (and many states') wiretapping statutes do not cover mobile tracking devices. Thus, the permissibility of installing and monitoring tracking devices is governed by general Fourth Amendment principles. There is no expectation of privacy in the movement of a vehicle on roadways. *United States v. Karo*, 468 U.S. 705 (1984); *United States v. Knotts*, 460 U.S. 276 (1983). As long as the officer installs the tracking device from a place where the officer has a right to be, no warrant is required. *United States v. McIver*, 186 F.3d 1119 (9th Cir. 2001); *State v. Jackson*, 46 P.3d 257 (Wash. App. 2002), *aff'd*, 76 P.3d 217 (Wash. 2003). Some courts impose a requirement for a warrant for monitoring based upon their respective state constitutions. *State v. Campbell*, 759 P.2d 1040 (Or. 1988). If the device is installed under the hood or within the car itself, or if officers must violate a legitimate expectation of privacy, a warrant to install is required. *United States v. Gbemisola*, 225 F.3d 753 (D.C. Cir.), *cert. denied*, 531 U.S. 1026 (2000); *United States v. Hufford*, 539 F.2d 32 (9th Cir.), *cert. denied*, 429 U.S. 1002 (1976). Most courts rule that there is no expectation of privacy in the take-off, travel location, and landing of an airplane, and therefore a locator beeper may be installed without a warrant. *United States v. Bruneau*, 594 F.2d 1190 (8th Cir.), *cert. denied*, 444 U.S. 847 (1979).

Global positioning satellite tracking devices

A bumper beeper reveals only the current location of a vehicle or package and requires real-time tracking. A global positioning satellite (GPS) tracking device may be attached to a vehicle and later retrieved to document the historical travel path of the vehicle. Courts are just beginning to consider the use of GPS tracking devices. A GPS device may be attached to a vehicle without a warrant under the same principles governing the use of a bumper beeper. *United*

States v. Moran, 349 F. Supp. 2d 425 (N.D.N.Y. 2005). However, if the GPS device is used to track movement off public highways and away from public areas where live surveillance could occur, a warrant based upon probable cause *may* be required. *United States v. Garcia,* 2006 WL 298704 (W.D. Wis. 2006). One state decided the issue under its more restrictive state constitution and required a warrant to attach a GPS tracking device to a vehicle. *State v. Jackson,* 76 P.3d 217 (Wash. 2003).

Parcel tracking devices

A warrant is generally not required to place a tracking device in a parcel in transit. *United States v. Gbemisola,* 225 F.3d 753 (D.C. Cir.), *cert. denied,* 531 U.S. 1026 (2000). If an officer is lawfully able to open and examine the parcel, the expectation of privacy in the contents of that parcel is extinguished. *Illinois v. Andreas,* 463 U.S. 765 (1983). A warrant is required to open most packages; only internationally shipped parcels may routinely be opened without a warrant. *United States v. Ware,* 338 F.3d 476 (6th Cir. 2004); *United States v. Taghizadeh,* 87 F.3d 287 (9th Cir. 1996) (international mail may be opened for customs inspection without suspicion). Monitoring the transit of the parcel on roadways requires no warrant. *United States v. Knotts,* 460 U.S. 276 (1983). However, a warrant is generally required to monitor the parcel once it is delivered to a home or other place where there is a reasonable expectation of privacy. *United States v. Karo,* 468 U.S. 705 (1984).

Cell phone tracking

Real-time tracking of cellular phones is technologically simple and legally complex. A cell phone sends a continuous signal to cell towers so that the cell network will be able to quickly route calls to the cell phone. The network detects and records the signal strength and general direction of the originating signal and by doing so reveals the location of the cell phone within a range of a few hundred yards or less. The value of cell phone tracking was incontrovertibly demonstrated when Italian police quickly located one of the July 21, 2006, London bombing suspects by following a cell phone signal.

The use of a pen register device with caller identification capability can accurately locate the cell phone as it travels even when no call is active. When the Pen Register

Statute was passed, it included a restriction on using the authority of the statute, with its reduced cause standard, to provide location information for cell phones. 47 U.S. Code § 1002(a)(1). In a case where officers had already obtained a Title III wiretap for a cocaine dealer's cell phone, the officers dialed the phone and hung up immediately. This allowed the cell phone provider who was cooperating with officers pursuant to the wiretap order to provide the officers the cell phone's location at various intervals. The dealer claimed that the officers' actions violated federal law. The court ruled that obtaining the tracking information did not constitute a search because the information was used only to track the suspect's movements on public roadways. *United States v. Forest,* 355 F.3d 942 (6th Cir.), *cert. denied,* 543 U.S. 856 (2004). Unlike the following cases, no real-time tracking was involved.

In the recent past, federal law enforcement officers have attempted to use a combination of the Pen Register Statute and Stored Communications Act of the EPCA to obtain court warrants ordering cell phone companies to provide real-time cell phone tracking data without showing probable cause to suspect criminal activity. Though there have been mixed results, the trend is to disallow such warrants. *In the Matter of the Application of the United States of America,* 441 F. Supp. 2d 816 (S.D. Tex. 2006) (government could not obtain limited cell site information prospectively under the dual authority of the Pen/Trap Statute and the Stored Communications Act); *In re U.S. for an Order Authorizing Installation and Use of a Pen Register,* 415 F. Supp. 2d 211 (W.D.N.Y. 2006) (requiring showing of probable cause); *In re U.S. for an Order Authorizing the Disclosure of Prospective Cell Site Information,* 412 F. Supp. 2d 947 (E.D. Wis. 2006) (hybrid of Pen/Trap Statute used in combination with the Stored Communications Act does not authorize order requiring cell phone company to provide prospective cell site information, namely the locations of cell towers being used at commencement and termination of calls to and from a particular cell phone). Officers have been more successful when seeking only the location of the cell tower receiving a signal from a particular phone and not additional information that would allow triangulated location of the phone itself. *In re Application of United States for an Order for Disclosure of Telecommunications Records and Authorizing the Use of a Pen Register and Trap and Trace,* 405 F. Supp. 2d 435 (S.D.N.Y. 2005). One court has allowed real-time cell phone tracking where the target was using another party's cell phone. The court ruled that the portion of the Pen Register Statute that protects against use of a pen register to identify the location of a cell phone applies only to the actual subscriber of the cell phone service. *In the Matter of the Application of the United States of America for an Order Authorizing the Installation and Use of a Pen Register,* 415 F. Supp. 2d 663 (S.D. W. Va. 2006).

Pole cameras

A camera mounted in a place where an officer would have a right to be does not violate a legitimate expectation of privacy, and therefore, no warrant is required. *United States v. Jackson,* 213 F.3d 1269 (10th Cir.), *rev'd on other grounds,* 531 U.S. 1033 (2000); *State v. Augafa,* 992 P.2d 723 (Haw. App. 1999). These devices are often mounted on utility poles, and thus are called "pole cameras." Most courts view such devices as extensions of an officer's senses, like binoculars. *United States v. McIver,* 186 F.3d 1119 (9th Cir. 1999), *cert. denied,* 528 U.S. 1177 (2000). However, some courts find pole cameras to be unreasonable when they constantly monitor areas within the curtilage of the home. *United States v. Cuevas-Sanchez,* 821 F.2d 248 (5th Cir. 1987) (pole camera observing activities in a backyard was unreasonable intrusion).

CHAPTER 9

CANINE SEARCH AND SEIZURE

Probable cause on a silver platter
A sniff is not a search
Vehicle sniffs
Vehicle searches
Impounded vehicles
Roadblocks
Bus interdiction
Public parking lots and cars parked on public streets
School property and parking lots
School lockers
Package interdiction
Vehicle sniffs
Currency sniffs
Homes
Jail and prison sniffs
Boat interdiction
Storage lockers
Sniffs of persons
Detaining a vehicle to wait for a detector dog
Establishing reliability of the detector dog
Tracking-dog evidence
Arson detector-dog evidence

As Shakespeare famously observed: "A rose by any other name would smell as sweet." Likewise, methamphetamine, heroin, marijuana, cocaine and other illegal drugs would, by any other name, smell just as bad to a detector dog. Canine olfactory superiority is an established fact. Whereas humans possess a paltry five million scent receptors, some dogs have in excess of 200 million. Due to this unique canine trait, the United States Supreme Court and most state courts grant particular deference to the exceptional ability of trained and certified narcotics-detection dogs to detect illegal drugs.

Probable cause on a silver platter

The U.S. Supreme Court has ruled that a sniff of luggage located in a public place "did not constitute a search within the meaning of the Fourth Amendment." *United States v. Place,* 462 U.S. 696 (1983). A suspect aroused the suspicions of DEA agents in the Miami International Airport. They conducted a brief investigation and examined his airline ticket and driver's license. Agents declined the suspect's consent to search because they feared that he would miss his plane and the DEA would be liable for the cost of the ticket. The agents telephoned other DEA agents at New York's LaGuardia Airport to pass on their suspicions about the suspect. Once the suspect arrived in New York, he was met by DEA agents who again asked consent to search his luggage. This time he refused. The agents then detained the luggage and presented it to a trained drug-detection dog for a sniff. The dog gave an alert. ("Alert" is the term that describes the dog's behavioral change when the dog detects the odor of drugs that it is trained to identify.) Based on the dog's alert, the agents continued to detain the luggage and obtained a search warrant. A large quantity of drugs was found. The Court ruled that the dog's alert created sufficient reason for further detention of the luggage and probable cause to search. None of the traditional warrant requirement exceptions, such as search incident to arrest, plain view, automobile, exigency, or stop and frisk, applied to the *Place* circumstances. Therefore, the agents had to obtain the search warrant.

A sniff is not a search

A canine sniff is not a search because the sniff does not intrude on a legitimate expectation of privacy. *Illinois v.*

Caballes, 543 U.S. 405 (2005). Canine sniffs are not intrusive. The dog's sniff only reveals the presence of contraband and does not expose luggage (or other items sniffed) to public view. The Supreme Court consistently rules that citizens do not have reasonable expectations of privacy in contraband. *United States v. Jacobsen*, 466 U.S. 109 (1984). The *Place* Court noted:

> A canine sniff by a well-trained narcotics detection dog does not require opening the luggage. It does not expose noncontraband items that otherwise would remain hidden from public view, as does, for example, an officer's rummaging through the contents of the luggage. Thus, the manner in which information is obtained through this investigative technique is much less intrusive than a typical search. Moreover, the sniff discloses only the presence or absence of narcotics, a contraband item. Thus, despite the fact that the sniff tells the authorities something about the contents of the luggage, the information is limited. That limited disclosure also ensures that the owner of the property is not subjected to the embarrassment and inconvenience entailed in less discriminate and more intrusive investigative methods. Therefore, we conclude that exposure of Place's luggage, which was located in a public place, to a trained canine did not constitute a search within the meaning of the Fourth Amendment.

Lower federal courts and many state courts have relied on *United States v. Place* to establish a firm rule that a positive alert by a trained drug-detection dog creates probable cause to search and probable cause to arrest. "A dog alert is at least as reliable as many other sources of probable cause and is certainly reliable enough to create a fair probability that there is contraband. We therefore have held in several cases that a dog alert without more gave probable cause for searches and seizures." *United States v. Ludwig*, 10 F.3d 1523 (10th Cir. 1993). A small minority of courts in other states have required independent reasonable suspicion of drug activity, in addition to the alert, to establish probable cause. *United States v. Beale*, 731 F.2d 590 (9th Cir. 1983), *modified en banc*, 736 F.2d 1289 (9th Cir.), *cert. denied*, 469 U.S. 1012 (1984). Most courts hold to the majority view that "a drug-sniffing dog's detection of contraband **establishes probable cause, enough for the arrest**, more than enough for the stop." *United States v. Williams,* 726 F.2d 661 (10th Cir.), *cert. denied,* 467 U.S. 1245 (1984); *United States v. De Los Santos Ferrar,* 999 F.2d 7 (1st Cir.), *cert. denied,* 510 U.S. 997 (1993).

Vehicle sniffs

The sniff of the exterior of a vehicle lawfully detained is not a search. *Illinois v. Caballes,* 543 U.S. 405 (2005). Thus, a patrol officer can issue a citation or otherwise conduct business while a detector dog team sniffs the car and no reasonable suspicion for the sniff is required. "When the odor of narcotics escapes from the interior of a vehicle, society does not recognize a reasonable privacy interest in the public airspace containing the incriminating odor. Where government officials have lawfully detained a vehicle, a dog's sniff is not a search within the meaning of the Fourth Amendment." *Romo v. Champion,* 46 F.3d 1013 (10th Cir. 1995). As long as the vehicle is not detained beyond the time necessary to accomplish the purpose of the traffic stop, whether it be to issue a citation, wait for a licensed driver, or simply to give a warning, the exterior of the vehicle is free game for a sniff. Some courts have allowed a very brief detention without reasonable suspicion to accomplish a dog sniff when a dog was at the scene. *United States v. Martin,* 411 F.3d 998 (8th Cir. 2005); *United States v. Carpenter,* 406 F.3d 915 (7th Cir. 2005); *United States v. $404,905.00 U.S. Currency,* 182 F.3d 643 (8th Cir. 1999).

No consent is required for a canine sniff, even absent any reasonable suspicion, if the vehicle is otherwise lawfully detained. *United States v. Morales-Zamora,* 914 F.2d 200 (10th Cir. 1990). The scope of the sniff is limited to the outside of the vehicle. "An agent may not unlawfully enter an area in order to conduct a dog search. The warrantless entry of a car interior is unlawful unless there is probable cause to believe that it contains contraband." *United States v. Sukiz-Grado,* 22 F.3d 1006 (10th Cir. 1994).

Vehicle searches

Once the drug-detection dog has sniffed the target vehicle and has alerted officers to the odor of narcotics, there remains the question of whether a warrant is required to search the vehicle. The automobile search exception to the Fourth Amendment Warrant Clause may eliminate the need for a warrant. Losing the mobility (exigency) of the vehicle by towing or some other means does not destroy the validity of the search. *United States v. Ross*, 456 U.S. 798 (1982); *United States v. Hatley*, 15 F.3d 856 (9th Cir. 1994). An auto exception search extends to the trunk and containers. *California v. Acevedo*, 500 U.S. 565 (1991). An alert to the passenger compartment also provides probable cause to search the trunk of the car. *United States v. Rosborough*, 261 F.3d 731 (10th Cir. 2004). This doctrine applies to vehicles that may be used as homes—for example, motor homes and vans—as long as they are capable of mobility. *California v. Carney*, 471 U.S. 386 (1985).

Even though the automobile exception may allow a warrantless search, the officer should consider a warrant. A search for drugs conducted pursuant to a warrant allows officers freedom to meticulously search. If the search is pursuant to consent, the driver may withdraw consent when he sees officers disassemble the dashboard. The warrant may also provide significant protection against civil rights lawsuits that allege an unlawful seizure and search. Most important, searches under warrant place the burden of proving an illegal search on the defendant. Warrantless searches require the prosecution to prove that the search was unquestionably legal, and that the officers made no legal errors. Some prosecutors issue form warrants for automobile searches premised on a drug-dog alert. (*See Appendix.)*

Impounded vehicles

A vehicle impounded for any legitimate reason may be subjected to a detector dog sniff. *United States v. Rodriguez-Morales*, 929 F.2d 780 (1st Cir. 1991), *cert. denied*, 502 U.S. 1030 (1992). There is no requirement of reasonable suspicion for the sniff. *United States v. Jensen*, 425 F.3d 698 (9th Cir. 2005); *United States v. Jensen*, 425 F.3d 698 (9th Cir. 2005), *cert. denied*, ___ U.S. ___, 126 S. Ct. 1664 (2006); *United States v. Castro*, 166 F.3d 728 (5th Cir.), *cert. denied*, 528 U.S. 887 (1999); *State v. Kolb*, 674 N.W.2d 238 (Minn. App. 2004). One court has disapproved of conducting sniffs on all impounded vehicles, though the validity of the court's opinion is questionable following the Supreme Court decision in *Illinois v. Caballes*. *United States v. Tueller*, 349 F.3d 1239 (10th Cir. 2003).

Roadblocks

Assuming that the checkpoint is otherwise lawfully conducted, sniffs may be performed at a roadblock. *Merrett v. Moore*, 58 F.3d 1547 (11th Cir. 1995), *cert. denied*, 519 U.S. 812 (1996); *United States v. Morales-Zamora*, 914 F.2d 200 (10th Cir. 1990); *McCray v. State*, 601 S.E.2d 452 (Ga. App. 2004).

Bus interdiction

Checked luggage is treated the same as airline luggage; a sniff is not a search and requires neither probable cause nor reasonable suspicion. *United States v. Williams*, 365 F.3d 399 (5th Cir. 2004). However, sniffing a passenger's hand-carry items does require reasonable suspicion. *United States v. O'Neal*, 17 F.3d 239 (8th Cir.), *cert. denied*, 513 U.S. 960 (1994). Officers cannot order passengers to move off the bus and leave their belongings behind without creating a seizure. *United States v. Garzon*, 119 F.3d 1446 (10th Cir. 1997). However, officers can stand a few feet away from passengers disembarking with their luggage and allow passive sniffing. *United States v. Reyes*, 349 F.3d 219 (5th Cir. 2003) (dog sniff of passengers exiting bus from distance of four to five feet was not a search).

No seizure occurs when officers board a bus to conduct luggage and passenger-area sniffs if there is no associated detention. If the bus driver permits the officers to board, the sniff is conducted at a regular stop, it does not unreasonably delay the bus, and passengers are given no reason to believe that they must stay on board, there is no seizure. Since there is no seizure, no reasonable suspicion is required. *United States v. Jackson*, 390 F.3d 393 (5th Cir. 2004). During the course of the sniff, officers may move baggage to make it more accessible to a dog sniff. *United States v. Ward*, 144 F.3d 1024 (7th Cir. 1998); *United States v. Gant*, 112 F.3d 239 (6th Cir. 1997); *United States v. Gault*, 92 F.3d 990 (10th Cir.), *cert. denied*, 519 U.S. 939 (1996). But officers cannot manipulate the baggage to identify the contents by feel. *Bond v. United States*, 529 U.S. 334 (2000); *United States v. Nicholson*, 144 F.3d 632 (10th Cir. 1998). While manipulating the baggage to identify its contents is not allowed, merely compressing the baggage to expel air in preparation for a canine sniff is generally permitted. *United States v. Lovell*, 849 F.2d 910 (5th Cir. 1988); *State v. Lancelotti*, 595 N.W.2d 558 (Neb. App. 1999).

Public parking lots and cars parked on public streets

A sniff of cars parked in a motel parking lot does not require reasonable suspicion. *United States v. Ludwig*, 10 F.3d 1523 (10th Cir. 1993). Parking lots that are open to the public or that are in public view and not fenced are fair game for sniffs without suspicion. *United States v. Dunkel*, 900 F.2d 105 (7th Cir.1990) (even though parking lot was curtilage of private office, no legitimate expectation of privacy in parking lot that was open to tenants's guests and was not fenced), *vacated on other grounds*, 498 U.S. 1043 (1991); *United States v. Reed*, 733 F.2d 492 (8th Cir. 1984) (officer's initial entry into business parking lot was not a search where lot was bound on three sides by public streets and visible from streets on two sides, fenced gate was completely open to public street, and there was no indication that lot was private to owners and those specifically authorized); *United States v. Edmonds*, 611 F.2d 1386 (5th Cir. 1980) (finding no legitimate privacy expectation in business loading dock). A dog sniff of a car parked on a public street or alley does not require particularized reasonable suspicion. *United States v. Friend*, 50 F.3d 548 (8th Cir. 1995), *vacated in part*, 517 U.S. 1152 (1996).

School property and parking lots

Many agencies cooperate with school officials in sniffing student lockers. Some take the drug-detection dog through the hallways as a reminder to the students that school should be a drug-free environment and that illegal drug sales and possession will not be tolerated. "The dog's sniffing of student lockers in public hallways and automobiles parked in public parking lots does not constitute a search." *Horton v. Goose Creek Independent School District*, 690 F.2d 470 (5th Cir. 1982), *cert. denied*, 463 U.S. 1207 (1983). High school officials decided to conduct a sweep of the parking lot and asked for a police canine handler to assist and to conduct sniffs of students' parked cars. After the dog gave an alert on Myers' car, officers found a gun in the car. Relying on the recent Supreme Court decision in *Caballes* and Supreme Court standards for school premises searches, the Court ruled that the parking lot sniff and resulting search was lawful. *State v. Myers*, 839 N.E.2d 1154 (Ind. 2005), *cert. denied*, ___ U.S. ___, 126 S. Ct. 2295 (2006).

School lockers

Many agencies cooperate with school officials to have drug-detector dogs sniff student lockers. The Tenth Circuit has expressly authorized drug-detection dog sniffs of student lockers. *United States v. Venema,* 563 F.2d 1003 (10th Cir. 1977). Sniffing students is not a wise idea. *B.C. v. Plumas Unified School District,* 193 F.3d 1260 (9th Cir. 1999). However, at least one court disagrees and has approved random, widespread sniffs of the student body. *Doe v. Renfrow,* 631 F.2d 91 (7th Cir. 1980), *cert. denied,* 451 U.S. 1022 (1981). If asked to sniff students for drugs, just say "no."

Package interdiction

Many illegal drugs pass through mail and parcel services. Thousands of sniffs are performed each year in parcel distribution centers. When officers have reasonable suspicion to believe that a package contains contraband, they may detain that package for a reasonable length of time to investigate. *United States v. Dennis,* 115 F.3d 524 (7th Cir. 1997); *State v. Duhon,* 109 P.3d 1282 (Kan. App. 2005). The U.S. Postal Service has articulated a narcotics package profile. Profile factors include: (1) the size and shape of the package; (2) whether the package is taped to close all openings; (3) handwritten labels; (4) an unusual return name and address; (5) unusual odors coming from the package; (6) a fictitious return address; and (7) the package's destination. The package's city of origin and the recipient's identity are also key factors in developing reasonable suspicion. *United States v. Logan,* 362 F.3d 530 (8th Cir. 2004); *United States v. Cantrall,* 762 F. Supp. 875 (D. Kan. 1991). Other factors may include excess taping, cash payment for postage, and use of express mail services. *United States v. Smith,* 383 F.3d 700 (8th Cir. 2004) (package shipped via overnight delivery and marked for optional Saturday delivery); *United States v. Morones,* 355 F.3d 1108 (8th Cir. 2004) (package was sent by overnight delivery, shipper paid cash, no phone numbers were included, labels were handwritten, sender and recipient had same last name, package sent from source state); *United States v. Walker,* 324 F.3d 1032 (8th Cir. 2003) (package was delivered to airport by a person driving a vehicle rented by person who lived only 60 miles from airport, payment made in cash, and labels were handwritten); *United States v. Terriques,* 319 F.3d 1051 (8th Cir. 2003) (heavy taping and address irregularities); *United States v. Dennis,* 115 F.3d 524 (7th Cir. 1997) (express mail use).

Once there is reasonable suspicion to detain the package, delays of a single day are not unreasonable. *United States v. Dennis,* 115 F.3d 524 (7th Cir. 1997) (one-day delay reasonable); *United States v. Banks,* 3 F.3d 399 (11th Cir. 1993) (one day allowed), *cert. denied,* 510 U.S. 1129 (1994); *United States v. Allen,* 990 F.2d 667 (1st Cir. 1993) (five-hour delay reasonable). Once the dog alerts to the package, there is probable cause to obtain a search warrant. *United States v. Gomez,* 312 F.3d 920 (8th Cir. 2002).

If the package is not delayed beyond a few moments, a sniff may be performed without reasonable suspicion. *United States v. Demoss,* 279 F. 3d 632 (8th Cir. 2002) (20-minute detention did not create a seizure). The package may be taken off the conveyor belt to make a sniff more convenient. *United States v Gomez,* 312 F. 3d 920 (8th Cir. 2002). Any significant delay must be supported by reasonable suspicion. *United States v. Fuller,* 374 F.3d 617 (8th Cir. 2004), *cert. denied,* 543 U.S. 1073 (2005).

Vehicle sniffs

The sniff of the exterior of a vehicle lawfully detained is not a search. *Illinois v. Caballes,* 543 U.S. 405 (2005). Thus, a patrol officer could be issuing a citation or otherwise conducting business while a detector dog team sniffed the car, with no reasonable suspicion required. "When the odor of narcotics escapes from the interior of a vehicle, society does not recognize a reasonable privacy interest in the public airspace containing the incriminating odor. Where government officials have lawfully detained a vehicle, a dog's sniff is not a search within the meaning of the Fourth Amendment." *Romo v. Champion,* 46 F.3d 1013 (10th Cir. 1995). As long as the vehicle is not detained beyond the time necessary to accomplish the purpose of the traffic stop, whether it be to issue a citation, wait for a licensed driver, or simply to give a warning, the exterior of the vehicle is free game for a sniff. Some courts have allowed a very brief detention without reasonable suspicion to accomplish a dog sniff when a dog was at the scene. *United States v. Martin,* 411 F.3d 998 (8th Cir. 2005); *United States v. Carpenter,* 406 F.3d 915 (7th Cir. 2005); *United States v. $404,905.00 U.S. Currency,* 182 F.3d 643 (8th Cir. 1999).

No consent is required for a canine sniff, even absent any reasonable suspicion, if the vehicle is otherwise lawfully detained. *United States v. Morales-Zamora,* 914 F.2d 200 (10th Cir. 1990). The scope of the sniff is limited to the outside of the vehicle. "An agent may not unlawfully enter an area in order to conduct a dog search. The warrantless entry of a car interior is unlawful unless there is probable cause to believe that it contains contraband." *United States v. Sukiz-Grado,* 22 F.3d 1006 (10th Cir. 1994).

Currency sniffs

One of the key elements of forfeiting cash is to show a connection to illegal activity. Positive alerts by drug-detection dogs on currency suspected to be the fruit or instrumentality of the drug trade are reliable evidence that the money should be forfeited. *United States v. $242,484 U.S. Currency,* 389 F.3d 1149 (11th Cir. 2004). Though there are rumors that a great portion of the currency in circulation is tainted with drug residue, those claims can be effectively debunked with good expert witness testimony. *United States v. $141,770 U.S. Currency,* 157 F.3d 600 (8th Cir. 1998) (case explains poor science behind tainted currency claim). Detector dogs used for currency sniffs must be "proofed" on the odor of untainted currency.

Homes

"A man's house is his castle," said Sir Edward Coke, and few places enjoy a higher expectation of privacy. Some courts hold that a sniff of a doorway or exterior walls of a single-family residence constitute a search, thus requiring probable cause. *United States v. Thomas,* 757 F.2d 1359 (2d Cir.), *cert. denied sub nom. Fisher v. United States,* 474 U.S. 819 (1985); *State v. Rabb,* 920 So. 2d 1175 (Fla. App. 2006). Even though some courts have deemed the sniff of a residential exterior to be a "search," most courts have routinely imposed a reasonable suspicion standard, rather than probable cause, in measuring the lawfulness of such sniffs. *United States v. Beale,* 736 F.2d 1289 (9th Cir.), *cert. denied,* 469 U.S. 1072 (1984). Other courts have required neither reasonable suspicion nor probable cause for sniffs of publicly accessible areas around a home. *United States v. Brock,* 417 F.3d 692 (7th Cir. 2005) (sniff outside of private room door not a search when consent to sniff common areas granted by roommate), *cert. denied,* ___ U.S. ___, 126 S. Ct. 2306 (2006); *United States v. Roby,* 122 F.3d 1120 (8th Cir. 1997) (sniff in hotel hallway not a search); *State v. Davis,* 711 N.W.2d 841 (Minn. App. 2006) (sniff of apartment hallway is not a search and requires no suspicion); *People v.*

Dunn, 77 N.Y.2d 19 (1990), *cert. denied*, 501 U.S. 1219 (1991) (sniff at front door of apartment not a search); *United States v. Tarazon-Silva*, 960 F. Supp. 1152 (W.D. Tex. 1997), *aff'd*, 166 F.3d 341 (5th Cir. 1998) (sniff of dryer vent near driveway not a search); *United States v. Vasquez*, 909 F.2d 235 (7th Cir. 1990) (sniff of exterior of garage not a search), *cert. denied*, 501 U.S. 1217 (1991); *State v. Smith* 2004 WL 213395 (Tex. App. 2004) (sniff of garage door not a search), *cert. denied*, 544 U.S. 961 (2005). One court has applied a state constitution to rule that a sniff in a driveway requires reasonable suspicion. *State v. Tackitt*, 67 P.3d 295 (Mont. 2003). When a detector dog that is already lawfully inside a home spontaneously alerts to hidden drugs, the sniff is not considered a search and the drugs will be admissible in court. *United States v. Reed*, 141 F.3d 644 (6th Cir. 1998).

Jail and prison sniffs

Although some courts frown on general canine sniffs of persons, at least one court has approved the limited use of drug-detection dogs to sniff prospective visitors at correctional facilities. *Romo v. Champion*, 46 F.3d 1013 (10th Cir.), *cert. denied*, 516 U.S. 947 (1995). The court noted: "While the dog's sniff of plaintiffs' bodies was clearly more intrusive than its sniff of the vehicle, it nevertheless was reasonable in light of all the relevant circumstances. Again, plaintiffs' expectations of privacy were reduced because they were visiting a prison, and a dog's sniff of the area surrounding one's body is not terribly intrusive."

Boat interdiction

Coast Guard officers have the right to board any vessel in navigable waters to ensure compliance with all laws of the United States. 14 U.S. Code § 89(a); *United States v. Troise*, 796 F.2d 310 (9th Cir. 1986). Accordingly, the Coast Guard may take a drug-detector dog aboard on such inspections without any reasonable suspicion. *United States v. Todhunter*, 297 F.3d 886 (9th Cir. 2002).

Storage lockers

A detector dog may be used to sniff the exterior of storage units, assuming that officers can lawfully access the units. *United States v. Ortega-Jimenez*, 232 F.3d 1325 (10th Cir. 2000); *United States v. Mahler*, 141 F.3d 811 (8th Cir.), *cert. denied*, 525 U.S. 885 (1998); *United States v. Lingenfelter*,

997 F.2d 632 (9th Cir. 1993). One officer conducting training inadvertently discovered a cache of illegal drugs hidden in a storage locker, and the court admitted the drugs on the basis that the officer was lawfully in the area, invited by the storage unit owner. *State v. Slowikowski,* 743 P.2d 1126 (Or. App. 1987), *aff'd,* 761 P.2d 1315 (Or. 1988). One court has relied on its state constitution to rule that the sniff of an exterior door of a storage unit is a search requiring reasonable suspicion. *State v. Carter,* 697 N.W.2d 199 (Minn. 2005).

Sniffs of persons

A sniff of a person is a search and is generally to be avoided. Courts have not been offended by unintentional person sniffs, where a dog alerted to a person nearby. *United States v. Reyes,* 349 F.3d 219 (5th Cir. 2003) (dog four to five feet away from bus passenger alerted without the handler's intention to perform sniff), *cert. denied,* 540 U.S. 1228 (2004); *United States v. Garcia-Garcia,* 319 F.3d 726 (5th Cir.) (brief incidental contact to suspect's leg while dog sniffed aisle was not unreasonable), *cert. denied,* 539 U.S. 910 (2003).

Detaining a vehicle to wait for a detector dog

Once an officer decides to detain a vehicle for a sniff, how long is it constitutionally "reasonable" to wait for a drug-detection dog? Courts routinely approve detentions of 20 to 30 minutes. *United States v. Lebrun,* 261 F.3d 731 (8th Cir. 2001) (20 minutes not unreasonable); *United States v. Bloomfield,* 40 F.3d 910 (8th Cir. 1994) (one hour wait not unreasonable when dog was requested six minutes after initial stop), *cert. denied,* 514 U.S. 1113 (1995); *United States v. Villa-Chaparro,* 115 F.3d 797 (10th Cir.) (43-minute wait reasonable), *cert. denied,* 522 U.S. 926 (1997); *United States v. Frost,* 999 F.2d 737 (3d Cir.) (almost one hour wait reasonable), *cert. denied,* 510 U.S. 1001 (1993); *United States v. McFarley,* 991 F.2d 1188 (4th Cir.) (38-minute wait reasonable), *cert. denied,* 510 U.S. 949 (1993); *United States v. Alpert,* 816 F.2d 958 (4th Cir. 1987) (50-minute wait reasonable); *United States v. Borys,* 766 F.2d 304 (7th Cir.) (75-minute wait reasonable), *cert. denied,* 474 U.S. 1082 (1985); *LeMense v. State,* 754 P.2d 268, 274 (Alaska App. 1988) (approximately 30-minute wait reasonable).

However, in rural areas a drug-detection dog is often not available within that time frame. Courts focus on more than just the time delay; the critical factor appears to be the officer's diligence in getting a drug-detection dog to the scene. One court considered a 50-minute delay from the time of the stop to the arrival of the dog. The court noted that the stop occurred 31 miles from where the nearest drug-detection dog was stationed, and found that the delay was not unreasonable. *State v. Welch,* 873 P.2d 601 (Wyo. 1994). Another court explicitly ruled that the 50 minutes necessary to secure a drug-detection dog was not unreasonable when the dog was stationed 25 miles away. The court also noted that it could not expect that the police would have a dog available at a shorter distance, given the rural area. *United States v. Hardy,* 855 F.2d 753 (11th Cir. 1988), *cert. denied,* 489 U.S. 1019 (1989). Several courts have approved detentions of up to 90 minutes when the detention is supported by reasonable suspicion and the officer acts with due diligence to get the dog to the scene as soon as practical. *United States v. $64,765.00 U.S. Currency,* 786 F. Supp. 906 (D. Or. 1991). One court approved a detention of nearly two hours when a stop was made in the early-morning hours at a remote location near the Canadian border. *United States v. Maltais,* 403 F.3d 550 (8th Cir. 2005), *cert. denied,* ___ U.S. ___, 126 S. Ct. 1345 (2006).

Establishing reliability of the detector dog

While the dog's positive alert can alone constitute probable cause to search, the reliability of the particular dog must be established in court, much like an expert witness's credentials. Most courts that have considered questions of canine reliability have depended to some degree on the dog's certification. *United States v. Boxley,* 373 F.3d 759 (6th Cir.), *cert. denied,* 543 U.S. 972 (2004). There are several national and state certification programs available. Generally, if a dog's training is documented, and the dog is certified at the time of the sniff and has developed a successful track record, the court will inquire no further. Following are examples of evidence required to establish reliability of detector dogs:

- Court refused to authorize extensive defense requests for the police dog's training records, veterinary records, alert reports, and other miscellaneous documents. "We do not believe the documents were relevant because the dog was certified on the day in question and because the dog properly alerted to the presence of contraband. Indeed, had the dog's records indicated it had false-alerted in the past, defendant's ability to cross-examine would not have been enhanced because there is no doubt it correctly alerted in this instance." *United States v. Gonzalez-Acosta*, 989 F.2d 384 (10th Cir. 1993).

- General history of the dog's reliable performance is sufficient to establish reliability for a particular sniff. *United States v. $30,670*, 403 F.3d 448 (7th Cir. 2005) (drugs or currency found after 97.6 percent of alerts; drugs found after 70.1 percent of alerts).
- The prosecution need not provide the dog's training and performance records. The handler's testimony as to the dog's track record is sufficient. Training and performance records are relevant for assessing the weight to give to the dog sniff, but are not required. *United States v. Boxley*, 373 F.3d 759 (6th Cir.), *cert. denied*, 543 U.S. 972 (2004).
- Fact that dog was certified by a standards organization was sufficient to show reliability, and training records were not required in court. *United States v. Sundby*, 186 F.3d 873 (8th Cir. 1999).
- Reliability is acceptable when handler and dog completed all standard training procedures for drug-detecting teams and the dog was certified to detect a variety of narcotics, including marijuana and its derivatives, cocaine and its derivatives, heroin and its derivatives, and methamphetamine, even though dog located the odor of PCP and had not been certified to find PCP odor. *United States v. Outlaw*, 316 F.3d 701 (5th Cir. 2003).
- Despite handler's inability to state with precision what in-service training should be conducted, and despite failure to show training records, reliability established when canine unit supervisor testified that the dog was certified at the time of the sniff. *United States v. Hill*, 195 F.3d 258 (6th Cir. 1999), *cert. denied*, 528 U.S. 1176 (2000).
- The prosecution must show that the dog was trained to detect the odors of particular drugs, that the dog has had an acceptable success rate, how the dog is trained to indicate an alert, and that the dog alerted in the proper fashion on the time in question. *United States v. Delaney*, 52 F.3d 182 (8th Cir.), *cert. denied*, 516 U.S. 878 (1995).
- Completion of drug-detection school and certification of dog and handler sufficient to establish reliability. Reliability is generally presumed if a sniff results in probable cause to search, though the defense may always challenge the dog's reliability. *United States v. Sanchez-Pena*, 336 F.3d 431 (5th Cir. 2003).

- Records of training and certification of the dog must be provided to defense. *United States v. Cedano-Arellano,* 332 F.3d 568 (9th Cir. 2003), *cert. denied,* 540 U.S. 1137 (2004).
- Handler's testimony that dog was certified on day of sniff and had never given false indication sufficient to show reliability. *United States v. Lopez,* 380 F.3d 538 (1st Cir. 2004), *cert. denied,* 543 U.S. 1074 (2005).
- Court testimony of handler that dog was reliable sufficient for purposes of probable cause. *United States v. Robinson,* 390 F.3d 853 (6th Cir. 2004).

Tracking dog evidence

The Royal Canadian Mounted Police and other Canadian public safety agencies have used dogs to track suspects for many years with great success. Canadian officers often introduce evidence that the dog tracked a particular person as evidence of the person's involvement in a crime. Some of their U.S. counterparts are following suit. More than 30 states allow tracking evidence to be admitted in court. *State v. Buller,* 517 N.W.2d 711 (Iowa 1994) (listing 32 state court decisions). With the proper foundation, a tracking dog's actions can tie critical evidence to suspects, as well as simply locate the evidence. *Epperly v. Booker,* 997 F.2d 1 (4th Cir.), *cert. denied,* 510 U.S. 1015 (1993). Tracking dogs can directly identify suspects based on articles left at a crime scene. *United States v. Gates,* 680 F.2d 1117 (6th Cir. 1982), *cert. denied,* 465 U.S. 1069 (1984). A dog may provide probable cause to arrest a suspect who has fled from the scene when the dog tracks a scent and leads officers to the suspect. *Warren v. City of Lincoln,* 864 F.2d 1436 (8th Cir. 1987), *cert. denied,* 490 U.S. 1091 (1989).

Arson-detector dog evidence

An arson-detector dog can help identify the source and cause of a suspected arson fire. *United States v Marji,* 158 F.3d 60 (2d Cir.), *cert. denied,* 525 U.S.1048 (1998); *State v. Schultz,* 58 P.3d 879 (Utah App. 2002). Although the dog's indication of the presence of accelerants may not be admissible as substantive evidence that the fire was caused by arson, a properly trained and certified dog can locate evidence that might not otherwise be detected. Some courts allow evidence of the dog's indication as prima facie evidence that accelerants were present at the fire. *State v. Buller,* 517 N.W.2d 711 (Iowa 1994).

CHAPTER 10

CANINE USE OF FORCE

Find and bite, or find and bark?
Liability for a service dog bite
Are police service dogs equal to deadly force?
Misdemeanors
Felonies
Warnings
Unintended bites
Liability protection

Use of force principles regulating canine teams do not vary from the general laws and principles governing all law enforcement use of force. However, there are some unique force application situations with canine teams. Police service dogs are locator tools; they are not primarily intended for deployment as a force option. Unlike any other tool in an officer's array, service dogs can be recalled once deployed. Service dogs also cannot be taken away from the officer and used against the officer. Many courts have acknowledged that deployment of **a police service dog can prevent the necessity of using deadly force**. *Robinette v. Barnes*, 854 F.2d 909 (6th Cir. 1988).

When should (or shouldn't) a service dog be used to locate and/or capture a suspect? Keep in mind that the service dog's primary function is to locate—not to bite—the suspect. Though most service dog handlers have received special training in use of force, the following information will help officers know when they may properly request the assistance of a service dog to locate and apprehend a suspect.

Ancient Egyptian papyri show that the use of dogs as law enforcement tools is at least several thousand years old. The spiked collar popular in cartoon illustrations has its roots in ancient Greece and Persia, where dogs equipped with spiked harnesses were sent before the advancing army to attack cavalry mounts. The expression "dogs of war" can be traced to the Middle Ages, when dogs wore armor and were trained to nip at the legs of opposing knights' mounts.

There is nothing new about using police dogs to subdue criminal street gangs. Long before the advent of the Bloods and the Crips, the turn-of-the-20th-century Parisian gendarmes were using police dogs against roving gang members. A few years later, in 1907, a police dog program began in New York. The program lasted nearly 20 years. Between the mid-twenties and 1956, when the Baltimore Police Department launched a canine division, police dogs were virtually unseen in America, although their use was popular in England, France, and Germany. By the late fifties, police canine programs were re-established. A 1959 article in the IACP journal *The Police Chief* asked: "Use of Police Dogs a Fad?"

Find and bite, or find and bark?

Under a find and bite philosophy, the dog is trained to search for a suspect; upon locating the suspect, the dog is allowed to bite him or her. The dog is trained to release the suspect upon command, or to release the suspect once the suspect ceases to resist. The find and bark philosophy is similar to find and bite; the dog is trained to hold or circle the suspect and to maintain a constant bark until the suspect is secured by officers. The dog is not trained to engage the suspect unless: (1) the handler commands; (2) the suspect fights with the dog; (3) the suspect attempts to escape; or (4) the suspect takes aggressive action toward the handler. Critics of canine programs advocate a nationwide mandate on bark and hold training. The find and bark approach requires a superior canine and immediate supervision by the handler. Some trainers assert that find and bark–trained dogs are unpredictable when they locate a suspect after an aggressive search or encounter.

To date there has been only one broad-scale, scientifically validated study comparing bite and hold–trained dogs and bark and hold–trained dogs and the likelihood of a bite. In 2003, the University of Central Florida released a study concluding that a *bark and hold dog is more likely to bite a suspect* in the course of a deployment. The debate is certain to continue. Whatever the training approach for a police service dog, the underlying question following a dog bite is whether the deployment of the police service dog was justified by the circumstances.

Liability for a service dog bite

The mere fact that a police canine bites a suspect will not expose a department to civil liability. Most commonly, a plaintiff will allege excessive force. Excessive force complaints can arise in a number of contexts. A plaintiff may claim that the deployment of the police service dog is excessive relative to the degree of the offense. A few courts have held that use of a canine to apprehend a misdemeanor suspect who poses no threat to the officers or the public is facially unconstitutional. Allegations of excessive force may also arise from the actual bite, or from repeated biting after the apprehension. This can occur when the handler fails to promptly call the dog off or the dog fails to obey the command. An unintentional bite may also generate an excessive force complaint. Police service dogs are trained to protect their handlers, and a dog may mistakenly perceive a threat to its handler and attack without warning or command.

The critical issue in defending a dog bite where excessive force is claimed is whether the dog should have been deployed in the first place. As with any evaluation of law enforcement use of force, this calculation includes the factors of *Graham v. Connor. See Use of Force chapter.* The first step in deciding when to send a dog is an evaluation of the crimes allegedly committed by the suspect. Next, consider the degree of danger that the suspect poses to officers and the public. Finally, ask whether the suspect is actively fleeing or resisting arrest. Though not necessarily a factor imposed by courts, officers should also consider the age of the suspect and use particular caution in sending a dog to locate and/or apprehend a juvenile.

Are police service dogs equal to deadly force?

Officers responded to a burglar alarm at a Nashville auto dealer and found evidence of forced entry. The canine handler shouted two separate warnings for the suspect to surrender or the dog would be sent into the building. When the suspect did not surrender, the dog was sent to locate the suspect. A third warning was shouted once the dog was in the building. The handler followed but lost sight of his dog. After a few minutes, the handler found the dog biting the unconscious suspect's throat. The suspect later died of his wounds. This is the only reported and confirmed case of a fatal injury from a police service dog in the United States in at least the past 25 years. *Robinette v. Barnes,* 854 F.2d 909 (6th Cir. 1988).

The factors used to determine whether a particular force is deadly force include the intent of the officer to cause death or serious injury and the likelihood that the force will, in fact, result in death or serious injury. The court unequivocally stated that **use of the dog does not constitute deadly force**. The dog was well-trained and the handler and dog both received regular in-service training. Thus, the court found that the suspect's death was "an extreme aberration from the outcome intended or expected." The deployment of a properly trained police service dog does not constitute deadly force. Since the *Robinette* decision, numerous federal courts have considered whether police service dogs constitute deadly force. The strong majority of courts agree that a police service dog bite does not amount to deadly force. *Marquez v. City of Albuquerque,* 399 F.3d 1216 (10th Cir. 2005); *Dunigan v. Noble,* 390 F.3d 486 (6th Cir. 2004); *Kuha v. City of Minnetonka,* 365 F.3d 590 (8th Cir. 2003); *Jarrett v. Town of Yarmouth,* 331 F.3d 140 (1st Cir. 2003). Many courts agree with the *Robinette* premise that the use of police service dogs prevents the use of otherwise justified deadly force. *Mickle v. Ahmed,* 444 F. Supp. 2d 601 (D.S.C. 2006).

In *Smith v. City of Hemet,* 394 F.3d 689 (9th Cir.), *cert. denied,* 545 U.S. 1128 (2005), the Ninth Circuit Court of Appeals expanded the definition of deadly force by police to include force "that creates a substantial risk of causing death or serious bodily injury." The court noted: "While we have not in any of our prior cases found that the use of police dogs constituted deadly force, we have never stated that the use of such dogs cannot constitute such force." The natural questions arising from the decision include: "what risk is substantial?" and "what is serious bodily injury?" Because these are questions of fact, they become questions for a jury. Thus, one practical effect of *Smith* is that more cases may end up in a trial, rather than being booted out of court on a motion for summary judgment. Counsel for officers will likely argue that an officer's force could not constitute deadly force if there was not a "substantial risk" that the resulting "serious bodily injury" would actually result in death. Future Ninth Circuit decisions will shape definition of "substantial risk" and "serious bodily injury." In the meantime, *Smith* appears to be having little practical effect on police dog-bite litigation. *Thompson v. County of Los Angeles,* 47 Cal. Rptr. 3d 702 (Cal. App. 2006) (citing the *Smith* definition of deadly force and holding that police service dog use does not constitute deadly force).

Some years ago, the San Diego Police Department made a deliberate choice to increase the number of police canine teams in an effort to reduce shootings. Results show that the department has significantly reduced officer shootings of suspects armed with weapons other than firearms since the department bolstered its canine force. The department enjoyed a corresponding increase in public approval.

Misdemeanors

As a general rule, service dogs should not be used to locate or apprehend suspects who have committed only misdemeanors. *Jarrett v. Town of Yarmouth,* 309 F.3d 54 (1st Cir. 2002), *cert. denied,* 540 U.S. 1017 (2003); *Marley v. City of Allentown,* 774 F. Supp. 343 (E.D. Pa.1991), *aff'd,* 961 F.2d 1567 (3d Cir. 1992). A dog should never be used to locate and apprehend a non-violent misdemeanor suspect. Courts have carefully considered deployments in misdemeanors, primarily in cases where suspects flee from traffic stops. Following are some examples of misdemeanor deployments that have not resulted in liability, and the court's reasoning.

- **Traffic stop for driving with improper license plates** (a misdemeanor), leading to suspicion that the car could be stolen. After a short pursuit (a felony), the suspect ran into wooded terrain. The suspect left a large knife behind in the car, suggesting a propensity to carry weapons. The court ruled in favor of the officers because the suspect may have committed felony auto theft and did commit felony evading, may have been armed, presented a danger evidenced by fleeing, and potentially may have been waiting to ambush the officers. The most significant factors were flight and presumption of a threat to officers. *Miller v. Clark County,* 340 F.3d 959 (9th Cir. 2003).
- **Traffic stop for driving under the influence of alcohol.** A suspect failed to stop for emergency lights, then stopped, got out of the car, yelled at the officer, got back in the car and drove off. After stopping in a backyard, the suspect ran. The officer gave warnings and sent the dog. The suspect's femoral artery was punctured by the dog bite. The suspect's blood alcohol level was .344. The court found no liability. The court found that the suspect had initially committed a misdemeanor, compounded into a felony evading. The suspect posed an immediate threat through his continued flight on foot. *Tilson v. City of Elkhart, Ind.,* 96 Fed. Appx. 413 (7th Cir. 2004).
- **Traffic stop for failure to dim lights.** After stopping, the suspect ran into a swampy area of high grass for no apparent reason. A 30-minute track with a dog resulted in finding the suspect, who was briefly bitten. The court ruled that the bite was reasonable force because the flight led to several conclusions: the officers could reasonably assume that the suspect had committed some crime more serious than failure to dim lights; the suspect fled into a residential area where he could confront citizens; the suspect may have been armed. *Kuha v. City of Minnetonka,* 365 F.3d 590 (8th Cir. 2003).
- **Pedestrian stop for suspicion of underage alcohol consumption**. A college honor student and football player was walking home from a drinking party with a sack in his hand. When the suspect saw a patrolling officer, the suspect fled. The officer followed, taking his unleashed dog with him. The handler put the dog on a leash when it appeared that the dog had picked up the suspect's scent. There was no dog bite. The suspect, who was severely injured when he fell into a rocky creek bed, had barbiturates and amphetamines in his blood, as well as a blood

alcohol level of .227. The suspect claimed that using the unleashed dog to locate a misdemeanor suspect constituted excessive force. The court disagreed. *Dennen v. City of Duluth*, 350 F.3d 786 (8th Cir. 2003).

- **Pedestrian stop for intoxication.** An intoxicated man went to a fast-food restaurant late at night and demanded to be served. He challenged workers to fight and smacked a window. Returning home, he strapped on a large knife and began to walk to the liquor store, when he found officers looking for him. Thus far, he had committed only misdemeanors. The suspect ran from the officers. After a warning, the dog apprehended the suspect by a bite to the arm. Though the court found the crimes to be minor, officers reasonably believed that the suspect could have committed a burglary at the restaurant. The court ruled in favor of the officers because of the act of flight upon seeing officers and the possession of the large knife. The court repeated the doctrine that a dog bite does not constitute deadly force. *Vera Cruz v. City of Escondido*, 139 F.3d 659 (9th Cir. 1997), *cert. denied*, 525 U.S. 869 (1998).
- **Suspect fled after minor traffic violations.** The suspect fled on foot into a residential area. Officers knew that the suspect had a record for armed robbery and feared for the safety of the citizens. The suspect was seen hiding under a car and refused to come out. After warnings that a dog would be sent, a dog bit the suspect and pulled him out from under the car. The bite was ruled to be reasonable due to the flight and the reasonable fear for citizens' safety. *Shannon v. City of Costa Mesa*, 46 F.3d 1145 (9th Cir.), *aff'd sub nom. Shannon v. City of Santa Ana*, 516 U.S. 822 (1995).
- **Suspect attempted to climb a fence into a Grateful Dead concert.** The suspect approached a fence, apparently intending to climb it and enter concert grounds without a ticket. An officer some distance away shouted a quick warning and sent his dog to capture the suspect. The issue before the court was whether the plaintiff was entitled to a damage award without taking the case to a jury. The plaintiff argued that the law clearly stated that a deployment for a property crime misdemeanor was unreasonable. The court refused to grant the plaintiff judgment without a trial, but noted that all of the cases addressing dog-bite use of force involved crimes that were significantly more severe. *Mason v. Hamilton County*, 13 F. Supp. 2d 829 (S.D. Ind. 1998).

The recurrent lesson in these and similar cases is that **a service dog may be deployed on a misdemeanor suspect when the suspect flees or actively resists arrest in some way**. This is consistent with the three factors posed by *Graham v. Connor.* The first factor is the degree of the crime. The second is the degree and immediacy of the threat against officers and the public. The third factor is whether the suspect is actively resisting attempts to arrest or apprehend him, either by force or fleeing. These factors are considered in light of the totality of the circumstances known to the officers on the scene, not the 20/20 hindsight of a court.

Felonies

The use of a police service dog to apprehend felony suspects generally receives more favorable treatment in court. The more violent and threatening the felony committed, the more likely it is that the use of force will be ruled as reasonable. However, officers cannot simply equate the commission of a felony with a crime sufficiently serious to send a dog to apprehend the suspect. **Suspects who are suspected of a felony involving the use or threat of a weapon, assaultive behavior, or a threat of serious bodily injury or death, and who are actively fleeing or resisting, may be apprehended by a police service dog.** The following cases offer general guidelines for deployments on felonies.

- **Suspect was driving a stolen car and led officers on a pursuit.** The suspect threw a glass bottle at an officer, then fled on foot over a fence and into a truck yard, where he hid. Numerous warnings were shouted. A dog was sent. The dog bit the suspect and the suspect put the dog in a headlock. The canine handler dragged the entwined dog and suspect out from under a car. The court found the force to be reasonable because the crime was a felony, the suspect assaulted an officer, the suspect fled, the suspect ignored repeated warnings and commands to surrender, and the suspect continued to resist when located. This is one of many cases where the court discussed the issue of bite and hold and bark and hold dogs and refused to rule that the use of bite and hold dogs is unreasonable. *Quintanilla v. City of Downey*, 84 F.3d 353 (9th Cir. 1996), *cert. denied,* 519 U.S. 1122 (1997).
- **Armed bank robbery suspect hiding.** The suspect fled onto private property and was hiding in bushes. More than 20

warnings were broadcast from a helicopter's loudspeaker. A dog was sent to find the suspect, and the dog bit the suspect. The suspect fought the dog and was bitten again. It comes as no surprise that the court found the use of a service dog to find a fleeing, armed suspect who had committed a violent felony to be objectively reasonable. This case is the classic circumstance for proper use of a dog. Better that the dog find the suspect than officers face the risk of gunfire from a hidden suspect. *Mendoza v. Block*, 27 F.3d 1357 (9th Cir. 1994).

- **Suspect wanted only for driving under the influence of alcohol and driving with a suspended license**. As the officer checked the status of the suspect's license, the suspect fled into nearby woods. A citizen reported that the suspect had been in a neighbor's garage (thus committing a minor felony). A canine handler located the suspect and shouted a warning to stop or the dog would be sent. The suspect shouted at the officer and continued to flee. The dog quickly caught the suspect with one minor bite, and immediately released the suspect. The officer shouted at the suspect to remain still so that the dog would not bite again. The dog sat calmly. The suspect then bolted and began to run. The dog again stopped him. The court noted that the crimes were not particularly severe. The suspect was not charged with burglary of the garage. Nonetheless, the use of the dog was reasonable due to the flight. *Carey v. Cassista*, 939 F. Supp. 136 (D. Conn. 1996).

Warnings

Most canine deployment policies require that a verbal warning be given before releasing a dog to locate a suspect. Loud, repeated warnings not only encourage the suspect to surrender but also help avoid liability for any dog bite. *Matthews v. Jones*, 35 F.3d 1046 (6th Cir. 1994) (fact that warning was given made deployment objectively reasonable). The crucial issue in most dog-bite lawsuits is whether the dog should have been used in the first place. To that end, a warning greatly increases the reasonableness of the deployment, as the suspect makes the deliberate choice not to surrender. *Ruvalcaba v. City of Los Angeles*, 167 F.3d 514 (9th Cir.) (officers gave three warnings in both Spanish and English before releasing police dog into a closed theater), *cert. denied*, 528 U.S. 869 (1999). Warnings should be loud, clear, and repeated. *Vera Cruz v. City of Escondido*, 139 F.3d 659 (9th Cir. 1997), *cert. denied*, 525 U.S. 869 (1998).

There is no absolute constitutional right to any warning before the use of force, generally, or before the deployment of a service dog. *Kuha v. City of Minnetonka,* 365 F.3d 590 (8th Cir. 2003). Verbal warnings are always sound practice, unless giving a warning would plainly jeopardize officer safety. *Szalba v. City of Brooklyn Park,* 429 F.3d 1168 (8th Cir. 2005). However, courts have found deployments without warnings to be objectively unreasonable in circumstances where the suspect would not have known that police were present or where the suspect was effectively contained in a perimeter. Occasionally, officer safety may be compromised by shouting a warning, which would reveal the officer's location. Consider the possibility of a warning by loudspeaker from the perimeter. In the *Kuha* case, officers argued that a warning as they searched through tall grass would have posed a safety risk. The court suggested that a warning could have been shouted from a nearby hilltop, noting that "a jury could properly find it objectively unreasonable to use a police dog trained in the bite and hold method without first giving the suspect a warning and opportunity for peaceful surrender."

Warnings are particularly critical when the suspect may not be aware of officers' presence. Officers responding to a mistaken burglary report sent a dog into a residence without warnings, despite a department policy mandating loud verbal warnings. The dog found the lawful resident asleep in her bed and bit her in the face, crushing some of her bones. The victim suffered substantial injuries. The court refused to grant immunity to the officers due to the lack of warnings. *Vathekan v. Prince George's County,* 154 F.3d 173 (4th Cir. 1998). Similarly, another court found deployment without warnings to be unreasonable where the suspects were contained in a narrow alley. It did not help matters that one of the suspects was a pregnant teenage girl. *Kopf v. Wing,* 942 F.2d 265 (4th Cir. 1991), *rev'd following remand sub nom. Kopf v. Skyrm,* 993 F.2d 374 (4th Cir. 1993).

Unintended bites

Unintended bites happen. The bite may be intended by the dog, in response to a person's behavior, but not intended by the handler. For example, an officer stopped a suspect for driving under the influence of alcohol. The suspect became confrontational and abusive. In the course of the arrest, the suspect's wife tried to free the suspect from the officer's hold. The officer ordered his canine to assist and the dog bit the wife. Four backup officers arrived and the fight continued. When the suspect's wife once again jumped in, the dog bit her again, this time without any command. The court had little sympathy for the claim of excessive force. A department will not be liable for a dog's bite if the dog mistakenly believed that an officer was in danger. *Blais v. Town of Goffstown*, 406 A.2d 295 (N.H. 1979). Persons who attempt to interfere with a canine operation cannot claim excessive force when their own actions result in an unintended bite. Dogs are trained to protect their masters. *Dunigan v. Noble*, 390 F.3d 486 (6th Cir. 2004).

There is little litigation over truly unintentional bites. This may be because wise administrators act quickly to resolve the damages and preserve public relations. One effective technique used by several agencies is an instant settlement. The effectiveness of a settlement agreement and liability release depends on three elements. First, a supervisor must have immediate access to cash settlement funds (up to a predetermined amount) and an ability to charge emergency medical bills. Second, the agency's legal advisor must have a written settlement agreement prepared in fill-in-the-blank format. Third, the agency must settle with the bite victim promptly. This type of quick settlement may significantly reduce the cost of an unintended bite.

Liability protection

Some state laws extend special liability protection for canine programs. For example, Utah law offers liability protection for all political entities with police canine programs. Utah Code Ann. § 18-1-1. Many other states have criminal statutes designed to punish injury to police service dogs and their handlers. Ind. Code § 35-43-1-2; Mass. Gen. Laws ch. 272 § 77A; Or. Rev. Stat. § 164.369; Ohio Rev. Code Ann. § 2921.32.1. To be well-protected, an agency should require that the police service dog be certified for patrol duty by the state police standards and training agency. Canine teams that participate in multi-agency task forces should be certified to the highest standard of all participating agencies.

APPENDICES

APPENDIX A: HOMICIDE AND VIOLENT ASSAULT FIRST RESPONDER CHECKLIST

The following checklist is designed for first responders. The objective is to secure the scene, hold witnesses and suspects, and preserve evidence. The first responder can best serve the investigation by perfect preservation for detectives.

Initial Scene Response

- En route to the scene, observe vehicles and persons leaving. Drive with enough caution to arrive in one piece.
- Drive up only as close as *absolutely necessary*. Many crime scenes have been damaged by patrol vehicles driving through blood, over shell casings, or trace evidence.
- First priority is to preserve life, then isolate any non-injured suspects.
- Protect the scene, protect the scene, protect the scene.
- Don't overlook the possibility of a dying declaration. Ask: "who did this to you?" If the suspect's name is not known, obtain a description of height, weight, gender, race, hair, clothing, speech accents. The dying declarations will be powerful evidence in the eventual trial. If you leave to pursue the suspect, leave someone with the victim to listen for dying declarations.
- If this is clearly a death scene, only the single initial officer should enter the scene, unless there is a need for backup for safety purposes. Be careful not to walk through blood pools or disturb other evidence.
- As soon as the scene is safe, the backup officer should stand outside the scene. Do not move dead bodies, including those that are hanging. If a person is hanging, and first aid might be successful, cut the rope in a place that does not disturb any knots.
- Wear gloves to prevent cross-contamination.

- In assessing death, listen for breath sounds, heart sounds, and feel for a carotid pulse. Do not touch the body unnecessarily. Document where you touch the body and inform the medical examiner or coroner.
- If medical assistance is provided to the victim, insofar as possible, note where medical staff touch the victim. When resuscitation efforts are complete, ask medical staff to note or circle any punctures or other injuries caused by treatment. Request that medical staff bag and preserve syringes, bandages, etc.
- If medical staff cuts through clothing, instruct them to avoid bullet holes, bloodstains, or cuts to the clothing. Note the condition of the clothing before medical staff begins treatment.
- Note the condition and size of blood pools if the surface is porous or there is some disturbance to the blood pools.
- Establish large primary and secondary perimeters. Keep as many persons as possible outside of the perimeter. If necessary, enlist a citizen to assist with scene security until other officers arrive. No one ever regretted an excessively large perimeter.
- Consider potential escape routes and notify other officers of best perimeter containment posts.
- Generally, it is best to not interrogate suspects if investigators will be promptly responding. Do not give *Miranda* warnings unless there is an arrest and interrogation is necessary. It is more important to focus attention on securing the scene.
- Delay *arresting* any suspect if possible! Remember that arresting a suspect starts the clock for judicial probable cause review, appointment of legal counsel, and brings *Miranda* rules into play.
- As soon as practical, remove the suspect(s) from the scene to prevent destruction of evidence, influencing witnesses, and to stop the suspect from observing evidence that may later be used against the suspect.
- Do not allow the suspect to wash hands, eat or drink anything, or use the restroom.
- Mentally note the suspect's physical and mental condition.
- Do not be overly concerned about identifying victims. It is far more important to identify and locate the suspect.
- Assess needs and request additional officers for transport, isolation, and scene security.

- Assign an officer to accompany any injured suspect in the ambulance and in the treatment room (insofar as medical personnel permit), preferably with a tape recorder. This officer is responsible for maintaining custody of the suspect, recording any statements, collecting information from medical personnel, securing the injured person's property, and serving as the initial contact at the hospital.
- Identify and detain eyewitnesses and potential eyewitnesses. As soon as practicable, have eyewitnesses sequestered. Instruct them to not discuss the incident among themselves.
- Record names, addresses, and dates of birth, of *all* persons at the scene.
- Prevent anyone from smoking or otherwise contaminating or altering the scene.
- Assign an officer to accompany the injured officer, if any, to provide support, and to protect the officer from media and others.
- Assign a perimeter security officer to maintain perimeter integrity and begin a scene log.
- Protect the scene from rain, snow, blowing debris, if necessary.

Communications

- Limit radio traffic and statements that may be overheard. Request a clear radio channel from dispatch. Use telephones and cellular walkie-talkies. Don't use phones at the scene that may have evidentiary value, i.e., do not pick up a phone that may bear fingerprints or DNA.
- Make necessary notifications, or assign dispatcher to do so. Include command staff, public information officer, county or district attorney, investigators, crime laboratory team, medical examiner.
- Listen carefully to witnesses and ambient noises.
- Ask only questions necessary for immediate public safety and scene management, such as number of injured, triage questions, outstanding suspect and suspect vehicle descriptions, outstanding weapons, location of all involved officers and suspects, area of crime scene, location of any physical evidence or potential evidence.
- Mentally note the emotional condition of witnesses. Emotional condition may be an important factor in court credibility, and in using witness statements in court.

- Broadcast as much suspect information for outstanding suspects as possible. Consider roadblocks if appropriate.
- Note and/or tape spontaneous statements from witnesses/

Evidence preservation

- ***Preserve, don't collect***, unless absolutely necessary.
- If possible, hold your hands behind your back to keep from touching evidence.
- Protect fragile and easily disturbed evidence, such as scattered shell casings, etc.
- If there are tire or shoe prints, warn other officers and medical personnel to avoid damaging the prints.
- Even if the suspect is long gone, attempt to identify the suspect's route to check for discarded evidence, clothing, hair cuttings, shoe prints, etc.
- Sniff the air for unusual or distinctive odors, such as gunpowder, tobacco, marijuana, alcohol, perfume, chemicals, etc.
- Use booties and gloves to reduce transfer contamination.
- Do not touch weapons. Do not attempt to unload or make safe firearms. Weapons *always* hold trace evidence.
- Turn any running water off, if applicable; stop toilet from flushing.
- Note any scene alterations by emergency medical providers (in addition to alternations to the victim and clothing described above).
- Document condition of lights, restraints, water, toilets, etc. Which lights were on, and which were off?
- Will supplemental lighting or equipment be required?
- Will an additional evidence collection team be required? Should the Crime Lab be called to assist?
- Note temperature and thermostat settings.
- Consider secondary crime scenes, such as the suspect's vehicle, pursuit routes, emergency medical center.
- Note the position of windows, doors, cabinets, drawers, etc. Open or closed? How far? Were deadbolts engaged? Was there damage to doors and windows?
- Note any unusual sounds, transient lighting, or other phenomena.
- If there are numerous persons in the area, photograph and/or videotape the crowd. It may be helpful in identifying witnesses, as well as discrediting persons who later falsely claim to have witnessed the event.

- Watch your tongues! Do not contaminate witnesses' testimony by allowing witnesses to overhear officers or other witnesses.

Additional Initial Considerations

- As soon as sufficient staff is available, consider secondary crime scenes, such as the suspect's escape path, suspect's and victim's residences and/or work places, involved vehicles found away from the primary scene, site of the initial assault (if separate from the primary scene).
- If the reporting party or parties are not at the crime scene, locate them as soon as possible to obtain possible eyewitness statements.
- Identify emergency medical personnel who may have left the scene prior to officers and obtain statements.

APPENDIX B: OFFICER-INVOLVED FATALITY CHECKLIST

An officer-involved fatality (OIF), whether a shooting, traffic crash, or other type of fatality, presents unique investigative challenges. In addition to the unique investigative dynamics, an OIF generates additional, independent investigations by the county attorney, the venue agency (if the incident occurs in a jurisdiction other than the involved officer's employing jurisdiction), an administrative investigation, civil litigation or risk management investigation, and potentially a federal investigation covering civil rights issues. At least one investigation will focus on the question of potential criminal liability for the death. Another will examine whether agency policy was violated. Most incidents will also cause a review to prepare the agency's defense for the probability of a civil suit against the officer(s) and agency. These three types of investigation each will be operated under a different set of legal rules.

One view of OIF investigations represents an adversarial role for the involved officers and the investigators. Competent law enforcement administrators as well as police attorneys recognize that both the agency and the officer are best served by two fundamental investigative values: first, the investigation must be as thorough as possible, and second, nothing should prevent the officers from receiving prompt legal counsel as they participate in the investigative process. The philosophy and methodology of an OIF investigation is beyond the scope of this book. This section presents only a first responder's guide for an OIF (*see also In-Custody Death checklist*).

Initial Scene Response

- First priority is to preserve life, then isolate any non-injured suspects.
- Protect the scene, protect the scene, protect the scene.
- Treat like any homicide scene, establishing large primary and secondary perimeters. Keep as many persons as possible outside of the perimeter.
- Assess needs and request additional officers for transport, isolation, and scene security. Don't underestimate

staffing needs. Call other agencies for staffing support if necessary.

- Assign an officer to accompany the injured suspect in the ambulance and in the treatment room (insofar as medical personnel permit), preferably with a tape recorder. This officer is responsible for maintaining custody of the suspect, recording any statements, collecting information from medical personnel, securing the injured person's property, and serving as the initial contact at the hospital.
- Identify and detain eyewitnesses and potential eyewitnesses. As soon as practicable, have eyewitnesses sequestered. Instruct them to not discuss the incident among themselves.
- Record names, addresses, and dates of birth, of *all* persons at the scene.
- Prevent anyone from smoking or otherwise contaminating or altering the scene.
- Assign an officer to accompany the injured officer, if any, to provide support, and to protect the officer from media and others.
- Assign a perimeter security officer to maintain perimeter integrity and begin a scene log.
- Protect involved officer(s) from non-essential questioning by keeping the involved officer near the supervisor until an escort officer can be assigned and the escort's duties explained.

Communications

- Limit radio traffic and statements that may be overheard. Request a clear radio channel from dispatch. Use telephones and cellular walkie-talkies. Don't use phones at the scene that may have evidentiary value.
- Make necessary notifications, or assign dispatcher to do so. Include command staff, public information officer, county or district attorney, peer support network, investigators, crime laboratory team.
- Use proper terminology, like "involved officer" rather than "shooter."
- Limit questions to involved officers. Concentrate only on the information needed to manage the scene and coordinate response. The first responders, including first responding supervisors, do not have investigative responsibility. Ask only questions necessary for immediate public safety and scene management, for example, the number of in-

jured, triage questions, outstanding suspect and suspect vehicle descriptions, outstanding weapons, location of all involved officers and suspects, area of crime scene, location of any physical evidence or potential evidence.
- Broadcast as much suspect information for outstanding suspects as possible. Consider roadblocks if appropriate.
- Direct involved officers to not discuss the incident with other involved officers, or officers present for scene management. Ensure that your orders are given in a professional tone, preserving respect for the officer's dignity and emotional state.
- Direct scene management officers to not discuss the incident with anyone other than investigators, and to not question involved officers.
- Note and/or tape spontaneous statements from involved officers.
- Asking supportive questions, like "are you okay?" or "what can I do for you?" is humane, respectful, and appropriate and will not impair legal issues.

Evidence preservation

- ***Preserve, don't collect***, unless absolutely necessary.
- Protect fragile and easily disturbed evidence, such as scattered shell casings, etc.
- Use booties and gloves to reduce transfer contamination.
- Turn any running water off, if applicable; stop toilet from flushing.
- Note scene alterations by emergency medical providers.
- Document condition of lights, doors, restraints, water, toilets, etc.
- Will supplemental lighting or equipment be required?
- Will an additional evidence collection team be required? Should the Crime Lab be called to assist?
- Obtain a dying declaration from any critically injured person, if possible.
- Wait to remove the involved officer's weapon until a substitute weapon can be issued, and dignity can be preserved. Leave the involved officer's weapon in the holster (or in place on the ground), until the entire duty belt can be replaced. Don't remove magazines from pouch.
- Examine the weapons of officers present who did not shoot to ensure that the weapons have not been fired. Do not overlook back-up weapons.

- Locate and mark shooting position(s), and position(s) of suspects.
- Consider secondary crime scenes, such as the suspect's vehicle, pursuit routes, emergency medical center.
- Note the position of windows, doors, cabinets, drawers, etc. Open or closed? How far?
- Note condition of lights, and lights turned on or off by responding officers.
- Note any unusual sounds, transient lighting, or other phenomena.
- Instruct involved officers to not wash hands or face, or wipe off clothing, in order to preserve gunshot residue evidence and blood spatter or other physical evidence. If the officer has blood on his or her clothing, be sensitive to the probable desire to clean up and change as soon as reasonable (preserving the officer's clothing as potential evidence).
- If there are numerous persons in the area, photograph and/or videotape the crowd. It may be helpful in identifying witnesses, as well as discrediting persons who later falsely claim to have witnessed the event.

Additional Initial Considerations

Though the preceding steps must be accomplished promptly, they are time consuming. By the time the first responding supervisor has worked through the initial checklist, the investigative team should be on scene. However, the first responding supervisor should also be aware of these additional considerations.

- Involved officers should be sequestered as soon as possible, and in a supportive manner. Assign an uninvolved officer to take the involved officer (one escort per involved officer), to the officer's own station, unless circumstances will not allow.
- Order the involved officer to not talk about the incident except with investigators and legal counsel.
- The involved officer has likely just experienced the most traumatic event in his or her life to this point. Treat the officer accordingly.
- The escort officer should not ask the involved officer about the incident. The escort officer is responsible for transport, emotional support, protecting the involved officer from media and other intrusions, assisting the involved officer with physical needs like food, beverage, a com-

fortable and private location, and clean, comfortable clothes. The escort officer should ask supportive questions, and may help the involved officer recall the agency's investigative protocol.

APPENDIX C: IN-CUSTODY DEATH CHECKLIST

An in-custody death, no matter what the cause and who may bear responsibility, is at the top of every corrections manager's list of horrors. An "in-custody" death is any death occurring while a prisoner is incarcerated, being transported in a custodial circumstance, or being taken into custody. In-custody deaths generally mandate at least two, and sometimes three, separate investigations, each conducted independently, and each with its own objectives. First and foremost, the law enforcement agency with appropriate jurisdiction must thoroughly investigate each in-custody death to determine criminal responsibility. Deaths that appear to be incontrovertibly natural might later be ruled homicides following the autopsy, which is virtually mandatory in some jurisdictions for an in-custody death. The second mandatory investigation is to prepare for the inevitable civil suit. This investigation should involve corrections managers, legal counsel and risk management staff. A third investigation may be conducted by facility administration to consider breaches of policies and procedures.

The criminal investigation will likely be fully available as part of the public record. An investigation conducted with an eye toward civil liability principles and under the auspices of legal counsel or risk management will be non-discoverable as litigation preparation material. Investigators should work closely with legal counsel to protect the confidentiality of the investigation.

Investigative Approach

Sudden and unexpected in-custody deaths fall into several general categories: prisoner-on-prisoner force, use of restraints, use of force by officers, suicides and accidents. In each case initial investigative steps may mean the difference between a highly defensible civil case and an expensive settlement or judgment. Following is a checklist of essential investigative actions applicable for the majority of in-custody deaths, derived from the good and bad experiences of a risk manager and homicide prosecutor.

Initial scene response

- First priority is to preserve life, then isolate the suspect, and protect the scene
- Treat like any homicide scene
- Don't be too quick to conclude suicide
- Preserve reporting information

Entering the scene

- Record time of entry
- Preserve a single path of entry
- As soon as practicable, lock down inmates and insist on silence
- Leave hanging bodies in place, except as necessary for life-saving; do not cut knots
- Turn water off; stop toilet from flushing
- Note scene alterations by emergency medical providers
- Document condition of lights, doors, restraints, water, toilets, etc.
- Obtain a dying declaration

Preserving the scene for investigators

- Assess and isolate the perimeter, be very generous with perimeter exterior
- Assign a scene security monitor to exclude unnecessary persons and log entries
- Exclude rubberneckers, even (especially) ranking rubberneckers with no legitimate need to view the scene
- Use booties and gloves to reduce transfer contamination
- Don't forget that DNA and fingerprints really make cases sometimes! Beware of contamination

Initial notifications

- Command staff, Public Information Officer
- Will emergency response teams be needed to manage inmates?
- Internal investigators to assist outside criminal investigators
- Criminal prosecutor *experienced* with homicide investigation and familiar with corrections law
- Risk manager
- Adequate personnel for perimeter security, scene isolation and inmate interviews
- Create an investigative command post

Urgent investigative steps

- Isolate witnesses, don't allow interviews by inexperienced officers
- No nonessential scene alterations
- No smoking, water running, toilet flushing
- Hold the scene security officer, first officer on scene and initial reporting party for quick first interview by investigators
- Take copious instant photos to preserve the scene
- Reassess the scope of the perimeter
- Evaluate the need for secondary search areas, such as the victim's or suspect's work areas, cell, any area where the weapon (if any) could have been fabricated
- Promptly assign a senior correctional officer as liaison to criminal investigators, prosecutor and risk manager to avoid unnecessary confusion and improper initial conclusions

Initial approach to the suspect and witnesses

- Isolate, isolate, isolate *away* from the scene
- No washing or clothing change
- No interrogation by first responding officers
- Record all excited utterances, spontaneous declarations, and immediately note the suspect's physical and emotional state
- Tape all statements
- Note all physical and emotional behaviors, i.e., signs of sexual arousal, semen stains, intoxication, excitement, etc.
- No potty, use a catch toilet
- No sudden and unwarranted *Miranda* warning; wait for investigators
- Identify each person on the unit at the time of the incident, including trustees or others who may have had access to the unit

Initial Investigation Legal Considerations

The corrections manager can be a valuable investigative resource from the outset of the investigation. Most criminal investigators from an outside agency, and most prosecutors, have little knowledge of the peculiar search and seizure and interrogation legal doctrines applying to inmates. More often than not, the real legal expert is the corrections manager who deals with search and interrogation of inmates on a daily basis.

Inmate and Cell Searches

A "search" for Fourth Amendment purposes is any government activity that intrudes on a legitimate expectation of privacy. Thus, the question is where an inmate retains any expectation of privacy in the correctional environment. **The United States Supreme Court has consistently ruled that there is no expectation of privacy in a prison cell or common area, such as the day room.** "A right of privacy in traditional Fourth Amendment terms is fundamentally incompatible with the close and continual surveillance of inmates and their cells required to ensure institutional security and internal order . We believe that it is accepted by our society that loss of freedom of choice and privacy are inherent incidents of confinement." *Hudson v. Palmer,* 468 U.S. 517 (1984). The same doctrine applies to pre-trial detainees in county jail custody. *Bell v. Wolfish,* 441 U.S. 520 (1979).

Corrections authorities have a general right of strip searches for inmates (though not pre-trial detainees), including non-invasive body cavity inspection. *Bell v. Wolfish,* 441 U.S. 520 (1979). Body cavities may be searched by appropriate medical personnel upon reasonable suspicion, although an x-ray may be just as effective and can be conducted with little articulated suspicion. *Moore v. Carwell,* 168 F.3d 234 (5th Cir. 1999). Inmates have no protection against blood extraction for purposes of DNA testing. *Shaffer v. Saffle,* 148 F.3d 1180 (10th Cir.), *cert. denied,* 525 U.S. 1005 (1998). Even so, consider a warrant. The DNA evidence will not change, and a warrant shifts the burden of a suppression hearing to the criminal defendant. Blood and urine testing are also helpful to show intoxication, or lack of intoxication to defeat a defense of voluntary or involuntary intoxication.

Visitor searches

Those who voluntarily come to the institution and may be witnesses, suspects or accomplices in an in-custody death have surrendered significant privacy expectations by coming to the facility. **Visitors may be searched upon *reasonable suspicion,* not the traditionally required probable cause, of complicity in criminal activity.** Even a strip search of a visitor may be premised upon reasonable suspicion. *Burgess v. Lowery,* 201 F.3d 942 (7th Cir. 2000); *Romo v. Champion,* 46 F.3d 1013 (10th Cir.), *cert. denied,* 516 U.S. 947 (1995). With appropriate staff and privacy concerns met, even a body cavity search may be based on the lower standard of reasonable suspicion. *Spear v. Sowders,* 71 F.3d 626 (6th Cir. 1995). Remember, although the legal right may exist, strip searches and body cavity intrusions should be limited to times of true need, and accompanied by steps to preserve as much personal dignity as possible. These principles will be entirely foreign to most investigators and prosecutors accustomed to higher standards outside the prison setting.

Interrogation of inmates

Traditionally, *Miranda* warnings are required when *custody* (deprived of liberty in a significant way) and *interrogation* (questions or statements intended to elicit an incriminating response) are present. Just because an inmate is incarcerated, he or she may not be *in custody* for purposes of *Miranda.* An inmate may not be in custody until the inmate is subject to additional restraints beyond those normally imposed under the terms of incarceration. An additional restraint is "one that places a restriction on the inmate's freedom of action in connection with the interrogation and prevents him from leaving the scene of questioning by placing a further limit on his already restricted freedom of movement." *Commonwealth v. Larkin,* 708 N.E.2d 674 (Mass. 1999).

Factors tending to show that an inmate is not "in custody" include asking the inmate whether he or she would like to speak with investigators, interrogating in a day room or other non-lock down area, lack of pressure from investigators, offering coffee, telling the inmate that he or she could stop the interrogation by outside investigators at anytime by calling for a correctional officer. *United States v. Turner,* 28 F.3d 981 (9th Cir. 1994), *cert. denied,* 513 U.S. 1158 (1995); *Commonwealth v. Perry,* 733 N.E.2d 83 (Mass. 2000); *Commonwealth v. Larkin,* 708 N.E.2d 674 (Mass. 1999). Don't squelch voluntary and spontaneous statements. "*Miranda* does not protect an accused from a spontaneous admission made under circumstances not induced by the investigating officers or during a conversation not initiated by officers." *United States v. Hayes,* 120 F.3d 739 (8th Cir. 1997).

Aside from *Miranda,* there are Sixth Amendment right to counsel issues to consider. *Miranda* is a Fifth Amendment prophylactic rule designed to protect against compelled self-incrimination. It is not charge or case specific and the *Miranda* rights are always implicated by any custodial interrogation. An inmate in custody awaiting conviction or appeal may not be questioned about the crime for which the inmate is incarcerated, without permission of the inmate's lawyer. However, such inmates may be questioned without counsel about new criminal offenses (assuming *Miranda* concerns are satisfied). *Illinois v. Perkins*, 496 U.S. 292 (1990).

Appendix D: Asset Forfeiture Investigation

Asset forfeiture is a tool to assist law enforcement to curb the flow of illegal drugs in our communities. Americans spend an average of more than $60 billion on illegal drugs each year. Asset forfeiture helps take away the profit incentive in drug dealing, reduce the financial base for maintaining and expanding drug operations, and apply drug dealers' profits to public programs. A bank robber cannot keep the money stolen from a bank. Why should a drug dealer or illegal arms merchant be allowed to keep profits from sales of contraband?

An asset forfeiture case is a civil lawsuit against property, not persons. A drug dealer can be charged with the underlying crime at the same time that the drug dealer's nice car can be sued. Because asset forfeiture actions are civil, a preponderance of the evidence standard applies. Hearsay evidence may be admitted.

Forfeiture of illegal drugs and weapons is based on the contraband nature of the property. Property that can be traced to an illegal drug transaction is a proceed. Proceeds are forfeited on the basis that they are profits of illegal activities. Property that is used to facilitate illegal activities is also subject to forfeiture. Asset forfeiture may occur in either state or federal court. If state or local officers investigate the case and the charges are brought in state court, and there is property subject to forfeiture, then a state court forfeiture action is appropriate.

Additional questions must be asked when investigating a crime involving property potentially subject to forfeiture. Ask questions that connect the property to facilitation of the crime and profit from the crime. Consult with the government attorney assigned to prosecute civil forfeitures early in the investigation. Civil forfeiture lawsuits must often be filed within a short time after seizure of the property to be forfeited.

Seizure of a large amount of cash requires particular investigative efforts to connect the cash with facilitation of an illegal transaction or proceeds from an illegal transaction. Following are some suggested questions to ask at the time that the cash is discovered. In many cases suspects have disclaimed any ownership interests in huge sums of cash. A suspect who disclaims an ownership interest should be asked to sign a written disclaimer. *See below.*

Interview for seizure of cash

Is this your money? (**If the answer is "no," have the suspect sign a disclaimer form.**)
¿Es este dinero suyo?

Where do you work?
¿Donde trabaja?

How much are you paid?
¿Cuánto le pagan?

When did you get this money?
¿Cuándo obtuvo este dinero?

Where did you get this money?
¿De dónde obtuvo este dinero?

Who gave you the money?
¿Quién le dio el dinero?

How did you/do you contact this person?
¿Cómo contactó/contacta esta persona?

How do you know this person?
¿Cómo conoce a esta persona?

Have you met this person before? When? Where?
¿Ha reunido con (o conocido) esta persona antes? ¿Cuándo? ¿Dónde?

How much are you being paid?
¿Cuánto le están pagando?

Did you receive all of the money at the same time?
¿Recibió todo el dinero a la misma vez?

Have you exchanged any of the bills?
¿Ha intercambiado alguno de los billetes?

Did you wrap or repackage them?
¿Los envolvió o rempaquetó?

Did you count the money after receiving it?
¿Contó el dinero después de recibirlo?

What is the source of the money?
¿Cuál es la fuente del dinero?

What are you supposed to do with the money?
¿Qué está supuesto que usted debe hacer con el dinero?

Who arranged this transaction?
¿Quién arregló esta transacción?

How did you know the person who arranged the transaction?
¿Cómo conoció ala persona la cual arregló la transacción?

Have you met them before?
¿Usted le ha conocido a la persona anteriormente?

Have you spoken to the person since the exchange?
¿Ha hablado usted con la persona después del intercambio?

What identifying information about this person can you give me?
¿Qué información indicative me puede dar acerca de la persona?

Was there a receipt given for the money?
¿Fue dado un recibo por el dinero?

How much money is here?
¿Cuánto dinero hay aquí?

Disclaimer of Ownership of Currency

1. I, ________________________________, acknowledge that on ______________, 20__, $__________________ in currency was seized from me by law enforcement officers representing the following department(s): ______________________________________.

2. I hereby state that I am not the owner of this currency and have no claim for its return to me.

3. The owner of the currency is:

Name ______________________________
Address ____________________________
Telephone __________________________

4. The currency came into my possession under the following circumstances: (optional)

   ____

   ____

   ____

   ____

5. I have been advised and understand that by signing this Disclaimer of Ownership of Currency, that I am waiving my right to notice of seizure of this currency and that I do not have a right to file a petition or claim for return of the currency since it is not my money.

6. I am not under the influence of any drug, narcotic, alcohol, or medicine at this moment that would impair my judgment.

7. My signature below acknowledges that I have read and understand this document and I have no questions regarding it content.

MY SIGNATURE IS FREE AND VOLUNTARY.

____
Signature & date

______________________ ______________________
Witness Witness

Disclaimer of ownership of currency (Spanish)

Renuncia de Propiedad Monetaria

1. Tengo concimiento que el ________________________,
$ ___________________ Fueron confiscados de me persona, por oficiales de la policia de ________________________.
2. Yo declaro de que no soy el dueno de este dinero y que no tengo reclamo alguno a su devolusion.
3. El dueno de este dinero es:

Nombre ________________________________
Direccion ______________________________
Telefono _______________________________

4. El dinero llego a mi posesion a travez de las siguentes circunstancias: (opcional)

____

____

____

____

5. He sido avisado y entiendo que al firmar este renunciamiento de propiedad monetaria estoy renunciando a mi derecho de notificacion del confiscamiento de este dinero y de que no tengo el derecho de archivar un peticion o un reclamo al devolvimento den dinero ya que no me pertenece.
6. No estoy bajo las influencias de ninquna droga, narcotico, medicamento, o alcohol, en este momento; las cuales impedirian mi juicio.

MI FIRMA EN ESTE RENUNCIAMIENTO ES LIBRE Y VOLUNTARIA.

____

Firma y fecha

_________________________ _________________________

Testigo Testigo

Appendix E: Basic Spanish

The most essential element of speaking Spanish is the understanding that while the majority of the consonants are the same as in English the vowel sounds are unique and consistent.

Pronunciation Guide

Vowels	*Tricky Consonants*	
A -	(AH) as in "hat"	ll = y
E -	(EH) as in "hay"	z = s
I -	(EE) as in "he"	j = h
O -	(OH) as in "hoe"	ñ = ny
U -	(OO) as in "you"	h is always silent
Y -	(EE) as in "he"	rr is rolled

People

Spanish contains both a formal and an informal way of saying "you;" one ought to know that there are appropriate situations for both "usted" (formal) and "tú" (informal)

"Usted" is used to show respect when addressing people such as: Officials (municipal or otherwise), Elderly, Adults, Bosses, Organization Leaders, etc.

"Tú" is used when addressing close friends, children and pets. Thus the instances in which "tú" will be appropriate are rare and you will be understood by playing it safe and using "usted."

I	Yo	(YOH)	
HE	El	(Ehl)	
SHE	Ella	(EY-yah)	
THAT	Aquel	(ah-KAEL)	
THESE	Estos	(EYS-tohs)	
THEY	Ellos	(EY-yohs)	masculine
THEY	Ellas	(EY-yahs)	femine
THIS	Este	(EHS-tay)	
THOSE	Aquellos	(ah-KAY-yohs)	
YOU	Usted	(oo-STEHD)	formal
YOU	Tú	(TOO)	familiar
YOU	Ustedes	(oo-STEH-days) plural	
WE	Nosotros	(Noh-SOH-trohs)	
MISTER	Señor	(saen-YOR)	
MISSES	Señora	(saen-YOR-ah)	
MISS	Señorita	(saen-yor-EE-tah)	

Every noun is assigned a gender. Words ending in "o" are generally masculine and those that end in "a" are generally feminine. An article generally precedes a noun: "el" for masculine nouns and "la" for feminine nouns. When addressing or speaking about group of people/ things that are mixed in gender you will use the masculine articles "ellos" or "aquellos." Articles generally agree in gender and number with nouns.

Example: Los hombres (The men) vs. El hombre (The man) Aquéllos (Those guys)

Basic Interrogatives

WHO?	¿Quién?
WHAT?	¿Qué?
WHERE?	¿Dónde?
WHERE IS?	¿Dónde está?
WHEN?	¿Cuándo?
WHY?	¿Por qué?
HOW?	¿Cómo?
WHICH?	¿Cuál?
WHOSE?	¿De quién?
IS THERE?	¿Hay?
ISN'T THERE?	¿No hay?
IS IT?	¿Es?
ISN'T IT?	¿No es?

Obtaining Basic Information and Booking

What is your name?
¿Cómo se llama?

Write your name/address/phone number.
Escriba su nombre/ dirección/ número de teléfono.

Write your date of birth.
Escriba su fecha de nacimiento.

Are you a United States citizen?
¿Es usted ciudadano de Los Estados Unidos?

Of what country are you a citizen?
¿De que país es usted ciudadano?

Write the name and/or telephone number of your nearest relative.
Escriba el nombre y/o el número de teléfono de su familiar más cercano.

Write your social security or identification number.
Escriba su número de seguridad social o de identificación.

Do you have identification papers?
¿Tiene papeles de identificación?

Do you use any other name? Have you used any other name before? Write it.
¿Usa algún otro nombre? ¿Ha usado algún otro nombre antes? Escríbalo.

Have you ever been arrested before?
¿Ha sido arrestado alguna vez antes?

When?	Where?	Why?
¿Cuándo?	¿Dónde?	¿Por qué?

I am going to take your fingerprints.	Relax.
Le voy a tomar sus huellas digitales.	Relájese.

Clean your hands with this.
Límpiese las manos con esto.

I am going to take your photo.	Stand here.
Le voy a fotografiar.	Párrese aquí.

***Miranda* Warning (advisement of rights)**
YOU HAVE THE RIGHT TO REMAIN SILENT.
Usted tiene el derecho de permanecer callado.
IF YOU GIVE UP THE RIGHT TO REMAIN SILENT, ANYTHING YOU SAY CAN AND WILL BE USED AGAINST YOU IN A COURT OF LAW.
Si usted renuncia el derecho de permanecer callado, cualquier cosa que usted diga, se puede usar en contra de usted en una corte de ley.
YOU HAVE THE RIGHT TO TALK TO A LAWYER BEFORE WE TALK TO YOU AND TO HAVE HIM PRESENT WHILE WE TALK TO YOU.
Usted tiene el derecho de consultar con un abogado y tenerlo presente mientras le hablamos.
IF YOU CANNOT AFFORD TO HIRE AN ATTORNEY, ONE WILL BE APPOINTED TO REPRESENT YOUR PRIOR QUESTIONING.
En caso de que usted no tuviera suficientes fondos para ocupar su propio abogado, la corte le nombrará uno para usted sin costo alguno. También usted tiene el derecho de tenerlo presente, si desea.

YOU HAVE THE RIGHT TO STOP ANSWERING QUESTIONS AT ANY TIME.
Usted tiene el derecho de terminar la entrevista en cualquier momento.

DO YOU UNDERSTAND EACH OF THE RIGHTS EXPLAINED TO YOU?
¿Entiende usted cada uno de estos derechos que le acabo de explicar?
HAVING THOSE RIGHTS IN MIND, WILL YOU TALK TO ME?
Con esos derechos en mente, ¿hablará usted conmigo?
DO YOU WISH TO REMAIN SILENT?
¿Desea permanecer callado?
DO YOU WISH TO TALK?
¿Desea hablar?
DO YOU WANT AN ATTORNEY HERE?
¿Desea tener un abogado presente?

I UNDERSTAND MY RIGHTS AND KNOW WHAT I AM DOING.
Entiendo cuales son mis derechos, y sé lo que estoy haciendo.
I DO NOT WANT A LAWYER AND I AM READY TO GIVE A STATEMENT.
No quiero un abogado y estoy listo para dar una declaración.
NO PROMISES OR THREATS HAVE BEEN MADE TO ME.
No me han hecho promesas ni amenazas.
NO FORCED COOPERATION OR COERCION HAS BEEN USED AGAINST ME.
Ninguna forma de fuerza se ha empleado en contra de mí.
WHEN YOU SIGN THIS, YOU ARE NOT ADMITTING GUILT.
Cuando usted firma aquí, no está admitiendo culpabilidad.
BY SIGNING, IT MEANS YOU UNDERSTAND YOUR RIGHTS.
Al firmar indique que usted sí entiende sus derechos.

Traffic Stops and D.U.I. Investigations

Interrogative

Hello, how are you?	¿Hola, cómo está?
Who was the driver?	¿Quién era el chófer?
Were you driving?	¿Estaba usted manejando?
Do you speak English?	¿Habla inglés?
Is there anyone else here who speaks English?	¿Hay alguien aquí que habla inglés?
How fast were you going?	¿Cuán rápido iba?
Do you know why I stopped you?	¿Sabe por qué yo le paré?
Do you have a driver's license?	¿Tiene una licencia de manejar?

English	Spanish
Is this your car?	¿Es éste su propio carro?
Who is the owner of the current car?	¿Quién es el dueño del carro?
Is this your current address?	¿Es ésta su dirección actual?
What is your current address?	¿Cuál es su dirección actual?
What year is the car?	¿De qué año es el carro?
Do you have insurance?	¿Tiene seguro?
Do you have identification?	¿Tiene identificación?
What is your name?	¿Como se llama?
How do you spell your name?	¿Cómo se escribe su nombre?
Do you have a nickname?	¿Tiene algún sobrenombre?
Have you ever used any other names?	¿Alguna vez jamás ha usado algún otro nombre?
What is your mother's surname?	¿Cuál es el apellido de su madre?
Where do you work?	¿Dónde trabaja?
What kind of work do you do?	¿Qué tipo de trabajo hace?
Where are you headed?	¿Adónde va usted?
What is your social security number?	¿Cuál es su número de seguridad social?
Have you been drinking alcohol?	¿Ha estado bebiendo alcohol?
Have you taken any drugs?	¿Ha tomado alguna droga?

Declarative

English	Spanish
I didn't understand.	No entendí (or) comprendí.
I don't understand.	No entiendo (or) comprendo.
It doesn't matter.	No importa.
You have been stopped for . . .	Usted ha sido parado por . . .
Failure to wear your seat belt.	Falta de usar su cinturón.
Your car was weaving.	Su carro iba de lado a lado.
Expired car license.	Placa vencida.
Failure to use signals.	Falta de usar las direccionales.
Failure to stop at the traffic light/stop sign.	Falta de parar en el semáforo/alto.
Tinted windows.	Ventanas obscuras.
Illegal turn.	Vuelta ilegal.
The headlights/taillights. are not functioning	Las luces delanteras/traceras no funcionan.
The speed limit is _______ miles per hour.	El limite de velocidad es ______ millas por hora.
Your speed was ______ miles per hour.	Su velocidad fue ______ millas por hora.
You have violated a traffic law.	Usted ha violado una ley de tráfico.
I will come right back.	Ya vuelvo.
I am issuing you a citation.	Le estoy dando un citatorio.

When you sign here you are not admitting guilt.	Cuando firma aquí no está admitiendo culpabilidad.
Your signature is a promise to appear in court or pay the fine.	Su firma es una promesa para presentarse en la corte o pagar la multa.
You may go.	Está libre para irse.
You are arrested for driving while intoxicated.	Usted está arrestado por manejar mientras está intoxicado.
I am giving you a warning.	Le voy a dar una advertencia.

Imperative

Pull off the road.	Estaciónese fuera del camino.
Park over there.	Estaciónese allí.
Turn off the engine.	Apague el motor.
Back up.	Retroceda.
Brake.	Frene.
Enough!	¡Basta!
Slow.	Despacio.
Stop.	Alto.
Turn left/right	Doble izquierda/derecho.
Yield.	Ceda el camino.
Get it out.	Sáquela.
Step out of the car.	Bájese del carro.
Walk this line.	Camine esta línea.
Put one foot in front of the other.	Ponga un pie enfrente del otro.
Put your feet together.	Ponga los pies juntos.
Extend your arms.	Extienda sus brazos.
Put your head back.	Eche su cabeza hacia atrás.
Close your eyes.	Cierre los ojos.

Touch your nose with your right/left index finger.
Toque su nariz con el dedo índice derecho/izquierdo.

Don't move!	¡No se mueva!
Throw the keys out the window.	Tire las llaves por la ventana.
Put your hands against the windshield.	Ponga sus manos sobre el parabrisas.

Reach your hand out the window and open the door from the outside.
Saque su mano por la ventana y abra la puerta desde afuera.

Hands up!	¡Manos arriba!
Put your hands behind your head!	¡Ponga sus manos atrás de su cabeza!

Kneel!	¡De rodillas!
Lie flat on your front!	¡Acuéstese boca abajo!
Spread your legs.	Abra sus piernas.
Drive carefully.	Vaya con cuidado.

Vocabulary

Car	Carro
Citation	Citatorio
Drugs	Drogas
Alcohol	Alcohol
Highway Patrol	Policía de Patrulla
Stop sign	Alto (or) Señal de parada
Traffic light	Semáforo
Blame/fault	Culpa
Court	Corte
Ticket/fine	Multa
Signal (v)	Señalar
Cross (v)	Cruzar
Run over (v)	Atropellar
Carefully	Con cuidado
Speeding	Exceso de velocidad
Run a stop sign/stop light (v)	llevarse la luz roja
Weaving (v)	Yendo de lado a lado

Felony Stop

Hands up!	¡Manos arriba!
Hands on your head!	¡Manos sobre la cabeza!
Out!	¡Salga! (or) ¡Afuera!
Slowly!	¡Despacito!
Now!	¡Ahora!
Turn around!	¡Dése vuelta!
Walk backwards!	¡Camine para atras!
Stop!	¡Alto! (or) ¡Para!
Kneel!	¡De rodillas!
Down!	¡Abajo!
Separate your feet!	¡Separe los pies!
Don't move!	¡No se mueva!
Don't talk!	¡No hable!
Everybody out!	¡Todos afuera!
Drop it!	¡Déjela caer!

Search and Search Warrants

Police!	¡Policía!
We have a *search warrant*!	¡Tenemos una *orden de cateo*!
Open the door!	¡Abra la puerta!
Now!	¡Ahora!

Right Now!	¡Ahorita!
Freeze!	¡Quieto!
Drop it!	¡Dejéla caer!
Hands up!	¡Manos arriba!
You are under arrest!	¡Está arrestado!
May I search?	¿Puedo catear?
I am going to search your . . .	Voy a catear su . . .
Car	Carro
Building	Edificio
House	Casa
Person	Persona
That	Aquel
This	Esto
Understand?	¿Entiende? (or) ¿Comprende?
Answer "yes" or "no."	Conteste "si" o "no."
Is this yours	¿Es suyo?
Did you know?	¿Sabía?
Sign here.	Firme aquí.

Arrest

I am arresting you for . . .	Estoy arrestándole por . . .
I am putting you in handcuffs.	Estoy poniéndole esposas.
Get into the vehicle.	Súbase al vehículo.
Watch your head.	Cuíde su cabeza.

Questioning a Lost Child

What is your name?	¿Cómo te llamas?
How old are you?	¿Cuántos años tienes?
Do you know your telephone number?	¿Sabes tu número de teléfono?
Do you know your home address?	¿Sabes la dirección de tu casa?
What is your mom/dad's name?	¿Cómo se llama tu mamá/papá?
Did you go with a stranger?	¿Fuiste con un extraño?
Are you hurt?	¿Estás lastimado(a)?
Is your mom/dad coming for you?	¿Tu mamá/papá viene a recogerte?

Victim/Witness Interrogation

Who called the police?	¿Quién llamó a la policía?
Who is the victim?	¿Quién es la víctima?
Who saw what happened?	¿Quién vio lo que pasó?
When did it happen?	¿Cuándo pasó esto?

Write your name/address/phone number.
Escriba su nombre/dirección/número de teléfono.

Do you know the suspect? What is his or her name?
¿Conoce al sospechoso? ¿Cuál es su nombre?

Is the suspect a man or a woman?
¿Es el sospechoso un hombre o una mujer?

How old? ¿De cuántos años?
Show me how tall the suspect is. Muéstreme que tan alto es el sospechoso.

Is the suspect thin/average/stout/fat?
¿El sospechoso, es delgado/promedio/corpulento/gordo?

What color of skin/eyes/hair does the suspect have?
¿Qué color de piel/ojos/cabello tiene el sospechoso?

Is the suspect Latino/Anglo/African American?
¿El sospechoso, es Latino/Anglosajón/Negro?

Does the suspect have a beard/mustache/long hair?
¿Tiene el sospechoso un bigote/una barba/cabello largo?

Is there anything that is unique or distinguishing about the suspect?
¿Hay algo único o que distingue el sospechoso?

What color clothing was the suspect wearing?
¿Qué color de ropa llevaba el sospechoso?

Shirt	Pants	Jacket	Dress
Camisa	Pantalónes	Chaqueta	Vestido

Was there more than one suspect? ¿Había más de un sospechoso?
How many? ¿Cuántos?

Did the suspect leave on foot or in a vehicle?
¿El sospechoso se fue a pie o en vehículo?

What type of vehicle? ¿Qué tipo de vehículo?
Car? Truck? Motorcycle? ¿Carro? ¿Camión? ¿Motocicleta?

What color? Old or new? ¿De qué color? Viejo o nuevo?

Did you see the license plate number?
¿Vio usted el número de la placa licencia?

Did the suspect have a weapon?	Pistol?	Knife?	Rifle?
¿Traía un arma el sospechoso?	¿Pistola?	¿Cuchillo (or) Navaja?	¿Rifle?

Basic Greetings

Hello.
Hola.

Good morning/Good day.
Buenos días.

Good afternoon.
Buenas tardes.

Good evening.
Buenas noches.

How are you?
¿Cómo está usted?

Very well, thank you.
Muy bien, gracias.

You're welcome.	Yes.	No.	Maybe.
De nada.	Sí.	No.	Tal vez.

Do you speak English?
¿Habla usted inglés?

I speak a little.
Hablo un poquito.

Do you understand?
¿Entiende usted?

I don't understand.
No entiendo./No comprendo.

Speak slower please.
Hable más despacio, por favor.

Repeat, please.
Repita, por favor.

What is your name?
¿Cómo se llama?

What is your address?
¿Cuál es su dirección?

My name is . . .
Me llamo . . .

What is your telephone number?
¿Cuál es su número de teléfono?

How old are you?
¿Cuántos anos tiene?

Are you married?
¿Es casado(a)?

What happened?
¿Qué ocurrió?

Where?
¿Dónde?

When?
¿Cuándo?

I am officer . . .
Soy el (or) la comandante . . .

Spanish standard field sobriety tests

Horizontal gaze nystagmus

Lleves lentes de contactos? (Do you wear contact lenses?)

No haga nada hasta que te diga que empiece. Solo mireme a mi y escuche a mis instrucciones. (Don't do anything until I tell you to start. Just watch me and listen to the instructions.)

Parese con sus pies juntos u sus manos a sus lados. (Stand with your feet together and your hands down to your side.)

No se mueva la cabeza. (Don't move your head.)

Siga mi dedo con sus ojos, no se mueva la cabeza. (Follow my finger with your eyes only, don't move your head.)

Siga mi dedo hasta que te diga bien. (Keep watching my finger until I tell you to stop.)

One leg stand

Tiene algunas problemas medicas con sus piernas? (Do you have any medical problems with your legs?)

No haga nada hasta que te diga que empiece. Solo mireme a mi y escuche a mis instrucciones. (Don't do anything until I tell you to start. Just watch me and listen to the instructions.)

Mantenga sus manos a sus lados, parese en un pie y levante su otro pie unos seis pulgadas. (Keep your hands down to your side, stand on one foot and bring your other foot up six inches.)

Mantenga su pierna estracha y apunte con su dedo de pie. (Keep your leg straight and point your toe.)

Mire a su pie y cuente hasta treinta en voz alta. (Look at your foot and count to thirty slowly and out loud.)

No se preocupe si deja caerse solo que siga otra ves. (If you put your foot down just restart from where you left off.)

Comprende? (Understand?)

Puede empezar. (You may begin.)

Nine step walk and turn:
No haga nada hasta que te diga que empiece. Solo mireme a mi y escuche a mis instrucciones. (Don't do anything until I tell you to start. Just watch me and listen to the instructions.)

Mantenga sus manos a sus lados. (Keep your hands down to your side at all times.)

Ponga su pie derecho en frente de su pie izquierdo, poniendo su calcanar junto a su dedo de pie. (Bring your right foot in front of your left foot, heel to toe.)

No se mueve de esta posicion hasta que le diga a empieze la prueba. (Don't move from this position unit I tell you to begin the test.)

No haga nada hasta que te diga que empiece. Solo mireme a mi y escuche a mis instrucciones. (Don't do anything until I tell you to start. Just watch me and listed to the instructions.)

Si resbala empieze de nuevo en la posicion de antes. (If you slip just stand back into the same position.)

Ande nueve pasos por delante y vuelve aminando en una linea estrecha. (I want you to take nine setps down and nine steps back in a straight line.)

Cuente los pasos en voz alta. Si se olvida a que paso va, empiece de nuevo con uno. (Count the steps out loud, if you slip just keep going from where you left off.)

Cuando llega al paso nueve, de una vuélta, dejando un pie en su lugar y pisando con el otro para dar la vuelta. (When you get to step nine I want you to stop, pivot on your front foot , and with your back foot take several small steps to turn yourself around.)

Despues de dar la vuélta, ande los últimos nueve pasos, poniendo el calconar de un pie junto al dedo del otro pie. (After you turn around put your back foot heel to toe again and finish your next nine steps.)

Acuerdese de tener sus manos a sus lados, cuente en voz alta y mire a sus pies. (Remember to keep your hands down to your side, count out loud, and watch your feet.)

Comprende? (Understand?)

Puede empezar. (You may begin.)

Portable breath test

Abra la boca y levante la lengua. (Open your mouth and lift up your tongue.)

Esta maquina prueba su respiro. No le va a condenar, solo indica si usted ha tomado alcohol hoy. (This is a portable breath tester. It cannot convict you, it just gives me an indication if you have had any alcohol to drink.)

No haga nada hasta que te diga que empiece. Solo mireme a mi y escuche a mis instrucciones. (Don't do anything until I tell you to start. Just watch me and listed to the instructions.)

Quiero que respire fuerte y exhaloar en este tubo fuerte y cuanto que pueda. (Take a deep breath and blow into this tube as hard as you can and as long as you can.)

Comprende? (Understand?)

Inhale. (Inhale.)

Exhale. (Blow.)

Tiene que exhalar mas fuerte. (You need to blow harder than that.)

Arrest

Por favor, de una vuelta y ponga sus manos en su cabeza. (Turn around and put your hands on your head.)

Breath test

Quiero que usted exhale aqui muy fuerte Y por un largo tiempo. Usted tiene que hacer que la maquina emita un sondo constante. Si no lo hace, consideraré que usted haya rechazado tomar la prueba. (I want you to blow into this mouth piece as hard as you can and as long as you can. You need to make the machine produce a steady tone. Otherwise I will consider that you have refused to take the test.)

No exhale hasta que le diga. (Don't blow until I tell you to.)

Exhale ahora. (Blow now.)

Continue exhalando. (Keep blowing.)

La maquina indica que la cantidad de alcohol en su sangre es a ___ por ciento. El limite de acuerdo con la ley es punto zero ocho por aento. (The machine indicates that your alcohol content is at ___ percent. Point zero eight is the legal limit.

Citation issuance
Nececito que firme aqui en la lina. (I need you to sign your name here on the line.)

Su firme no dice que usted es culpable, solo que promete contactar el tribunal y que esta en cargo de la citacion. (Your signature does not mean that you are guilty, just that you will promise to contact the court and take care of the citation.)

Esta es us copia de la citacion. (This is your copy of the citation.)

Le voy a detener por estar borracho mientras manejando. (You are under arrest for driving while drunk.)

Other questions
Ha tomado alguna bebida alcoholica hoy? (Have you had any alcohol to drink today?)

Cuantas bebidas alcoholicas ha tomado? (How much alcohol have you had to drink?)

Donde trabaja? (Where do you work?)

Cual es su numero de seguridad social? (What is your social security number?)

O donde vive? (Where do you live?)

Que es su direccion? (What is your address?)

Que es su numero de telefono? (What is your telephone number?)
Spanish Admonitions and Interview Questions for Impaired Driving Investigations

Chemical test questions
Mr. or Ms.[Subjects Name], do you understand that you are under arrest for:
Sr. o nombre de Ms.[Subjects], ¿Entiende usted que usted está bajo detención para:

___ Driving under the influence of alcohol and/or drugs or with a measurable amount of a controlled substance or drug metabolite in your body?
¿El conducir bajo influencia del alcohol y/o de las drogas o con una cantidad mensurable de una sustancia o de un metabolite de drogas controlada en su cuerpo?

___ An alcohol offense under 21 years of age?
¿Una ofensa del alcohol bajo veintiun años de edad?

___ Violation of conditional driving license?
¿Violación de una licencia de manejar condicional?

___ Commercial driver license offense?
¿Ofensa de la licencia de conductor comercial?

Response if any: ____________

I hereby request that you submit to a chemical test to determine the alcohol (drug) content of your blood/breath. I request that you take a [Type of Test] test.

Solicito por este medio que usted someta a una prueba química para determinar el contenido del alcohol (droga) de su sangre/aliento/orina/boca. Solicito que usted tome la prueba de [tipo de prueba].

___ The following admonition was given by me to the subject before the chemical test was administered:

Test results indicating an unlawful amount of alcohol, drug or a controlled substance or its metabolite in your breath/blood/ urine in violation of the law, or the presence of alcohol and/ or drugs sufficient to render you incapable of safely driving a motor vehicle may, result in denial, suspension, revocation or disqualification of your driving privilege or refusal to issue you a license.

Resultados de la prueba que indican una cantidad ilegal de alcohol, droga o una sustancia controlada o su metabolite en su respiración, sangre/orina/boca en violación de la ley, o la presencia de alcohol y/o de las drogas suficientes para hacerle incapaz con seguridad de conducir un vehículo de motor puede, da lugar a la negación, a la suspensión, a la revocación o a la descalificación de su privilegio de manejar o de negación de publicarle una licencia.

What is your response to my request that you submit to a chemical test? Response:

¿Cuál es su respuesta a mi petición de que usted someta a una prueba química?

If the subject refuses the test, read the following:

___ The following admonition was given by me to the subject:

If you refuse the test(s) or fail to follow my instructions the test(s) will not be given. However, I must warn you that your driving privilege may be revoked for ___ months for a first refusal or ___ months for a subsequent refusal with no provision for limited driving. After you have taken the test(s), you will be permitted to have a physician of your own choice administer a test(s) at your own expense, in addition to the one(s) I have requested, so long as it does not delay the test or tests requested by me. I will make the test results available to you, if you take the test(s).

Si usted rechaza la prueba o falla deseguir mis instrucciones, la prueba no será dada. Sin embargo, debo advertirle que su privilegio de conduirse pueda revocar para ___ meses para una primera denegación o ___ meses para una denegación subsecuente sin la disposición para conducir limitado. Después de que usted haya tomado la prueba, le permitirán para hacer que un médico de su propia opción administre una prueba en su propio costo, además de el que yo he solicitado, siempre y cuando no lo hace retrasa la prueba o las pruebas pedidas por mí. Pondré los resultados de la prueba a disposición usted, si usted toma la prueba.

Unless you immediately request a test(s), the test(s) cannot be given. Response if any:

A menos que usted solicite inmediatamente una prueba, la prueba no puede ser dada.

If the subject claims the right to remain silent or the right to counsel, read the following:

___ The following admonition was given by me to the subject:

Your right to remain silent and your right to counsel do not apply to the implied consent law which is civil in nature and separate from the criminal charges. Your right to remain silent does not give you the right to refuse to take the test(s). You do not have the right to have counsel during the test procedure. Unless you submit to the test(s) I am requesting, I will consider that you have refused to take the test(s). I warn you that if you refuse to take the test(s), your driver's license can be revoked for ___ months with no provision for a limited license.

La su derecha de permanecer callado y la su derecha de aconsejar no aplican al consentimiento la ley implicada que es civil en naturaleza y a parte de las cargas criminales. La su derecha de seguir siendo silenciosa no le da la derecha de rechazar tomar la prueba. Usted no tiene la derecha de tener consejos durante el método de prueba. A menos que usted someta a la prueba que estoy solicitando, consideraré que usted ha rechazado tomar la prueba. Le advierto que si usted rechaza tomar la prueba, su licencia de driver's se pueda revocar por ___ meses sin la disposición para una licencia limitada.

Investigative interview questions

Were you operating vehicle?
¿Usted funcionaba el vehículo?

Where were you going?
¿Adónde usted iba?

What street or highway were you on?
¿Adónde usted iba?
Direction of travel?
¿Dirección del recorrido?

Where did you start from?
¿De dónde usted salen?

When?
¿Cuándo?

What time is it now?
¿Cuándo ahora está?

What it today's date?
¿Qué él fecha de hoy?

Day of Week?
¿Qué día de la semana es él?

What city or county are you in now?
¿Qué ciudad o condado está usted en ahora?

What were you doing during the last three hours?
¿Qué usted hacía durante las tres horas pasadas?

Have you been drinking?
¿Usted ha estado bebiendo?

What?
¿Qué?

How much?
¿Cuánto?

Where?
¿Dónde?

When did you have your first drink?
¿Cuándo usted tiene su primera bebida?

Last drink?
¿Bebida pasada?

Are you under the influence of an alcoholic beverage (drugs) now?
¿Ahora está usted bajo influencia de una bebida alcohólica (drogas)?

Are you taking tranquilizers, pills, medicines or drugs of any kind?
¿Usted está tomando los tranquilizantes, las píldoras, las medicinas o las drogas de la clase?

What kind?
¿Qué clase?

When did you have the last dose?
¿Cuándo usted tiene la dosis pasada?

Are you ill?
¿Es usted enfermo?

(If subject was in a crash, ask these questions):

Were you involved in a crash today?
¿Estaba usted implicado en un desplome hoy?

When?
¿Cuándo?

Have you had any alcoholic beverage or drugs since the crash?
¿Ha tenido usted bebida alcohólica o drogas desde el desplome?

If so, what?
¿Si es así qué?

When?
¿Cuándo?

How much?
¿Cuánto?

You have the right and obligation to contact the local drivers license office and schedule a hearing and appear before them to contest the citation.
Usted tiene la derecha y la obligación de entrar en contacto con la división local de la licencia de conductores y de programar una audiencia y de aparecer antes de ellas para disputar la citación.

Appendix F: VCCR Mandatory Notification Nations

Antigua and Barbuda
Armenia
Azerbaijan
Bahamas, The
Barbados
Belarus
Belize
Brunei
Bulgaria
China (not applicable to people who carry "Republic of China" passports issued by Taiwan)
Costa Rica
Cyprus
Czech Republic
Dominica
Fiji
Gambia, The
Georgia
Ghana
Grenada
Guyana
Hong Kong
Jamaica
Kazakhstan
Kiribati
Kuwait
Kyrgyzstan
Malaysia
Malta
Mauritius
Moldova
Mongolia
Nigeria
Philippines
Poland
Romania
Russia
Saint Kitts and Nevis
Saint Lucia Saint Vincent and the Grenadines
Seychelles
Sierra Leone
Singapore
Slovakia
Tajikistan
Tanzania
Tonga
Trinidad and Tobago
Turkmenistan
Tuvalu
Ukraine
United Kingdom
USSR
Uzbekistan
Zambia
Zimbabwe

The State Department also maintains a 24-hour help line to assist officers in dealing with persons who claim diplomatic immunity. In a case of a crime alleged to be committed by a person claiming diplomatic immunity, the officer should immediately verify immunity through one of the cards listed above, and/or by calling the State Department. The phone number is 202-647-1985 (0815 - 1700, Eastern Standard Time) or after hours, 202-647-7277.

Appendix G: State Department Contact Information

The best way to notify the State Department of an arrest of a foreign national is a phone call, immediately followed with a faxed copy of the arrest report. They can be reached at:

Office of the Assistant Legal Adviser for Consular Affairs L/CA,
Room 5527A
U.S. Department of State
Washington, D.C. 20520
Phone 202-647-4415 Fax 202-736-7559

For urgent matters after business hours, officers may call the State Department Operations Center at 202-647-1512. The State Department also distributes, at no cost, pocket cards with phone numbers of the State Department help desk, sample language to inform detainees of VCCR and treaty rights, and a list of mandatory notification nations.

Following are the VCCR notices suggested by the State Department:

When Consular Notification is at the Foreign National's Option
As a non-U.S. citizen who is being arrested or detained, you are entitled to have us notify your country's consular representatives here in the United States. A consular official from your country may be able to help you obtain legal counsel, and may contact your family and visit you in detention, among other things. If you want us to notify your country's consular officials, you can request this notification now, or at any time in the future. After your consular officials are notified, they may call or visit you. Do you want us to notify your country's consular officials?

When Consular Notification is Mandatory
Because of your nationality, we are required to notify your country's consular representatives here in the United States that you have been arrested or detained. After your consular officials are notified, they may call or visit you. You are not required to accept their assistance, but they may be able to help you obtain legal counsel and may contact your family and visit you in detention, among other things. We will be notifying your country's consular officials as soon as possible.

Appendix H: Sample Descriptions and Nexus Paragraphs

Controlled substance warrant descriptions

Any and all controlled substances, drug paraphernalia of any sort, drug cultivation tools and devices, packaging materials, scales or measuring devices, pipes and other smoking and ingestion devices, instructional literature or books showing the cultivation, manufacture, distribution or use of controlled substances, records of drug transactions and profits, including all electronic media and reading devices such as computers, diskettes, tapes, monitors and printers. Further stated such controlled substances as more particularly described as:

Marijuana, a green leafy substance in dried form. Further to include materials used to package marijuana, specifically, plastic sandwich bags; materials for using marijuana, including but not limited to, rolling papers, small sheets of thin paper often found with adhesive on one side, pipes, used to smoke marijuana, clips used to hold a marijuana cigarette while being smoked. Further to include personal notes and records of narcotic transactions, listing names, dates, prices, quantity sold and/or amounts owed.

Cocaine, a controlled substance in white, powdery, crystalline form. Further to include materials for packaging cocaine, specifically paper sheets cut from magazines, lined paper, and other paper types, plastic drinking straws, cut and uncut; items for ingesting or inhaling cocaine, including but not limited to hollow tubes for snorting cocaine, small spoons for snorting cocaine, mirrors used for cutting and snorting cocaine, razor blades used for cutting and separating cocaine; paraphernalia and equipment for manufacturing crack cocaine, including, but not limited to, propane or butane torches or other heat sources, baking soda for separating the cocaine base, small jars or vials for cooking, pots for boiling and trays or mirrors for drying cocaine. Further to include personal notes and records of narcotic transactions, listing names, dates, prices, quantity sold and/or amounts owed.

Methamphetamine, a yellowish white powdery substance. Further to include materials for packaging methamphetamine, specifically small plastic baggies; paraphernalia for using methamphetamine, including hollow tubes for snorting methamphetamine, small spoons for snorting methamphetamine, mirrors for holding methamphetamine while being snorted, razor blades for cutting methamphetamine into lines, hypodermic syringes for injecting methamphetamine, glass or tubular pipes for heating methamphetamine, scales for weighing methamphetamine; "cut," a light-colored powdery substance used to dilute the methamphetamine. Further to include personal notes and records of narcotic transactions, listing names, dates, prices, quantity sold and/or amounts owed.

Lysergic acid diethylamide (LSD), a controlled substance in liquid form or soaked into paper and divided or serrated into approximately 1/4O size stamps or squares often bearing a variety of designs or colors as well as being plain or solid colored. Further to include packaging LSD, specifically squares of tin foil used to wrap the LSD stamps, clear plastic baggies used to carry the LSD in small liquid vials, such as Murine or food coloring type vials; paraphernalia for using LSD, including, but not limited to, liquid eye droppers used to drop liquid LSD into the eyes. Further to include personal notes and records of narcotic transactions, listing names, dates, prices, quantity sold and/or amounts owed.

Heroin, a brown-colored, rock like substance. Further to include materials for cutting and diluting heroin, including milk sugar, a white powdery substance in crystalline form, quinine, a white powdery substance in crystalline form; equipment for weighing and packaging heroin, specifically, scales for weighing heroin, consisting of an instrument with pans and weights and measures attached to horizontal beams marked to show gram, ounce, pound, and kilogram quantities; clear plastic baggies with self-sealing sealing tops, balloons, small spherical rubber bags designed to be inflated; paraphernalia for using heroin, including, but not limited to, hypodermic syringes with needle for injecting heroin, bent spoons for heating and melting of narcotics, tie strings for cutting off blood circulation, includes shoe strings, twine, rope, pieces of rubber. Further to include personal notes and records of narcotic transactions, listing names, dates, prices, quantity sold and/or amounts owed.

Gamma Hydroxy Butyrate, a clear liquid, somewhat thicker than water. Also called GHB, G, Jib, Scoop, Liquid E, Tranquili G, Liquid X, Ladies' Viagra, Grievous Bodily Harm, Easy Lay, Gamma 10, Salty Water, GH Buddy, Aminos, Blue Nitro, Blue Thunder, Thunder Nectar, Revivarant, Remforce, Firewater, Invigorate, sodium oxybate, Fantasy, Midnight Blue, Verve, Rejoov, G-riffick, Eclipse, GHGold, Soap, Vita G, Dormir, Enliven, FX, Serenity, Inner G, Zen. Generally administered in liquid form, added to beverages. Often carried and stored in film canisters, dropper bottles, hair spray, liquid candy bottles, food coloring, breathe mint containers (may also be liquid LSD), vanilla bottles, Gatorade bottles, hand lotion pump dispensers.

Methylenedioxy-methamphetamine, a solid in pill or powder form. Also known as MDMA, Ecstasy, X, E, Euros, XTC, Smurfs, Hug Drug, and also referred to by names of cartoon characters and/or various brand markings that may be embossed on MDMA tablets. Administered by mixing with candy, such as Skittles, Pez, or embedded in Tootsie Rolls. Often accompanied by lollipops and hard candy, infant pacifiers and candy pacifiers (to avoid grinding of teeth), eucalyptus inhalants (to enhance sensation of burning nasal passages), balms and lotions, lighting devices, particularly light sticks, and fans and feathers and other colorful, decorative accessories.

Ketamine, a veterinary tranquilizer, also known by brand names Ketalar, Ketajet, Ketaset, generally appearing in liquid form, but may be found in powder form. Administered by evaporating the liquid and inhaling the remaining powder residue, or dipping cigarettes into the liquid and smoking the cigarettes. Also known as Special K, Ket, Kat, or Vitamin K.

Mushrooms, such as mushrooms native to Mexico and Central America and sometimes grown in the United States, a hallucinogen, containing the chemicals psilocybin and psilocin. Further to include personal notes and records of narcotic transactions, listing names, dates, prices, quantity sold and/or amounts owed.

Peyote, a cactus button containing mescaline, from the fleshy portion of the peyote cactus, native to Mexico and southwest United States, a hallucinogen. Further to include personal notes and records of narcotic transactions, listing names, dates, prices, quantity sold and/or amounts owed.

Clandestine lab, a hidden makeshift laboratory where chemicals are compounded, synthesized, concentrated, purified, separated, extracted, or other physical or chemical processing, or conversion, for the purpose of producing an illegal substance, or where chemicals used in the manufacturing of illegal substances are stored, distributed, or transported. Further to include: laboratory equipment, including, but not limited to glassware, beakers, separator funnels, condenser columns, thermometers, plastic funnels, filters, Pyrex dishes, heating mantles, torches, matches, rubber tubing, vacuum pumps, Ph testing strips, drug recipes, chemistry books, drawings, etc.; chemicals, including, but not limited to, benzyl chloride, methylamine (gas cylinder or a 40% solution in water), phenyl-2-propanone, aluminum (foil, wire, pellets), hydrocyhloric acid, iodine, magnesium sulfate (anhydrous), phosphorous, sodium chloride, ethyl alcohol (ethanol), and isopropyl alcohol. Further to include personal notes and records of narcotic transactions, listing names, dates, prices, quantity sold and/or amounts owed.

Sexual assault and child abuse warrants

In some cases of sexual assault, the suspect's possession of pornography may be helpful to show intent. *State v. Dalphond,* 585 A.2d 317 (N.H. 1991). In other cases, physical evidence such as weapons, sexual toys, restraint devices, lubricants, will be available to corroborate the victim's statement. A search warrant may also be used for the simple task of verifying the victim's description of the crime scene if the report is delayed and officers are not able to immediately gain access to the scene.

Search warrants are one of the least-utilized–but most productive–investigatory tools in child abuse cases, particularly in sexual abuse cases. Child abuse cases always benefit from corroboration of the child's story and much of the corroboration can come in the form of physical evidence. In physical abuse cases, consider search warrants for the weapon used to injure or threaten the child, and portions of the flooring, items of furniture (whether seizing or photographing) and stairways when the defense is that the child fell and was accidentally injured.

Documenting that the child victim has accurately described the crime scene or instrumentalities will provide evidence that can be used to bolster credibility. For example, in one case a detective executed a search warrant and found a pink lotion bottle that the child had described. The child testified that the suspect lubricated the genitals with this lotion. The jury was able to conclude that since the child accurately recalled one detail (the lotion bottle), the child accurately recalled the sexual conduct and the jury convicted the defendant.

Search warrants can reveal evidence of associated crimes, such as child pornography, computer bulletin board pornography, and may well produce evidence of other victims or multiple perpetrators. There is not a problematic staleness issue with photographs and videos; perverts tend to hold on to such stuff. A search warrant may also be used defensively to defeat a later claim that the child gained her sexual knowledge from pornography. If no pornography is found or if the pornography does not show the acts that the child describes, this claim is weakened.

Child sexual abusers, whether a clinically-defined pedophile or not, often have pornographic videotapes, magazines and photographs that should be sought. Consider a warrant for items used to groom the child as a victim, photographs of the victim (clothed or not), drugs or alcohol used to intoxicate the victim, sexual toys and aids, petroleum jelly and other lubricants. Work records may corroborate that the suspect had opportunities to spend time with the victim. Telephone records, address books and correspondence will show communication with the victim. A warrant may be used to seize bedding, photograph rooms and seize household items that the child described as being in the scene of the crime.

The child's ability to describe the surroundings and circumstances of the abuse will dictate the specificity with which the officer can describe the things being sought. However, when an officer details his or her relevant investigative experience and training to recite such facts that sexual abusers rarely discard child pornography and that they often keep photographic records of their victims, the scope of the search and permissible seizure will be broadened. *United States v. Rabe*, 848 F.2d 944 (9th Cir. 1988). Such recitation of expertise and training also will help overcome staleness problems when the pornography was observed in the distant past by the child or another.

The affiant officer should recite his or her experience in great detail, specifying the length of time assigned to child abuse investigations, all relevant training and seminars, number of similar cases investigated, number of victim and suspect interviews completed, knowledge of child abuse laws, training and lectures presented, past search warrants in child abuse cases, and special honors or recognition received for child abuse investigation.

Drug detector canine resumé

Although many courts have ruled that the alert by a trained drug detector canine creates probable cause to search, some indicia of reliability of the canine should be included in the affidavit. The trend appears for courts to be willing to suppress evidence obtained following a canine sniff and alert if there is not a basis for evaluating the canine's reliability before the magistrate that issued the warrant. Following is a sample canine resumé. This is model language and the format must be adapted to the particular dog's training and certification.

K-9 Monty is a male four-year-old German Shepherd acquired by the County Sheriff's Office Narcotics Unit immediately following Monty's initial training at the K9 Academy for Law Enforcement, Delta, British Colombia, Canada. Monty received 16 weeks of pre-service training in the detection of controlled substances and he is trained to detect and locate the odors of methamphetamine, cocaine, heroin and marijuana, and their derivatives. Monty successfully completed his pre-service training in June of 2001, and was certified as a narcotics drug detector canine immediately upon graduation by the California Narcotic Canine Association.

Monty has participated in annual International Police Canine Conferences sponsored by the K9 Academy for Law Enforcement every year since his pre-service training. Monty has been certified in the detection of the odors of methamphetamine, cocaine, heroin and marijuana, and their derivatives by the United States Police Canine Association, North America Police Working Dog Association, California Narcotic Canine Association, and the POST Canine Program. Monty receives an average of five hours per week of in-service training, approximately one-half of which is devoted to the detection of controlled substances. Monty is trained in accordance with the standards of the United States Police Canine Association.

Monty is frequently used to search houses, warehouses, business facilities, automobiles, packages, school lockers and buses for the presence of controlled substances. Since his placement into service, Monty has been handled by Officer John Smith, a ten-year veteran of the Sheriff's Office. Monty has been used by the City Police Department, Highway Patrol, Division of Adult Probation and Parole, Bureau of Land Management Law Enforcement Services, Bureau of Indian Affairs Law Enforcement Division, and various other state, federal and municipal agencies.

Monty has been trained to be an aggressive alert dog, meaning that he will show a heightened emotional state when he detects the odors of controlled substances. Monty will scratch and bite at the location where he detects such odors. In 98.5% of cases where Monty has demonstrated an alert indicating the scent of controlled substances, either controlled substances have been found at that location or officers have affirmed that controlled substances were recently at the location, leaving their distinctive scent.

Appendix I: Telephonic Warrant Form

The following dialogue must be audio-recorded. Read the following to the magistrate, word for word, after completing:

STATE OF ____________________, Plaintiff, versus _____________________, Defendant.

Affidavit in Support of Telephonic Search Warrant, prepared by _____________________.

I am in telephonic contact with Judge/Magistrate ______________ and I am recording the entire conversation. I, ________________, being sworn state as follows:

1. I am a peace officer in the State of _____________. I have been a police officer for the last _____ years. For all of those years I have been employed by the _________________. For the last ____ years, I have been assigned to the ____________ division. My duties there have included the investigation of ____________________ (the type of crime under investigation). During my career I have been involved in the investigation and/or arrests of at least _____ persons for crimes such as ____________________ (the type of crime under investigation). I attended the Police Academy and am currently a certified police officer. During my career, I have attended many hours of in service training that includes training into the investigation of __________________.
2. The property for which a search warrant is sought is described as follows:

   ____

3. The grounds for issuing a search warrant, as provided by state statute, are as follows: the property is evidence of illegal conduct (or was unlawfully acquired or is unlawfully possessed, or is used to conceal or commit any crime).
4. I have probable cause to believe, and do believe, that the property is located on the premises known or described as: _____________________, address __________________________. (Describe the entire property, including vehicles, garages, barns and any other outbuildings)

5. The facts to establish the grounds for the issuance of a search warrant are: (State the factors for probable cause)

   ____

   It is now ____ a.m./p.m. on the ____ day of ______________, 200__. I am signing the affidavit, under oath, and in the telephonic presence of Judge/Magistrate ____________________.

____

AFFIANT

Your honor, may I sign you name to the affidavit, indicating that I have sworn to the contents of the affidavit?

____

JUDGE/MAGISTRATE

(You should now tell the magistrate that you will read the proposed warrant)

Proposed Order for Search Warrant

It is ordered that a search warrant be issued for the articles and places described in the above affidavit, for an immediate search in the daytime (or any time day or night) and upon notice (or without notice) (If the magistrate authorizes night time or no-knock service, you should ask the magistrate to state a specific finding supporting such authorization).

DATE SIGNED: TIME SIGNED:

____

JUDGE/MAGISTRATE

(You should then read the Warrant to the magistrate)

STATE OF ______________, Plaintiff, versus ___________________, Defendant.
Search Warrant.

TO ANY PEACE OFFICER IN THE STATE OF ________________:
Proof by Affidavit was made before me this day by _____________ that there is probable cause for issuance of a search warrant, as more fully set forth in the affidavit, a copy of which is attached hereto and incorporated herewith.

You are therefore commanded to make immediate search **(in the daytime) (anytime of the day or night)**, of the person of:
of the vehicle described as:
of the premises described as:
for the following property:
If you find any of the property described above, or any part thereof, bring it before me immediately at this court and make return to the court.

You (are) (are not) authorized to execute this search warrant without giving prior notice of your authority and purpose.
(Ask the magistrate for authorization to sign the warrant in the magistrate's name)

DATE SIGNED: TIME SIGNED:

____
JUDGE/MAGISTRATE

Service:
Date/Time:
Served by Whom:
Location Served:

Appendix J: Affiant Training and Experience Resumé Guide

Name and Rank ______________________________

Present assignment and date ______________________________

Previous assignments and dates ______________________________

____

Formal academic degrees earned or in progress ______________

Academy attended ________ Date completed ____________

Law enforcement experience prior to present employment ________

____

Military service ______________________________

Post-academy training ______________________________

Recent in-service training ______________________________

Drug Investigator or DEA Academy graduate ______________

Crime Scene School ______________________________

Task force membership/experience ______________________

Instructor experience ______________________________

Expert witness certification ______________________________

Number of search warrants prepared ____ Warrants executed ____

Warrants related to type of crime under investigation __________

Previous controlled substances warrants ________________

Warrants resulting in seizure of controlled substances/stolen property

____

Awards/Commendations ______________________________

Professional society membership ______________________

Appendix K: Location Description Guides

Residences

Street address ____________________________________

City/County/Area ____________________________________

Owner ____________________________________

Tenant or occupant ____________________________________

Single/multiple dwelling ___________ Number of units ___________

Apartment designation ________ Building designation ____________

Direction that front/main entrance faces ____ Number of stories _____

Construction type: Brick _____ Frame _____ Aluminum siding _____

Stucco_____ Log _____ Concrete block _____ Wood siding _____

Vinyl siding _____ Other ____________________________

Architectural type:

Rambler/ranch ____ Split level ____ Split entry ____ Gambrel ___

Colonial____ Salt box____ Townhouse____ Mobile home____

Pre-fab____ Other ____________________________

Dominant color ______ Trim color _____ Shutter/door color ________

Roof type ________ Shingle/metal color _____ Tar/pebble _________

Attached/detached garage ___ Size ________ Color ______________

Garage door type ____________ Other outbuildings ______________

Driveway location and type ____________________________

Sidewalk location and type ____________________________

Fence location and type ____________________________

Other distinctive features ____________________________

Additional factors for rural locations:

Rural route box number ____________________________

Name or markings on mailbox ____________________________

Property commonly known as ____________________________

Name of ranch ____________________________

Direction and distance from mailbox ____________________________

GPS reading ____________________________

Nearest utility pole marker or mile marker _____ Direction _________

Nearest intersection or landmark ________________________________

Direction and distance to nearest intersection ______________________

Additional factors for business locations

Signs and marquees ________________ Awnings _________________

Type of business ____

Parking area location ____

Street level designated as __________ Outbuildings ______________

Attach drawings or photographs as available and necessary for clarity.

Appendix L:
Quick Checklist for Search Warrant Affidavit

- **Caption.** Have you included the proper title of the court which will issue the warrant?
- **Affiant.** Have you described your training and experience and told the court about your prior search warrant experience?
- **Description.** Have you particularly described the place to be searched? Have you particularly described the person or things to be seized? Have you discussed the curtilage and outbuildings?
- **Probable cause.** Have you given the court sufficient information to conclude that there is probable cause to believe that fruits, instrumentalities or evidence of a crime will be found?
- **Notice.** Will the warrant be served with notice, or is it a no-knock warrant? Have you given the court reasons to issue a no-knock warrant?
- **Time.** Is the warrant to be served at night? Have you provided a justification for night time service?

TABLE OF CASES

INDEX

W